Quixotic Desire

Psychoanalytic Perspectives on Cervantes

EDITED BY

Ruth Anthony El Saffar

AND

Diana de Armas Wilson

Cornell University Press

ITHACA AND LONDON

This book is published with the aid of a grant from the
Program for Cultural Cooperation between Spain's
Ministry of Culture and United States Universities.

First published 1993 by Cornell University Press.

International Standard Book Number 0-8014-2823-8 (cloth)
International Standard Book Number 0-8014-8081-7 (paper)
Library of Congress Catalog Card Number 93-13360

Printed in the United States of America

*Librarians: Library of Congress cataloging information appears
on the last page of this book.*

⊗ The paper in this book meets the minimum requirements of the
American National Standard for Information Sciences–Permanence of
Paper for Printed Library Materials, ANSI Z39.48–1984.

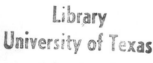

Contents

Acknowledgments

The task of assembling and editing a collection of this sort requires the support and cooperation of more people than a page or two of text could ever adequately represent. We are especially grateful for the seed money from which this project was allowed to take root, provided by the Program for Cultural Cooperation between Spain and the United States, and for a subsequent subvention to Cornell University Press to help offset publication costs. We thank the University of Denver for a Faculty Research Grant that funded a professional indexer.

We also thank Peter Rudnytsky for the careful attention and helpful commentary he lavished on the introduction to this book; Joshua McKinney for his unstinting labors on the translation of Maurice Molho's article from the Spanish; Ralph di Franco, for his hand in those labors; Carol Taylor—wizard of the faculty computer lab at the University of Denver—for leading us safely through a labyrinth of microbytes to the familiarity of the printed page; Anne J. Cruz, for sharing much expert advice on editing a collection, the fruits of her trio of edited volumes; and María Antonia Garcés, for the generous expenditure of time that brought us into contact with contributors we might not otherwise have included here. Diana Wilson thanks her husband, Douglas B. Wilson, for his generous aid and counsel at various crises during the difficult birth of this book.

Telephone calls across continents and oceans, flurries of express packages, frantic conversions of floppy—and not-so-floppy—disks are all part of the long-distance coordination of collaborative work

ix

such as this. Our effort was both complicated and facilitated by the technologies that have made a village of our globe. We offer thanks across the ethers to the many unknown and unnamed people who engineered our electronic contacts with one another.

Of course, none of the work on this volume could have been completed without the good will and ready support of the writers whose essays appear in these pages. We are grateful for the many hours our contributors have given to the volume and for the mines of insights with which they have enriched it.

Finally, we thank Edward Friedman and Edward Dudley for the kind, helpful, and extensive readings they gave our collection when it was still a foundling in search of a home. Their support was instrumental in finding us the shelter of Cornell University Press, and their suggestions crucial for improving the overall condition of the ungainly but well-loved child they first met in manuscript form.

R. A. E. S.
D. de A. W.

Note on Texts

Because of the number of different contributors to this volume and the large selection of editions of the works of Cervantes available, we have limited citation from *Don Quixote* to notation by part and chapter number (e.g., II.10). For other works of Cervantes—for example, the *Persiles*, stories from the *Exemplary Novels*, and plays from Cervantes's *Interludes*—textual references to the Spanish originals are given in the footnotes by each contributor.

All quotations from Cervantes's works appear in both Spanish and English. Unless otherwise noted, the translations into English were supplied by the contributors. Well-known translations of *Don Quixote*—such as those by John Ormsby, Samuel Putnam, and J. M. Cohen—frequently provided the basis from which modifications and modernizations were made, as indicated by the contributors in each specific case. One contributor was able to consult, in manuscript version, the translation of *Don Quixote* by Burton Raffel (Bantam, forthcoming 1994).

Foreword

Max Hernández

This is an ambitious, provocative, disquieting, and important book. The essays gathered and edited by Ruth Anthony El Saffar and Diana de Armas Wilson around Miguel de Cervantes's oeuvre open new vistas, reach into unsuspected recesses, and add significant dimensions to its reading. By invoking the literary origins of psychoanalysis, the collection seems to propose guidelines for a programmatic approach to literature. In several of the essays the unsettling aspects and the radical implications of the concept of the unconscious undermine disciplinary boundaries, build unexpected bridges, shift apparently immovable references. It is as though the editors, having assumed the quixotic task of fighting the windmills of canonical reading and hierarchical systems of all sorts, show how *lack* haunts the pages of literature.

In the more general context of the psychoanalytic studies of literature, what is most salient in the majority of the essays is a vehement postmodern sensibility. Some, though not others, question the keystone of psychoanalytical theory to which Freud gave primary and lasting form: the Oedipus complex. Thus, the reading of Cervantes's fiction since Freud has allowed for the deconstruction of what is regarded as a "Freudian fiction." This may be more promising for literary criticism in that it helps to avoid facile *prêt-à-porter* interpretations along the lines that some exercises in applied analysis have shown. If this reading often assumes the stance of a fully ideologized account of psychoanalysis—a sort of new psychoanalytic gospel according to the literary critics—it is not a gospel that requires psycho-analysis to *submit* to the literary perspective.

Let us turn for a moment to the analytic situation. There, both the analyst and the analysand are faced with another quixotic task: to look for the unreason with which their reason is affected, to right actual or imagined wrongs, to redress real or fictive injuries. The clinical situation teaches us a plain lesson: one has to learn to accept uncertainty, to tolerate the experience of not knowing, to develop what Keats called a "negative capability." Only thus will it be possible to find new avenues for understanding and different ways of modulating conflict. Analyst and analysand aspire to a truth often emerging from the emotional experience of the encounter, even if it is an ever-changing kernel of truth left behind the shifting objects of desire.

This excursion to the private domains of the couch may seem out of place here. Some readers might ask: How does the practice of analysis contribute to the reading of books? Why has someone whose insights are rooted in the clinical tradition, and whose views often differ from those sustained by some of the authors in this volume, written this foreword? Let me answer by recalling a brief passage from *Don Quixote*.

Prior to his second sally, Don Quixote "fue a ver sus libros; y como no hallaba el aposento donde le había dejado, andaba de una en otra parte buscándole [went to consult his books, and not finding his library where it ought to be, he wandered from one room to another, looking for it]" (I.7). Most of his books have been burned, and those which have escaped the ardent censorship of the priest and the barber have been walled up and plastered in the "aposento de los libros [library]": such is the cruel remedy for the hidalgo's madness that his friends have devised. After a fruitless search for his library, having suffered what Francisco Ayala thinks may well have been the gravest of all his disappointments, the old hidalgo stays at home. For a fortnight he talks, perhaps sensibly, with the priest and the barber. Meanwhile, he is secretly enlisting Sancho Panza as the companion of his adventures. The knight-errant and his squire leave home suddenly. Loss of his avenue into the imagination sets the stage for Don Quixote's second sally.

In this brief episode Cervantes calls our attention to one of the multiple, mysterious, and definitive correspondences between what is written in the words of fiction and the figurations of insanity. But he also states something more specifically related to the singularity of the knight's quest: what Don Quixote was looking for was *doubly* inaccessible, buried in the "aposento" and locked in the text "de los

libros." In this way we arrive at the precise locus where the essays
of this collection converge. The scholars gathered together here are
searching, like the knight himself, for the walled-up door and the key
to a contemporary understanding of the great Spanish writer. They
are looking, in other words, for the secret passage connecting life
with the written word which one tries to rediscover through the act
of reading. That is what this volume is about.

Montaigne once said we are only interpreters of interpretations.
This seems unavoidable. Reading some of the essays in this collection,
one comes up against problematic areas. There are instances less
postmodern than pre-oedipal. At times, those authors who challenge
the assumptions of the oedipal model do not question their own. Each
of these polemical essays contains, nonetheless, some fascinating insights, and each ignites the desire to continue reading. In this mood
one finds oneself turning page after page. One is surprised, amused,
shocked. One goes back to Cervantes and returns once more to the
essays. Then one finishes reading the book and sees that the fragments of the hero, the madness of the hidalgo, the anguish of the
women, and the colloquial barking of the dogs all acquire a sort of
plural, polyphonic, multilayered, conflicting harmony. If one may
disagree with some of the interpretations, one can only admire the
scholarship, appreciate the ingenuity, and respect the audacity that
is bound in these pages.

Introduction

Ruth Anthony El Saffar
and Diana de Armas Wilson

Freudian theory offers the one model of reading we have
that can claim to make a text speak more than it knows.

—Peter Hulme

◆

Like Corneille's M. Jordain with his prose, Cervantes's texts have
always been speaking psychoanalysis. Long before notions of discontinuity, deconstruction, and the displacement of desire had entered our critical repertoire as instruments of textual decoding, readers
of Cervantes groped for a lexicon adequate to the analysis of his
maddeningly elusive and insistently heteroglossic works. The multiple narrative filters refracting the "true history" of the knight's deeds
in *Don Quixote* or the unresolved question of the dogs' origins in "The
Colloquy of the Dogs"—to draw from only the two Cervantine texts
most frequently invoked in this collection—induced doubt in Cervantes's readers not only about such issues as reliability, intention,
authorship, and referentiality but also about the status of fiction and
the nature of identity.

Cervantes's critics have long found themselves dazzled by his narrative virtuosity and its resistance to totalizing interpretive systems.
Cervantes may have been "speaking psychoanalysis" all along, but
can psychoanalysis, better than any other critical approach, speak
him? Are not Cervantes's texts, because of their polyvalent nature,
bound to have the last word? Is not theory finally dismembered by
its own hounds once its predatory disposition has been unmasked?
Whether structuralist or Marxist, New Historicist or psychoanalytic,
the theory that insists on preconceived formulations and seeks with
nets and traps, if not indeed with bludgeons, to master its quarry

1

becomes ultimately the object of its own hunt. Were the contributors of this volume to stay wedded to issues such as penis envy, breast deprivation, castration anxiety, or any of the other stalwarts of classic Freudian theory, the tools of psychoanalysis would surely have become traps. The effort here, however, not only to allow the insights opened up by Freud to read Cervantes but also to allow Cervantes to read Freud, sponsors a more flexible use of the psychoanalytic perspective than the one that has so often left readers, especially those in the Hispanic critical tradition, skeptical.

The prime psychoanalytic question addressed throughout this volume has to do not with meaning or intention or characterization per se but rather with what drives material generally analyzed according to categories such as plot, character, narrator, sequence, closure, or levels of discourse. Psychoanalysis challenges the identification of any symbolic system with its manifest content, displacing attention from what is presented to what remains hidden. To see in Cervantes and Freud, as well as in the readers of both, the play of desire as it erupts across our texts is to make the move that undermines the easy identification of one thing with another. Desire, together with the signifiers in which it appears and through which it hides, becomes, therefore, the object of psychoanalytic inquiry. The text becomes a complex web of intersecting forces designed to tell an *Other* story, a story of that which cannot be told. Cide Hamete, the Arab narrator of *Don Quixote*, reminds us of that story when he asks the reader to praise him not for what he wrote but for what he has refrained from writing.[1] The Freud who alerted himself to jokes and slips of the tongue (as opposed to the Freud who imposed his phallic interpretation on Dora's discourse), the Lacan who carefully listened to the suturings and omissions in the signifying chains of his patients' narratives, and the Irigaray who minutely rereads Freud's "Femininity" all stand as reminders of the attention to the text required in studies whose intent is the unmasking of desire.

If psychoanalysis as a praxis of criticism has often failed readers by making facile translations of one system of symbolization into another, or by presupposing and imposing on the text an already formed "solution" driven by the interpreter's unconfessed imperialistic desire, it can also fail by getting lost in the free play of an intertextuality that renders critical commentary an extension of the text itself. Psy-

---

1. The translator reports of Cide Hamete: "Pide no se desprecie su trabajo, y se le den alabanzas, no por lo que escribe, sino por lo que ha dejado de escribir [He asks that his labors may not be despised, and that he be praised, not for what he writes, but for what he has refrained from writing]" (II.44).

choanalysis works as a valuable and viable critical mode because—in its best moments—it posits, in both literary and interpretive texts, that the psyche functions as an organizing principle, constantly creating itself through the images and lexicons out of which it gains material expression.

Rejecting, like postmodernist readers, the assumption of a definitive or authoritative reading, psychoanalytic criticism nonetheless assumes a grounding in the unconscious. Such a grounding moors the reading in matter that, however inaccessible to exact formulation, nonetheless makes sense of the otherwise unchecked play of the signifier. Absent from the text, yet present in its silences, elisions, and breaks, is that Other so often invoked in Cervantes's texts as the "devil who never sleeps." Both the source and the end of the pulsions of desire, that Other drives the stories on and tosses the characters from event to event.

The fifteen essays collected in this volume, many of them drawing on post-Freudian theories, regard the making of fiction and the exploration of psychic processes as convergent enterprises that belong to a single imaginative venture. The collection itself was generated, to borrow a phrase from one of its contributors, at "that precarious meeting place between disciplines" as well as at "the permeable border between languages."[2] Engendered in that "in-between," Cervantes and psychoanalysis have become inseparable from each other. Their new mode of blending precludes the reductionist readings of the past: Cervantes's tales are no longer, or at least not simply, assimilated to the Oedipus complex, a tendency of earlier couplings of psychoanalysis and literature. Far different today than when it first entered academic writing in the 1920s, or even when it re-emerged as a critique of formalism in the 1950s, psychoanalysis, now part of a general postmodern sensibility, is rediscovering its origins in literature.

The essays in this collection are gathered into sections designed to reflect, as closely as possible, the different approaches of the contributors. The sections themselves are ordered so as to tell a story about drifts and trends in psychoanalytic criticism at the end of the twentieth century. In the last part of this introductory essay—after a description of each essay in order of appearance—we elaborate on those drifts and trends, noting their impact on what we see as the ongoing dialogue between Cervantes and Freud.

2. See Andrew Bush's essay, "The Phantom of Montilla," in this volume.

◆

In tribute to the Freud who brought psychoanalytic thinking into twentieth-century discourse, Part I, "The Discourse of Affiliation," opens this book with an examination of the still mysterious and secret affinities between the founder of psychoanalysis and the founder of the modern novel, offering insights into how the stories of both writers complement, refract, and serve to explain the one to the other. Although it is possible to trace Freud's fascination with *Don Quixote* in letters from 1883 to his fiancée, Martha Bernays, his enthusiasm for Cervantes began long before. When, as a boy, Freud and his school friend Eduard Silberstein founded a secret and exclusive "Castilian Academy," the young Sigismund identified himself with one of Cervantes's talking dogs. In his correspondence with Silberstein, whom he fulsomely addressed as his "Queridísimo Berganza," Freud signed off with the royally canine "Ich, Scipio." In playing the authoritarian Cipión to his friend's loquacious Berganza, Freud was already assuming the superior role of protopsychiatrist, the posture of listener and, at strategic moments, critic. One confidential letter to Silberstein even bore, in garbled but endearing Spanish, Freud's imperious warning: "No mano otra toque esa carta [Let no other hand touch this letter]."[3]

What moved the young Freud to replay, with so much secrecy, a text whose motivating theme is foundational shame? What attracted him to a fiction in which Cervantes explodes all the rituals of avoidance of the obscene? How did the writing that he portrayed to his "little princess" Martha as "coarse" serve to illuminate Freud's study of psychic processes?[4] León Grinberg and Juan Francisco Rodríguez address these questions in their essay "Cervantes as Cultural Ancestor of Freud," showing Cervantes to be one of Freud's major precursors. The two Madrid psychoanalysts reveal in their study that various formative elements of psychoanalysis were coalescing in the crucial summer of 1883, when Freud read and commended *Don Quixote* to his fiancée. A whole repertoire of key psychoanalytic concepts coincided with Freud's early reading of Cervantes's "Colloquy of the Dogs," an event that Grinberg and Rodríguez closely historicize. Cervantes provided the literary frame that led to Freud's identification of himself with the dog Cipión, whose attitude of psychoanalytic

---

3. See Peter Gay, *Freud: A Life for Our Time* (New York: Doubleday, 1989), 22. For a more detailed description of these formative events, see León Grinberg and Juan Francisco Rodríguez, "Cervantes as Cultural Ancestor of Freud," in this volume. See also S. B. Vranich, "Sigmund Freud and 'The Case History of Berganza': Freud's Psychoanalytic Beginnings," *Psychoanalytic Review* 63 (1976): 80.

4. Gay, *Freud*, 45.

listening Freud incarnated. Freud's theoretical transpositions of many of Cervantes's sexual allegories are revealed in this study of the history of the "future creator of psychoanalysis."

Much as he left us a legacy of openness and exploration of territories hitherto unrecognized, Freud also became in his own right an institution, causing a considerable body of Freudian thought to be appropriated (or perhaps misappropriated) as dogma. In Part II, "The Discourse of Desire," the reader will find essays that focus not only on Freudian theory but also on the ways in which desire itself enacts its evasions and disruptions of social codings and prescriptions.

Psychoanalytic theory most successfully avoids its own dogmatisms, hierarchies, and orthodoxies when informed by the liminal god Hermes, whose shapeshifting gives him access to the regions of soul otherwise resistant to observation and penetration. Hermes, the god of thieves and travelers as well as exegetes, is by nature wary of and attuned to the Other, surviving not by acts of power and authority but by a suspension of self which is the essence of the analytic attitude. Long before psychoanalysis itself became a lens by which to see the hungers and rages of infancy pushing at the borders of social intercourse and proper behavior, Cervantes's Hermetic character/narrators—Chirinos and Chanfalla, Pedro de Urdemalas, Ginés de Pasamonte, Campuzano, Cide Hamete, Periandro—were opening up territories within which the mechanisms of power and dominance could be exposed as fictions. Like Chanfalla and Chirinos in Cervantes's "Wonder Show" ("El retablo de las maravillas"), the psychoanalytic critic peoples the stage on which his or her performance takes place with the images that desire projects onto it. Such desire, as Anthony Cascardi makes clear in the opening essay of Part II, "The Archaeology of Desire in *Don Quixote*," is predicated on the replication of hierarchical distinctions.

Looking back on the wreckages made by historicist and existentialist readings, Cascardi explains the relation between history and desire through the psychoanalytic concept of archaeology. An archaeology of desire presupposes that origins are never fully recoverable: "Desire tends to gather around a series of substitutes for what has been hidden or eclipsed, although not entirely lost." For Cascardi, the "modernity" of *Don Quixote* is shown by its complex instancing of both the problem of desire and its literary representation in the early modern world. Cascardi's Cervantes is bothered not so much by the loss of the heroic ethos as by the self-destructive forms of desire that such an ethos can (and still does) generate. Concerned to find an alternative to such forms of desire, blindly pursued in the name of heroic aims, Cervantes eschews any idealist reshaping of the past, in the style of the *comedia*, with its sacrificial codes of honor. Such a pernicious economy of desire is best exemplified for Cascardi by the interpolated tale in *Don Quixote*, part I, "The Curious Impertinent," in which objects of desire are presented with the specific aim of being excluded or destroyed. Here, desire "recognizes and reincorporates precisely what it would seem to exclude." Cascardi's study locates Cervantes's modernity in his ability to articulate "the hidden mobility of desire."

The question of desire—of what drives discourse, fiction, theory, culture—also informs the second essay in Part II, Diana de Armas Wilson's comparative study of two dream interpreters, Artemidorus of Daldis and Sigmund Freud. Her "Cervantes and the Night Visitors: Dreamwork in the Cave of Montesinos" shows how Cervantes absorbs and replies to Artemidorus even as he anticipates Freud. Cervantes's fictional dreams, from *La Galatea* (1585) through the *Persiles* (1616), are precognitive and anxiously libidinized. If the use of precognition for his literary dreams makes Cervantes a descendant of Artemidorus, his foregrounding of sex/gender negotiations makes him a precursor to Freud. Don Quixote's convulsive dream in the Cave of Montesinos, where he constitutes himself as the liberator of various mummified chivalric heroes of Carolingian romance, peers beyond its own historical moment to Freudian dream theory. But it is Artemidorus, Wilson argues, who helps explain why economics and calculation surface in Don Quixote's manifest dream. The Cave of Montesinos dream thus stands at an intersection in western oneiric history. Resistant to interpretation even from within the text itself, Don Quixote's dream of indebtedness to an enchanted and needy Dulcinea reveals the constraints of desire emerging with early modern capitalism.

In the final essay in Part II, Carroll B. Johnson turns the analytic lens away from Freud—and Cervantes—to focus directly on the desire that hides within the interpreter's own discourse. In "Cervantes and the Unconscious," Johnson reviews the traditional approaches to the question of the unconscious in texts—attempts to probe the unconscious of the author or the characters—before addressing the relations between Cervantes's text, its critical readings, and "the censored chapter," in Lacanian terms, of Johnson's own unconscious. In this essay Johnson aims to explore various manifestations of the unconscious in the reader, seeking to account both for the troubling diversity of interpretations of Cervantes's works and for the rigor and tenacity with which these critical readings are championed. Johnson's claim that the ultimate cognitive objective is not knowledge about the text but knowledge about the reader is followed by an autobiographical account of the vagaries of his own unconscious and their possible bearing on Cervantes studies. Johnson compares his reading of Don Quixote's descent into a lake of boiling pitch (I.50), for him a fantasy of aggressive phallic sexuality, with Ruth El Saffar's reading, in which she sees the episode as a fantasy of maternal nurturing. While acknowledging that both interpretations help his unconscious to speak, he also recognizes an unwillingness on his part to relinquish the interpretation that best attends to his own unconscious structuring.

If Part II of the book gathers together essays that confront, in one way or another, the question of the unconscious as the source of the unconfessed desires that energize theory making and identity formation, as well as the production of dream-material, Part III, "Fragmented Heroes, Fragmented Texts," focuses on images of fragmentation as they appear in specific instances in *Don Quixote*. Fragmented heroes and texts belie the illusions of a unified self and a single correct interpretive reading which have motivated earlier critical theories. The discovery of permeable surfaces, of chinks in the armoring by which we assure ourselves of a stable reality, allows for openings into that place of the Other, openings that concern so many of the contributors to this volume.

Part III begins with Anne J. Cruz's essay, "Mirroring Others: A Lacanian Reading of the *Letrados* in *Don Quixote*." Her study addresses the confrontation between Don Quixote and the humanist figures of authority, many of them risible, who take a leading role in structuring the narrative of *Don Quixote*. Cruz examines all these "educated men"—the village priest (a graduate of Sigüenza), the members of the Argamasilla Academy, Sansón Carrasco, Don Diego de Miranda, the humanist guide to the Cave of Montesinos—as mirror images of Don Quixote. These characters function, in Cruz's reading, as a series of Lacanian "A-fathers," figures who represent the Symbolic order, one of the meanings of the Other within Cervantes's text. Through her use of Lacanian mirror-stage theory, Don Quixote's various encounters with the *letrados* are traced until the hero (re)enters the Symbolic, at the novel's closure, with his restoration to sanity.

In " 'The Whole Body of Fable with All of Its Members': Cervantes, Pinciano, Freud," Mary Malcolm Gaylord examines Cervantes's exposure of the contradictions at the core of orthodox plotting. These contradictions adumbrate, for Gaylord, Freud's account of a contest between a repressing consciousness and an irrepressible unconscious. Gaylord examines the "strappado" or wrist-hanging episode in chapter 43 of *Don Quixote*, part I, during which the "stretched-out" hero suffers excruciating, as well as conspicuously eroticized, torments.

Don Quixote's vainglorious proffering, to two playful "semidamsels,"
of his hand as a "heroic extremity" results in his finding himself
caught in a bind, his body fused with the very shape of his story.
Through its identification of Don Quixote's tortured body with "the
whole body of fable with all of its members"—the canonized fictional
anatomy of the prose epic—this episode, elucidating the Freudian
rhetoric of displacement, makes one set of members into figures for
the other. Cervantes gives us here a new rhetoric of sexual tropes,
of versions of the mind destined to become new figures. Gaylord
examines Cervantes's cunning series of master metaphors—"members," "extremities," "dismemberments"—to show how physical as
well as textual bodies in Cervantes are held together and torn apart
by the violent forces of desire.

The object of George A. Shipley's essay, "Sancho's Jokework," is
to account for Sancho's clumsy story of Lope Ruiz, the moral goatherd, and Torralba, the mustachioed and scorned shepherdess who
chases him in *Don Quixote* (I.20). Shipley deploys Freud's categories
in *Jokes and Their Relation to the Unconscious* to elucidate his reading of
this strange Cervantine episode. Sancho's "bad joke" of a story—with
its repetitive mechanism of the never-ending tale of the goat ferry,
projects onto his heroine Torralba his own clinging anxieties. The
goatherd Lope, by the same token, stands in Sancho's story for Don
Quixote's upright morality. Read through the grid of Freud's *Jokes*,
Sancho's story may be freshly seen as an aggressive spoof designed
to reflect in distorted miniature his own dilemma, and at the same
time to humiliate a master he unconsciously resents.

In Part IV, "The Other's Story," each of the contributors takes up
a figure not from among the "major" characters of *Don Quixote* but
from within the interpolated tales. The emphasis here is on how
secondary characters and events expose, in their dispersal and marginality, the desires and iconoclasms embedded within the work as
a whole.

Ruth El Saffar's essay, "In Marcela's Case," focuses on female desire
as emblematic of an alternative economy radically at odds with dominant patriarchal values yet consonant with the unconscious drives
shown to be present in *Don Quixote*. El Saffar argues that critical
studies of the Marcela episode themselves perpetuate the struggle for
gender dominance, since nearly all male critics attack the position of
freedom Marcela takes, while nearly all female critics support it. Reading Marcela as a figure for the Artemis who represents both warrior
and Great Mother characteristics, El Saffar suggests that, through
Marcela, Cervantes is exploring the roots of culture and identity for-

mation in a way that challenges the patriarchal norm. Drawing on Freudian and post-Freudian efforts to explain female psychosexual development, she proposes that many of these accounts are weakened by an unacknowledged fear of the Great Mother in her negative aspects, a fear that works to divert attention away from the regions of the psyche in which this threatening figure dwells. Marcela exposes those diversionary fictions of human development and culture.

In "Against the Law: Mad Lovers in *Don Quixote*," Carlos Feal sees Cardenio's madness as rooted in the extent of his submission to other men. Feal employs various psychoanalytic tools for conceptualizing different episodes. An opening Lacanian analysis explicates how Cardenio escapes the Symbolic order, founded on the Law of the Father, and regresses to the level of the Imaginary, the dual mother-child relation. Cardenio's fall into the Imaginary—underlined by the Foucauldian notion of madness as "the absence of work"—is enriched by a Freudian reading of (Wolf Man) Cardenio as a voyeur of the "primal scene." Feal also invokes Erich Neumann to negotiate the labyrinthine Sierra scene. At the close, both the Terrible Father and the Terrible Mother are shown to be dethroned in Cervantes's text, as the laws of pleasure or desire (*leyes del gusto*) finally assert themselves.

Remarking on the fondness of psychoanalysis "for peering into dark dwellings from which Platonists had once fled," Eduardo González, in "Curious Reflex, Cruel Reflections: The Case for Impertinence," examines the male need to encage, to "suck into a bottle," his female. González himself places the feminine—including a female descendant of the romance-besotted Don Quixote, Henry James's "cage-girl"— in three concluding boxes. These captivity narratives gloss the central concern of his essay, the "cognitive greed" of Anselmo, the hero of "The Curious Impertinent." González constructs a composite view of Anselmo from the parallel notions of weddedness—marriage both with its "sacred glow" and its "special breed of wretchedness"—and divorce or parting, including parting with portions of wealth, autonomy, and freedom. González sees Anselmo as an "incest-haunted spouse," a man out on a "hell-bent search for the flawed woman (and mother) in Camila," who is "only a mirror of spouse hysteria." The "hysteric" mode in Cervantes's tale—a mode of "emanation of ancestral mysteries from a primal core, from an oracle"—leads to an exploration of "hysterogamy," González's term for the "union and constant rumble . . . between the adult child and some buried but still festering parental corpse."

In " 'The Captive's Tale': Race, Text, Gender," Paul Julian Smith suggests that the interpolated tale traditionally regarded as Cervantes's semiautobiographical captivity narrative be read instead as a narrative of de-territorialization. Rereading this tale (I.39–41) in the light of the work of the gay theorist Guy Hocquenghem, Smith shows how Cervantes interrogates oppositions. Smith, who sees anal desire within patriarchy as diverted into social or financial investments, draws out of Cervantes's text a desublimated homosexuality. His essay opens and closes with the Moorish woman Zoraida, who functions as an Other, moving between two paradigms: she is not only an object of exchange among males—apparently destined for the closure of marriage, reproduction, and entry into the patriarchal order—but also an Arab, a Muslim, and a betrayer of the father. In addition to Zoraida, the Murcian renegade joins those North African marginals in Cervantes's narrative "who refused to be assigned to one side or the other of the paradigm." As Smith unravels the knots of race, text, and gender, he argues for a shift in our reading of "The Captive's Tale" from a phallic to an anal mode. This mode, Smith suggests, may be transposed into an "annular" group mode, a circle that causes phallic hierarchies to collapse.

Part V, "The Mother's Story: Incorporation and Abjection," takes the reader out of the mesmerizing realm of *Don Quixote* and into what have often, misleadingly, been called Cervantes's secondary works. Drawn, as so much recent psychoanalytic reading is, by the allure of the mother, the contributors in this section have focused almost exclusively on that most horrific and suppressed of figures, the witch or negative mother. It is her story, the darkest in the patriarchal construction of social roles, that is investigated as these writers take a long look at the witch Cañizares of "The Colloquy of the Dogs," and at the wily procuress of Cervantes's most outrageous and most disputed story, "The Pretended Aunt" ("La tía fingida").

Maurice Molho's "Cervantes and the 'Terrible Mothers' " opens this section. The "Terrible Mothers" he addresses are a group of iron-willed and overwhelming women who appear in both Cervantes's life and his writings—mothers who dominate men of diminished virility. Suggesting that a Terrible Mother lurked in Cervantes's unconscious, Molho focuses on a series of mothers, beginning with Cervantes's own "supervirile" mother, Leonor Cortinas. The question of why Cervantes displaced his mother's name, Cortinas, with the substitute name Saavedra, making his authorial name a crucible for erasure and repression, is for Molho an issue rife with parental fantasies. The second mother he examines is the witch Montiela in "The Colloquy of the Dogs," an absent mother rejected by her canine son Cipión and—her maternity monstrously figured by the "double-sexed" witch Cañizares—by Berganza, too. Although the attitudes of the two dogs appear to be different, Molho sees their motivations as similar: maternal disavowal, whether intellectual or emotional, is the structural name of the game. Molho continues his discussion with a look at the phallic women in the "The Wonder Show," Juana Macha and Teresa Repolla, women whose names reveal not only their virile qualities but also, as a corollary and structural constant, the infravirility of the men in their families. The last, and the most limited, of the phallic mothers is Teresa Panza, whom Molho examines through the onomastics of her name, through her material concerns, and through her dominating sense of the "reality principle."

In the second essay of Part V, " 'The Pretended Aunt': Misreading and the Scandal of the Missing Mothers," Mary S. Gossy takes a close look at the ways in which literature, as well as the critics who interpret it, continues to be caught in the requirement of culture that the mother be suppressed. Gossy's rereading of "The Pretended Aunt," a tale so scandalous as to have been generally voted out of the Cervantine canon, suggests that the story's presentation of a woman active in the pursuit of her own economic and sexual needs threatens patriarchal norms, as well as the venerable image of Cervantes that many critics have cultivated. Even more threatening than the figure of the procuress, however, is that of the mother destined to be left in silence and obscurity. By calling attention to the figure of the absent mother so neglected in critical commentary on the tale, Gossy brings to light the absence that founds culture, righting and rewriting in the process the history of her own critical encounter with the text.

Finding in Nicolas Abraham and Maria Torok the theoretical tools to argue that "The Colloquy of the Dogs" is an "incorporation," Andrew Bush shows, in "The Phantom of Montilla," how an enigmatic text may remain symbolic, subtended by a metaphor whose unity is recoverable. With useful assistance from Poe and Shakespeare, Bush elaborates on Abraham and Torok's revision of the Freudian death drive, their theories of the Phantom and the Crypt. These "theories of readability" counter not only Lacan's mechanism of "foreclosure," which sees the genesis of psychosis as strictly illegible ("a gap in sense and a senseless gap") but also his postulate of the Nom-du-Père. But it is Bush's replicative coinage of the "ouïe-de-la-mère"—saying yes (oui) to the mother through a hearing (ouïe)—which allows him to read Cervantes's protagonist-dogs as embodying "the figurative expression of the mother's unconscious." Bush argues that Abraham and Torok's concept of the Phantom permits deci-

pherment—the recovery, through transgenerational and translinguistic orientation, of determinate, if not always verifiable, meaning.
The Phantom, Bush persuades us, is "at large" in the "Colloquy."
She is the witch Cañizares, his titular Phantom of Montilla, whose
enigmatic prophecy is misinterpreted by the dogs, condemned from
birth to "incorporate" instead of to "introject"—to reenact the bizarre
acts of a cryptic family drama. Bush closes his essay with a fictive
"prehistory" of incest in the family from Montilla. This little psychodrama, a prospectus for a one-act play (*entremés*) conjectured from
social history, turns on the father's seduction of the daughter. The
mother's discovery of the incest indicts the daughter as the offending
agent of the family's fall. The violated daughter then secretly mothers
a haunted son who, in hallucinatory moments, believes himself to be
a dog, a "beast of (his mother's) burden." The closure of this essay,
in the mode of what Barbara Johnson calls "hard-working word play,"
elucidates what for centuries has remained a senseless gap: those
enigmatic words Cervantes claimed to have "engendered" in the
"Colloquy"—that "flesh has gone to flesh."

Finally, María Antonia Garcés, in "Berganza and the Abject: The
Desecration of the Mother," approaches the "The Colloquy of the
Dogs" from the perspective of Julia Kristeva's elaboration of Freudian
and Lacanian psychoanalysis, proposing that its central episode—the
episode of the witch Cañizares—represents the discourse of the
Other, that is, the subject of the unconscious. Cañizares stands for
that opacity of the signifying system (the slips, the vacillations, the
dreams) that constitutes Berganza as subject. Garcés also amplifies
the sexual allusions in Cervantes's text, until recently elided by most
critics. Much of her essay is devoted to the notion of abjection, as
defined by Julia Kristeva's theories of the accession to language in
Powers of Horror. The depiction of the witch Cañizares surpasses the
traditional image of woman as whore in order to posit the feminine
as "abject." Illustrating a dramatic attempt at separation, at constituting a unity, the abject appears as that terrifying emptiness that
marks the first split between what is not yet an ego and what is not
yet an object, as Kristeva argues in *Tales of Love*. As that uncanny
"object that functions as a magnet of identification," ensuring the
advent of a subject for an object, the abject is intimately linked to the
birth of language. Garcés reads "The Colloquy of the Dogs" as a
profound reflection not only on the question of human desire, but
also on the problem of origins: the origin of being, and especially the
origin of language.

♦

The order of the sections is designed to follow a shift in keeping with developments in psychoanalytic theory itself. Psychoanalysis since Freud has been largely occupied with delving into that area most neglected in his work, the area of the mother-child dyad from which the father is by and large excluded. The emphasis among object relations theorists on the mother marks a movement away from Freud's paternal, oedipal emphasis, a movement reflected also in our organization of the volume. To the degree that fascination with and focus on the mother can also be found in the later works of Cervantes, one could say that Cervantes anticipated the shift in psychoanalysis itself from father-focus to mother-focus. It is in this light that, in the concluding section of this introduction, we want to consider not only the Freud who read Cervantes but also the Cervantes who continues to read Freud.

Nothing reveals better than the one-act play "The Wonder Show" Cervantes's deflation of the illusion of father-rule so desperately embraced by the dominant social order. In the play, two sexually and socially amorphous theater directors, Chirinos and Chanfalla, take their imaginary show from town to town, exposing as they do the anxieties of social and sexual identity that govern the perceptions of their audiences. As Maurice Molho points out in his essay in this volume, the onomastics of "The Wonder Show" give away what the theater directors reveal through their self-reflexive stagecraft: that beneath the posturing of legitimacy through which the fiction of order and identity is enforced lies another order entirely, the order of mother-rule. As in his other interludes, or in short novels such as "The Jealous Extremaduran" ("El celoso Extremeño") and "The Call of Blood" ("La fuerza de la sangre"), to name only a few of the works in which the pretensions of honor are deflated, in "The Wonder Show" Cervantes gives us a glimpse of the maternal-sexual-imaginative power that in fact controls the social order.

Chirinos and Chanfalla tell the town magistrates and their families that only those people whose fathers are Old Christian (not crypto-Jewish) and sovereign, sexually, in their own homes will be able to see the dramas about to be presented. Although the theater masters have no show at all, everyone participates desperately and spontaneously in creating one, out of fear of being exposed as illegitimate or socially fraudulent. The fear that Chirinos and Chanfalla expose in the town magistrates has everything to do with the status of the father. Might he be tainted by racially inferior ancestry? Is he *really* he father? The question of legitimacy, as the theater masters show, haunts the social order and drives its activities.

The fact that the response to the fear of exposure is universal among the townspeople suggests that in Cervantes, as in modern psychoanalytic theory, the subject is a construction ever in the process of defending itself against the revelation of its own fictive nature. The psychoanalytic emphasis on the central importance of the father in bringing the child out of maternal symbiosis and into culture shows the fragility of the culture into which the child is introduced, and the massive pressures just under the surface that threaten to disrupt it. Through psychoanalytic theory, the divided, decentered subject so clearly exposed in Cervantes's writings becomes a subject available to critical discourse.

Animating the essays of this volume is the shared supposition, informed by a variety of psychoanalytically inspired theories, that Cervantes repeatedly challenges the assumptions of that paternal power which the dominant social order promulgates as a norm. By seeking in the romances of chivalry the heroic and invulnerable father, Don Quixote finally learns the emptiness of that image and those models. In an especially poignant expression of the despair that marks his shift in character from part I to part II, he protests that "this whole world is tricks and devices, one against the other. I can do no more" (II.29).[5] The discovery of the empty signifier—that the "real" does not inhabit the signs that seek to capture it—makes of all order, all convention, all system a substitute, an image that reflects nothing more than the desire of the subject for that which is always Other. Cervantes's use of theater, of the play within the play, of narratives within narratives, of stories, characters, and narrators whose origins remain foreign or uncertain, repeats the theme of psychoanalysis that it is *lack* that haunts the subject and, by extension, the social and theoretical order. All systems, including language, are constructed to disguise that lack.

Out of that lack Freud also made his own story of psychoanalysis. Turning psychoanalytic method on itself, many post-Freudians whose work is used in this volume have asked one question: What does Freud's founding story of the Oedipus complex, with its accompanying use of the castration complex and the boy's introjection of the incest-prohibiting superego, *not* tell? Based on an idealization of the mother-son bond, Freud writes a story of a boy's forced, unwanted separation from the all-loving mother. In that story the boy gives up

5. "Todo este mundo es máquinas y trazas, contrarias unas de otras. Yo no puedo más" (II.29).

his desire for his mother only because of the threat of a powerful father.[6] The desire the male child represses because of his fear of castration is what Freud, reading himself into the myth of Oedipus, took to be every boy's desire to remain one with the mother. The "positive" resolution of the Oedipus complex, according to this interpretation, brings the boy into identification with the father and therefore into the laws of the culture, the principal one being the law prohibiting incest.

Since the success of the enforcement of the father's law depends on the power of his threat, the acquisition of identity, conferred as a mantle once the son has given up his wish to remain one with the mother, assumes a mother worthy of desire, and a father strong enough to enforce separation from her. But what if neither is true? What if the boy, as Berganza and Cipión show in "The Colloquy of the Dogs," in fact finds the mother repugnant? (Cipión finds laudable Berganza's refusal to let the woman who says she is their mother kiss him: "You did well. It is no gift, but rather a torment to let yourself be kissed by an old lady.")[7] What if she "had a lively temper and was impatient, self-willed, and sharp-witted," as Freud's son Martin describes his grandmother Amalia Freud?[8] Could there be, in the overpowering, loquacious, and sometimes terrifying mothers Cervantes wrote into Don Quixote and "The Colloquy of the Dogs" a flavor of the problematic in the bond of mother and son that Freud insisted on calling "altogether the most perfect, the most free from ambivalence of all human relationships"?[9] And if the father is a Vi-

6. In "The Shell and the Kernel," trans. Nicholas Rand, Diacritics 9 (1979): 16–28, Nicolas Abraham and Maria Torok take up the question of the lie of the Oedipus complex, the story of the boy's guilty desire to be free of the mother which the invention of the threatening father is designed to disguise. For a discussion, see Esther Rashkin, "Tools for a New Psychoanalytic Literary Criticism: The Work of Abraham and Torok," Diacritics 18 (1988): 31–52. Madelon Sprengnether, in "(M)other Eve: Some Revisions of the Fall in Fiction by Contemporary Women Writers," in Feminism and Psychoanalysis, ed. Richard Feldstein and Judith Roof (Ithaca: Cornell University Press, 1989), 298–322, also sees repression lying behind the psychoanalytic myth of Oedipus, reading in Freud's idealization of the all-good mother a repression of her powerful negative aspects.

7. "Bien hiciste; porque no es regalo, sino tormento, el besar ni dejar besarse de una vieja" (291). Citations in Spanish come from Juan Bautista Avalle-Arce's edition of the Novelas ejemplares, vol. 3 (Madrid: Clásicos Castalia, 1982). The English translation is our own. María Antonia Garcés, in her essay "Berganza and the Abject," discusses at length the question of mother-incest in the "Colloquy."

8. See Gay, Freud, 504.

9. The reference is from "Femininity," in The Standard Edition of the Complete Psychological Works of Sigmund Freud, ed. and trans. James Strachey, 24 vols. (London: Hogarth Press, 1953–74), 22:133. Further references to the Standard Edition will be abbreviated SE with volume and page number. As the editors of the Standard Edition point out, comments similar to the

ennese Jew whom German teenagers succeed in taunting and humiliating,[10] or an impoverished barber-surgeon of possibly *converso*
origin unable to support his family,[11] could it not be that the idealized
strong father, like the all-good mother, is more a wish than a reality,
a wish that Cervantes, more willingly than Freud, was able to "smile
away"?[12]

What if the story of Oedipus, like the story of Amadís of Gaul,
becomes a fiction, a substitute, designed by men—Freud, let us say,
and, to draw from literature, Don Quixote—who would otherwise
find themselves at the mercy of Medusa, the all-powerful, engulfing,
castrating mother whom the fictions of the nuclear family seek to
deny and contain. Melanie Klein and Julia Kristeva, as well as Abraham and Torok, all suggest for Freud what Maurice Molho has suggested for Cervantes: that it is the mother's desire and power, not
that of the compensatorily invoked fathers, against which the "hero"
seeks to defend.

So powerful is the insistence on the father's rule in Freud that he
sees the incest prohibition as foundational to culture. In both *Totem
and Taboo* and *Moses and Monotheism* he sought, through a historical
reconstruction, to account for the universality of the Law of the Father.
As Rosalind Coward has argued, however, Freud's theories of culture
and human development were heavily influenced by the late-
nineteenth-century debate regarding the universality of patriarchy.[13]

---

one quoted in "Femininity" can also be found in *Group Psychology and the Analysis of the Ego*
(*SE* 18:69–143), *Introductory Lectures on Psycho-Analysis* (*SE* 16 and 17), and *Civilization and Its
Discontents* (*SE* 21:64–145).

10. Peter Gay, among other biographers of Freud, makes much of the incident, which
"stung" Freud into developing "fantasies of revenge"; see *Freud*, 12.

11. Cervantes's biographer William Byron calls proofs of Cervantes's Jewish ancestry "cir-
cumstantial and inconclusive," noting also that "while they can be countered, they cannot
be dismissed"; see *Cervantes: A Biography* (Garden City, N.Y.: Doubleday, 1978), 24. A much
more positive presentation of Cervantes's likely status as a *converso* is offered by Américo
Castro, whose entire *Cervantes y los casticismos españoles* (Madrid: Alfaguera, 1966) is devoted
to the subject.

12. The reference here is an echo of Lord Byron's remark in *Don Juan* 13.11 that Cervantes
"smiled Spain's chivalry away."

13. Coward points out that anthropological studies in the second half of the nineteenth
century brought to western Europe questions about the universality of the patriarchal family
which provoked a "most violent controversy." The controversy produced "a mass of speculation not just on the history of the relations between the sexes, but also on the meanings
of the different forms of sexual ordering"; see Rosalind Coward, *Patriarchal Precedents: Sexuality and Social Relations* (London: Routledge and Kegan Paul, 1983), 10. Freud was both
deeply influenced by and highly aware of these debates, and clearly situated himself on the
side of patriarchy as a founding institution of culture. See chapters 7 and 8 of *Patriarchal
Precedents* for a detailed account of Freud's theories and their relation to the concept of
patriarchy.

He clearly positioned his theories against those of writers such as J. J. Bachofen and J. F. McLennan, who proposed a matriarchate at the foundations of human culture. Jacques Lacan's structuralist reading of Freud also tends toward a universalizing of the Law of the Father by associating the foreclosure of the father with psychosis.

Whether the rule of the phallus, as Lacan repeats the Freudian gesture of father-dominance, is universal or historically conditioned, the structures of the psyche described by psychoanalysis in the twentieth century were clearly in place in the sixteenth and seventeenth centuries in Spain. Cervantes's "Wonder Show" exposes the fact that power among the men who rule the towns of Spain is based on the notion that one is one's father's son, and that the father is himself a man of power. The fear that such an idealization of the father may be unwarranted controls the population. The fiction of father-rule persists, however, because it seems preferable to submission to the Furies that seem to dwell in the realm of the mother.

The contributors to this volume express, albeit in vastly different ways, what we see as a common vision of the Cervantine unconscious, one that undermines the Freudian story of Oedipus in ways similar to the work of post-Freudian writers such as Melanie Klein and Abraham and Torok. Klein's excavations in the pre-oedipal realm reveal the origins of the Terrible Mother in the child's frustration and rage when she fails him. Although she is a source of gratification, her power to reject allies her with Kali and Medusa and all the mythological figures that portray the monstrous aspects of woman. It is precisely those aspects—the terrifying, death-dealing, rejecting aspects of the mother/goddess—and the corresponding failure of the father to rescue the son from her that Cervantes exposes in his works.

Versions of the son's possession by the mother are revealed in Feal's study of Cardenio, Bush's and Garcés's analyses of the dogs in the "Colloquy," El Saffar's discussion of Grisóstomo, and Molho's reading of Cervantes himself. Emphasizing the power, albeit occluded, of the feminine in the unconscious of Cervantes's texts are the essays of Gaylord, Gossy, and El Saffar. The impulse to bottle or cage that feminine power that threatens to engulf men is the object of González's text, while Shipley alludes to the male impulse to flee from that power. Other contributors emphasize not so much the terror, madness, and death that await men who face the feminine unprotected as the failures of the male characters fully to enter the father's world. That is the basis of the studies offered here by Cruz and Smith.

At the beginning of this introduction we asked what may have caused Freud both to read and to conceal his attachment to precisely the two works most frequently tapped by our contributors for psychoanalytic insight. Given his secret boyhood fascination with "The Colloquy of the Dogs" and his passionate attachment as a young man to *Don Quixote*, could it have been that Freud saw exposed in Cervantes, as he also did in his early work with hysterics, the Gorgon side of the mother which his theory of Oedipus was later designed to repress?

If the Other is the unconscious, and if that unconscious is the territory marked out by desire for and fear of the mother, Cervantes anatomizes the repression, by both the social order and classical psychoanalysis, of the mother's story, that is, the story of the outlawed son still in possession of and possessed by the mother. Luce Irigaray's observation that psychoanalysis remains fixated in the anal stage, or alternatively the phallic stage,[14] underscores the point that the Cervantes whom Freud read as a young man also reads him. The "coarseness" of *Don Quixote* against which the founder of psychoanalysis warned Martha Bernays may have reflected his desire to keep his fiancée within the bounds of a cultural norm which, at the same time, he enjoyed seeing Cervantes undermine. The Cervantes who showed the horrific, witchlike aspects of the mother may well have appealed to the adolescent Sigismund, just as the Cervantes who deflated the romances of chivalry may have amused a young doctor beginning to explore the question of hysteria. From the later Freud, however, the founder of psychoanalysis who abandoned the paternal seduction theory and built his theory of psychosexual development around the story of Oedipus, we hear nothing more of Cervantes.

Although the contributors to this volume have themselves identified with different roles with respect to the family romance unveiled in Cervantes's work—a point central to Carroll Johnson's study—all work together to illuminate the nature of that romance. The mother whom Cipión in "The Colloquy of the Dogs" repudiates has a tragic secret that cripples her sons. The secret the subject both knows (Berganza) and denies (Cipión) is that the mother has been seduced into a social order that is built out of the denial of her being. She, and the story of the child's seduction by the father which she cannot tell, is the outlaw who must forever be ruled. Her revenge is to rule, in her turn, her son. What Cervantes allows us to see—through, for example, the witch's narrative in "The Colloquy of the Dogs"—is how

---

14. See Luce Irigaray, *Speculum of the Other Woman*, trans. Gillian C. Gill (Ithaca: Cornell University Press, 1985), for an extended exposition of this point.

the toxins of anger and envy infect the child. Through psychoanalytic readings that scrutinize what the author "refrained from writing" for a story of identity the culture cannot tell, we find the fiction of father-rule and mother-love disrupted along with many of the other fictions of the patriarchal family.

I

The Discourse
of Affiliation

1

Cervantes as Cultural Ancestor of Freud

León Grinberg and
Juan Francisco Rodríguez

El hidalgo fue un sueño de Cervantes
Y don Quijote un sueño del hidalgo.
El doble sueño los confunde y algo
Está pasando que pasó mucho antes.

—Jorge Luis Borges, "Sueña Alonso
Quijano"

Siegfried Bernfeld, who has made such brilliant contributions to the history of Freud and psychoanalysis, once wrote that "the fantasies of his childhood and the daydreams of his adolescent period, insofar as they are known to us, do not reveal anything about Freud as the future creator of psychoanalysis."[1] In this essay, however, we attempt to prove that it is possible to trace the formation of the "future creator of psychoanalysis" by paying careful attention to a marginal underground current that flows through his literary and philosophical interests rather than to his more official and more overt concerns. In such an investigation one should never lose sight of Freud's own references to formative events in his life: "My deep engrossment in the Bible story (almost as soon as I had learnt the art of reading) had, as I recognized much later, an enduring effect upon the direction of my interest."[2] His later engrossment in Goethe's essay on nature must

1. This essay is a radically revised version of a longer study by Drs. León Grinberg and Juan Francisco Rodríguez that appeared in the *International Journal of Psycho-Analysis* 65 (1984): 155–68. The reference to Siegfried Bernfeld is from "Freud's Scientific Beginnings," *American Imago* 6 (1949): 133.

2. *The Standard Edition of the Complete Psychological Works of Sigmund Freud*, ed. and trans.

also have had an enduring effect on his interest, since Freud decided to study medicine after reading it. From this point of view it is fitting that, many years later, in 1930, Freud was to receive the Goethe Prize for the literary quality of his work, an award that was a source of great satisfaction to him. The analysis of texts, authors, and characters appears, as is well known, throughout Freud's work. One has the impression that literary, biblical, and mythical subjects were a permanent source of creative inspiration for him. Although the literary aspect of Freud's interests has been commented on in hundreds of articles and from multiple perspectives, we believe that more can be said, particularly with regard to Freud's seldom-noted involvement with various works by Cervantes.

Motivated by his interest in science and research, as well as by his aversion to practical medicine, Freud worked as a researcher at the Brücke Institute until June 1882, when the director advised him, in view of his meager financial prospects, to go into private practice. Although, in his autobiography, Freud associates his decision to abandon scientific research with the advice of his teacher Ernst von Brücke, there was, perhaps, another influence at work. In this very same month of June 1882 Freud had fallen in love with Martha Bernays, and he needed to earn a living if he was to marry and provide for a family. As a result, Freud left the Institute and entered the General Hospital of Vienna with the intention of studying for two years the various specialties that would prepare him for the practice of general medicine.

In November 1882, when Freud was working in the Division of Internal Medicine under Professor Nothnagel, his colleague and mentor Josef Breuer told him about the case of Anna O. This case aroused in him an enormous interest, and he felt the need to comment on it over and over again. In May 1883 Freud left his parents' house to reside in the psychiatric clinic run by Theodor Meynert. He remained in the psychiatry department until October, when he switched to dermatology. In the five months between May and October which amounted to his entire psychiatric experience, Freud was to make the crucial choice to specialize in neurology, a decision that led to his studies in hysteria and psychoanalysis.

According to Ernest Jones, Freud was studying acute hallucinatory psychosis when "he obtained the vivid impression of the wish-fulfillment mechanism he was to apply so extensively in his later

James Strachey, 24 vols. (London: Hogarth Press, 1953–74), 20:8. Further references to the *Standard Edition* will be abbreviated *SE*, with volume and page number.

investigations of the unconscious."[3] It may have been his interest in the problem of hallucination that led Freud to read Flaubert's *Temptation of Saint Anthony*. From his letters to Martha, we know that Freud was reading Flaubert's work during a trip with Breuer. On July 26, 1883, Freud wrote to Martha: "What impresses one above everything is the vividness of the hallucinations, the way in which the sense impressions surge up, transform themselves and suddenly disappear. . . . One understands it better when one knows that Flaubert was an epileptic and given to hallucinations himself."[4]

Once he became interested in the subject of hallucinatory phenomena, it is not surprising that Freud would want to read *Don Quixote*, since the delirious fantasies and possible hallucinations of its protagonist would enable him to continue his reflections on the subject. Indeed, Freud comments on the book several times to Martha in letters dated August 22 and 23 and September 8, 1883.[5] In the letters to Martha, one also finds references to Anna O. Freud comments on her on August 5, and on October 31 he relates the episode of the transference-love with Breuer. On November 11 Freud discusses with Martha the impossibility of a patient's falling in love with him ("For that to happen one has to be a Breuer"),[6] alluding by implication once again to the very absorbing case of Anna O.

It seems evident that Freud spent the summer of 1883 occupied with the two literary texts that, as we know from Jones's remark, had made the greatest impression on him as a young man. We believe that there is a significant correlation between Freud's arrival at the psychiatric clinic, his discovery of wish-fulfillment through the acute hallucinatory psychosis known as Meynert's amentia, his interest in the hallucinations of Saint Anthony and Flaubert, his fascination with the delirious world of Don Quixote, and his involvement with the case of Anna O., who suffered from intense hallucinations and whose pregnancy and hysterical delivery were understood as hallucinatory. This catalogue of events enables us to understand that, already by 1883, a central core of psychoanalytic thought was forming in Freud's mind. Before then, Freud had devoted himself to the study of histology and anatomy of the nervous system, about which he published

3. Ernest Jones, *Sigmund Freud: Life and Work*, 3 vols. (London: Hogarth Press, 1953), 1:72.
4. Ibid., 192.
5. A selection of Freud's letters appears in *Briefe, 1873–1939*, ed. Ernst Freud and Lucie Freud (1960); the English version appears as *Letters of Sigmund Freud, 1873–1939*, trans. Tania Stern and James Stern (New York: Basic Books, 1961). References to Freud's correspondence will be given by date and addressee of his letters.
6. Jones, *Life*, 247.

five papers. Although he continued to publish works on these topics for another ten years, and gave no public evidence during that time of his thoughts on hysteria, we can reasonably claim to establish contact with "the future creator of psychoanalysis" at this point.

It is in the crucial summer of 1883 that *Don Quixote* takes on its singular importance. In his letter to Martha of August 22 Freud writes: "This same kind of gay moodiness, as I would like to call it, also leads me to my not making good use of my time: I read a lot, fritter away much of the day. For instance, I now possess *Don Quixote* . . . and concentrate more on it than on brain anatomy." In other words, Freud feels guilty for neglecting what he considers to be his official duties for the sake of what we might now call his psychoanalytic interests. But, as a vehicle for expressing this personal conflict, Cervantes's *Don Quixote* is particularly apt, for it is precisely this book that most vividly captures the variance between reality and fantasy, a conflict in which Freud himself felt totally immersed.

We know, in fact, from his autobiographical references that neither at that time nor indeed in his later life, did Freud feel any particular predilection for his career as a doctor. He notes in his autobiography that he was moved, rather, "by a sort of curiosity, which was, however, directed more towards human concerns than towards natural objects" (*SE* 20:8). Later he adds: "In my youth I felt an overpowering need to understand something of the riddles of the world in which we live and perhaps even to contribute something to their solution" (*SE* 20:253). It is evident that these dreams, channeled through his research at the Brücke Institute, were quixotic, since Freud does not seem to have sufficiently taken into account their reality. Indeed, Jones's account highlights the idealistic nature of Freud's youthful dreams of scientific dedication.

> He was twenty-six. He did not want to be a physician. Yet he was in a blind alley, with practically no future prospects of ever earning a livelihood. The lack of foresight, and indeed of a sense of reality, seems so foreign to the Freud we knew later, who was always alive to the practical issues of life. From his subsequent accounts of the happenings one could get the impression that it was only Brücke's homiletic intervention that suddenly woke him out of a dream, the dream of idealistically serving the cause of science irrespective of mundane considerations.[7]

7. Ibid., 68.

Martha Bernays played a role in awakening Freud from his dream of research. In a letter of October 9, 1883, Freud clearly points to the existence of this conflict between his scientific work (at this moment, for him, laboratory research) and his love for Martha when, as we mentioned earlier, on falling in love, he had been forced to think about and to take into account mundane necessities. Freud states in this letter that research is a dream and his love for Martha a reality. On another occasion he writes that brain anatomy (research) was the only serious rival Martha ever had, and when, in December 1885, he abandons the laboratory of La Sâlpetrière, he confirms this to himself again, saying that he could overcome his love for science only to the extent that it was an obstacle between him and Martha. Here Freud is struggling against the new scientific interest—psychopathology— which had begun to take on importance for him as a result of his contact with Jean Martin Charcot. This interest, which threatened to absorb him in 1885, had already engaged his thoughts two years earlier, as we have seen, for it was in the summer of 1883 that he first became interested in hallucinations, delusions, and wish fulfillment in Saint Anthony, Don Quixote, and Anna O. These interests had more remote antecedents. In other words, in the summer of 1883 Freud's mind was in conflict between his psychopathological interests and brain anatomy. His efforts to become a neurologist were resisted by his fascination with psychoanalytic research.

The conflict seems to us to be most revealing. In one of his letters to Martha, Freud identifies with Don Quixote: "We were all noble knights passing through the world caught in a dream."[8] We know about his dreams of glory (his interest in Hannibal and so on), and his fantasy of making some brilliant discovery (his adventure with cocaine, so quixotic in many ways, would begin in April 1884). During the three years in question, while engaged in hospital work, Freud was constantly occupied with "the endeavour to make a name for himself by discovering something important."[9]

The themes of wish fulfillment, transference, cathartic method, and the possibility of explaining hallucination and delirium were all being developed unconsciously during the period of Freud's engagement to Martha. At the same time, he was himself living out the conflict between his own desires and dreams and the difficulties he came up against in trying to fulfill them, a conflict that stimulated him to self-analysis. Thus, it is logical that *Don Quixote* would interest him more

8. Cited ibid., 191.
9. Ibid., 86.

than brain anatomy because, while Cervantes expressed his own personal conflict, he also offered some very important keys to understanding it. If this universal conflict posited by Cervantes—between fantasies and dreams on the one hand and realities on the other—could be understood by Freud himself and explained to the world, this achievement would carry along with it the glory he had dreamed of and would at the same time resolve his personal conflict.

Cervantes presents madness as a complex but intelligible phenomenon in terms of human motivations. This must have been a tremendously important stimulus or reinforcement for Freud, who had set for himself precisely the project of making sense of, or finding a meaning for, dreams, symptoms, and ultimately madness itself. Don Quixote not only talks about "la razón de la sinrazón"—"the reason for the unreason" which would be the ultimate goal of Freud's entire work—but also constantly gives proof that deeds, actions, and words can be understood if one pays attention to the motivations that cause those reactions. This would largely explain the success of *Don Quixote*, insofar as the reasons behind irrationality can be understood: if madness has its rational aspect, if reason can be understood, the gap between sanity and insanity is narrowed or disappears, for there is a certain compatibility between madness and reason.

When Freud was studying psychiatry with Meynert in the summer of 1883, however, no one saw the possibilities for comprehending the symptoms of neurosis and psychosis. Nobody saw "the reason for the unreason." Surely this was what led Freud to talk, on the one hand, about "useless psychiatry" and, on the other, about how he had wasted his time reading *Don Quixote*. The similarity of thought between Cervantes and Freud now becomes clear. Freud was going to do in the scientific world what he found Cervantes doing in the literary one. That is, he was going to restore the status of fantasy and subjectivity in a post-Cartesian world which had tried to deemphasize those factors, and to discover and study the laws and mechanisms by which psychic reality is governed. In short, Freud's contact during the summer of 1883 with the world of Don Quixote deeply affected the future creator of psychoanalysis. Jones tells us that this contact was a *re*reading of *Don Quixote*. Perhaps closer research into Freud's *first* contact with Cervantes might tell us even more about the birth of psychoanalysis. To take that closer look, we must now consider "The Colloquy of the Dogs" ("El coloquio de los perros").

Freud writes about his first contact with Cervantes in a letter to Martha on February 7, 1884. He recalls that as a boy he had read "The Colloquy of the Dogs" together with his friend Silberstein. The two of them had founded a "Castilian Academy," of which they were the sole members, and called each other by the names of the dogs, Freud taking on the role of Cipión, Silberstein that of Berganza. Freud describes his relationship with Silberstein as very close and intense: "We used to be together literally every hour of the day that was not spent on the school bench."

"The Colloquy of the Dogs," the last of the twelve *novelas* from Cervantes's 1613 collection *Exemplary Novels*, begins in a frame tale called "The Deceitful Marriage" ("El casamiento engañoso"). A soldier named Campuzano tells a friend that, while recuperating from syphilis in a hospital, he overheard and wrote down a dialogue between two dogs named Cipión and Berganza, who spoke all night at the foot of his bed while they thought he was sleeping. The question of what is fantasy and what is reality, so important to Cervantes, is evident from the beginning of this story, which was so fascinating to Freud. The problem lends particular conviction to the idea that Cervantes is a cultural ancestor of Freud's. Cervantes's story, in effect, begins with the discussion of whether dogs can actually talk, whether the whole story might be merely the dream of the convalescent patient Campuzano, or whether it might be a fantasy spun out of his imagination. The theme of fantasy and its power to usurp reality recurs in various forms as a leitmotif as Berganza's story unfolds. Thus, for example, when the witch Cañizares describes her participation in the witches' sabbaths, she explains:

> Hay opinión que no vamos a estos convites sino con la fantasía, en la cual nos representa el demonio las imágenes de todas aquellas cosas que después contamos que nos han sucedido. Otros dicen que no, sino que verdaderamente vamos en cuerpo y en ánima; y entrambas opiniones tengo para mí que son verdaderas, puesto que nosotras no sabemos cuándo vamos de una o de otra manera, porque todo lo que nos pasa en la fantasía es tan intensamente, que no hay diferenciarlo de cuando vamos real y verdaderamente.

> [People say that we attend these gatherings only in our imagination, and that the devil calls up before our mind's eye the image of all those things which we afterwards relate as though they had happened. Others disagree, and say that we really go in body and soul. For my part, I believe both these opinions to be true, even though we don't know when we go in one form or the other, for everything that happens to us in our fancy is so intense that there's no difference between it and what really and actually happens.][10]

10. Miguel de Cervantes, *Novelas ejemplares*, ed. Franciso Rodríguez Marín, 2 vols. (Madrid:

The witch tells Berganza that he and Cipión are actually human children, transformed at birth because of envy. She also discusses the possibility of undoing the enchantment. In other words, the themes of enchantment and transformation so prevalent in *Don Quixote* are also present in "The Colloquy of the Dogs." There are many other quixotic themes in the "Colloquy," such as the references to language, instinct and reason, aggression, deceit, and corruption, as well as a perfect description of idealization in the ironic criticism of the pastoral world as described in the literature of the period. Thus, a whole repertoire of the key themes of psychoanalytic thought was already an object of interest for Freud as a young student.

But there is something even more suggestive for the history of psychoanalysis in "The Colloquy of the Dogs," since this short work is cast in the form of a dialogue with a very peculiar structure. The story portrays Berganza narrating his life to Cipión throughout the night. In this atmosphere, free from external distractions, Berganza begins by confessing:

> Y aun de mí, que desde que tuve fuerzas para roer un hueso, tuve deseo de hablar, para decir cosas que depositaba en la memoria, y allí, de antiguas y muchas, o se enmohecían, o se me olvidaban. Empero ahora, que tan sin pensarlo me veo enriquecido deste divino don de la habla, pienso gozarle y aprovecharme dél lo más que pudiere, dándome priesa a decir todo aquello que se me acordare, aunque sea atropellada y confusamente.

> Ever since I was big enough to gnaw a bone, I have wanted to talk and say things I had stored up in my memory which, growing old or dim there, either rusted away or were forgotten. But now, finding myself endowed with this divine gift of speech, I intend to enjoy it and profit from it to the fullest, making haste to say everything I can remember, even though it comes out all higgledy-piggledy.]
> (213)

To which Cipión replies: "Habla hasta que amanezca . . . que yo te escucharé de muy buena gana, sin impedirte sino cuando viere ser necesario [Talk until morning . . . for I'll listen with great pleasure, without interrupting you unless I think it necessary"] (214). This attitude of psychoanalytic listening is sustained by Cipión throughout the entire narration, as he encourages Berganza, for example, to delve

Espasa-Calpe, 1975), 2:296–97. Further references to the "Coloquio" are to this edition and will be cited in the text.

further into his problems: "Antes, Berganza, que pases adelante, es bien que reparemos en lo que te dijo la bruja, y averigüemos si puede ser verdad la grande mentira a quien das crédito [Before you go on, Berganza, it would be well for us to give thought to what the witch told you, and to find out whether the great lie you believe can be true]" (309). Although Cipión does not interpret the facts, he listens and maintains an attitude of guidance and encouragement perfectly in keeping with the character and personality of Freud. This may explain why Freud identified with Cipión in his game with his boyhood friend Silberstein. According to Freud's letters to Martha, the role of listener was characteristic of his place in his personal relations with Silberstein. In reality, Cipión's attitude in the "Colloquy" is similar to one that the "pre-psychoanalyst" Freud would adopt with his patients in his *Studies on Hysteria*. It is from such an ethico-pedagogical position that Cipión pressures his "patient" Berganza to recall the many traumas, abandonments, and abuses he suffered throughout his life. Speaking of such previously unmentioned events would constitute an actual catharsis. The psychoanalytic atmosphere becomes more intense as we observe how Berganza begins to enquire about his true identity. Along with his "therapist" Cipión, Berganza seeks out the truth regarding his origins and life story.

It is not difficult to see in the story of Cipión and Berganza how the seed of psychoanalysis was planted in the adolescent Freud. The seed already contained the essential themes of reality and fantasy: the interplay and distinction between them, as well as the fundamental question of fantasy that imposes itself as reality, essential for an understanding of the unconscious. Cervantes's story also evokes the problems of instinct and reason and other phenomena such as idealization and its origins. The "Colloquy's" staging of the conversation enshrined in silence, moreover, also contains the obscure intuition of a model, a prototype, one might say, of the psychoanalytic situation. Ultimately, as we see it, Berganza's night-long recounting to Cipión of the "dog's life" closely models what Freud himself would actually put into practice in 1890 when he began to use the cathartic method.

In the known and overt history of Freud, Freud-Silberstein or Cipión-Berganza would be the first of his famous dialogues. That fascinating series would continue with the dialogues of Freud-Martha, Freud-Breuer, and Freud-Fliess, to culminate in the great dialogue that is self-analysis: Freud-Freud. Years later, when the design of his work was more perfectly thought out, Freud was to say that if some outside observer were to reflect on the analytic situation and ask what was happening between analyst and analysand, Freud would reply that they were simply having a dialogue. If we consider the work of the person who wrote these words and created the psychoanalytic dialogue, it is difficult not to attach a great deal of significance to this dialogue of the dogs. Placed at the very beginning of a series of decisive dialogues in the evolution of the Freudian creation, Cervantes's "Colloquy" seems to invite us to see it as a condensation, in the mind of the adolescent Freud, of all his later advances. Thus, in the episode of the Castilian Academy we may draw an extremely important conclusion: that a form of psychoanalysis existed for Freud even before the appearance of Breuer and Anna O. Incidentally, we should not overlook the fact that *Don Quixote* is, for some authors, essentially a long dialogue, or, as Salvador de Madariaga puts it, "the most wonderful dialogue ever written in any language."[11]

It was a mystery to the family how and when Freud learned Spanish, until he himself revealed, in a letter to Martha dated February 7, 1884, that he had learned it secretly, late in 1883. He kept his secret probably for the same reason that he felt guilty about reading *Don Quixote* during the previous summer. Both enterprises interfered with his official obligations and duties, and with his schoolwork on brain anatomy. The fact that the adolescent son of a poor Viennese Jewish family living in straitened economic circumstances had set himself to studying Spanish must have seemed as extravagant and senseless as the adventures of Don Quixote himself, who, we might recall, began his sallies at dawn, secretly and unbeknownst to anyone. It was impossible, in 1883, for Freud to confess to impulses that would be felt as manic or quixotic. These impulses also explain his fascination and identification with the figure of Don Quixote and the resultant threat of ending up himself as a mad gentleman tilting at windmills.

In their interesting work concerning this episode, J. E. Gedo and E. S. Wolf make the astute observation that Freud, in his games with Silberstein, adopted the name of Cipión or Scipio, a name perfectly in accord with his youthful dreams of grandeur. The historical events recalled in this essay enable us to understand how the adolescent Freud, in assuming for himself the role of Cipión, was expressing his quixotic dream of being a great man and conquering the world by creating psychoanalysis. In this creation, "The Colloquy of the Dogs" was to play, as we have seen, a decisive role. In summary, we agree that the Castilian Academy "prefigured in its core the whole psy-

---

11. Commentaries by Salvador de Madariaga in *El ingenioso hidalgo Don Quijote de la Mancha* (Buenos Aires: Editorial Sudamericana, 1962), 126.

choanalytic enterprise." Cipión's role of listening to the story of Berganza's life and making occasional comments to facilitate the flow of the narrative "has left its stamp on the professional activity of the psychoanalyst."[12]

12. J. E. Gedo and E. S. Wolf, "Freud's *Novelas ejemplares*," in *Freud: The Fusion of Science and Humanism: The Intellectual History of Psychoanalysis*, ed. J. E. Gedo and G. H. Pollock (New York: International University Press, 1976), 98.

II

The Discourse of Desire

2

The Archaeology of Desire in *Don Quixote*

Anthony J. Cascardi

A storm is blowing from Paradise.
—Walter Benjamin

What are the shapes of modern desire, and how are these displayed in Cervantes's texts? I take as my point of departure the central insight of contemporary psychoanalysis that neither the thinking subject nor the literary text can ever be accepted as fully "present" to itself, but that there always exists an absent and potentially troubling extension that a text, like the subject, is never quite capable of articulating but never fails completely to exclude.[1] If *Don Quixote* invites a psychoanalytic reading—which is to say, a reading in light of the fundamental insight that psychoanalysis provides—it does so not because its characters are more or less susceptible to the procedures of a diagnostic analysis than those of any other text, or because of some psychological peculiarity of its author, but rather because of the particular emphasis that Cervantes places on the strange visibility of these exclusions, gaps, and lacks.[2] To be sure, psychoanalysis can be used as a reductive

1. This increasingly accepted view has its origins not in the simple rejection of Hegel, as is sometimes presumed, but rather in the extension of the Hegelian dynamic of desire: the dependence of the *cogito* on the positing of desire may not be directly grasped in immediate experience, as Hegel presupposed, but it is nonetheless interpreted by another consciousness situated in the seemingly endless stream of signs. Desire is not so much a felt or intuited phenomenon as a deciphered (inter)dependence that becomes visible as a form of intertextuality.

2. "Impediment, failure, split. In a spoken or written sentence something stumbles. . . . Discontinuity . . . is the essential form in which the unconscious first appears to us as a phenomenon—discontinuity, in which something is manifested as a vacillation." Jacques Lacan, "The Freudian Unconscious and Ours," in *The Four Fundamental Concepts of Psycho-Analysis*, trans. Alan Sheridan (New York: Norton, 1981), 25. For one example of the case

means for explaining the motives of characters in terms of existential projects regulated by normalized patterns of desire, or for diagnosing an author in terms of a preestablished conception of the psychosexual genealogy of the self. But only the smallest and least interesting fraction of the insights of psychoanalysis can be summarized in such terms; and when used principally as a key for deciphering the meaning of the projected symbolic shapes of womb and phallus, psychoanalysis serves mainly to reinforce a static view of personality, to reduce the power of desire to trouble our procedures of reading, and ultimately to negate the central insights that it has furnished for the interpretation of literary texts.

Don Quixote presses us to move beyond the bounds of a psychoanalytic reading of the type that would be content simply to decode a series of sexual signs or situate the author within the various sexual fields suggested by his predilect symbols, and propels us instead toward a rereading of itself in relation to other texts in such a way as to restore their forgotten potential for mobilizing desire. In other words, we are impelled to take *Don Quixote* as a fully "modern" text and to judge its effects in this way because Cervantes's novel represents an exemplary instance of the transformation of the relationship between two conceptually distinct, historically locatable structures of desire into a more complex and pervasive tension between two ways of reading texts. And yet we are also drawn to understand *Don Quixote* as a historically embedded work, as positioned within the large-scale transformation I have elsewhere described in terms of the social and historical conflict within early modern Spain between the "old" and the "new."[3] *Don Quixote* may legitimately be situated within this shifting historical field to the extent that it articulates the eclipse of the "heroic" order of society dominated by the values of caste and represented in the chronicles, the ballads, and the romances of chivalry, by a newer, relatively less static (but also more prosaic) order controlled by the values of social class. The effects of this historical change may be interpreted according to the

---

against the psychoanalysis of authors, readers, and characters, see Peter Brooks's comments on Freud's *Beyond the Pleasure Principle* in "Freud's Masterplot," where he argues that "we can read *Beyond the Pleasure Principle* as a text concerning textuality and conceive that there can be a psychoanalytic criticism that does not become—as has usually been the case—a study of the psychogenesis of the text (the author's unconscious), the dynamics of literary response (the reader's unconscious), or the occult motivations of the characters (postulating an 'unconscious' for them)." *Reading for the Plot* (New York: Vintage Books, 1985), 112.

3. See Anthony J. Cascardi, "The Old and the New: The Spanish *Comedia* and the Resistance to Historical Change," *Renaissance Drama*, n.s., 17 (1986), reprinted in *Renaissance Drama as Cultural History*, ed. Mary Beth Rose (Evanston, Ill.: Northwestern University Press, 1990), 401–28.

contrasting social codes in which desire is fixed. The shift from the values of "caste" to those of "class" corresponds to the change from a highly stratified society and the forms of desire proper to it to a society differentiated along horizontal lines and in increasingly functional terms. Some of the consequences of this shift within early modern Spain become visible in, among other ways, the creation of a series of culturally ambiguous, displaced, or "marginal" groups (e.g., the *moriscos, conversos*, and *pícaros*) whose identity cannot be located either in terms of the social order that has been eclipsed or in terms of the emergent order but which is constituted in the differential space between these two. Additionally, these consequences are written into the recurrent conflicts between Don Quixote and the other characters in Cervantes's work. Whereas Don Quixote construes every opposition as some manifestation of the hierarchical division of society into two groups—the worthy and the unworthy, or the noble and the base—the others are apt to find themselves positioned within a network of relationships whose effects are increasingly controlled by the circulation of capital and whose desires are structured by the upward mobility promised by a system of "free" economic exchange. Thus, in contrast to Don Quixote, a figure such as Teresa Panza desires principally the economic means to improve her family's situation in society and to better her lot. Sancho's desires, which are modeled on those of Don Quixote, remain opaque to her. Consider Teresa's exchange with Sancho at the conclusion of part I:

"¿Qué bien habéis sacado de vuestras escuderías? ¿Qué saboyana me traéis a mí? ¿Qué zapaticos a vuestros hijos?"
"No traigo nada deso," dijo Sancho, "mujer mía, aunque traigo otras cosas de más momento y consideración."
"Deso recibo yo mucho gusto," respondió la mujer; "mostradme esas cosas de más consideración y más momento, amigo mío. . . . ¿Qué es eso de ínsulas, que no lo entiendo?"

["What profit have you got out of your squireships? Have you brought me a skirt? Or some pretty shoes for the children?"
"I haven't brought any of that, wife," said Sancho, "although I bring other things of greater value and importance."
"I'm very glad of that," replied his wife. "Show me these things of greater value and importance, my friend. . . . But tell me, what is this about isles? I don't understand you."](I.52)[4]

4. English translations in this chapter are from J. M. Cohen, *The Adventures of Don Quixote* (Harmondsworth: Penguin Books, 1950).

This passage may stand as an example of the ways in which two distinct modes of historically conditioned desire come into conflict with each other throughout the text. By reading the passage in historical terms, we may be able to overcome the limitations of those critics of Cervantes's novel who fail to recognize their own idealizing denials of history as extensions of the very quixotism that is (pre)figured in Cervantes's text. And yet *Don Quixote* also suggests that as long as we remain content to read literature with the principal aim of using history to fill in what remains unexpressed within a given discourse, we will have falsified and reduced the mobilizing function of desire, which ensures the dynamism of history itself. In short, the simple, historicizing correction of quixotic idealism fails to see that the effort to locate meaning in historical terms may constitute an attempt to reduce the disorienting effects of desire and to restrict our interest in reading to a narrow, hermeneutic purview.

As we shall see in further detail later in this chapter, the relationship between history and desire may more accurately be explained in light of the psychoanalytic concept of archaeology.[5] This concept leads to an alternative way of reading texts. If the notion of archaeology suggests, on Freud's own account, an investigation into concealed origins,[6] then the premises of an archaeology of desire must be that origins are never fully recoverable and that desire tends to gather around a series of substitutes for what has been hidden or eclipsed, although not entirely lost.[7] And rather than think of desire as the

5. Paul Ricoeur provides a lengthy discussion of this concept in *Freud and Philosophy: An Essay on Interpretation*, trans. Denis Savage (New Haven: Yale University Press, 1970), 439–52.

6. See Freud's lengthy comparison, in *Civilization and Its Discontents*, of the psyche to the archaeological remains of ancient Rome, where he concludes that "what is past in mental life *may* be preserved and is not *necessarily* destroyed." Sigmund Freud, *Civilization and Its Discontents*, trans. James Strachey (New York: Norton, 1961), 20. Even more interesting is Freud's analysis in *Delusion and Dream* of the archaeologist Dr. Norbert Hanold, a fictional character from Wilhelm Jensen's *Gradiva* (1903) who suffers from a lack of desire for living women, and who regards them all as objects of marble and bronze. In Hanold's love for Gradiva, his desire congeals around an object that substitutes for something archaic that has been hidden or eclipsed but not entirely lost. In a dream that takes place in old Pompeii on the day of the eruption of Vesuvius, Hanold sees Gradiva stretched out on the steps of the temple, where she becomes covered by a rain of ashes; her face turns as white as marble and comes to resemble a bas-relief. Gradiva turns out to be Fraulein Zoë Bertgang, the archaeologist's childhood sweetheart. On Freud's account, Hanold's dream represents a "disappearance plus preservation of the past." Sigmund Freud, *Delusion and Dream and Other Essays*, trans. Harry Zohn, ed. Philip Rieff (Boston: Beacon Press, 1956), 73. My thanks to Diana de Armas Wilson for the reference to *Delusion and Dream*.

7. By an extension of this logic, then, even what we may perceive as the most archaic moments of consciousness or culture are best viewed as forgotten or repressed, and therefore as having the power to demonize or haunt the present, just as the romances of chivalry have demonized Don Quixote.

ground of an absent satisfaction (the interpretation of which might well demand a hermeneutic response), we would do better to think of desire as historical, insofar as history is the source of those imaginary objects around which a desire in search of origins tends to coalesce. If customarily we think of history as a means of articulating our relationship to the past, then a work such as *Don Quixote* complicates that picture and suggests that the "movement" of history toward the future is driven by the pressure of a desire *for* the origins we imagine as located in the past. History then appears not so much as the framework in terms of which the meaning of a given text may be revealed, but rather as the source of those displacements whose traces can be glimpsed in the form of discontinuities or gaps within a text. In the case at hand, an investigation of the archaeology of desire in *Don Quixote* may best proceed by a remapping of the historical displacement of the "old" by the "new" in terms of the strange productivity of "archaic" desires within a cultural space that believes itself to be overcoming archaism by normalizing desire through the processes of world disenchantment, societal rationalization, and historical self-assertion.[8] The success of such an undertaking depends on our ability to resist the static models of desire, and their associated patterns of personality, in terms of which the (historical) distinction between "old" and "new" has customarily been aligned.

THE EXISTENTIAL MODEL OF DESIRE AND THE CERVANTINE CRITIQUE

We may perhaps begin from the proposition that a strictly historical analysis of *Don Quixote* leads quite naturally to a series of existential conclusions about the nature of personality centering on the impossibility of satisfying heroic desires in the modern, disenchanted world. Don Quixote "remembers" epic society as a place where it was possible to invoke the principles of virtue and justice and to make judgments according to unambiguous ethical criteria. Accordingly, Don Quixote attempts to "reread" the modern world in terms of the categorical oppositions between the noble and the base. His own claims of absolute goodness and exemplariness are counterbalanced by his repeated and categorical condemnations of his enemies as unworthy, ignoble, or vile. In addition, he imagines the possibility of existence

8. For further discussion of historical self-assertion in relation to the problem of modernity, see Hans Blumenberg, *The Legitimacy of the Modern Age*, trans. Robert M. Wallace (Cambridge: MIT Press, 1985), and A. J. Cascardi, *The Subject of Modernity* (Cambridge: Cambridge University Press, 1992).

in a world of unambiguous values, faithfully transmitted through the chronicles, the ballads, and above all the romances of chivalry.

Seen from the perspective of an existential understanding of desire, heroic society may appear to offer its members the security of a stable identity and the "metaphysical comfort" of values derived as if from first principles. But this model of desire, although historical, meets with a series of internal limitations, which *Don Quixote* rapidly takes into account. First, "heroic" society severely restricts the mobility of desire in the construction of personality and therefore limits the possibilities of what the self may be. The controlling institutions of such a society remain closed to the majority of its ordinary members, who cannot aspire to the condition of nobility which heroic action requires. In terms of the comic, deflationary impulse of *Don Quixote*, "epic" society also sets for its heroes a series of extraordinary goals whose contingencies it chooses to ignore. Such heroes may be momentarily exalted, and the ordinary members of this society may find themselves temporarily ennobled and empowered by the hero's exemplary deeds. But the hero is bound eventually to be deflated, and the nonheroic individuals of this society may find themselves deceived when they discover that the hero is not in fact an ultimate source of empowerment but a human artifact who expresses in a contingent way their own interests, desires, and fears. In the judgment of at least one critic, these members of society would have done better to seek this empowerment through the criticism and revision of their ordinary experiences, beliefs, and practices rather than in the quixotic pursuit of heroic ideals.[9]

From an existentialist point of view, *Don Quixote* represents a successful correction of the heroic ideal insofar as Cervantes is compelled to redirect his hero's failures and succeeds in transforming these into sources of authentic self-creation. Thus, for a critic such as Américo Castro, who existentializes José Ortega y Gasset's doctrine of the circumstance, "*Don Quixote* shows us that the reality of existence consists in receiving the impact of all that can affect man from without, and in transforming these influences into outwardly manifest life processes. The illusion of a dream, devotion to a belief—in short, the ardently yearned for in any form—becomes infused in the existence of him who dreams, believes, or longs; and thus, what was before transcendency without bearing on the process of living becomes em-

9. Roberto Mangabeira Unger, *Passion: An Essay on Personality* (New York: Free Press, 1984), 56. Cervantes's supreme awareness of this danger stands at the heart of his ambivalence toward the theater of his day, especially that of Lope de Vega. See Cascardi, "The Old and the New."

bodied into life."[10] As it later takes shape in what Georg Lukács describes in *The Theory of the Novel* as the "novels of disillusionment," the existential correction of the heroic ideal comes under the pressure of an extreme skepticism about the possibilities for the satisfying desire and achieving human virtue in the modern world. Indeed, it would seem on this account that the controlling anxiety of the novel as a genre is dominated by a permanent loss of faith in the existence of an "original" context for desire rather than by the hope for its recovery.

When evaluated as an experiment in existential projection, however, works of modern fiction in general, and *Don Quixote* in particular, are powerless to reorient desire from within. At best, characters in the novel achieve an ambiguous *desengaño* that leads them to positions of self-irony or, in the case of Don Quixote, to a normalized relationship with the world that can be achieved only at death. This evidence suggests that the existentialist interpretation of desire in *Don Quixote*—through which Castro reconstitutes Cervantes's post-heroic protagonist as justified and redeemed by his own free self-assertion— has in some ways failed to come to terms with the ways in which desire and its consequences are represented in the text. Moreover, it appears that Cervantes is not so much troubled by the success or failure of the heroic ethos, by the disappearance of the conditions of heroism from the modern world, or by the outcome of the struggle between the pressures of normality and heroic ideals as he is concerned to find an alternative to the self-destructive and potentially sacrificial forms of desire that may be pursued in the name of heroic ends. (I have argued elsewhere that the *Persiles* represents Cervantes's idea of a solution to this same problem.)[11] Not only in Don Quixote, but also in the figures of Fernando and Dorotea, and in the tale of "The Curious Impertinent," Cervantes takes as the object of his concern the potentially violent, self-sacrificing forms of desire characteristic of a social order predicated on the replication of hierarchical distinctions and on the preservation of such distinctions through notions of racial purity or "cleanliness of blood." Thus, at the conclusion of her tale Dorotea represents herself as having been sacrificed to the requirements of society's unyielding law of honor. To transgress boundaries in Dorotea's world is to allow oneself to be touched by alien matter and to experience abjection. Because she has been "de-

10. Américo Castro, "Incarnation in Don Quijote," in *An Idea of History*, ed. and trans. Stephen Gilman and Edmund L. King (Columbus: Ohio State University Press, 1977), 26.
11. See A. J. Cascardi, "Reason and Romance: An Essay on Cervantes's *Persiles*," *MLN* 106 (1991): 279–93.

filed" by Fernando, Dorotea must exile herself and deny both herself and her parents any hope for reconciliation: "Es tanta la vergüenza que me ocupa sólo el pensar que, no como ellos [mis padres] pensaban, tengo de parecer a su presencia, que tengo por mejor desterrarme para siempre de ser vista que no verles el rostro, con pensamiento que ellos miran el mío ajeno de la honestidad que de mí se debían de tener prometida [I am so overwhelmed by shame at the mere thought of appearing in their presence, so different from the daughter they had supposed me, that I think it would be the lesser evil to banish myself for ever from their sight rather than look them in their face and know their thoughts. For they will consider that I have lost the honor they had the right to expect of me]" (I.29). In "existential" terms, Dorotea's task is to find a place for herself within the order of society as it stands; indeed, this is the interpretation that Américo Castro has given of her.[12] Yet it would seem more important to say that Cervantes rejects the attempt simply to reproduce the existing social order through a resolution of crises such as Dorotea and her family suffer. Indeed, Cervantes seems to suggest that what Dorotea suffers is like a wound that cannot be repaired, at least not within the framework of the existing historical or social world; accordingly, Dorotea more closely resembles those "marginal" groups whose desires cannot be accommodated within the framework of social relations as they exist.

Similarly, Cervantes resists attempts to situate the self in relation to the dominant social order through an idealist reshaping of the past or the resurrection of an archaic symbolic law, as the *comedia* and its sacrificial code of honor attempted to do. Consider in this regard "The Curious Impertinent," which compels us to associate the structure of violence and sacrifice with the *comedia*-like patterns of desire that lead to self-destructive suspicion and jealousy. Camila, Lotario, and above all Anselmo resemble *comedia* characters who are caught in sacrificial patterns of desire. Indeed, Anselmo refers to the way in which he has fashioned his own dishonor, describing himself at the conclusion of the tale in *comedia*-like terms as the "fabricador de mi deshonra [maker of my own dishonor]" (I.35). Hierarchical systems of desire organized around the values of caste tend to increase the occasions for violence by establishing clear lines of demarcation around desire's possible objects and by demanding that certain of these objects be

12. See Américo Castro, "La ejemplaridad de las novelas cervantinas," in *Hacia Cervantes* (Madrid: Taurus, 1967), 451–74.

valued more highly than the rest. "Camila es finísimo diamante [Think of Camila as a rare diamond]," says Lotario. He continues:

> Mira que no hay joya en el mundo que tanto valga como la mujer casta y honrada, y que todo el honor de las mujeres consiste en la opinión buena que de ellas se tiene. . . . La honesta y casta mujer es arminio, y es más que nieve blanca y limpia la virtud de la honestidad. . . . Es asimesmo la buena mujer como espejo de cristal luciente y claro; pero está sujeto a empañarse y escurecerse con qualquiera aliento que le toque. Hase de usar con la honesta mujer el estilo que con las reliquias: adorarlas y no tocarlas. Hase de guardar y estimar la mujer buena como se guarda y estima un hermoso jardín que está lleno de flores y rosas, cuyo dueño no consiente que nadie le pasee ni manosee; basta que desde lejos y por entre las verjas de hierro gocen de su fragrancia y hermosura.

> [There is no jewel in the world so precious and chaste as a virtuous woman, and the whole honor of women lies in their good reputation. . . . The chaste and virtuous woman is an ermine, and the virtue of chastity is whiter and purer than snow. . . . A good woman is also like a mirror of clear and shining glass, which is liable to be stained and dimmed by every breath which touches it. A chaste woman must be treated like holy relics, which are to be adored but not touched. A good woman must be guarded and prized like a beautiful garden full of flowering roses, whose owner does not allow anyone to walk in it or to touch them; enough that they enjoy its fragrance and beauty from afar off through its iron railings.] (I.33)

The objects of desire in such instances are not simply exalted; they are exalted as part of a sacrificial logic, which is to say, they are elevated *in order to be excluded or destroyed*, and the economy of this desire depends on their destruction. This is paradigmatically the case with the identity of women who, like Camila, are positioned (typically by men) as the supreme repositories of "value"; they become "heterogeneous," in Georges Bataille's sense of the term, although they remain necessary for the exclusionary system they validate and are thus positioned as its (sacrificial) victims.[13] At the same time, societies

13. See Georges Bataille, "The Psychological Structure of Fascism," in *Visions of Excess: Selected Writings, 1927–1939*, trans. and ed. Alan Stoekl (Minneapolis: University of Minnesota Press, 1985), 137–60. In my view this complicates the picture of male "traffic" in the love of women presented in Diana de Armas Wilson's study "Passing the Love of Women: The Intertextuality of 'El curioso impertinente,' " *Cervantes* 7 (1987): 9–28.

of caste tend to interpret the values proper to them not as historically contingent constructs but as having the force of nature. Thus Lotario argues that the principles of conjugal honor and cleanliness of blood have a warrant that extends to the creation of woman in Genesis and to the biblical institution of matrimony.

> Cuando Dios crió a nuestro primero padre en el Paraíso terrenal, dice la divina Escritura que infundió Dios sueño en Adán, y que, estando durmiendo, le sacó una costilla del lado siniestro, de la cual formó a nuestra madre Eva; y así como Adán despertó y la miró, dijo "Esta es carne de mi carne y hueso de mis huesos." Y Dios dijo: "Por ésta dejará el hombre a su padre y madre, y serán dos en una carne misma." Y entonces fue instituido el divino sacramento del matrimonio, con tales lazos, que solo la muerte puede desatarlos. . . . Y aquí viene que, como la carne de la esposa sea una mesma con la del esposo, las manchas que en ella caen, o los defectos que se procura, redundan en la carne del marido, aunque él no haya dado, como queda dicho, ocasión para aquel daño. . . . Y como las honras y deshonras del mundo sean todas y nazcan de carne y sangre, y las de la mujer mala sean deste género, es forzoso que al marido le quepa parte dellas, y sea retenido por deshonrado sin que él lo sepa.

> [When God created our first father in the earthly paradise, Holy Scripture tells us that He caused a deep sleep to fall on him, and in his sleep took one of the ribs of his left side and created our mother Eve; and when Adam awoke and looked on her, he said: "This is now bone of my bone and flesh of my flesh." And God said: "Therefore shall a man leave his father and his mother, and they shall be one flesh." Then was instituted the divine sacrament of marriage, whose bonds are soluble only by death. . . . Hence it arises that, as the flesh of the wife is one with the flesh of the husband, the blemishes which fall on her or the defects she incurs recoil upon the flesh of the husband, although, as I have said, he may be in no respect the cause of the trouble. . . . Now as all this world's honors and dishonors spring from flesh and blood, and the bad wife's are of this kind, part of them must inevitably fall on the husband; and he must be considered dishonored, even though he does not know of it.] (I.33).

Within a framework such as Américo Castro's, the violence of desire in "The Curious Impertinent" is to be explained simply as the product of the historical anxieties generated over purity of blood. But the anxieties of "The Curious Impertinent" outstrip the purely historical and existential frameworks in which Castro and other critics have attempted to situate them insofar as they are at once exorbitant, excessive, and hyperbolic. For instance, Lotario warns Anselmo in copious terms about the destruction that he, Lotario, will precipitate:

> Mira, pues ¡oh Anselmo!, al peligro que te pones en querer turbar al sosiego en que tu buena esposa vive; mira por cuán vana e impertinente curiosidad quieres revolver los humores que ahora están sosegados en el pecho de tu casta esposa; advierte que lo que aventuras a ganar es poco, y que lo que perderás será tanto, que lo dejaré en su punto, porque me faltan palabras para encarecerlo.

> [Reflect, then, Anselmo, on the danger you expose yourself to in seeking to disturb your good wife's peace! Consider what vain and foolish curiosity it is that prompts you to stir the passions which now lie quiet in your chaste wife's breast. Be warned that you stand to gain little and to lose so unspeakably much that words fail me to express its value.] (I.33)

For his part, Anselmo is driven to seek confirmation of facts that he knows already and in advance to be true: ("Deseo que Camila, mi esposa, pase por estas dificultades, y se acrisole y quilate en el fuego de verse requerida y solicitada, y de quien tenga valor para poner en ella sus deseos [I want my wife Camila to pass through the ordeal, and be purged and refined in the fire of temptation and solicitation by someone worthy of her]" (I.33). In this respect, both Anselmo and Lotario come to resemble the split (Lacanian) subject, who is divided between the *sujet d'énonce* and the *sujet d'énonciation*. To say this much is not to "diagnose" the subject in Lacanian terms as split. Indeed, Anselmo anticipates and thereby nullifies the force of a purely diagnostic reading of this curious deflection of truth by desire into discourse by characterizing his own attempt at self-destruction as a process of contamination, and by comparing his desire for self-defilement to that of a female eating malady, "enfermedad que suelen tener algunas mujeres, que se les antoja comer tierra, yeso, carbón y otras cosas peores, aun asquerosas para mirarse, cuanto más para comerse [an illness common in women, which makes them long to eat earth, chalk, coal, and other worse things, loathsome to the sight and much more loathsome to the palate]" (I.33).[14] Indeed, it is only when we see that the "sacrificial" violence of caste societies is inten-

---

14. See the fascinating discussion of this passage in Wilson, "Passing the Love of Women."

sified by the tendencies of its members both corporeally and psych-
ically to re-incorporate what has been excluded as alien, ignoble,
dishonorable, or base that the "psychoanalytic" significance of "The
Curious Impertinent" can be made clear over and above its existential
value as an "exemplary" text. In this case, the exemplary "meaning"
of what might be taken as a cautionary tale is overwhelmed by the
very exorbitance of the "example" and by the procedures of narrative
discontinuity by which it is interpolated into the larger text. As in
several of the *Novelas ejemplares*, "The Curious Impertinent" offers an
example of a case in which desire recognizes and reincorporates precisely what it would seem to exclude. What remains for us to inves-
tigate is the more general principles by means of which this and other
such examples are "sutured" into Cervantes's text.

The Mediations of Desire and the Critique of Imitation

On the basis of the cases presented thus far, it would seem that
the "existential" reading of *Don Quixote* to which a simple historicism
might lead fails principally in its inability to recognize Cervantes's
response to the conflicts generated by two distinct ways of reading
desire. More important than any alignment of the structures of desire
along the historical lines designated by "caste" or "class" is Cervantes's ability to locate the hidden mobility of desire everywhere
within the societies we may call, respectively, "heroic" and "modern," or "old" and "new." The historical and existential interpretations of *Don Quixote* tend to neglect the (always already) mediated
nature of desire, on which the psychoanalytic understanding of archaeology depends. Insofar as it is through mediation that desire
displays its complex relationship to an "archaic" past, the purely
historical and existentialist interpretations of *Don Quixote* fail also to
come to terms with the modernity of Cervantes's work. Indeed, it
seems inaccurate to say that *Don Quixote* represents either the absolute
failure of the heroic ethic or the achievement of existential or "novelistic" freedom, as Castro has argued. Rather, *Don Quixote* represents
a form of post-epic literature in which the concept of an archaic, heroic
world as providing an immediate and undifferentiated ground of
desire is shown to be self-limiting insofar as it relies on the naive
conception of an "original" context of desire and on the possibility
of establishing an unmediated relationship to the historical past. More
precisely in Cervantes's case, the discovery of the prior mediation of

historical experience by desire as shaped by literature and other cultural forms, is articulated through a critique of reading. This is the point of Cervantes's insistence on the mediating function of the romances of chivalry throughout *Don Quixote*, and it serves to align the exoteric intention of the novel as stated in the famous closing passage of part II ("poner en aborrecimiento de los hombres las fingidas y disparatadas historias de los libros de caballerías [to arouse man's contempt for all fabulous and absurd stories of knight errantry]" [II.74]) with the mobility of desire displayed throughout the text. More specifically, the Cervantine understanding of our relationship to history as mediated by desire is directed against those modes of reading that would attempt to negate the power of desire through the promise of a direct or unmediated relationship with the past.[15]

In setting out to imitate the practices of the knights-errant of chivalry, Don Quixote reenacts the drama of modernity's need simultaneously to displace and to assume the authority of the past. The problem of the cultural reproduction of authority—of achieving cultural "maturity," of entering the world of the fathers, while displacing the dominant authority of the past—emerged with particular force during the early modern age, when cultures began to become particularly conscious of their own contingency in historical terms.[16] During the European Renaissance, the concept and practice of imitation served as a stabilizing response to the problems generated by the increasing preoccupation with authority and desire in history. At the beginning of *Don Quixote*, Part I, the as yet unnamed hero adopts the practice of imitation as a means of modeling his desire according to the (textual) examples of illustrious predecessors. Taken at face value, imitation is designed to stabilize the play of desire and offers a self-projective means of displacing the past.

> Le pareció convenible y necesario, así para el aumento de su honra como para el servicio de su república, hacerse caballero andante, y irse por todo el mundo con sus armas y caballo a buscar las aventuras y a ejercitarse en todo aquello que él había leído que los caballeros andantes se ejercitaban, deshaciendo todo género de agravio, y

---

15. On the subject of mediated desire, see René Girard's classic study *Deceit, Desire, and the Novel*, trans. Yvonne Freccero (Baltimore: Johns Hopkins University Press, 1965).

16. See Hans Blumenberg, *The Legitimacy of the Modern Age*, trans. Robert M. Wallace (Cambridge: MIT Press, 1983); and A. J. Cascardi, "History, Theory, (Post)Modernity," in *After the Future*, ed. Gary Shapiro (Albany: SUNY Press, 1990), 1–16. It might be argued that the problem of entering the modern age was more intensely felt in the Spain of the Golden Age than elsewhere in Europe because the embeddedness of and cultural attachment to the reigning order of society were particularly deep in Spain.

poniéndose en ocasiones y peligros donde, acabándolas, cobrase eterno nombre y fama.

[It appeared to him fitting and necessary, in order to win a greater amount of honor for himself and serve his country at the same time, to become a knight-errant and roam the world on horseback, in a suit of armor; he would go in quest of adventures, by way of putting into practice all that he had read in his books; he would right every manner of wrong, placing himself in situations of the greatest peril such as would redound to the eternal glory of his name.] (I.1)

If history has the power not only to provide models of action and belief but also to control and demonize the present, then the practice of imitation may be regarded as one way of coming to terms with the incalculable power of history by allowing us to recuperate loss in terms of an exemplary discourse; ideally, the past might then be successfully incorporated or absorbed into the present age and the work of "archaeology" might be brought to an end. But as *Don Quixote* abundantly shows, the practice of imitation cannot serve adequately to recuperate losses or to stabilize desire in historical terms. Indeed, in *Don Quixote* the practice of imitation constructs the possibility of a (literary, historical) present as a function of an insatiable desire *for* the past; since this desire cannot conceivably be fulfilled, history has a predominantly disorienting effect. From the very start it becomes clear that the objects of Don Quixote's imitations are variable rather than fixed. In the early chapters of part I the hero calls to mind and proposes to imitate the figures of the epic (e.g., the Cid), the fictional heroes of chivalric romance (Amadís de Gaula and others), as well as figures drawn from the Moorish novel (Rodrigo de Narváez and Abindarráez) and from the ballad tradition (the Marqués de Mantua). This jumbled array—which replicates the confusion of origins surrounding the creation of the Cervantine text, with its multiple authors and variants—suggests that the "original" models of Don Quixote's desire have somehow been lost or eclipsed, and that these figures have broken loose from the organizing structure that history once provided. Indeed, it is only through the introduction of the conceptual category of romance that this heterogeneous variety of imitative models drawn from the past is later brought under critical control.

According to Lukács in *Theory of the Novel*, the chivalric romances against which *Don Quixote* was in the first instance a polemic and which it parodied had lost the "necessary transcendent relationship" to the original oneness or "totality" of life in of the epic world. But as long as the rise of the novel is seen to depend on the absolute loss of an original totality rather than on the transformation of the idea of such a totality into desire's archaeological "source," we are unable to comprehend the mediating function of literary romance. Lukács went on to say of the romances that "their mysterious and fairy-tale like surfaces were bound to degenerate into banal superficiality."[17] I would suggest, however, that the "degraded" quality of romance stems from the temptation to restore and repossess "epic" values and thus to refuse to acknowledge as lost the proposed objects of desire. Throughout *Don Quixote* Cervantes makes a concerted effort to expose the fantasies of romance as anachronistic or out of place and discontinuous in the disenchanted modern world. As Michael McKeon has argued in connection with the early English novel, the category of "romance" was originally unstable; not only is it possible to detect antiromance elements within romance, but romance itself passes through a series of seemingly infinite permutations, as the term shifts in emphasis from "heroic" to "amorous."[18] Only in the shift in reading from history to desire could the novel come to be established as a term of categorical opposition to the romance. Indeed, in historicizing the novel, McKeon fails to draw the more general conclusion that would seem warranted by the texts at hand: that novelistic or "quixotic" desire is desire in search of a lost or forgotten—not to say "romantic"—object, the effect of which is to transform the "real" world into a series of phantasms or substitute appearances of an "original" that remains inaccessible to consciousness.

In addition, the jumbled array of figures offered as the possible models of Don Quixote's desire introduces an essential discontinuity into the Cervantine text, one that is prefigured by the discontinuities set forth in the prologue to part I, which, it bears noting, is itself already, initially, discontinuous with the main body of the text; it is this discontinuity that suggests the modernity of Cervantes's stance with respect to the problem of desire itself. As John Lyons has explained in a study of the theory and practice of example in the Renaissance, the discontinuity of example, which may be viewed as a discursive or rhetorical manifestation of the disruptive effects of desire, arises from the fragmentary status of the "original," that is, from the model's status as a fragment excised from another, perhaps lost,

---

17. Georg Lukács, *Theory of the Novel*, trans. Anna Bostock (Cambridge: MIT Press, 1971), 103.

18. Michael McKeon, *The Origins of the English Novel: 1600–1740* (Baltimore: Johns Hopkins University Press, 1987), 52–64. Both modes, heroic and amorous, are at work in, among other places in *Don Quixote*, the story of the captive's relationship with Zoraida (I.39–41).

unlocatable, or untotalizable "whole."[19] Indeed, the essential discontinuity implicit in the very concept of *eximere* (to cut out) would suggest that all examples are the sites of a possible, projected, absent, or denied satisfaction; all examples are extracted from one context and placed into another within which they make desire visible by virtue of their own exteriority.

The principal effect of example is to introduce a series of troubling separations or gaps within the apparently homogeneous contours of character and text; in the case of *Don Quixote* these commence with the name of its hero and the forgotten place of his birth. The discontinuity of example applies as well to the textual surface of the (exemplary) work, since a shuttling back and forth between different rhetorical modes or levels of discourse—between "history" and "fiction," "prologue" and "narrative," "fiction" and "theory"—is the way in which the discontinuity that underlies exemplification may be felt as a textual effect. Indeed, it would appear on even a cursory inspection that the discontinuities associated with the quixotic principle of exemplification pervade Cervantes's text, which is a sutured work, a "detotalized whole" that seems to be composed principally of such gaps. These range from the rhetorical discontinuities just mentioned to large-scale discontinuities such as those that are introduced in relation to the genesis of the manuscript and the genealogy of the printed text, as signaled by the break in Don Quixote's adventure with the Vizcaíno in part I, chapter 8. The discontinuous quality of Cervantes's text governs as well the procedure of interspersing or intercalating seemingly autonomous narrative segments (for instance, the stories of Fernando and Dorotea, the "Curioso impertinente," and the captive's tale) within the framework of the larger narrative.

Consider once again the case of the "The Curious Impertinent" in this regard. In "existential" terms the point of the story seems to be that Anselmo comes to recognize, just in time to save himself, that he is ultimately responsible for the destruction of himself, his wife, and his friend. This "existential" point, however, is offset by the sheer exorbitance of the tale and by the priest's concluding remarks: "No me puedo persuadir que esto sea verdad; y si es fingido, fingió mal el autor, porque no se puede imaginar que haya marido tan necio, que quiera hacer *tan costosa experiencia* como Anselmo, [There is something unconvincing about it. If the author invented it he did it badly, for it is impossible to believe that there could be a husband so stupid

---

19. John Lyons, *Exemplum: The Rhetoric of Example in Early Modern France and Italy* (Princeton: Princeton University Press, 1989), esp. 31–32.

as to want to make the *very costly experiment* Anselmo did]" (I.36;
emphasis added). The case for a purely existential reading of the story
is furthermore upset by virtue of the fact that the narrative "staging"
of the tale allows Cervantes to highlight a series of coincidental motives and acknowledgments shared by the protagonists of the tale
and those who hear it read. We notice this as figures such as Cardenio
and Dorotea, who listen to the tale, are allowed to see their own
abrogation of responsibility and the consequences of that breach re-
fracted in the lives of Anselmo, Lotario, and Camila. As a consequence, the mediated quality of desire at work in the self-
representations of Fernando and Dorotea is brought to the fore. Indeed, characters such as Fernando, Dorotea, and Anselmo can best
be read as repetitions of previously shaped structures of literary desire; it is only when the narratives of these characters are juxtaposed
and seen as fragmentary that the rhetorical effect of the interruption
of "The Curious Impertinent" by Don Quixote's battle with the wi-
neskins, or the surprising appearance of Luscinda and Fernando at
the end of the tale, can be felt. As a result of these and similar in-
terruptions, it becomes impossible to say which elements of the text
are "continuous" and which are not.

Now, let us return to the specific question of Don Quixote's imitation of examples at the beginning of part I. It is customary to think
that the novel as a genre requires the assertion of the self qua individual and to believe that self-assertion can be achieved only through
the supersession of all relationships to imitative models drawn from
the past. This would be an appropriate enough conclusion to draw
from the case of a character such as, for example, Robinson Crusoe,
whose narrative begins with his attempted rejection of the authority
of the father.[20] But the example of *Don Quixote* would suggest that
the eclipse of imitation as a normative practice for containing the force
of desire in relation to the past in fact generates a *proliferation* of
models, none of which can satisfy the desire that self-assertion demands. Thus, in response to a question concerning his identity, Don
Quixote replies in quasi- epic terms by claiming to appropriate all
models of desire for himself: "Yo sé quien soy . . . y sé que puedo ser
no sólo los que he dicho, sino todos los doce Pares de Francia, y aun
todos los nueve de la Fama, pues a todas las hazañas que ellos todos
juntos y cada uno de por sí hicieron, se aventajarán las mías [I know

20. Although there is not enough space to demonstrate the point here, it nonetheless
bears noting that Robinson's narrative in the end conforms more closely to the father's law
than to the shape of his modern desire.

that I am capable of being not only the characters I have named (e.g. the Cid, Baldovinos, and Abindarráez), but all the Twelve Peers of France and all the Nine Worthies as well, for my exploits are far greater than all the deeds they have done, all together and each by himself]" (I.5). Similarly, when confronted with the demand that a work of art imitate and pay homage to preexisting forms, the "author" of *Don Quixote* is counseled to buttress his modernizing efforts by reproducing—or, more accurately, by excerpting and citing—the various modes of discourse that historically have licensed literature, even if these are occasions of discontinuity and disruption rather than signs of an authentic or legitimate belief in the authority of the past:

> Vengamos ahora a la citación de los autores que los otros libros tienen, que en el vuestro os faltan. El remedio que esto tiene es muy fácil, porque no habéis de hacer otra cosa que buscar un libro que los acote todos, desde la A hasta la Z, como vos decís. Pues ese mismo abecedario pondréis vos en vuestro libro; que, puesto que a la clara se vea la mentira, por la poca necesidad que vos teníades de aprovecharos dellos, no importa nada; y quizá alguno habrá tan simple que crea que de todos os habéis aprovechado en la simple y sencilla historia vuestra; y cuando no sirva de otra cosa, por lo menos servirá aquel largo catálogo de autores a dar de improviso autoridad al libro.

> [Let us come now to references to authors, which other books contain and yours lacks. The remedy for this is very simple; for you have nothing else to do but look for a book which quotes them all from A to Z, as you say. Then you put this same alphabet into yours. For, granted that the very small need you have to employ them will make your deception transparent, it does not matter a bit; and perhaps there will even be someone silly enough to believe that you have made use of them all in your simple and straight-forward story. And if it serves no other purpose, at least that long catalogue of authors will be useful to lend authority to your book at the outset. Besides, nobody will take the trouble to examine whether you follow your authorities or not.] ("Prólogo," part I)

Indeed, it would not be too much to claim that modern literature begins when the "catalogue of authors" mentioned by Cervantes comes to be the heterogeneous site of a fragmented and inevitably unfulfillable desire rather than the model of an "exemplary" relationship to the inheritance of the past.[21]

---

21. The "formlessness" of the text is reproduced in the claim that this text is similarly authorless. I refer to the passage in the prologue to part I that reads: "Yo, aunque parezco

As with the case of Don Quixote's mixed bag of models in part I, it is on the basis of a perceived marginality or secondariness with respect to the past that the peculiarly modern nature of desire within *Don Quixote* is made manifest. It can be said that Cervantes comes to realize that literature may be historical and that desire may be disruptive, but that the course of literary history may not necessarily be progressive. As a result, the "modernity" of *Don Quixote* must find expression in the spaces already occupied by preexisting forms. Thus, when the Cervantine narrator affirms his iconoclastic desire in the famous concluding passage of part II, he frames the purpose of his writing with respect to the books of the past rather than in terms of the desire to shape something radically new, but not because what might be "new" has yet to be invented; his purpose is stated in retrospective terms and so suggests that, strictly speaking, there may be no radically new forms for the modern writer to create. To be sure, Henry Fielding later would claim to have authority over a "new province of writing" (*Tom Jones* 2:1), but Fielding's *Joseph Andrews* was itself written "in imitation of Mr. Cervantes"; like Cervantes's boast in the prologue to the *Novelas ejemplares* that he was the first in Spanish to "novelize," these assertions of literary modernity can be carried out only through the repetition of preexisting texts.[22]

LITERARY HISTORY AND LITERARY DESIRE

If we think of *Don Quixote* as offering some of the most complex examples of the problem of desire and its literary representation in the modern world, it becomes increasingly clear that Cervantes's novel is both sustained and troubled by the mobile and potentially disruptive nature of desire, but that our conventional methods of reading are designed principally to deaden desire's disorienting effects. Indeed, while an appreciation of the motive force of desire may be central to an understanding of *Don Quixote* in the light of the fundamental insights that psychoanalysis provides, readers of the novel characteristically seek to normalize and control desire by attempting to submit literature to the "higher" authority of a theoretical discourse. The fact of fiction's ultimate inability to redeem desire—or, for that matter, to afford any ultimate justifications of its own

---

padre, soy padrastro de don Quijote [I, though in appearance Don Quixote's father, am really his stepfather]."

22. Some of the ambiguities of originality in Cervantes have been discussed by John G. Weiger in *The Substance of Cervantes* (Cambridge: Cambridge University Press, 1985), esp. 41–83, and by E. T. Aylward in *Cervantes: Pioneer and Plagiarist* (London: Tamesis Books, 1982).

status as a secondary, mediated, and therefore potentially degraded world discontinuous with our own—is the occasion for the inclusion within *Don Quixote* of a seemingly authoritative theoretical discourse. With the theoretical efforts of the barber and the canon of Toledo near the conclusion of part I (47–48), Cervantes recognizes the temptation to legitimize the literary mediations of desire by passing desire through the crucible of rational judgment. The problem of desire would in this case be "resolved" by an appeal to the discursive norms of unity and verisimilitude of the sort that are invoked earlier by the priest in order to reduce the ec-centricity (or im-pertinence) of the "Curioso impertinente." Yet it seems that despite these efforts a quixotic "remainder" is left to threaten and demonize the achievements of literary theory as represented in Cervantes's text. Indeed, the canon admits that he has himself attempted to author a perfect romance, taking care nonetheless to discipline himself in the process ("guardando en él todos los puntos que he significado [observing in it all the points I have mentioned]"; I.48), and Don Quixote provides a particularly extravagant example of the power of desire to overwhelm the efforts of theory in the form of the fantastic adventure of the Caballero del Lago. Consider this summary of the canon's reaction to Don Quixote's discourse on the Knight of the Lake: "Admirado quedó el canónigo de los concertados disparates que don Quixote había dicho, del modo con que había pintado la aventura del Caballero del Lago, de la impresión que en él habían hecho las pensadas mentiras de los libros que había leído [The canon was astonished at this well-reasoned nonsense of Don Quixote's, at his description of the adventure of the Knight of the Lake, and at the impression made on him by the deliberate lies in the books he had read]" (I.50). In short, as the reflection of a typically modern predicament, fiction's attempt to reorient desire by coming to full theoretical consciousness and control of itself may result in the appeal to an independent theoretical discourse, but this appeal is in turn deflected by desire's affective force.

This predicament forms the context surrounding issues that have been addressed by the revisionist methods of criticism developed in response to latter-day barbers, canons, and priests—methods that attempt to take to heart the insights of contemporary psychoanalysis into the deflections of desire. Revisionism and other "strong forms" of reading attempt to correct the deficiencies of conventional literary history, according to which the imputed claim of *Don Quixote* as the founding example of the modern novel derives from the simple rejection of the authority of tradition in establishing aesthetic norms.

Ian Watt, for instance, had claimed that "previous literary forms had reflected the general tendency of their cultures to make conformity to traditional practice the major test of truth: the plots of classical and Renaissance epic, for example, were based on past history or fable, and the merits of the author's treatment were judged largely according to a view of literary decorum derived from the accepted models of the genre. This literary traditionalism was first and foremost challenged by the novel."[23] As a characterization of modern writing, Watt's account might at best provide us with a Cartesian reading of Descartes, who from one point of view attempts to resist the claims of history by arrogating to himself the invention of a new mode of philosophical discourse. Descartes may have hoped that his project of rational self-assertion would serve as a bulwark against the disorienting effects of desire in history and as an absolute defense against the demonic presence of the past. For Cervantes, by contrast, discourse is always historical, but modern discourse is uniquely so insofar as it is unable to recover the original referents for our desires, which are themselves literarily and historically defined.

To be sure, the claims of modern writing as a progressive attempt at the containment of desire through new ways of form making may serve as mere covers for a sense of the displacement that stems from the persistence of a past whose immediate authority has been lost. But all such "modern" form making must be subordinate to the procedures of "creative," "quixotic," or other revisionist kinds of reading, which are also iconoclastic, or form breaking, in their struggles to overcome the past. The result of this tension is a literally infinite and fragmentary species of desire that undermines any view of literary history as constituting the stable ground of modernity's relationship to the past. In contrast to their archaic analogues in the canon of sacred texts, works of modern literature can best be seen as responding to an overwhelming accretion of unfulfillable desire in history, which renders the task of autonomy or self-consciousness that is necessary to the constitution of modernity nearly impossible to achieve.[24] Hence Cervantes's intense but impossible project to "compete with Heliodorus" in the making of the *Persiles*.

23. Ian Watt, *The Rise of the Novel: Studies in Defoe, Richardson, and Fielding* (1957; reprint, Berkeley: University of California Press, 1964), 13.

24. In the analysis of one Bloomian critic: "Because the secular canon is never fixed and the 'religion' of humanism never fully revealed, salvation or the achievement of poetic desire remains a salvation for one in which the poets are in a direct and intensely personal competition—the achievement of one detracts from all the others, and the higher the canon elevates the greats of the past, the greater the burden on the poetic future." Jean-Pierre

As a modern writer Cervantes is hurled toward the future while the trajectory of his writing is deflected by the stormy accumulation of literary desire in the past. One is reminded in this connection of Walter Benjamin's description of the *angelus novus*, whom he sees as advancing toward the future with a visage that remains turned toward the wreckage of the past: "Where we perceive a chain of events, *he* sees one single catastrophe which keeps piling wreckage upon wreckage, and hurls it in front of his feet. The angel would like to stay, awaken the dead, and make whole what has been smashed. But a storm is blowing from Paradise; it has got caught in his wings with such violence that the angel can no longer close them. This storm irresistibly propels him into the future to which his back is turned, while the pile of debris before him grows skyward."[25] Insofar as historical (not to say revisionist) interpretation of *Don Quixote* recognizes the possibility of literary and cultural "progress" in terms of the impossibility of a return to the fullness of an archaic past which it struggles also to deny, it may provide a way to come to terms with some of the insights into the nature of desire that psychoanalysis provides. Indeed, we might well think of *Don Quixote* itself as a radically revisionist work. One measure of its modernity lies in its ability to embarrass any mode of reading that fails to recognize the lost quality of the objects of desire or to acknowledge the always already mediated nature of our relationship to the past.

Mileur, *Literary Revisionism and the Burden of Modernity* (Berkeley: University of California Press, 1985), 130.

25. Walter Benjamin, "Theses on the Philosophy of History," in *Illuminations*, trans. Harry Zohn, ed. Hannah Arendt (New York: Schocken Books, 1969), 257–58.

3

Cervantes and the Night Visitors: Dream Work in the Cave of Montesinos

Diana de Armas Wilson

Que toda la vida es sueño, / Y los sueños, sueños son.
—Pedro Calderón de la Barca

A fresh perspective on the Cervantine dream is in order for the twenty-first century—one that might wriggle out of the conceptual grip of crude Freudianism (what Freud himself called the American "commerce in couches") without wandering into the sterile camp of modern neuroscience (the REM neurophysiologists).[1] Such a change of venue would involve thinking about the psychoanalysis of dreaming more playfully, not so much on the basis of its clinical beneficiaries as on that of its literary precursors. "The monument of psychoanalysis must be traversed—not bypassed," Roland Barthes writes, "like the fine thoroughfares of a very large city, across which we can play, dream, etc."[2] In my attempts to traverse the monument of psychoanalysis en route to the Cave of Montesinos, I have been consulting,

---

1. In an attempt to dethrone Freud's dream theory, Allan Hobson has theorized a dreaming brain that is spontaneously active, both seeing and moving, during REM sleep, and that fires off electrochemical signals at recurrent, even predictable, intervals. Hobson's claims are widely regarded as limited and premature: his wish to establish a physical theory of consciousness, using dreams as the bridge across the mind-body chasm, has been attacked by his fellow physiologists, by traditional psychoanalysts, and by a new generation of dream interpreters, who share with Hobson his anti-Freudian stance but little else. See Hobson, *The Dreaming Brain* (Cambridge: Harvard University Press, 1988). On the alternative to the "commerce in couches," see Julia Kristeva's remarks in "Psychoanalysis and the Polis," in *The Kristeva Reader*, ed. Toril Moi (New York: Columbia University Press, 1986), 303.

2. Roland Barthes, *The Pleasure of the Text*, trans. Richard Miller (New York: Hill and Wang, 1975), 58.

by way of a map, the text of one of Freud's most vivid precursors: the second-century Hellenistic dream interpreter Artemidorus of Daldis (Daldia). Freud, who allowed that Artemidorus furnished western culture with "the most complete and painstaking study of dream-interpretation as practiced in the Graeco-Roman world," took his title *Die Traumdeutung* (*The Interpretation of Dreams*) from Artemidorus's *Oneirocritica*.[3] Both Artemidorus and Freud assume what moderns call the cleavage of the subject (conscious/unconscious), with the unconscious (psyche) either talking to the dreamer, as in Artemidorus, or waiting to be discovered down the "royal road" of dreams, as in Freud.[4] Both interpreters agree with Aristotle that dreams are not heaven-sent.[5] Both privilege allegorical dreams that require decoding—dreams that use condensation and displacement to veil significant events—over direct dreams. And both recognize the notion of the "day's residues," already a topos in Epicurean literature.[6] As Artemidorus puts it: "A man will not dream about things to which he has never given a thought."[7]

Freudian dream theory, by contrast, is generatively challenged by Artemidorus, whose culture-specific categories, as we shall see, appear to invert the oedipal model of personality. Artemidorus offers us not only a non-Freudian typology of dreaming but also a different cultural model of dream interpretation, not a Viennese but a Mediterranean configuration based on urbanized Greek-speaking clients

3. *The Standard Edition of the Complete Psychological Works of Sigmund Freud*, ed. and trans. James Strachey, 24 vols. (London: Hogarth Press, 1953–74), 4:98n. Further references to the *Standard Edition* will be abbreviated *SE*, with volume and page number. See also 37–38, 130, 131, 389n., and 645n. in the Avon reprint of vols. 4 and 5 of *SE*. For Freud's mention of Artemidorus, see *SE* 4:3, 4, 98, 99; 5:86, 354, 606, 685; 11:174; and in 15:86, 236. Freud's own bibliography for *Die Traumdeutung* cites Artemidorus in two versions: a German translation (Vienna, 1881) and an abridged English one (London, 1644).

4. "The interpretation of dreams is the royal road to a knowledge of the unconscious activities of the mind" (*SE* 5:608).

5. In *De divinatione per somnum*, Aristotle thought it ridiculous to maintain that it was the gods who sent dreams. See *On Prophecy in Sleep* 1.462B 20–22; 2.463B 12–15; 2.464A 20–22. Freud sees Aristotle as claiming that dreams are not divine but "daemonic," since nature is "daemonic" rather than divine. In the first edition of his *Interpretation of Dreams* (1900), Freud admitted to difficulties with the Greek distinction between "daemonic" and "divine": "No doubt this distinction has some great significance if we knew how to translate it correctly." An apology followed here, suppressed in later editions: "My own insufficient knowledge and my lack of specialist assistance prevent my entering more deeply into Aristotle's treatise" (37n.).

6. According to Seneca, "The sleeper's visions are as turbulent as his day." See *Ad Lucilium epistulae morales*, trans. Richard M. Gummere, 3 vols. (Cambridge: Harvard University Press, 1917), I.56.6.

7. Artemidorus, *The Interpretation of Dreams* (*Oneirocritica*), trans. Robert J. White (Park Ridge, N.J.: Noyes Press, 1975), 67–68, n.6. Further references to Artemidorus are to this edition and will be cited by book and section number.

from what is now western Turkey. Closer to our Cervantine dreamer, however, Artemidorus' treatise was considered throughout the sixteenth century "Europe's most popular guide to dream interpretation."[8] How does Cervantes, to use a Bakhtinian phrase, absorb and reply to Artemidorus?[9] Might the Hellenistic tradition of dream interpretation have found its way into Cervantes's texts, in the slow but sure-footed manner that Cervantes's talking dogs (themselves the stuff of a dream) found their way into Freud's writing?[10] These questions, relating temporally remote conventions, strategically bracket Cervantes between Artemidorus and Freud. My aim, then, is to stage a fresh confrontation—a mock colloquy—between these framing dream interpreters, ancient and modern. Such an exchange provides a useful heuristic tool, allowing us to infiltrate Cervantes's dreamworld with new questions.[11] This colloquy of oneiromancers may also reveal where Cervantes's fictions, with respect to dreaming, leave us as postmodernist readers. Are we, too—as Renaissance romance writers never tired of telling us—such stuff as dreams are made on?

Although I have elsewhere acknowledged the rootedness of texts in the contingency of history,[12] space here allows me only to nod to sixteenth-century international dream culture. About a century before Cervantes's dreaming heroes Don Quixote and Persiles (not to mention his "dream dogs" Cipión and Berganza) would convert their readers into armchair oneiromancers, Artemidorus' Greek *Interpretation of Dreams* was published in a Latin translation. This publishing

8. Richard L. Kagan, *Lucrecia's Dreams: Politics and Prophecy in Sixteenth-Century Spain* (Berkeley: University of California Press, 1990), 36–37.

9. See Julia Kristeva on Mikhail Bakhtin's notion of writing "as a reading of the anterior literary corpus and the text as an absorption of and a reply to another text," in "Word, Dialogue, and Novel," in *Desire in Language: A Semiotic Approach to Literature and Art*, ed. Leon S. Roudiez, trans. Thomas Gora et al. (New York: Columbia University Press, 1980), 69.

10. As a young man, Freud appropriated the secret name Cipión—"Ich, Scipion"—in private correspondence with his boyhood friend Edward Silberstein. See the essay in this collection by León Grinberg and Juan Francisco Rodríguez, entitled "Cervantes as Cultural Ancestor of Freud." See also S. B. Vranich, "Sigmund Freud and 'The Case History of Berganza': Freud's Psychoanalytic Beginnings," *Psychoanalytic Review* 63 (1976): 80.

11. Cervantes's thought on dreaming may have been opaque, or at least artfully disintegrated, even to himself. His representations of dreams are not unlike that rooster represented by Orbaneja, that (premodernist) painter from Ubeda whose fragmented style makes Don Quixote so anxious about his own *historia*: "Tendrá necesidad de comento para entenderla [It will require a commentary to be understood]" (II.3). Miguel de Cervantes, *El ingenioso hidalgo Don Quijote de la Mancha*, ed. Andrés Murillo, 2 vols. (Madrid: Clásicos Castalia, 1978), 64. Further references to *Don Quixote* are to this edition and will be cited in the text. All translations are my own.

12. See, for example, the opening chapters of Diana de Armas Wilson, *Allegories of Love: Cervantes's 'Persiles and Sigismunda'* (Princeton: Princeton University Press, 1991).

event occurred in 1518, two years after the publication of the important Jewish text on the Interpretation of Dreams, the *Pitron chalomot*.
The Latin *Oneirocritica*, essentially a defense of dream interpretation
against its critics, was rapidly translated into various vernacular languages.[13] I know of one dual-language edition of Artemidorus bound
together with an Arabic text by Achmet ibin Sirin, a volume that
sounds like one of those lost manuscripts awaiting discovery by Cervantes in a Toledo marketplace.[14] But apart from its multiple translations, Artemidorus' text also spawned a great number of
Renaissance "dream-books," widely circulated manuals that served
as a major source of popular lore about dreams.

Early modern Europe viewed dreams either as diagnostic tools,
courtesy of Galen, or as media for prognostication, owing to the
dissemination of the works of professional Hellenistic dream interpreters such as Artemidorus. In Hapsburg Spain (Cervantes's Spain),
dream prognosticators were the bane of village priests, who, as confessors, found themselves in direct competition with all the local
sabias, or "wise-women," who operated cottage industries in sooth-
saying. This gendered rivalry between Spain's male confessors and
its legions of female "oneirocriticas" invites comparison, and perhaps
contrast, with the ancient competition between dream interpreters
and rabbinic authorities in the Judaic tradition.[15] According to an
estimate by Amador de Velasco y Muñeco, an astrologer arrested in
1578 by the Inquisition, there were "over ten thousand" freelance
dream interpreters in Spain alone, all working hard for a living (like
Freud).[16] The frenzy for divination included the casting of horoscopes,
a practice whose increasing popularity is disparagingly avouched by
Don Quixote himself: "Que no hay mujercilla, ni paje, ni zapatero
de viejo que no presuma de alzar una figura, como si fuera una sota
de naipes del suelo [There is not a servant girl nor a page boy nor an
old cobbler who won't undertake to cast a horoscope as if it were the
easiest thing in the world]" (II.25). An intense popular interest in
precognition had earlier moved Juan Luis Vives to inveigh against

13. Steven R. Fischer, "Dreambooks and the Interpretation of Medieval Literary Dreams,"
Archiv für Kulturgeschichte 65 (1983): 3. The *Oneirocritica* was not available in Spanish until
1918, as Kagan notes in *Lucrecia's Dreams* 186, n. 6.

14. Carol Schreier Rupprecht mentions this manuscript in an excellent essay recalling our
own culture's participation in a long tradition of oneirics; see "Our Unacknowledged Ancestors: Dream Theorists of Antiquity, the Middle Ages, and The Renaissance," *Psychiatry Journal
of the University of Ottawa* 15 (1990): 119.

15. Ken Frieden shows, throughout *Freud's Dream of Interpretation* (Albany: SUNY Press,
1990), how dream interpreters posed a threat to the ancient rabbis.

16. Cited by Kagan, *Lucrecia's Dreams*, 186, n. 9.

free-market dream interpreters "who predict the future for as little as a *blanca*."[17] Cervantes's gypsy seer Preciosa, the heroine of "La gitanilla," would doubtless fit into this entrepreneurial camp.

Almost four centuries later and in another country, Freud would assume, although with far more profundity and ambivalence, a similarly antiprophetic stance. Some of Freud's remarks make him an odd bedfellow for both the Epicurean philosophers, who were skeptical of the typology of predictive dreaming, and the Christian humanist Vives, who was unhappy with the marketing of "futures." Because the interesting tension in Freud's speculative thought both questions and tests Artemidorus (and not only Artemidorus) on the value of precognition, my dialogue of dream interpreters must begin with a prologue on Freud and the future.

THE INTERPRETATION(S) OF DREAMS

"I have never been able to find anything to confirm the prophetic nature of dreams," Freud announced in his *Five Introductory Lectures*, delivered almost a decade after the publication, at the very threshold of the twentieth century, of *Die Traumdeutung* (1900).[18] But what Freud declared himself unable "to confirm" he was also, as we shall see, unable to renounce: the kind of deciphering practiced not only by Spain's homely *sabias* and *beatas* but also by all the major traditions of dream interpretation in antiquity, from the Bible and the Talmud to the philosophy and literature of classical Greece and Rome. Although classical antiquity "confirmed" (to use Freud's own verb) his discovery of psychoanalysis by furnishing him with the Oedipus legend (*SE* 4:261), Freud did not return the honor. His response to the classical traditions of oneiromancy was agonistic: if he identifies himself as "a partisan of antiquity" (*SE* 11:7), it is to rewrite antiquity's notions of precognition.

The infancy of dream interpretation in western culture includes not ✓ only the Greco-Roman classica but also the Judaic tradition. From

17. Vives's high-minded humanist disdain for the prophetic tallied with his stance against the use of dreams for divination in his commentary on Cicero's *Dream of Scipio*. See Juan Luis Vives, "Sueño de Escipión," in *Obres completas*, ed. Lorenzo Riber, 2 vols. (Madrid: Aguilar, 1947), 1:609. See also Macrobius Ambrosious Theodosius, commentary on *The Dream of Scipio*, trans. William Harris Stahl (New York: Columbia University Press, 1952).

18. In 1931, in his preface to the third (revised) English edition of *The Interpretation of Dreams*, Freud would insist that his revolutionary "dream book" contained "the most valuable of all the discoveries" he had made: "Insight such as this falls to one's lot but once in a lifetime" (*SE* 4:xxxii).

Talmudic dream interpretation we learn that "a dream that is not interpreted is like a letter that is not read."[19] The exemplary biblical dream interpreter is, of course, Joseph: among the half dozen references to the Bible in Freud's dream book, three nod to Joseph's interpretation of Pharaoh's dream.[20] That this dream—of seven lean kine following and then devouring seven fat kine—could be interpreted to forecast seven years of famine following seven years of plenty was an example for Freud of "symbolic" dream interpreting, the kind of procedure that "inevitably breaks down" when faced with confused or unintelligible dreams (*SE* 4:97).

What Freud struggles with here, however, is not only Joseph's symbolic technique, his substitution of food for kine, but also his premonitory tactics—his transposition of Pharaoh's dream "into the future tense."[21] If dreams divine the future, Freud thinks that they are only "ostensibly prophetic" (*SE* 5:625), that the explanation for the phenomenon lies "within the bounds of natural psychology" (*SE* 4:65). By the close of his dream book, Freud seems ready to articulate this psychological explanation more fully. It would be "truer" to say, he writes, that dreams give us a knowledge of the past instead of the future, "for dreams are derived from the past in every sense." This totalizing claim, however, is instantly qualified by a concessive utterance that dismantles all distinctions—past, present, future—of linear time: "Nevertheless the ancient belief that dreams foretell the future is not wholly devoid of the truth. By picturing our wishes as fulfilled, dreams are after all leading us into the *future*. But this future, which the dreamer pictures as the *present*, has been moulded by his indestructible wish into a perfect likeness of the *past*" (*SE* 5:621).[22] It is this "perfect likeness," then, that moves Freud to look to the drea-

---

19. See Frieden, *Freud's Dream*, 75. Frieden remarks the absence of Talmudic dreams in Freud's *Collected Works*—dreams notably rich in the very qualities we have come to associate with Freudian dream interpretation: troping, condensation, and literary insights. Freud's bibliographical footnote to dream interpretation in the Jewish tradition is read by Frieden as a smokescreen for other issues. See especially Frieden's chapter 4, "Freud: Demystification and Denial," 95–132.

20. See part C of *The Dream Work*, where Freud privileges Josephus over Joseph as an interpreter of Pharaoh's dream (*SE* 4:334). See also "Affects in Dreams," in *The Dream Work*, part H, where Freud acknowledges his oneiromantic identification with the biblical Joseph: "The name Josef plays a great part in my dreams. . . . My own ego finds it very easy to hide itself behind people of that name, since Joseph was the name of a man famous in the Bible as an interpreter of dreams" (*SE* 5:484, n. 2).

21. After its meaning has been "arrived at by symbolic interpretation," Freud sees the act of transposing a dream "into the future tense" as "a remnant of the old prophetic significance of dreams" (*SE* 4:97).

22. Emphasis added. On Freud's formula for "obscure and confused dreams" as "*disguised fulfilments of repressed wishes*," see *SE* 5:674.

mer's infancy—to his or her "childhood experience," as a source from which dreams reproduce material (*SE* 4:15). Freud's child, then, to borrow Wordsworth's poetic inversion, becomes father to the dreaming man. Looking back on *The Interpretation of Dreams* in the opening paragraph of *Delusion and Dream* (1906), Freud writes that although he is "far from accepting in dreams a prevision of the future," he could not, nevertheless, "completely reject the connections of dreams with the future." For dreams have revealed themselves to him as wish fulfillments: "and who could dispute that wishes are preponderantly concerned with the future?"[23]

Although it is impossible to systematize Freud on precognition, what is clear from his writings is that childhood concerns are replayed throughout the course of life under different guises and disguises. Unlike Freud, however, Artemidorus posits a psychic apparatus that seems not only remote from the past but also resolutely future-oriented. As the title of his book makes clear, Artemidorus is remembered for his *oneirocritica*—his criticism of the *prophetic* class of dreams.[24] The etymology of the Greek term *oneiros*, however, reveals a curious grounding in the present: the prophetic dream "tells what is real." How the prophetic future coexists with the "reality" of past and present, the kind of coexistence we find in Cervantes's fictional dreams, bears pondering. John J. Winkler wondered, for instance, "which is the stranger supposition—that the unconscious mind is aware of momentous changes in the offing or that it is obsessed with the remote events of one's childhood." Whether remote past events were not, indeed, linked with the future was actually a concern of Plutarch's, in an argument in which he moved "from the strangeness of our powers of memory to the reasonableness of precognition."[25] Plutarch's cognitive move here from the past to the future seems vaguely pre-Freudian. But the same move is curiously replicated by Cervantes, whose dreaming protagonist, as I will show, shuttles with ease between memory and precognition, between the hallucination

---

23. Sigmund Freud, *Delusion and Dream and Other Essays*, ed. Philip Rieff, trans. Harry Zohn, from the second edition of Freud's *Gesammelte Schriften* (Boston: Beacon Press, 1956), 25–26. Further references to *Delusion and Dream* are to this edition and will be cited in the text.

24. Not all dreams qualified for Artemidorus' predictive theory, however: the majority of his clients came to him reporting ordinary *enhypnia*—literally "something in one's sleep" (*Oneirocritica* 1.1)—dreams that were merely reminders of the dreamer's present state of affairs, allegories of the reigning cultural anxieties of the age of the Antonines.

25. John J. Winkler, *The Constraints of Desire: The Anthropology of Sex and Gender in Ancient Greece* (New York: Routledge, 1990), 26n., citing Plutarch. I am indebted to this brilliant anthropological study for illuminating the economically determined values assigned to sexuality by Greek-speaking Mediterranean males in antiquity.

of an obsolete chivalric past and the terrible intuition of a progressively disenchanted—and wish-fulfilled—future.

Another major tension between Artemidorus and Freud is identified by Freud himself, when he remarks that his own technique differs from the ancient method in that it "imposes the task of interpretation upon the dreamer himself" (*SE* 4:98n.).[26] Given that dreamers are not always available for interpretive comment, however, especially when they are fictional characters, Freud's avowed distinction from the ancients breaks down the moment he himself psychoanalyzes Dr. Norbert Hanold, the hero of Wilhelm Jensen's novel *Gradiva*. Although for his clients' dreams Freud privileges the "decoding method" of interpretation (*SE* 4:97), for "artificial dreams constructed by imaginative writers," he approves the "symbolic" procedure. In *Delusion and Dream* he speaks of such fictional dreams as "those dreams which have never been dreamed" (25). Although such dreams can be interpreted just as though they had been dreamed "by real people," as Freud remarks in a footnote added to *Die Traumdeutung* in 1909, the task of interpretation obviously cannot be imposed "upon the dreamer himself" (*SE* 4:97n.).

But the most instructive, and perhaps the most entertaining, distinction between Artemidorus and Freud rests on the value each assigns to sexuality. Although the sexual question has been, as Paul Ricoeur rightly protests, "too much the center of the discussion" about Freud, the notion of sexual *disguise* or *camouflage*, in the sense of a "*violence done to the meaning*," bears recalling in the context of Artemidorus.[27] In Freud's dream—"a psychosis of short duration" (*SE* 22:15–16, 221, 244–45)—the infantile impulses "excluded from conscience" come to "revisit the dreamer in a camouflaged form" (*SE* 5:396). The many elongated stand-ins for the phallus in Freudian dreams are altogether too well known to rehearse here. When, in a rare appearance, the male organ is featured *un*disguised in *The Interpretation of Dreams*, Freud draws attention to the way sexual repression trans-

26. The classicist John J. Winkler considers Freud to have launched a "misguided attack" on Artemidorus, based perhaps on "a hasty and partial reading" and resulting in a "false verdict." The most significant feature of Artemidorus' interpretive system, according to Winkler, is that the symbols of any coded dream "are drawn by the soul from the individual dreamer's own cultural experience—not from the language of the gods, nor from any universal Book of Meanings." The dreamer essentially collaborates with the dream interpreter in that the latter must know "what is specific to the identity of each individual dreamer—wealth, social and marital status, occupation, health, age, and so forth." Artemidorus is "in the business of translating people's messages to themselves." See ibid., 28–30n.

27. Paul Ricoeur, *Freud and Philosophy: An Essay on Interpretation*, trans. Denis Savage (New Haven: Yale University Press, 1970), 95 and 92.

poses genitals to the face, nose, or teeth—to "unobjectionable parts
of the body" (*SE* 5:387). The breasts of a dreamer's mother, in Freud,
appear camouflaged as "two pears" (*SE* 5:372). Dreaming of a secret
liaison with a lady committed to another man is regarded as a "Typical
Example of a Disguised Oedipus Dream" (*SE* 5:398–99n.). Indeed,
"disguised" dreams of incest with one's mother, in Freud's view,
"are many times more frequent than straightforward ones" (*SE* 5:398).
Freud is careful not to universalize sexual interpretation: "The assertion that all dreams require a sexual interpretation, against which
critics rage so incessantly, occurs nowhere in my *Interpretation of
Dreams*" (*SE* 5:397). What Freud finds it "fair to say," however, is
"that there is no group of ideas that is incapable of representing sexual
facts and wishes" (*SE* 5:372).

For Artemidorus, by contrast, one might say that there is no group
of ideas that is incapable of representing *economic* facts and wishes.
Although Artemidorus provides us with a document based on inter-
views with thousands of clients ("a kind of ancient Kinsey report,"
according to Winkler), even a superficial reading of the *Oneirocritica*
will disappoint readers in search of second-century *aphrodisia*. The
basic principles of meaning employed by Mediterranean dreamers of
early antiquity to interpret the erotic stun us with their hard-core
practicality. Again and again, Artemidorus reads the sexual dream as
an economic signifier of profit or loss. The *Oneirocritica* swarms with
examples. When a childless woman dreams that her breasts fall off,
for instance, it signifies "financial embarrassment" (1.41). Hellenistic
dreams about the penis, a polyvalent signifier, turn out to be especially humdrum: "Because it alternately expands and contracts," Artemidorus explains, it may correspond either to "wealth and
possessions" or to "poverty, servitude, and bonds." At one point he
even speaks of "the necessary part" of the man, informing us par-
enthetically that "this is what the penis is called," and then equating
it with a man's "financial obligations" (1.79).[28] Dreams about "intercourse with prostitutes who work in brothels" mean an expense of
spirit and a waste of money: "For men who frequent these women
feel ashamed and spend their money as well" (1.78). Sex with one's
wife is interpreted as auspicious because "men take pleasure both in
love-making and also in success" (1.78). Sex with one's servants signifies, unabashedly, that the dreamer "will derive pleasure from his

28. Artemidorus writes in the tradition of the two penis dreams in the earliest extant
dream book, the Chester Beatty Papyrus III, which may date as far back as the Twelfth
Dynasty (c. 2000-1790 B.C.E.): "If a man sees his penis becoming large in a dream, it is good;
it means his possessions will multiply" (cited in the notes to the *Oneirocritica*, 75n.).

possessions" (1.78). Sex with one's mother—a charged dream in both
Sophocles and Freud—is not uncomplicated in Artemidorus, where
it admits of "many different interpretations." (1.79). One it does *not*
appear to admit, however, is Plato's, whose attitude toward such a
dream is one of heavy moral censure: "When a man through sleep
has parted company with all shame and sense, he does not shrink
from incest" (*Republic* 9.571c). The incestuous dream in Artemidorus,
however, far from being shameless, is considered auspicious for any
craftsman or laborer, "for we ordinarily call a person's trade his
'mother' " (1.79). Sex with one's mother is viewed as unlucky if she
is standing during the act, which would then signify "constraint,"
that is, the inability to afford a bed or a mattress (1.79). The dream
of incest is even more inauspicious if one's mother is kneeling, since
her immobility would then signify "great poverty" (1.79). The blue-
collar mother, in short, seems to work overtime as a signifier for her
son's business life.

Artemidorus wraps up his section on incest dreams with an amaz-
ingly dismissive closure: "So much, then, for sexual intercourse"
(1.80). If Artemidorus, unlike Freud, tends to de-eroticize sexual
dreams, it may be because his clients, unlike Freud's, are dreaming
in a scarcity economy, where external threats are the stuff that dreams
are made on. Innumerable dreams in Artemidorus signify empty toil,
prostitution, indigence, poverty, suffering, working in the mines, or,
even worse, *not* working in them—"unemployment along with fear
and drudgery" (1.43). The signifying dreamworld in the *Oneirocritica*
stubbornly circulates around a man's business and his standard of
living. Because blood is a symbol of money, dreams of losing blood
are bad (good, however, for doctors) (1.61). Dreams of flying like a
bird—which Freud traces back to the sexual feelings generated by
"childish romping" (*Hetzen*); (see *SE* 4:272; 5:392–93)—signify for Artemidorus success in business projects (1.4). Even a dream as gendered as a sex-change transformation is allegorized into economics:
it is auspicious for a poor man or a slave to change into a woman in
his dream, Artemidorus writes, "for a woman's work is lighter" (1.50).

From Artemidorus, in short, we learn that second-century dreamers
did not dream—did not think—in the same way that we do about
sexuality, that the laws of a dream's exegesis are products of their
time. What the soul (personified throughout Artemidorus' text as
"psyche") relayed to Hellenistic dreamers were messages for external
prosperity. The culturally determined value assigned to sexual matters, in other words, turned on a "calculus of profit": as Winkler puts
it, "Sex, like food and clothing, provides material with which the soul

can talk to us about the truly important things in life, such as whether we will come into money, whether my wife will be . . . hard-working, whether I will win or lose a lawsuit."[29] Sex for Artemidorus' dreamers, in short, was a screen, a predictable disguise, for the issues that *really* mattered.

CERVANTINE DREAMERS

What are the issues that really matter for Cervantes's dreamers? The subjectivity of the Cervantine dreamer would seem to be constituted differently from that of the economically driven dreamer in Artemidorus' text. How radically do the schemas of valuation change between Rome's Silver Age and what has been reified as Spain's Golden Age? Could the doctrines of austerity formulated in the fourth century by numerous enthusiasts of asceticism—church fathers such as Augustine and Jerome—have caused such a radical change in dream life? At what point do we begin to document the emergence of a western guilt culture? These questions show us promising avenues of reflection. The "more rigorous" style of dreaming that Michel Foucault depicts for late antiquity, only a few centuries after Artemidorus, may be another of those Foucauldian "grand narratives" which, like his work on madness, need further scrutiny: "an increased anxiety concerning sexual conduct, a greater importance accorded to marriage and its demands, and less value given to the love of boys."[30]

The fictional dreamer in Cervantes is sexually anxious in a precognitive kind of way. As early as *La Galatea* (1585), Lisandro announces that his dream of being pinned under a tree was both monitory and prophetic: "No eché de ver entonces que la fortuna en sueños me

---

29. Winkler, *Constraints*, 37, 27. "The goal of decoding soul's premonitory messages about the future is largely directed at external changes of wealth, health, and social status" (30).

30. Saint Jerome, for instance, declared that "all sexual intercourse is unclean," as Elaine Pagels reminds us in "The 'Paradise of Virginity' Regained," *Adam, Eve, and the Serpent* (New York: Random House, 1988), 94. Michel Foucault, *The Care of the Self*, vol. 3 of *The History of Sexuality*, trans. Robert Hurley (New York: Random House, 1988), 36. Foucault foregrounds the multiple forms of "penetration" in Artemidorus' text—"a man's book that is addressed mainly to men." Defined as the sign of "winners" in the "games of mastery" being replayed in the dreams of late antiquity, penetration constitutes "the very essence of sexual practice, the only form, in any case, that deserves attention and yields meaning in the analysis of dreams." Foucault sees married men as having all the power in late antiquity: "In this world the married man can also have his mistress, avail himself of his servants (boys or girls), and frequent prostitutes" (28–35). See also John Winkler's Foucauldian reading of sexual significance in Artemidorus as phallocentric, as characterized by an "invasive protocol" (*Constraints*, 40).

mostraba lo que allí a poco rato despierto me había de suceder [I could not see then that fortune was showing me in dreams what would happen to me, a short time later, when awake]."[31] And as late as the *Persiles* (1617), the hero recounts a dream in which a personified puppet called SENSUALIDAD threatens him with some future disaster: "Costarte ha, generoso mancebo, el ser mi enemigo [It will cost you dearly, young man, to be an enemy of mine]."[32] Cervantes would seem to assume, along with the ancients, that the psyche is by its very nature "prophetic," that it is mysteriously aware of future events in a cost-effective sort of way. But the Cervantine psyche is also anxiously libidinized. If Cervantes's use of auguries and economies makes him a descendant of Artemidorus, his foregrounding of sex and/or gender negotiations makes him a precursor of Freud. Sexual significance in Artemidorus, as Winkler rightly notes, did not "take us very far into the domestic sphere, in which husbands and wives and lovers negotiated their relationships."[33] Cervantes's fictions, by contrast, focus intensely on these negotiations: one need only think of "El curioso impertinente," in which Anselmo laments the "tan costosa experiencia [very costly experiment]" of pushing his wife into his best friend's bed. The Cervantine dreamer, then, looking both backward to Artemidorus and forward to Freud, stands at an intersection of western cultural history, at a moment in the early modern period when love and cash, to borrow Javier Herrero's striking compound in the context of "La ilustre fregona,"[34] are competing for cultural expression.

THE CAVE OF MONTESINOS

Although Don Quixote's dream-vision in the Cave of Montesinos has been exhaustively analyzed by critics,[35] Carroll Johnson was per-

31. Miguel de Cervantes, *Là Galatea*, in *Obras completas*, ed. Angel Valbuena Prat, 12th ed. (Madrid: Aguilar, 1962), 621.

32. Miguel de Cervantes, *Los trabajos de Persiles y Sigismunda*, ed. Juan Bautista Avalle-Arce (Madrid: Clásicos Castalia, 1969), 243.

33. Winkler, *Constraints*, 39, 41.

34. Javier Herrero, "Emerging Realism: Love and Cash in *La ilustre fregona*," in *From Dante to García Márquez: Studies in Romance Literatures and Linguistics, Homenaje for Anson Conant Piper*, ed. Gene H. Bell-Villada, Antonio Giménez, and George Pistorius (Williamstown, Mass.: Williams College, 1987), 47–59. See also María Antonia Garcés's instructive compounding of love and gold in "Zoraida's Veil: The Other Scene of 'The Captive's Tale,' " *Revista de estudios hispánicos* 23 (1989): 65–98.

35. See, inter alia, Philip Stephan Barto, "The Subterranean Grail Paradise of Cervantes," *PMLA* 38 (1923): 401–11; T. Earle Hamilton, "What Happened in the Cave of Montesinos?"

haps the first Hispanist to apply the criteria of psychoanalysis rigorously to measure the hero's pathologies: his "arrested psychosexual development" as well as his "chronic inability to interact successfully with women." Johnson's strong reading of Don Quixote as a middle-aged psychotic with an unconscious passion for his niece—it was "Sobrina" who was "lurking at the latent level" of the Cave of Montesino's dream—was, predictably, anathema to scholars of an encomiastic persuasion, many of whom still venerated Don Quixote as a Christ figure.[36] But "Sobrina" permitted the constitution of new theories: she energized a whole new generation of readers who were curious (in a scarcely disinterested way) about the connections between obsessive reading and the operations of desire, including the desire to give dreams meaning.

It is desire, we know, that throws Don Quixote's dream back on the side of libido, an energy that Cervantes personifies in the later *Persiles* dream.[37] But to see Don Quixote's dream as the accomplishment of a *repressed* desire—that is, as a disguised wish fulfillment—is to ask what Don Quixote desires ("Dear God, what *does* he want?") as well as to produce our own field of interpretation. Don Quixote tells us, repeatedly, that the object of his desire is "la sin par Dulcinea [the peerless Dulcinea]," who is the "única señora [sole lady]" of his most secret thoughts (II.9). Carroll Johnson tells us that the object of Don Quixote's desire is his niece. I would argue that the object of Don Quixote's desire is the studious avoidance of its own fulfillment. It is an object best expressed through his alter ego Cardenio, whose strange precognition of unpleasure becomes a self-fulfilling prophecy for Don Quixote: "Me parecía que lo que yo desease jamás había de tener efeto [It seemed to me simply that what I desired was never to

in *Proceedings of the Comparative Literature Symposium*, 2 vols. (Lubbock: Texas Tech College, 1968), 1:3–18; Robert Hollander, "The Cave of Montesinos and the Key of Dreams," *Southern Review* 4 (1968): 756–67; Alban K. Forcione, "The Cave of Montesinos," *Cervantes, Aristotle, and the "Persiles"* (Princeton: Princeton University Press, 1970), 137–46; Peter N. Dunn, "La cueva de Montesinos por fuera y por dentro: Estructura épica, fisonomía," *Modern Language Notes* 88 (1973): 190–202; Gethin Hughes, "The Cave of Montesinos: Don Quixote's Interpretation and Dulcinea's Disenchantment," *Bulletin of Hispanic Studies* 54 (1977): 107–13; E. C. Riley, "Metamorphosis, Myth, and Dream in the Cave of Montesinos," in *Essays on Narrative Fiction in the Iberian Peninsula in Honour of Frank Pierce*, ed. R. B. Tate (Oxford: Dolphin, 1982), 105–19; Anthony J. Cascardi, "Cervantes and Descartes on the Dream Argument," *Cervantes* 4 (1984): 109–22.

36. Carroll B. Johnson, *Madness and Lust: A Psychoanalytical Approach to "Don Quixote"* (Berkeley: University of California Press, 1983), 158, 167. To Johnson, indeed, we owe the early claim, increasingly validated in recent years, that Cervantes "anticipated with uncanny accuracy many of the discoveries of modern clinical psychiatry" (8).

37. See Ricouer, *Freud and Philosophy*, 91.

come to pass]" (I.27). Cervantes foreshadows Freud's theory that, in our dreams, desire can mold the future into a perfect likeness of the past. A desire ensnared by literacy—a desire not to desire—molds Don Quixote's disenchanted future into a "perfect likeness" of a fictional Carolingian past, where the dreamer constitutes himself among the mummified figures of the exhausted dead.

The ties between the oneiric and the archaic are made visible in the Cave of Montesinos, owing to a convulsive dream that peers beyond its own historical moment to Freudian dream theory. Don Quixote's role as dreamer may be enlightened by Freud's analysis, in *Delusion and Dream*, of another fictional dreamer, Dr. Norbert Hanold, the hero of *Gradiva*. As a "foot-fetishist" radically alienated from the female gender, Dr. Hanold is a docent of archaeology whose "fetishistic erotomania" has, for readers of *Don Quixote*, one especially resonant symptom: "He has no interest in living women" (66–68). The basic premise of the narrative of *Gradiva*, says Freud, is that its hero's interest has been "transferred to women of stone or bronze" (67). A kind of early modern Norbert, Don Quixote also has no interest in living women: his interest has been transferred to women of paper or print. He has fabricated, as a safe love object, a woman who resembles those textual ladies who, in Sansón Carrasco's phrase, are "estampadas e impresas [in print]" (II.73). Freud's claim, in *Delusion and Dream*, that storytellers "usually know many things between heaven and earth that are not yet dreamt of in our philosophy" (27) is borne out by Cervantes, who already "knew" what Freud had to unearth from *Gradiva*: that the male rejection of eroticism generates anxiety dreams of earth burial, encavement, or entombment; that such an encavement is an unconscious exteriorization of a cryptic formation within the ego; and that the healing figurative expression of the dreamer's trauma is embodied in an endangered and therefore "needy" female. The Cave of Montesinos, Don Quixote's cryptic formation, is sexually allegorized by Sancho's flippant remark—a deeply ironic one, if we consider Don Quixote's rejection of eroticism—about his master's long stay in the cave: "Que ya pensábamos que se quedaba allá para casta [We had begun to think you were staying down there to found a family]" (II.22). In the dreams of Don Quixote and Dr. Hanold—both "creatures of a writer," as Freud would put it (33)—psychic ex-cavation for the male requires a transference of interest from the fetish to the female. In both texts this interest is metaphorized as a debt.

The hero of *Gradiva* wishes unconsciously "to have been buried two-thousand years ago in the Villa of Diomede" in Pompeii (49).

"There is no better analogy for repression," Freud explains in a later passage, "than the burial which was the fate of Pompeii and from which the city was able to rise again through work with the spade" (61). Don Quixote wishes unconsciously to have been buried some eight hundred years before, in the Carolingian past with "los doce Pares de Francia [the Twelve Peers of France]" (I.5). An equally powerful analogy for repression is the fate of those superannuated chivalric figures, enchanted by Merlin for upwards of five hundred years within the Cave of Montesinos. Although the wishes of both Don Quixote and Dr. Hanold are fulfilled in their respective dreams, only the latter is "excavated from the ashes" of his repression. Or as Freud elaborates it, "Our archaeologist is snatched out of his alienation from love and admonished to pay the debt with which all of us are charged from birth" (71). Don Quixote's alienation from love is too far gone. He cannot "pay the debt." The thrust of his journey is toward death.[38]

Don Quixote encounters death when he meets a cry of players all dressed up to enact "The Parliament of Death" ("Las cortes de la muerte") in Part II, chapter 11. At that moment, tellingly, he reveals to us a rare glimpse of his past: "Desde mŏchacho [since childhood]," he says, "fui aficionado a la carátula [I was fond of plays]." As people grow up, Freud explains in "Creative Writers and Day-Dreaming," they seem to give up such playful pleasures: "But whoever understands the human mind knows that hardly anything is harder for a man than to give up a pleasure which he has once experienced. Actually, we can never give anything up; we only exchange one thing for another. What appears to be a renunciation is really the formation of a substitute or surrogate" (SE 9:145–53). Don Quixote's surrogate for his childhood pleasures would seem to be an addiction—emblematized by the phantasmagoric "Cortes de la Muerte" encounter—to death-inducing fictions. It is not until his later confrontation with the chivalric Durandarte, as Helena Percas de Ponseti has cogently argued, that Don Quixote sees his own death grotesquely prefigured.[39] In Freudian terms, then, the future and the past coalesce in the Cave of Montesinos when Don Quixote meets Durandarte resting upon his marble cenotaph. This flesh-and-blood figure with his heart of "carne

38. Harry Sieber credits Jorge Luis Borges with this insight in "Literary Time in the 'Cueva de Montesinos,' " MLN 86 (1971): 268.

39. Helena Percas de Ponseti, "La cueva de Montesinos," Revista hispánica moderna 34 (1968), 379–93. Durandarte's mummified heart—described as "amojamado" (dried up)—echoes the earlier description of Don Quixote himself, in part II, chapter 1, as "tan seco y amojamado que no parecía sino hecho de carne momia [so dried up and withered that he seemed to have been turned into a mummy]" (ibid., 384).

momia" (mummified flesh) is the unconscious expression of the silly, superannuated, and "heartless" chivalric lover which Don Quixote is himself becoming.

His meeting with Dulcinea, newly arrived among the enchanted dead, expresses some equally disturbing psychoanalytic knowledge. In keeping with Freud's principle of contradiction in dream life,[40] Dulcinea has turned into her opposite, the coarse and needy peasant girl recycled by Sancho (*his* opposite). The dream here witnesses to the culturally produced idea of Golden Age woman, a binary notion articulated by Sancho when, in trying to remember the exact words of Don Quixote's love letter to Dulcinea, he converts with a mala-propism a "soberana señora [sovereign lady]" into a "sobajada señora [overmassaged lady]." It is a version of this latter "lady" who ma-terializes in Don Quixote's dream as a down-and-out farm girl trying to pawn a cheap petticoat ("un faldellín de cotonía"). The "sovereign lady" has been "enchanted," which is another way of saying that she has succumbed to Sancho's interpretive desires. If Don Quixote's desires cannot "come to pass"—to borrow from Cardenio's lament—it is because they are not, and never were, *his*. They were all borrowed desires, on loan from Amadís or, after a crash course in chivalry, from Sancho.[41] As a subject of desire, Don Quixote "can't afford" his own desires.

It is at this point in the dream that Artemidorus, with his sharp eye for the calculus of debt, supplements Freud as an interpretive aid. When the enchanted Dulcinea approaches Don Quixote for a loan of six *reales*, against collateral in the form of her slip, he finds himself short by two *reales*. He even wishes aloud, in a kind of gross disparity, that he were a Fugger ("un Fucar"), a German banker, in order to relieve her economic distress. In Carroll Johnson's Freudian reading the most plausible interpretation of this dream is that, al-though Don Quixote "invests" all he has in the enchanted Dulcinea, four *reales*, his failure to produce the requested six coins signifies his

40. "Ideas which are contraries are by preference expressed in dreams by one and the same element." According to Freud, "the alternative *'either—or'* is never expressed in dreams." Because these alternatives exist in dreams without canceling each other out, "an 'either-or' used in *recording* a dream is to be translated by 'and.' " See *The Freud Reader*, ed. Peter Gay (New York: W. W. Norton, 1989), 158–59.

41. Even the desire to visit the Cave of Montesinos may be borrowed from the Knight of the Grove's fictional trip, at the bidding of his Casildea, to the Cavern of Cabra (II.14). For a splendid reading of why Cardenio's desires do not "come to pass," see Edward Dudley, "The Wild Man Goes Baroque," in *The Wild Man Within*, ed. Edward Dudley and Maximillian E. Novak (Pittsburgh: University of Pittsburgh Press, 1972), pp. 115–39.

"fear of impotence."[42] Resistant readers may ask why, in this dream, the money has to stand in for sexual prowess, or indeed for any other signified: why can't a *real* be just a *real*? But even Artemidorus (brought back from the dead to interpret this dream) would not allow the luxury of a pure signifier here. The concession that sometimes a *real* is just a *real* may have served for simple *enhypnia* or diagnostic dreams. But in Don Quixote's complex *oneiros*,[43] sex is already linked with the discourse of debt. The linkage may be illuminated by Foucault's reminder that "there exists in Greek—and in many other languages as well, to varying degrees—a very pronounced ambiguity between the sexual meaning and the economic meaning of certain terms." By playing on "the polysemy of the vocabulary of debt," Artemidorus uses words that signify both being "bound to pay" and "pressed by a sexual need."[44]

There exists in Spanish, too, a pronounced ambiguity between the sexual and the economic. One finds it, for example, in the phrase "perder crédito," conventionally used for fallen women who "lose credit," an ambiguity exploited by Cervantes in his astonishing representations of seduced or deflowered women such as Dorotea or Feliciana de la Voz, women who have lost their "chaste treasure." Feliciana, indeed, begins her narrative in the *Persiles* by opting to forgo "el crédito de honrada [the credit of a chaste woman]" in order to tell her *caso*.[45] She "pays" to talk, in other words, foreshadowing those sexually distressed females who, like Dora, also had to pay for a "talking cure." In the light of these linguistic ambiguities, Cervantes's dreamers invite special scrutiny. Why are his two main heroes dreaming through a "vocabulary of debt"? In Don Quixote's dream, Dulcinea's handmaid pertly reminds him of his indebtedness: "Todo eso, y más, debe vuestra merced a mi señora [All this, and more, your worship owes my lady]" (II.23). The sexual meaning of his debt is signaled by the cheap underwear, the cotton "faldellín," he is offered as a pawn. Dreaming at that ambiguous intersection of the sexual and the economic, Don Quixote anticipates the later hero of the *Persiles*, who dreams about a "debt" he may owe to the personification of "SENSUALIDAD." But although the dreaming hero of

42. Johnson, *Madness and Lust*, 158.
43. For example, "It is natural for a man who has stuffed himself with food either to vomit or to choke" in his dreams (*Oneirocritica* 1.1). Don Quixote has stuffed himself with impossible dreams, with mediated (and antiquated) desire.
44. Foucault, *Care of the Self*, 27–28.
45. Cervantes, *Persiles*, 292.

the *Persiles* tries to convert his debts into credits—a conversion that Kenneth Burke claims all of us do in both literature and dreams[46]— Don Quixote attempts no such conversion.

Indebted as Don Quixote claims to be to Dulcinea, his dream reveals certain "constraints of desire" in that he cannot provide her with even a temporary loan. The dream figure of Montesinos, a faded aristocrat, is obliged to remind the hero that even the enchanted have debts, that economic need is ubiquitous: "Que esta que llaman necesidad adondequiera se usa [That which is called need is to be found everywhere]" (II.23). Economic need (*necesidad*), in short, must receive star billing in Cervantine dreams as it did in Artemidorus. As the product of scarcity economies in which calculation and ambiguity are normal practices, the "need" that we find in the dreams of late antiquity takes up its abode, once again, within the cultural formations of Cervantes's troubled Hapsburg age. Edmund Burke's lament, on the occasion of Marie Antoinette's death, that the age of chivalry was gone—"succeeded by economists and calculators"—did not take into account the age before chivalry, the centuries of late antiquity, when economics and calculation were regularly signified in dream interpretation.

Nor did Burke take into account Cervantes, an early modern writer, whose avowed aim, long before the age of Marie Antoinette, was to topple the codes of chivalry. One way to subvert the ideological function of these codes was to mention money—and not merely in reminding Don Quixote that he should carry it, along with clean shirts, on his quests. The displacement, within the Cave of Montesinos dream, of Don Quixote's wish to be Amadís, a chivalric hero, with the wish to be a Fugger, a German banker, marks the passage from feudal pretensions to early modern capitalism, to the rise of "Don Dinero [Sir Money]," Francisco de Quevedo's well-known personification. In a suggestive insight based on his reading of "La gitanilla," Robert ter Horst writes that "the core event in Cervantine fiction comes to be what it will be in later fiction—a transaction, an instrument of exchange, a deal." But this core event also bears out Robert Bly's remark, in a more popular context, that "the psyche likes to make deals."[47] The deals negotiated by the Cervantine psyche reveal that dreams are the paradigm of all the brave stratagems of our needs

---

46. Burke writes that in literature, as in dreams, we all attempt to convert our debts into credits. See Kenneth Burke, *The Philosophy of Literary Form* (Berkeley: University of California Press, 1973), 17. I am indebted to George Shipley for this reference.

47. Robert ter Horst, "Une saison en enfer: *La gitanilla*," *Cervantes* 5 (1985): 111. Robert Bly and Keith Thompson, "What Men Really Want," in *Challenge of the Heart: Love, Sex, and Intimacy in Changing Times* (Boston: Shambhala Publications, 1985), 106.

and desires. Cervantes's writing records the parallels between dreaming, making fictions, and making deals.

And so I interpret Don Quixote's dream as an oneiric dream experience, in that those missing reales tell "what is real" in Artemidoran terms—and perhaps what is "real," too, in Lacanian terms of the Real Order, that elusive domain of the inexpressible, where the subject meets with both sexuality and death. After this kind of dream encounter, where his unconscious expresses what is forbidden to him as a speaking subject, Don Quixote begins to lose the stability of his identity. Artemidorus could have warned him that the "character and disposition" of the enchanted Dulcinea would function as a symbol "of things that will happen to the dreamer" (1.78), of the systematic disenchantment of his world. No longer able to afford the price of his illusions, Don Quixote is forced to relinquish them, along with his invented identity. When, after a series of debilitating blows to his narcissism, Don Quixote finally accepts that he will never see Dulcinea, he ceases to be Don Quixote. Seen from his deathbed, then, the Cave of Montesino's dream qualifies as an oneiric or future-directed dream.

But what is special about *Don Quixote* is that the oneiric is pressed into service in *and* out of dreams. Indeed, it haunts the rest of the events in part II, "events whose truth is always subject to interpretation," as Ruth El Saffar has noted.[48] Don Quixote's dream takes on the status of a fiction within a fiction, as the text begins to thematize interpretation. A series of dream interpreters is internalized in the narrative, making literal a desire for interpretation triggered by Don Quixote himself, when he raises what Anthony Cascardi calls "one of the most persistent skeptical worries in connection with this adventure: our ability to tell dreams from wakefulness."[49] Having "awakened" from sleep into his dream-vision itself, and having attempted a routine exercise of all his senses in order to certify the stability of his identity, Don Quixote links his past to his present: "que yo era allí entonces el que soy aquí ahora [that I was the same there and then as I am here and now]" (II.23). What he is "here and now" is an interpretant whose subjective stability is rooted in desire. It is desire that makes him describe a grotesque nightmare as deeply fulfilling, indeed, as "la más sabrosa y agradable vida y vista [the

48. In a section aptly called "Don Quixote's Symbolic Undoing," Ruth El Saffar mentions the "oneiric quality" of the events the hero encounters in part II. See El Saffar, *Beyond Fiction: The Recovery of the Feminine in the Novels of Cervantes* (Berkeley: University of California Press, 1984), 92.
49. Cascardi, "Cervantes and Descartes on the Dream Argument," 109.

most delightful and agreeable vision]" any human being had ever experienced (II.22). And it is desire that makes him call into question, in a surprising deal with Sancho, the veracity of his own dream: "Pues vos queréis que se os crea lo que habéis visto en el cielo, yo quiero que vos me creáis a mí lo que vi en la cueva de Montesinos [If you want me to believe what you saw in the heavens, I want you to believe what I saw in the Cave of Montesinos]" (II.41). Knowing the truth or falsehood of this dream is, of course, not necessary to its interpretation.[50] What is disclosed in this dream is a truth about the state of Don Quixote's desire—what Julia Kristeva would call a "mad truth": "a truth which is true in a different way than objective reality because it speaks a certain subjective truth, instead of a presumed objective truth."[51] But even Cervantes's Lotario knew that lovers are only as truthful as they are "incapable of expressing what they feel" ("siempre quedan tan cortos como verdaderos") (I.34). Subjective truth is unspeakable. Its operations are *pre-* or *trans-meaning*, to borrow Kristeva's terminology for those nondiscursive phenomena that elude the language function, that cut "through language, in the direction of the unspeakable."[52]

Apart from the dreamer himself, Cervantes invites the narrator, a divining monkey, and a Magic Head into the text, like consultants, to further interpret what they would all seem to regard as unspeakable. The narrator Cide Hamete, in a handwritten márginal note, questions the plausibility of the events Don Quixote describes, exonerating himself of all responsibility for the dream's "apocryphal" nature ("Yo no tengo la culpa"). He even credits a rumor about the hero's supposed deathbed retraction of his dream (II.24). The Magic Head (who repeatedly insists it cannot judge desires: "que yo no juzgo de deseos") remains tantalizingly noncommittal: "A lo de la cueva . . . hay mucho que decir: de todo tiene [There is much to be said on the score of the cave: it's got everything]" (II.62). Even the divining monkey, that staple Renaissance symbol of *lascivia*, replies, unhelpfully, that parts of the dream are false ("falsas") and parts credible ("verisímiles") (II.25).

Readers who posit themselves as interpreters scarcely wish to rush in where monkeys fear to tread. An interpreter of the Cave of Mon-

---

50. See Sieber's "Literary Time in the 'Cueva de Montesinos,' " 269n.

51. On the *folle vérité*, or "mad truth," of delirium, see Kristeva, "Psychoanalysis and the Polis," 308.

52. Julia Kristeva, *Tales of Love*, trans. Leon S. Roudiez (New York: Columbia University Press, 1987), 29.

tesinos dream will fear becoming, as Percas de Ponseti explains, "one more character in the book."[53] But the exasperated Arab historian, writing in the margins of Cervantes, assigns the work of decipherment to us: "Tú, letor, pues eres prudente, juzga lo que te pareciere, que yo no debo ni puedo más [You, prudent reader, judge for yourself, for I should not, nor cannot, do more]" (II.24). In other words, "Reader, you decide." Readers down the ages have decided that the Cave of Montesinos dream may be interpreted as, among other things, a Christian allegory of the harrowing of hell; a parody of the classical trip to the underworld; an imitation of an Arthurian trip to Merlin's cave; an oddly malicious theatrical farce constituting Don Quixote's revenge on Sancho; and, more recently, a terrible pre-Freudian intuition of the hero's anguished psyche. The decades to come will usher in new interpretations from other "prudent" readers.

In an attempt to thematize interpretation, then, Cervantes builds a specific role for his reader into his work: the role of oneiromancer. Instead of providing meaning by way of the stability of the interpretive position, however, Cervantes focuses on the meaning of the interpretive position itself. Kristeva's claim that, with Freud, the dimension of *desire* appears "for the first time in the citadel of interpretive will" ignores the work of Cervantes as Freud's literary precursor.[54] Although Cervantes's pre-Cartesian dreamer is not yet a cogitating subject for whom the "truths" of empirical science can be known, he makes a giant cognitive leap toward the postmodern crisis of reason. *Don Quixote*—which has been called "a treatise about how meaning gets into things"[55]—introduces the desire to *give* meaning to dreams rather than to *find* it there. Thus dream interpretation—the paradigm

53. Cervantes's calculated avoidance of clarity—his programmatic "ambiguity"—is, for Percas de Ponseti, his most original trait: "The moment the critic commits himself to a clear-cut, single explanation of what happened in the cave of Montesinos he becomes, for future readers, one more character in the book"; Helena Percas de Ponseti, "The Cave of Montesinos: Cervantes' Art of Fiction," in the Norton Critical Edition of *Don Quixote*, ed. Joseph R. Jones and Kenneth Douglas (New York: W. W. Norton, 1981), 994. I am deeply indebted to Percas de Ponseti's various generative essays on the Cave of Montesinos dream. See, for example, "La cueva de Montesinos," *Revista hispánica moderna* 34 (1968): 376–99; and, for a more detailed study of Cervantes's sources, her *Cervantes y su concepto del arte* (Madrid: Gredos, 1975), 448–583. I thank her, also, for her useful reading of this essay.

54. Kristeva, "Psychoanalysis and the Polis," 306. Cervantes showed marked signs of resistance to the dawning of the scientific enlightenment. As Alban Forcione explains in the context of Galileo's antifantasy stance: "Cervantes saw a major adversary in those who would inhibit the fantasy with notions derived from science." See Forcione, *Cervantes, Aristotle, and the "Persiles"* (Princeton: Princeton University Press, 1970), 143n.

55. Guy Davenport, "Foreword" to Vladimir Nabokov, *Lectures on Don Quixote*, ed. Fredson Bowers (New York: Harcourt Brace Jovanovich, 1983), xvi.

in Cervantes for all interpretation—is made endlessly renewable. Does Don Quixote's cash deficit mean his fear of impotence, à la Freud; or vice versa, à la Artemidorus; or something altogether different? Reader, *you* decide.

4

Cervantes and
the Unconscious

Carroll B. Johnson

Noli foras ire, in te ipsum redi, in interiore homine habitat veritas.

—Saint Augustine

Apprends à te connaître, et déscends en toi-même.

—Corneille

Who in the world knows anything of any other heart—or of his own?

—Ford Madox Ford

Traditionally, psychoanalytic critics have tended to approach the question of the unconscious in texts in one of two basic ways. The first is to consider the text as a manifestation of the author's unconscious. In this approach the critic assumes that the material the author has banished from his or her own consciousness returns in a disguised form. Ruth El Saffar has done this in her study of *La Galatea* in *Beyond Fiction* (1984), and, more recently, in an article titled "In Praise of What Is Left Unsaid."[1] She, and other psychoanalytic critics who work in the same fashion, regard the various characters and their interpersonal dilemmas as signs of intrapsychic conflicts that really belong (in this case) to Cervantes and his inner struggle with the norms of his resolutely patriarchal society. The second traditional approach is

1. Ruth El Saffar, *Beyond Fiction: The Recovery of the Feminine in the Novels of Cervantes* (Berkeley: University of California Press, 1984); and "In Praise of What Is Left Unsaid," *MLN* 103 (1988): 205–22.

to consider that the characters' behavior, like our own, is the result of both conscious and unconscious motivation, and to attempt to tease the unspoken motivation out of the discourse, as John Weiger and I have both attempted to do.[2]

The procedure in both cases is to look for gaps in the discourse which reveal the presence of something concealed beneath the visible surface, or, in El Saffar's phrase, something left unsaid. The goal of a psychoanalytical reading of a literary text is to recover the "repressed" or "censored" content lying below the surface of the discourse, content that determines, finally, the form of that discourse. Cervantes's discourse presents gaping holes, such as, for instance, the unnarrated first fifty years of Don Quixote's life. The characters' discourse presents similar gaps in the form of apparently unmotivated behavior and incongruously fallacious reasoning. For example, when Don Quixote leaves home for the first time, he addresses Dulcinea in a soliloquy and laments her having ordered him out of her presence. Since he was not in her presence to begin with, however, if he wanted to avoid her, he needed only to stay where he was. His precipitous departure must therefore be the result of some unconfessed motivation, some unidentified need to get out of his house and away from the members of his household. Again, at the beginning of part II, when he has gone to El Toboso precisely to find Dulcinea and present himself to her, he agrees first to delay the search until it is too dark to see and then to reduce the search force by half. His willingness to sabotage his own mission in this way suggests that he is in fact not as keen to pursue the search as he himself believes.

In one case the critic attempts to probe the unconscious of the author, in the other that of the characters. In both cases the result is not actual knowledge but more or less reasonable inference, depending on the critic's training and sensitivity; and that result may be more or less illuminating depending on the same factors and on the degree of receptivity the critical community is willing to concede. A third approach to psychoanalytic criticism, which likens the reader and the text to the analyst and analysand in the clinical experience of transference, has been advanced by Peter Brooks.[3] Brooks observes that in any successful analysis, the patient becomes his or her own analyst and the analyst becomes the patient. This bears, I think, on my ob-

2. John G. Weiger, *The Individuated Self: Cervantes and the Emergence of the Individual* (Athens: Ohio University Press, 1979); Carroll B. Johnson, *Madness and Lust: A Psychoanalytical Approach to Don Quixote* (Berkeley: University of California Press, 1983).

3. Peter Brooks, "The Idea of a Psychoanalytic Literary Criticism," in *The Trial(s) of Psychoanalysis*, ed. Françoise Meltzer (Chicago: University of Chicago Press, 1988), 145–60.

servations here. The fact is that the only unconscious about which I can ever hope to speak with any authority is my own, not Cervantes's and not Don Quixote's. Unfortunately, like everyone else, I have no direct access even to my own unconscious. Jacques Lacan's insistence that "the unconscious is the discourse of the Other" means that my own unconscious is impenetrable to me, that it speaks to me through someone who is not me. In the case that interests us here, this Other is the text, both in its original form and in the form of the critical readings that surround it. As I read the text, the text is simultaneously reading me. In this essay, therefore, I deal with the relations between Cervantes's text, its critical readings, and my own unconscious, which Lacan has defined as "the censored chapter of my history."[4] The goal of psychoanalysis is to recover at least some of the censored material and allow it to assume its rightful place in the discourse. My goal here is to explore various manifestations of the unconscious in the reader, with a view to accounting for the maddening diversity of interpretations of Cervantes's works, and the tenacity with which the differing interpretations are championed. I try to use the discourse of the Other to shed a little light on an unconscious I can never really hope to know in full. Whatever insights I glean are offered as an example of how the process works. What results, in other words, is not a particular content to be generalized or a position to be taken as normative. The ultimate cognitive objective is not knowledge about the text, therefore, but knowledge about the reader, which means knowledge about oneself. Such knowledge can be counted on to be painful and embarrassing. If it were not, there would have been no need to repress it in the first place. If one is a literary critic, the dissemination of at least part of this painful and embarrassing self-knowledge becomes an unavoidable aspect of one's legitimate professional activity.

It would be superfluous to point out that, for many critics, the reader has come to supersede the text as the locus of critical interest, and it would be equally superfluous to pass in review the various current forms of reader-response criticism. I do feel impelled to point out some interesting coincidences, however, between the kind of psychoanalytic reading I hope to exemplify here and socio-ideological readings, especially those of a Marxist orientation. The premise common to both is that what is most important is that which is left unsaid,

4. Jacques Lacan, "La psychanalyse et son enseignement," *Bulletin de la Société Française de Philosophie* 2 (1957): 67, and "Fonction et champ de la parole et du langage en psychanalyse" (1957), in *Ecrits I* (Paris: Seuil, 1966), 136.

in one case the censored chapter of the author's or reader's history, and in the other the unchallenged assumptions, unverbalized because unacknowledged, that constitute ideology proper. Terry Eagleton summarizes the essential postulate of Marxist criticism when he notes that "ideology is present in the text in the form of its eloquent silences, its significant gaps and fissures."[5] The goal of both Marxist and psychoanalytic reading strategies is thus the same: to make the unspoken speak. In addition, both reading strategies involve the assumption that something in a particular text reaches out to a particular reader in ways that he or she is not aware of and hooks some aspect of his or her identity or personality, producing an effect whose cause is not apparent to the reader, but which accounts for the reader's particular interpretation and the tenacity with which it is defended. The question is, which particular things in the text have this power in which particular readers?

Louis Althusser coined the term "ideological interpellation" to account for this aspect of the text's impact on the reader. A text calls out to a reader as a gendered subject, as a member of a class, as a participant in a particular moment in history, and so on. Although the specificity of the reader's embodiment begins to answer the question of why interpretations diverge so wildly, since it remains on the level of consciousness, it does not account for such embarrassingly incompatible readings of *Don Quixote* as those offered by, say, James A. Parr and myself, both fiftyish white men of generally capitalist persuasion, living in the same city at the same time.[6] James Iffland has used Althusser's notion of ideological interpellation to good advantage, however, to account for at least some of the myriad interpretations of *Don Quixote* in two studies.[7]

José Barchilón and Joel Kovel, both practicing psychoanalysts, consider that as a result of a similar interpellative transaction below the level of consciousness, the reader's unconscious "resonates harmonically, as it were, with the unconscious of the characters (or resists resonance)."[8] Similarly, Norman N. Holland believes that the text reaches out to what he calls the reader's individual "identity theme,"

5. Terry Eagleton, "Machery and Marxist Literary Theory," in *Against the Grain* (London: Verso, 1986), 14.

6. Parr's disagreements with *Madness and Lust* are set out with unflinching rigor in James A. Parr, *Don Quixote: An Anatomy of Subversive Discourse* (Newark, Del.: Juan de la Cuesta, 1988), 86.

7. James Iffland, "Ideological Interpellation in *Don Quixote*," *Journal of the Midwest Modern Language Association* 20 (1987): 17–36, and 20 (1987): 9–27.

8. José Barchilón and Joel Kovel, "*Huckleberry Finn*: A Psychoanalytical Study," *Journal of the American Psychoanalytic Association* 14 (1976): 222.

which is hooked below the level of consciousness by something he or she identifies with in, for example, a particular character or situation.[9] Although the notion of identity may be momentarily out of fashion, Holland's hypothesis bears directly on the question underlying the title of John Allen's book *Don Quixote: Hero or Fool?* We all approach character through some aspect of ourselves, and we see something of ourselves (or resist seeing it) in Don Quixote, although I think Allen had in mind a more conscious identification with or rejection of the character.[10]

The question then becomes whether we are in fact dealing with something in the text or something originating in ourselves which we project onto the text, where we then proceed to "discover" it. The second possibility is unacceptable to us because it runs counter to our perception of ourselves as objective seekers after truth. It also becomes awkward to ask a granting agency for money to fund our "research" if research is defined as some kind of subjective self-indulgence. We therefore have a powerful vested interest in believing that we are always investigating objectively verifiable properties of the text. This vested interest (which has its own unconscious and ideological dimension) tends to blind us to the real source of our divergent interpretations—in ourselves—because we are forced to keep looking for it in the text. Shakespeare's observation that "the fault, dear Brutus, is not in our stars" seems particularly apt here. David Bleich has made a valiant effort to legitimize the proposition that the identity of the questioner defines the kind of questions he or she asks of the text, and that this in turn defines the possible answers.[11]

The historian Peter Loewenberg considers the researcher's own psychic investment in the facts under investigation a form of countertransference, the introduction of the therapist's unconscious feelings into the therapeutic situation: "The anxious clinging to 'hard' facts and the refusal to view 'facts' in any but what is interpreted as the 'obvious' way—i.e., in the manner which a given researcher can tolerate and therefore 'see'—is the scholarly analogue to the psychoanalyst's countertransference." Loewenberg further considers this unconscious investment inevitable in any investigation carried out by

9. Norman N. Holland, "Unity—Identity—Text—Self," in *Reader-Response Criticism, from Formalism to Post-Structuralism,* ed. Jane Tompkins (Baltimore: Johns Hopkins University Press, 1980), 118–32.

10. John J. Allen, *Don Quixote: Hero or Fool?*, vol. 1 (Gainesville: University Presses of Florida, 1969); vol. 2 (Gainesville: University Presses of Florida, 1979).

11. David Bleich, *Subjective Criticism* (Baltimore: Johns Hopkins University Press, 1978).

a human agent. "All research," he observes, "is unconsciously self-relevant, regardless of how distant it appears to be from the self on a detached scholarly level." The trick, he says, is to "bring the countertransference feelings into consciousness and to *use them as a tool of perception.*"[12] I think Loewenberg's use of the notion of countertransference is applicable to Bleich's critical approach, which denies all authority to the text and celebrates instead the reader's projection onto it of his own psychic proclivities. In a more recent effort to rehabilitate the text, Michael Steig also insists on the primacy of the reader's unconscious search for mastery over his or her inner demons: "Most of us appropriate limited areas of literature . . . in order to reach our desired goals. We seek to still questions, to reduce anxiety, to stabilize our relation to the literary work."[13]

The foregoing discussion leaves unexplored the vagaries of my own unconscious and their possible bearing on Cervantine studies. Before stretching myself out on the couch, I want to offer Don Quixote himself and Don Diego de Miranda as examples, within the text, of readers whose unconscious conflicts are manifested, or at least hinted at, by their reading. Don Quixote throws himself into his reading in an effort to deny or sublimate his unconscious conflicts. Instead of learning something about himself—that is, instead of being read by the text, as Lacan puts it so succinctly—he effects an imaginary identification with the knights-errant and finds, through them, a provisional solution to his psychic conflicts. Don Quixote's unconscious appears to be engaged by something in the text, and he certainly seems, to me at any rate, to project his own inner conflicts onto his reading material. When he is called on to discuss the romances of chivalry, for example, he invariably limits himself to recalling certain erotic episodes (especially concerning Lancelot, Guinevere, and the dueña Quintañona), from which we can infer a special interest on his part in such encounters. Don Diego, in contrast, does not actually read at all, but confines himself to the action of "leafing through" (*hojear*) certain books in his larger-than-average library. By keeping the books at bay, he hopes to forestall the possibility of finding out anything about himself, or about the worth of his values, that would make him uncomfortable. He does not give the text the opportunity to read him. Both Don Quixote and Don Diego, then, are engaged

12. Peter Loewenberg, *Decoding the Past: The Psychohistorical Approach* (Berkeley: University of California Press, 1969), 12.

13. Michael Steig, *Stories of Reading: Subjectivity and Literary Understanding* (Baltimore: Johns Hopkins University Press, 1989), 30.

and defined by the act of reading, the former by attraction and the latter by repulsion.

These reflections bring me to my own experience, which I want to exemplify by reference to *Don Quixote*, part I, chapter 50. In that episode Don Quixote elaborates a fantasy in the style of the romances of chivalry, involving a descent into a boiling lake, an underwater palace, and scores of beautiful damsels who undress the knight and cater to his every desire. I have always read this episode as a fantasy of aggressive phallic sexuality, a manifestation of that part of Don Quixote's psyche which he works so hard to deny but which keeps slipping through the chinks in his defenses. Such a reading seems to be reasonable speculation with respect to Don Quixote's unconscious, and it has the potential to enrich our understanding of his character. But if Holland or Bleich and Loewenberg and Steig are to be believed, how I read this episode offers real knowledge about me and my own unconscious. The text has read me, reached out and hooked a potentially embarrassing aspect of my psyche hitherto unacknowledged, which is to say repressed, by me, brought it into view, and made it speak. I am forced to acknowledge my own participation in Don Quixote's fantasy.

This is bad enough, but the worst is yet to come. In the summer of 1988 I heard a talk by Ruth El Saffar in which she made reference to the same episode. Imagine my surprise when she identified it as a fantasy of maternal nurturing, the polar opposite of my reading. I immediately ascribed her aberrant interpretation to the fact that she is a woman and therefore cannot understand men and male motivation the way I can, and that she is a Jungian and therefore obsessed with the ideas of nurturing and earth-mothering. That is, I explained her behavior (or explained it away) in terms of Althusser's ideological interpellation or Holland's identity theme. As her talk progressed, however, I was forced to recognize that in order to reach my interpretation, I had had to ignore, indeed blind myself to, major facts of the text. The descent into the lake is clearly an entry into the vagina, with the attendant masculine fears described as early as 1932 by Karen Horney.[14] The undressing clearly reduces Don Quixote to the status of a dependent child, something (since it is *his* fantasy) he must want. He does not do anything *to* the women; they do things *for* him, such as bathing and feeding him. I am forced to conclude that Don Quixote seems to be tired of being an adult man living in the fast lane, that

---

14. Karen Horney, "The Dread of Women" (1932), in *Feminine Psychology* (New York: W. W Norton, 1967), 133–46.

he wants to return to the womb and be mothered. This revelation renders all the more pathetic his frantic flight from housekeeper and niece into the ruggedly masculine, superphallic world of armor, lances, and horses.

My blindness to what is in fact obvious on the surface of the discourse cannot be explained in terms of reading as a man versus reading as a woman, or of reading as a Freudian versus reading as a Jungian. These categories do not explain anything; they are merely visibles that betray unconscious choices already made. (To *be* a man or a woman is the result not of choice but of chromosomes, but to *read* as one or the other *is* a matter of choice.) My blindness must ultimately be explained as a function of my own psychic economy. For reasons unknown to anyone, though soon to be discovered by me and my analyst, it was important to me to deny certain impulses in myself—perhaps a certain weariness with the responsibilities of masculinity, or perhaps a still unresolved aspect of my relation to my mother. What these particular impulses are is not relevant here. What is important is the effect of the discourse of the Other, that is, Cervantes's text interpreted by El Saffar, on my psyche. Quite simply, my unconscious has been made to speak—again. The new discourse is concerned with a deeper layer of repression buried beneath the first, which opened up when I discovered my participation in a fantasy of phallic domination over several women at once. There has been produced a kind of analogue to the triangular situation posited by Lacan consisting of the patient, the analyst, and the "Third," or what they sometimes jointly generate. As Shoshana Felman explains it: "The Other is in a position of a Third, in the structure of the psychoanalytic dialogue: it is a locus of unconscious language, sometimes created by a felicitous encounter, by the felicitous verbal coincidence between the unconscious discourse of the analyst and the unconscious discourse of the patient."[15]

The only explanation for Don Quixote's strange fantasy lies in his unconscious. The fantasy is, first, a manifestation of his unfulfilled and unfulfillable need to be a man among women. For years I had read this episode with my own unconscious resonating in harmony with what I took to be Don Quixote's, blind exactly as he is blind to what may be the real nature of his/my fantasy about the knight who jumps into the boiling lake in answer to a fragile but strangely compelling female voice. Owing to the discourse of another reader (whose

15. Shoshana Felman, *Jacques Lacan and the Adventure of Insight: Psychoanalysis in Contemporary Culture* (Cambridge: Harvard University Press, 1987), 125–26.

reading, like mine, is a function of her own particular combination of what she wants to find and what she is afraid she might find in the text), my unconscious has been made to speak. I am on the road to enhanced self-knowledge. My admiration for Cervantes's capacity to create fictitious people who act as though they had an unconscious just as I do has been increased (if that is possible). And, finally, my appreciation of the excitement inherent in the reading process, that peculiar combination of eagerness and a sense of danger, has been heightened.

But, in the end, I still find myself loath to give up my reading of the episode as a fantasy of phallic domination, partly because of the telltale shock of recognition I experienced when I discovered it. The desire for phallic domination is real, and not simply a camouflage for the more deeply repressed fantasy of nurturing discovered by El Saffar. Since her reading is a function of her unconscious, as mine is of my own, it would seem that she unconsciously edited out the domination just as I eliminated the nurturing. As I continue to read and be instructed by feminist theory, I discover that men typically experience a simultaneous desire to dominate and to be nurtured by women, and that this desire is reinforced by cultural expectations. Women are expected to nurture not just children but adult men as well. And of course they are expected to provide sexual satisfaction for the same men. Alice Miller has called this expectation "the masculine dream, as seductive as it is absurd, of being coddled by women like a baby and at the same time commanding them like a pascha."[16] This, it seems to me, is what Don Quixote is finally fantasizing. I should point out that this double and conflictive version of male entitlement reappears, already played for laughs by a precocious feminism, in the film director's fantasy in Federico Fellini's 8½ (1962) of an evening at home with all the women in his life. I do not know why Professor El Saffar does not dwell on the domination aspect of Don Quixote's fantasy, but it seems to me that her insistence on only the nurturing aspect must be as significant as my own inability to see it at all.

Impressions to the contrary notwithstanding, I am not trying to emulate Byron by dragging "the pageant of my bleeding heart" into print for everyone to marvel at. My model has instead been Freud, who in order to discover the mechanisms of everyone's dreams had to think deeply, and in public, about his own. The revelation of my unconsciously determined blindness to a perfectly visible aspect of Cervantes's text has, I hope, a paradigmatic value. It offers an expla-

16. Alice Miller, *The Drama of the Gifted Child* (New York: Basic Books, 1981). 89.

nation of why different readers read differently which surpasses the only apparently scientific notion of "competent" and "incompetent" readers, "correct" and "misguided" readings, for it suggests that we are all prisoners of powerful unconscious motivations. And because I am unaware of the true provenance of my own consciously held ideas—that is, that they are the product of an attempt to obliterate some thought so anxiety provoking that I cannot bear even to think it—the bulldog tenacity with which I cling to them is also explained. One might proceed, not without some risk, to hazard some generalizations about, for instance, the need experienced by certain readers to drain from Cervántes's work all traces of anything approaching seriousness in the sense of personal relevance, the need of other readers to hold up Don Diego de Miranda as a role model, or to insulate themselves from experience behind masses of well-documented trivia, or to make Cervantes the spokesman for either a kind of left-wing Erasmian liberalism or the rigid social conformity endorsed at Trent. None of us can discover by ourselves the unconscious motivation of our most cherished readings of Cervantes. But if we can allow ourselves to listen to one another, even in the silence of only apparently solitary reading, we may find we are hearing ourselves.

III

Fragmented Heroes, Fragmented Texts

5

Mirroring Others: A Lacanian Reading of the
Letrados in Don Quixote

Anne J. Cruz

In life, we do this at every moment: we appraise ourselves
from the point of view of others, we attempt to understand
the transgredient moments of our very consciousness and
to take them into account through the other.

—Mikhail Bakhtin

—El que de mí trata—dijo don Quijote—, a pocos habrá
contentado.

—Miguel de Cervantes

Having failed miserably in his own bureaucratic career and achieving
only a modest reputation as a playwright and poet, Cervantes held
a jaundiced view of *letrados*—the growing number of so-called nobil-
ities of the robe and of the sword whose university education prepared
them mainly for official posts.[1] Indeed, his criticism of these "educated

1. According to Richard Kagan, by the sixteenth century the term *letrado* in Spain referred
to two general categories: civil servants and churchmen trained in law, and humanist scholars
whose education stressed classical letters. Although he makes the distinction between
"largely legal" and "largely literary" training received by the letrados, he suggests that such
a division may be illusory, as these categories "formed a single, hybrid program"; Richard
Kagan, *Students and Society in Early Modern Spain* (Baltimore: Johns Hopkins University Press,
1974), xix–xx. Ottavio Di Camillo believes the reason to be that the medieval letrados were
the precursors of the fifteenth-century humanists; see his "Humanism in Spain," in *Renaissance Humanism: Foundations, Forms, and Legacy*, ed. Albert Rabil, Jr. (Philadelphia: University
of Pennsylvania Press, 1988), 55–108. See also Francisco Márquez Villanueva's review of
Janine Fayard, *Les membres du Conseil de Castille a l'époque moderne, 1621–1746* (Geneva, 1979),
and Jean-Marc Pelorson, *Les 'letrados' juristes castilans sous Philippe III: Recherches sur leur place*

men" in a novel about the misreadings of an unscholarly hidalgo is yet another example of masterfully Cervantine irony. The complex roles of the letrados in *Don Quixote* are however, due to far more than the author's distrust or, what has been stressed most often, the paradoxical nature of the novel. Figures such as the priest, the Knight of the Green Coat, and Sansón Carrasco have previously been considered the mouthpieces of conservative ethical values and of a normalcy opposed to Don Quixote's madness.[2] But as I hope to demonstrate, the letrados who appear in the text take an essential part in structuring its narrative. In Lacanian terms they represent one of the meanings of the Other, the Symbolic order in *Don Quixote* which imposes control on and attempts to stabilize the delusionary experiences of its protagonist.[3]

Yet the strength of both text and character lies in their resistance to social imperatives. What Lacanian theory allows us to see in the narrative is the contradictions that generate from oppositions, which in turn illuminate both its internal dynamics and the externalized narrative of history. As Juliet MacCannell has pointed out, Jacques Lacan's categories of the Imaginary, the Symbolic, and the Real inhere in social structures as much as in the novel. Noting how he has historicized the Freudian universals, she comments that "there are key nameable historical turning points in which the elaboration of these symbolic structures deepens or weakens, expands or subsides. What Freud could do for individual psychic histories Lacan does for the psychic history of his particular culture."[4] And, we might add,

---

dans la société, la culture et l'état (Poitiers, 1980), which I have been unable to consult but which, according to Márquez, present a critique of these professionals; Francisco Márquez Villanueva, "Letrados, consejeros y justicias," *Hispanic Review* 53 (1985): 201–27. In his prologue, Cervantes purposely sides with the less educated against the letrados when he ironically criticizes his own text as "ajena de invención, menguada de estilo, pobre de concetos y falta de toda erudición y doctrina, sin acotaciones en las márgenes y sin anotaciones en el fin del libro, como veo que están otros libros [devoid of invention, meager in style, poor in conceits, wholly wanting in learning and doctrine, without quotations in the margin or annotations at the end like other books I've seen]."

2. See, for example, Oscar Mandel, "The Function of the Norm in *Don Quixote*," *Modern Philology* 55 (1958): 154–63; Alberto Sánchez, "El Caballero del Verde Gabán," *Anales cervantinos* 9 (1961–62): 169–201; and Randolph Pope, "El Caballero del Verde Gabán y su encuentro con Don Quijote," *Hispanic Review* 47 (1979): 207–18.

3. The "Other" for Jacques Lacan holds various meanings: in the mirror stage, the relationship with the Real Other or mother; the unconscious as the discourse of the Other; and the father, the Symbolic order representative of the cultural character of the Other.

4. Juliet MacCannell, "Oedipus Wrecks: Lacan, Stendhal, and the Narrative Form of the Real," in *Lacan and Narration: The Psychoanalytic Difference in Narrative Theory*, ed. Robert Con Davis (Baltimore: Johns Hopkins University Press, 1983), 910–40. See also her *Figuring Lacan: Criticism and the Cultural Unconscious* (London: Croom Helm, 1986).

for the baroque as well. In *Don Quixote*, the relations between the knight and authority figures such as Sansón Carrasco exemplify the critique of culture—in literature as in society—that Lacan's incisive reading of Freud carries out so persuasively.

By repositioning historical periods as layered strata that impinge on one another, the novel's critical discourse not only realigns them as discontinuous epistemes, anticipating Michel Foucault's attack on historical continuity and synthesis—and therefore his critique of a "unified" subject—but also brings them into question.[5] *Don Quixote* demonstrates how its own language is already inscribed within a particular system, despite the spaces or gaps that open between the Foucauldian epistemes. Through its many-layered narratives, the Symbolic order in the text—more properly, *of* the text—already prefigures (by signifying) Don Quixote's adventures. Don Quixote's misreadings, however, reveal his inability to distinguish between objects and words, between signified and signifier. It is for this reason that Foucault has called him the "hero of the Same": "All those written texts, all those extravagant romances are, quite literally, unparalleled: no one in the world ever did resemble them; their timeless language remains suspended, unfulfilled by any similitude. . . . If he is to resemble the texts of which he is the witness, the representation, the real analogue, Don Quixote must also furnish proof and provide the indubitable sign that they are telling the truth, that they really are the language of the world. It is incumbent upon him to fulfil the promise of the books."[6]

That Don Quixote ultimately fails to fulfil this promise is, of course, one of the messages of *Don Quixote*. Foucault views him as "alienated in analogy," a disordered player of the Same and of the Other.[7] In his psychotic struggles the knight articulates the impossibility of the autonomous self. Yet it is also from this perspective that Foucault's judgment of the novel as "the first modern work of literature" can be understood. Surrounded from the start by novels of chivalry, Don Quixote as subject is constituted by language, that is, an *ordered* language. His unconscious, as Lacan's famous maxim makes clear, is already the language of the Other—in this case the archaic chivalric

5. "Continuous history is the indispensable correlative of the founding function of the subject: the guarantee that everything that has eluded him may be restored to him"; Michel Foucault, *The Archaeology of Knowledge* (New York: Harper Torchbooks, 1972), 12.

6. Michel Foucault, *The Order of Things: An Archaeology of the Human Sciences* (New York: Vintage, 1973), 46–47.

7. Ibid., 49.

discourse of the knightly narratives—although it is a language that emanates as well from his desire for the Real.[8] Following Lacan's L-schema, the chivalric adventures already form part of the order of the signifier. Fredric Jameson has attempted an explanation of this schema: "The subject's conscious desire, which he understands as a relationship between the desired object (a) and his ego or self (a'), is mediated by the more fundamental relationship between the real subject (S) and the capital A (*Autre*) of the Other, language or the Unconscious."[9] The dynamics of the L-schema—the movement of desire—positions the A as both source and fulfillment of the communications between self and desired object. Thus, Don Quixote's desire for what he perceives chivalric desire to be informs his unconscious from the first. Insofar as he reads, he partakes of a symbolic system, one that awakens in him the primary need to imitate the Other as he visualizes the exploits of the knights-errant. By naming himself Don Quixote, he strains to become the Other without intervention from the Nom-du-Père, the Name of the Father that would order his imaginary universe through paternal denial, the "non-du-père." Nonetheless, the act of naming—significantly, his own patronymic Quixote—is never totally his but is displaced among the different narrators of the text.[10] Oscillating by degrees between the Imaginary and the Symbolic in parts I and II, Don Quixote never fully separates from, or integrates with, the chivalric narratives.

Don Quixote's moments of madness are signaled by the reappearance of the Other's language in "pure" form. They are triggered when he is opposed by the Symbolic order, at which time, according to Lacan, the Name-of-the-Father is foreclosed: "It is the lack of the Name-of-the-Father in that place which, by the hole that it opens up in the signified, sets off the cascade of reshapings of the signifiers from which the increasing disaster of the imaginary proceeds, to the point at which the level is reached at which signifier and signified

8. According to Alan Sheridan, the Real should not be confused with reality. Although linked to the Symbolic and the Imaginary, the Real remains excluded from analytic experience. It is, rather, what is impossible, what cannot be symbolized; it describes that "which is lacking in the symbolic order, the ineliminable residue of all articulation," that which "may be approached, but never grasped"; Jacques Lacan, *Ecrits: A Selection*, trans. Alan Sheridan (New York: W. W. Norton, 1977), ix–x.

9. Fredric Jameson, "Imaginary and Symbolic in Lacan: Marxism, Psychoanalytic Criticism, and the Problem of the Subject," in *Literature and Psychoanalysis: The Question of Reading, Otherwise*, ed. Shoshana Feldman (Baltimore: Johns Hopkins University Press, 1982), 366.

10. Among the various names offered by the different narrators are Quijada, Quesada, Quejana, and Quijano. According to James Parr, the quest for the proper name would complement the search for an authentic text; see his *Don Quixote: An Anatomy of Subversive Discourse* (Newark, Del.: Juan de la Cuesta, 1988), 93–94.

are stabilized in the delusional metaphor."[11] The opposition stemming from the Symbolic propels the novel forward, as each of the knight's encounters with authority figures confirms the "disaster" of the Imaginary.[12] Ellie Ragland-Sullivan explains that "psychotic episodes occur when the intrinsic lack of this key phallic signifier . . . is challenged within the Symbolic order. The confrontation topples the mental house of cards supporting the subject's identity. . . . The primordial ideal ego has substituted itself for *je* and the ego ideal has taken the Other's place."[13] Repeatedly Don Quixote attempts to revert to the imaginary ideal ego of the medieval chivalric knight with whom he identifies. Repeatedly he is placed in situations where he faces what Lacan calls the A-father, that is, a "real" father, some specific concrete father figure, not even necessarily his own, but one representing the social order.

The A-fathers, the figures of authority that Don Quixote takes on, should be situated, according to Lacan, in a third position relative to the imaginary dyad o-o', that is, "ego-object" or "reality-ideal," its tension inducing an "eroticized aggression" which forms a Lacanian oedipal relation.[14] Lacan's triangle superimposes itself upon the Freudian model:

superego (phallic metaphor)

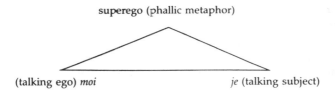

(talking ego) *moi*   *je* (talking subject)

Through castration, or separation trauma, the *moi* of the ego ideal gives in to the *je*; to Ragland-Sullivan, the phallic superego is "the paradoxical agent of psychic health and social adaptation as well as the harbinger of repression and censorship."[15] The *moi* and the *je*

11. Lacan, *Ecrits*, 217.

12. It is because of statements such as these that Lacan has often been accused of supporting the oedipal myth. He does not condone the cultural metaphor but instead points out its causes and consequences.

13. Ellie Ragland-Sullivan, *Jacques Lacan and the Philosophy of Psychoanalysis* (Urbana: University of Illinois Press, 1986), 198–99.

14. In one of his references to literary theory, Lacan states that this conjuncture will become more evident if analyzed through novelized structures, since their "situations," he says, are the novelist's "true resource" in that they make possible the "emergence of depth psychology," where, he adds, "no psychological insight would enable him to penetrate"; Lacan *Ecrits*, 217.

15. Ragland-Sullivan, *Lacan and Philosophy*, 57.

however, are correlatives; the *moi* informs the talking subject, while the *je* provides a sense of unity. Lacan has indicated that the role of the *je* is to temper, through rules and cultural conventions—in other words, through the superego or phallic metaphor—the *moi*'s intention to obliterate difference and perpetuate sameness.[16]

Don Quixote's famed ambiguity lies in his inability to remain solely within the "reality-ideal" dyad. A *loco entreverado*, his is a partial madness informing a discourse that points to the Other as fictional past in its psychotic moments as much as it reflects the Other in the historical present of rational speech. As we shall see, the knight's experiences with the letrados, who attempt to impose social codes on him, reenact the Lacanian mirror stage, whose failures then result in his inadequate individuation. The formation of Don Quixote's psyche breaks down, and, rather than a mature interrelationship obtaining among categories, there occurs a serious imbalance, which Jameson perceives as "the degradation of the Symbolic to an Imaginary level."[17] But it is also the resistance of the Imaginary to the Symbolic. As Lacan states: "For the psychosis to be triggered off, the Name-of-the-Father, foreclosed, that is to say, never having attained the place of the Other, must be called into symbolic opposition to the subject."[18] Don Quixote's psychosis is brought forth when he is confronted by contemporary figures of authority; in rejecting them he intends a wholeness by foreclosing these signifiers of death and separation.

In the novel's critique of baroque culture, Don Quixote's sameness bridges the gaps that open up between historical periods, all the while questioning and exposing their differences. Moreover, through the knight's confrontations with the letrados, his Lacanian A-fathers, the narrative is split in two directions: into a linear, symbolic mode recognizing difference and temporality, one that imposes masculine order on the text; and into a circular, imaginary mode that emphasizes discontinuity and oscillation, reflecting feminine values even as it searches for them.[19]

16. Jacques Lacan, *Séminaire* 1:218, quoted in Ragland-Sullivan, *Lacan and Philosophy*, 59.
17. Jameson, "Imaginary and Symbolic in Lacan," 351.
18. Lacan, *Ecrits*, 217.
19. Ronald Schleifer alludes to the two narrative modes in his essay "The Space and Dialogue of Desire: Lacan, Greimas, and Narrative Temporality," in Davis, *Lacan and Narration*, 874. Ruth El Saffar's finely nuanced study of the knight's search for the feminine, *Beyond Fiction: The Recovery of the Feminine in the Novels of Cervantes* (Berkeley: University of California Press, 1984), illuminates Don Quixote's obsession with Dulcinea. While partially complementing hers, my own analysis necessarily limits itself to the confrontation between Don Quixote and the letrados as figures of authority and the text's resultant narrative structure. For a further critique of the limits of phallocentric narratologies, see Susan Wimsatt's

The first of the letrados encountered by Don Quixote is indeed a Father: the priest whose literary *auto de fe* destroys much of Don Quixote's library, censoring the names of those knights whom Don Quixote wishes to emulate. A graduate of Sigüenza (an ironic allusion to the undistinguished degrees conferred by minor universities), the scholarly priest would often discuss the merits of the fictive knights of chivalry with Don Quixote. The scrutiny of those same narratives serves to ridicule the priest's pedantic critical stance as much as it presages Don Quixote's negative reception as a living text in part II. Moreover, it effectively separates the knight from the ranks of the letrados. As Luis Murillo has observed, Don Quixote's library collection indicates his limited interest in poetry and fiction, unlike the novel's other hidalgo, Diego de Miranda, the Knight of the Green Coat—and unlike Cervantes's other mad protagonist, the licentiate Vidriera.[20]

The priest's attempts to control and limit Don Quixote's readings to those he believes beneficial are ultimately futile. Don Quixote has, after all, already read the novels. And ironically, while literally burning his books, the priest stokes Don Quixote's imaginary fires by creating a scenario from a novel of chivalry: in search of his library, the knight is to believe that a "wise" enchanter has spirited it away along with the rest of his books. This piece of fiction, fabricated by the priest, immediately brings on one of Don Quixote's psychic delusions:

Así es—dijo don Quijote—; que ése es un sabio encantador, grande enemigo mío, que me tiene ojeriza, porque sabe por sus artes y letras que tengo de venir, andando los tiempos, a pelear en singular batalla con un caballero a quien él favorece, y le tengo de vencer,

---

provocative article "Coming Unstrung: Women, Men, Narrative, and Principles of Pleasure," *PMLA* 105 (1990): 505–18.

20. In her discussion of "El licenciado Vidriera," Ruth El Saffar suggests that the licentiate's failure as an intellectual may refer to the tensions among New and old Christians in securing positions, with the latter obtaining increasing numbers of posts despite their lack of education; Ruth El Saffar, *Novel to Romance: A Study of Cervantes's 'Novelas ejemplares'* (Baltimore: Johns Hopkins University Press, 1974), 60, n. 55. While Cervantes may have had the controversy in mind when ridiculing the intellectual pretensions of the *académicos* and the *bachiller* Sansón Carrasco in *Don Quixote*, it does not seem to be an issue with Don Diego de Miranda or with his son Lorenzo, whose background is that of old Christian *labriego* stock. It seems more likely that Cervantes would criticize all the intellectuals—whether old or New Christians—who contributed to or went along with the growing corruption of the state. See José Antonio Maravall, "From the Renaissance to the Baroque: The Diphasic Schema of a Social Crisis," in *Literature among Discourses: The Spanish Golden Age*, ed. Wlad Godzich and Nicholas Spadaccini (Minneapolis: University of Minnesota Press, 1986), 3–40.

sin que él lo pueda estorbar, y por esto procura hacerme todos los sinsabores que puede; y mándole yo que mal podrá él contradecir ni evitar lo que por el cielo está ordenado.

["That's it," said Don Quixote, "and he is a sage magician, a great enemy of mine, who has a grudge against me because he knows by his arts and lore that in time I am to engage in singular combat with a knight whom he favors and whom I shall conquer despite his efforts, and for this reason he endeavors to do me all the ill turns that he can, but I promise him it will be hard for him to oppose or avoid what is decreed by Heaven, and he will be unable to prevent it."] (I.7)

Don Quixote here structures his future adventures within narrative time. Now, his relationship with his knightly Other (the dyad o-o') constitutes the Imaginary, which, with the emergence of the subject, generally results in the emergence of temporality, in turn becoming the condition of the Symbolic as narrative. Ronald Schleifer has written that the "emergence of temporality itself as a concept . . . is recognized simultaneously with the emergence of the subject. . . . Thus temporality is not a pole in a binary opposition, but arises out of such an opposition; it is *the condition of the Symbolic*." He continues: "The psychotic, in a world of things, 'disavows' time altogether."[21] In Don Quixote's readings the Imaginary's potential (its conversion to the Symbolic) is blocked, since the separation that would divert his attention to the Law, to an understanding of his metaphoric role, never completely ensues. The narrative will be advanced metonymically, not by its sense of time but by its desire to repeat itself: enchanters will themselves be conjured up whenever and wherever an explanation is needed. The text's circular repetition becomes symptomatic of a confused sense of time, according to Schleifer. But such repetition also signals the Imaginary's search for the feminine.

This repetition is itself inscribed within a larger "master" narrative, that of the novels of chivalry. The signified of part I slides into part II as signifier, its narrative repositioning itself in a linear fashion. The text assumes a structure that will be redirected by the circularity of desire, at which disjunction the Imaginary emerges as paradox articulated in the language of the Other. Narrative time is thus both circular and linear. Ruth El Saffar has pointed out that the end of part I offers little promise of order restored, that Don Quixote continues

---

21. Schleifer, "The Space and Dialogue of Desire," 876–77.

to be locked in his vision of himself as knight.[22] After the second
sally, at the end of part I, Don Quixote returns home without knowing
where he is, although the text specifies the exact number of days it
takes for him to reach the town, and the day and the hour when he
crosses the town square to be delivered finally to his housekeeper
and niece:

> [Y] a cabo de seis días llegaron a la aldea de don Quijote, adonde
> entraron en la mitad del día, que acertó ser domingo . . . en tanto
> que el ama y sobrina de don Quijote le recibieron, y le desnudaron,
> y le tendieron en su antiguo lecho. Mirábalas con ojos atravesados,
> y no acababa de entender en qué parte estaba.

> [At the end of six days . . . [they] entered [the town] about the middle
> of the day, which it so happened was a Sunday. . . . Don Quixote's
> housekeeper and niece took him in and undressed him and laid
> him on his old bed. He looked at them, his eyes crossed, and still
> could not figure out where he was.] (I.52)

Part I closes, then, with the promise of continuity, both linear and
circular, in its presentation of another set of A-fathers.

Seeking information on Don Quixote's rumored third sally, the
"autor desta historia" ends part I with a not-so-gentle jab at the
supposed intellectual community of La Mancha, whose members of
the Argamasilla Academy, he finds, have eulogized Don Quixote,
Sancho Panza, Dulcinea del Toboso, and Rocinante in a series of
poems deposited in a lead box and buried in an ancient hermitage.
That the *académicos*, with the blatantly parodic pen names of Moni-
congo, Paniaguado, Caprichoso, Burlador, Cachidiablo, and Tiquitoc,
all exert their dubious talent in Don Quixote's honor is not so important; what draws our attention is that one of them—whose name
in this instance remains foreclosed, unknown to us—is given the task
of deciphering the illegible poems in the collection which might shed
light on Don Quixote's further adventures.

Indeed, the last sentence of part I assures us not only that this
unnamed *académico* (whose unwritten Name is thus that of the Father)
accomplishes the difficult task of making out the unreadable poems
by sheer guesswork—"a costa de muchas vigilias y mucho trabajo [at
the cost of many sleepless nights and much toil]"—but that he, like
any promotion-conscious academic, intends to publish them to discover the possibility of a second book: "con esperanza de la tercera

---

22. El Saffar, *Beyond Fiction*, 85–86.

salida de don Quijote [expecting to find out about Don Quixote's third sally]." If Cervantes's part I mocks the academician's scholarly authority, it nevertheless proffers the hope that he will uncover more publishable material. The text therefore assigns the continuation of the narrative to a Father, all the while desacramentalizing the letter by poking fun at the Law.

In part II, Don Quixote again confronts a series of A-fathers, but more important, he must come face to face with his own image as it has been set down in part I. Foucault's "hero of the Same" has been, if anything, too successful; his confrontations with the Other are at once with himself—yet not completely. Don Quixote's third sally is also due to a letrado, this time one who will involve himself fully in Don Quixote's adventures. Sansón Carrasco appears on the scene as a recently graduated *bachiller* from the University of Salamanca. As the son of a laborer, barely attaining minor orders, the young Carrasco is undoubtedly a caricature of the growing numbers of students produced by the proliferation of universities in the sixteenth century whose main incentives were to attain civil or ecclesiastical office.[23]

Again, Cervantes disparages the power of the letrado in his portrait of this aggressive, moon-faced youth, at the same time assigning him the "authoritative" role of reader and literary critic. Sansón's first intellectual task is to assess critically the recently published part I of *Don Quixote*, thereby imposing on the text both a logical order and a rational interpretation. In his judgment that "los niños la manosean, los mozos la leen, los hombres la entienden y los viejos la celebran [children pore over it, youths read it, grown men understand it, and old people praise it]" (II.3), Sansón Carrasco gives us the first reader-response criticism of the text. Sansón also assumes a textual critic's function when he questions the narrative's "loose ends": the whereabouts of Sancho's ass and the one hundred *escudos*, whose stated expenditure by Sancho falls within the category of the Real (II.4).[24] Nor is Sansón's critical task limited to part I; he projects his role of editor for what he imagines will be a forthcoming part II: "Yo tendré cuidado—dijo Carrasco—de acusar al autor de la historia que si otra vez la imprimiere, no se le olvide esto que el buen Sancho ha dicho;

23. Kagan, *Students and Society*, 78–81.

24. By contrast, Sancho's desire for the *ínsula*, where he will assume the power of governor, corresponds to the Imaginary and the Symbolic. Sansón comments: "—Mirad Sancho . . . que los oficios mudan las costumbres, y podría ser que viéndoos gobernador no conociésedes a la madre que os parió [Take care, Sancho. . . . Honors change manners, and perhaps when you find yourself a governor you won't know the mother that bore you]" (I.4). Don Quixote seems to be aware that Sancho's desire to govern, to become a Father, supplants his desire for the love of "the mother that bore" him.

que será realzarla un buen coto más de lo que ella se está" ["I will take care," said Carrasco, "to impress upon the author of the history that, if he prints it again, he must not forget what worthy Sancho has said, for it will raise it a good six inches higher"] (II.4). But, ultimately, Carrasco's main function will be to propel the narrative forward, not to dwell on its literary merits.

Unlike the two previous sallies, therefore, Don Quixote's last excursion is encouraged from the start by an unlikely participant. Called on by the housekeeper in an effort to avert the knight's impending departure, Sansón Carrasco appears to her a compelling figure whose persuasive powers alone can detain Don Quixote. The housekeeper and the niece form part of Don Quixote's restrictive retinue: with the priest and the barber, they wish nothing more than to keep the knight at home. Yet as the only female nurturers, they belong to the creative female principle repressed by Don Quixote and supplanted by the imago of Dulcinea.[25] The *bachiller*, who had already pledged to keep secret Don Quixote's departure eight days hence, patronizingly sends the housekeeper home to cook for him, suggesting that, to keep the knight from leaving, she pray to Saint Apollonia on the way. The prayer to Saint Apollonia, patron saint of toothaches, contains an erotic subtext that can hardly be ignored.[26] In this passage Sansón Carrasco construes a hierarchy of private versus public spheres and relegates the housekeeper to the feminine, sexualized realm of desire. As the Nom-du-Père, the Law, the force (and fear) of castration—of alienation from desire—underlies all of Sansón's seemingly paradoxical actions. The housekeeper's concerns meet with derision as Sansón arrogantly stresses his superior education: "Yo sé lo que digo, señora ama, váyase, y no se ponga a disputar conmigo, pues sabe que soy bachiller por Salamanca, que no hay más que bachillear [I know what I am saying, mistress housekeeper. Go, and don't set yourself to argue

---

25. Don Quixote's sexual fears and desires have been addressed by, among others, Louis Combet, *Cervantes ou les incertitudes du désire* (Lyons: Presses Universitaires de Lyons, 1981); Carroll Johnson, *Madness and Lust: A Psychoanalytical Approach to 'Don Quixote'* (Berkeley: University of California Press, 1983); and Ruth El Saffar, "Sex and the Single Hidalgo: Reflections on Eros in *Don Quixote*," in *Studies in Honor of Elias Rivers*, ed. Bruno M. Damiani and Ruth El Saffar (Potomac, Md.: Scripta Humanistica, 1989), 76–93. My essay views Don Quixote's desire for woman as analogous with his desire to become the "m/Other." Dulcinea substitutes for this desire in his Imaginary quest for his *moi* as knight-errant

26. The sexual connotations of teeth are well known; in *La Celestina*'s fourth act, for example, the bawd asks Melibea to pray to Saint Apollonia to relieve Pleberio's toothache, a scarcely veiled reference to Melibea's giving in to the young man's sexual desires. See M. Dominica Legge, "Toothache and Courtly Love," *French Studies* 4 (1950): 50–54; and Javier Herrero, "The Stubborn Text: Calisto's Toothache and Melibea's Girdle," in Godzich and Spadaccini, *Literature among Discourses*, 132–47.

with me, for you know I am a graduate of Salamanca, and one can't bachelor more than that]" (II.7). Yet Sansón's playful pun on *bachillear* underscores as well his own overweening pride in an increasingly useless degree.[27]

Carrasco's role in controlling the narrative is evident in his manipulation of Sancho; his pretense in accompanying Don Quixote elicits an unintentionally ironic commentary from the knight regarding Carrasco's intellectual and physical prowess, which in turn persuades Sancho to change his own mind:

> Mira quién se ofrece a serlo, sino el inaudito bachiller Sansón Carrasco, perpetuo trastulo y regocijador de los patios de las escuelas salmanticenses, sano de su persona, ágil de sus miembros, callado, sufridor así del calor como del frío, así de la hambre como de la sed, con todas aquellas partes que se requieren para ser escudero de un caballero andante.

> [See now who offers to become one [a knight], none other than the illustrious bachelor Sansón Carrasco, the perpetual joy and delight of the courts of the Salamancan schools, sound in body, discreet, patient under heat or cold, hunger or thirst, with all the qualifications requisite to make a knight-errant's squire!] (II.7) [28]

But it is Sansón as *letrado*, and not Sancho, who makes too lofty a companion; the narrative continues, then, with Don Quixote and Sancho Panza again in the dark, still in search of Dulcinea.

Luis Murillo notes that in part II, Aldonza Lorenzo is no longer mentioned as the pretext for Dulcinea; instead, the woman with whom Don Quixote claims to be in love is even further dissociated from reality.[29] Murillo's perceptive reading of this passage points to the contradiction in which Don Quixote (and the narrative) finds himself: "Quixote must inevitably feel driven to disenchant his lady and this personal or private obligation will be drawn in conflict with his public image and social role as deliverer or redeemer, all of this

27. As a *bachiller*, Sansón holds only a first degree. Kagan points out that by the seventeenth century, few *bachilleres* could count on obtaining government posts, since standards for such posts were on the rise; Kagan, *Students and Society*, 91.

28. Sansón's control is further indicated by the role he plays in Don Quixote's arrangements for the sally: "Y con parecer y beneplácito del gran Carrasco, que por entonces era su oráculo, se ordenó que de allí a tres días fuese su partida [and by the advice and with the approval of the great Carrasco, who was now their oracle, it was arranged that their departure should take place in three days' time]" (II.7).

29. Luis Andrés Murillo, ed., *El ingenioso hidalgo Don Quijote de la Mancha*, vol. 2 (Madrid: Editorial Castalia, 1978), 93, n. 2.

bound inescapably to his relationship with Sancho."[30] The drive that impels the knight's quest emanates from the Imaginary; yet not only is he unable to disenchant Dulcinea, but he must himself remain caught within the circular boundaries of his own desire. Sansón Carrasco's project to confront Don Quixote as the Other in his guise of the Knight of the Mirrors returns the narrative (and Don Quixote) full circle. Thus, we arrive again at the mirror stage.

Lacan's mirror-stage theory corresponds to the psychological development of the human infant, whose first six months are relegated to the pre-mirror stage of a fragmented body image.[31] Ragland-Sullivan describes it as "a dialectical instance in development, which permanently situates the human subject in a line of fiction and alienation."[32] The mirror stage, then, prepares the subject's trajectory from the pre-mirror to the Imaginary, and to the Symbolic: "The *mirror stage* is a drama whose internal thrust is precipitated from insufficiency to anticipation—and which manufactures for the subject, caught up in the lure of spatial identification, the succession of phantasies that extends from a fragmented body-image to a form of its totality that I shall call orthopaedic—and, lastly, to the assumption of the armour of an alienating identity, which will mark with its rigid structure the subject's mental development."[33] It is clear, however, that such a stage need not occur only in infancy. Since the structuring of the psyche is always incomplete, the stage will necessarily be repeated. Because the mirror stage must be understood as "a metaphor for the vision of harmony of a subject essentially in discord," this harmony is never attained, and the mirror stage will "disrupt the seeming autonomy and control of the speaking subject later in life."[34]

The episode of Sansón Carrasco as Knight of the Mirrors immediately follows two humiliating events in which even Don Quixote's

---

30. Luis Andrés Murillo, *A Critical Introduction to 'Don Quixote'* (New York: Peter Lang, 1988), 142.

31. Lacan, *Ecrits*, 4.

32. Ragland-Sullivan, *Lacan and Philosophy*, 17.

33. Lacan, *Ecrits*, 4.

34. Ragland-Sullivan, *Lacan and Philosophy*, 27. The passage through the mirror stage is one from the state of nature to that of culture that never totally obtains. Ragland-Sullivan states that "the imagistic and fantasmatic subject of identifications continues, nonetheless, to coexist (in a double inscription) with the subject of language and cultural codes throughout life" (29). It is important to note that Lacan himself views the mirror stage as a strategy he developed in opposition to the increasing popularity of the supposedly autonomous ego, whose "successful adaptation to society" he disparages as "a phenomenon of mental abdication that was bound up with the ageing of the psychoanalytic group in the diaspora of the war, and the reduction of a distinguished practice to a label suitable to the 'American way of life' "; Lacan, *Ecrits*, 306–7.

psychosis falls short: his frustrated encounter with the peasant girl whom Sancho had introduced as Dulcinea, and an all too real confrontation with a fictional devil. Finally face to face with his lady, Don Quixote finds that he cannot reconcile her imago with the round-faced peasant reeking of garlic.[35] Because his pathological depression is exacerbated by the confrontation of his Imaginary with the imaginary Others externally imposed on him, Don Quixote's self-image again suffers when he is overtaken by the boisterous Parliament of Death, whose costumed players refuse to participate in a chivalric adventure. After challenging them for their affront, Don Quixote and Sancho retreat under threat of stoning. What these events have in common is their role in fomenting Don Quixote's dejection and degradation. The psychic fragmentation of his fragile ego is then made visible in the episode of the Knight of the Mirrors.

Don Quixote's temporal unawareness is evinced by the narrative's plunging again into darkness. The beast fable that follows on the friendship between Rocinante and Sancho's ass may prefigure Don Quixote and the Knight of the Mirrors's relations as it does their squires', but it also serves to measure the distance between animal instinct and human behavior. Don Quixote's empathy with the Knight of the Forest, as the text first names the "Other" knight who appears singing of unrequited love, is due to the apparent similarity between them. As the knight tells his story under cover of darkness, we learn that his lady, Casildea de Vandalia, had required him to perform a number of Herculean tasks. Don Quixote is shocked to hear that the task of which the knight is most proud is his supposed victory over Don Quixote himself: "Pero de lo que yo más me precio y ufano es de haber vencido en singular batalla a aquel tan famoso caballero don Quijote de la Mancha, y héchole confesar que es más hermosa mi Casildea que su Dulcinea. [But what I most pride myself upon is having vanquished in singular combat that famous knight Don Quixote de la Mancha, and made him confess that my Casildea is more beautiful than his Dulcinea.] (II.14). Furthermore, the Knight of the Forest has appropriated Don Quixote's knightly reputation: "Y habiéndole vencido a él, su gloria, su fama y su honra se ha transferido y pasado a mi persona [And now that I have vanquished him, his

---

35. As is the case with Sansón Carrasco, who doubles as a fictive knight to do real battle with Don Quixote, Dulcinea's apparition here forms part of Sancho Panza's attempts to control the knight. Like Carrasco, Sancho projects onto Don Quixote's Imaginary; Andrew Bush rightly observes that the peasant girl functions as a prop in the *comedia* of Sancho's staging. I am grateful to him for commenting, in a personal letter to me, on the analogies in these episodes.

glory, his fame, and his honor have passed and are transferred to me]" (II.14). In this oral tale, narrated by Carrasco with the purpose of engaging Don Quixote in a battle over their ladies, it is the Other who attempts to invert the Lacanian triangle: Sansón projects from his *je* to Don Quixote's *moi*, his ideal ego. But the reversal is stymied: Don Quixote's *moi* already occupies the position of the *je*. As Ragland-Sullivan remarks, psychotic truth refers "to the importance of language and the Oedipal Law in structuring normal discourse."[36] Don Quixote's delusional discourse thus speaks the truth: "Habéis de saber que ese don Quijote que decís es el mayor amigo que en este mundo tengo, y tanto, que podré decir que le tengo en lugar de mi misma persona [I would have you know that this Don Quixote you speak of is the greatest friend I have in the world, so much so that I may say I take him to be myself]" (II.14).

Daybreak allows for (di)vision and differentiation: the narrative changes from oral to visual apperception as Don Quixote observes his rival transformed into the Knight of the Mirrors. *Cervantistas* have usually taken this knight to represent some sort of *dédoublement* of Don Quixote.[37] Carroll Johnson asserts, for instance, that the knight is Don Quixote's mirror image: "He overtakes Don Quixote and Sancho in the woods at night, and when dawn comes we see that his armor is covered with tiny mirrors. He is thus a literal mirror image of our hero, who sees himself reflected in the newcomer's outfit."[38] Yet, while it is tempting to view the episode as a program of therapy in which the older knight will be defeated by the younger, such an interpretation would have us accept Carrasco's false identity without understanding its function. Don Quixote is indeed reflected in the Knight of the Mirrors's outfit, but not in one piece. Rather, the small, moon-shaped mirrors (*lunas*) of the suit break up the totality of the image to reflect a fragmented knight, one whose own mind is unraveled precisely by the lack of a phallic signifier which, according to Lacan, would have served to break up his fusion with the Other—in this case with the chivalric order internalized in his readings and in the Imaginary wanderings of part I. The fragmented reflection in the mirrors thus confirms Don Quixote's psychosis, as the encounter between the two knights results in yet another failed mirror stage.

36. Ragland-Sullivan, *Lacan and Philosophy*, 200.

37. Robert Alter, for example, sees the disguised Carrasco as a "reflexion" of Don Quixote; see his *Partial Magic: The Novel as a Self-Conscious Genre* (Berkeley: University of California Press, 1975), 22.

38. Carroll Johnson, *Don Quixote: The Quest for Modern Fiction*, Masterwork Studies no. 44 (Boston: Twayne Publishers, 1990), 64.

The joust between the two illustrates the confrontations between the Symbolic and the Imaginary: as the figure of authority, the Knight of the Mirrors states a condition to Don Quixote—that whoever loses will remain at the winner's mercy—which both initiates and recapitulates the struggle. Don Quixote accepts, since he considers the game rules part of the chivalric code. Under these conditions his unexpected victory not only releases him from having to return home to await a cure for his madness but also, as an act of *méconnaissance*, forfeits any approach to the truth. Don Quixote refuses to "see" the knight's real identity, attributing his resemblance to Sansón to yet another trick played on him by his enemies.[39] The Symbolic order has been repressed, as the knight's feat frees his fragmented ego ideal to continue its quest.

He enjoys little respite, however, from the series of A-fathers. Don Quixote next comes across the Knight of the Green Coat, whose appearance has been taken as another mirror image of Don Quixote and as his literary (and literate) opposite.[40] But again, the figures of Don Diego de Miranda and his son are less Don Quixote's reflection than a displacement of his relationship with an A-father to a real father-son conflict. Carroll Johnson has rightly stressed the decadent aspects of such an hidalgo's life by the beginning of the seventeenth century.[41] As Don Diego's library leaves little doubt that he fulfils the requirements of a letrado, his outmoded social role seems to question that of the latter as well. Although he is himself a leisured country squire, his disappointment in his son's literary interests re-

39. Don Quixote's "blindness" also ensures Sansón's continuing his education: "Y si no fuera por los pensamientos extraordinarios de don Quijote, que se dio a entender que el bachiller no era bachiller, el señor bachiller quedara imposibilitado para siempre de graduarse de licenciado [Had it not been for the extraordinary fancies of Don Quixote and his conviction that the bachelor was not the bachelor, señor bachelor would have been incapacitated forever from taking his degree of licentiate]" (II.15).

40. Francisco Márquez Villanueva has written on the positive views elicited by the Knight of the Green Coat in particular; his careful study proposes instead a "paradoxical" reading of the passage, with both men seen as figures of madness: "Presenciamos el espectáculo de ver al uno vivir en plenitud su locura cuerda, rebosante de riesgo, y al otro su cordura loca, acolchada de precauciones. . . . Si la locura de don Quijote pretende vivir en el mundo de los libros de caballerías, el Verde Gabán, con no menor trastienda literaria, intenta crear la utopía neoepicúrea en un rincón de la Mancha e ilustra 'quijotescamente' lo que sería la vida real de un personaje de los *Colloquia*, de un Glición o un Eusebio [We witness the spectacle of one man living to the full his sane madness, overflowing with risk, and the other his mad sanity, padded with precautions. . . . If Don Quixote's madness presumes to live in the world of chivalric novels, the Man of the Green Coat, with no less of a literary storeroom, intends to create a neo-Epicurean utopia in a corner of La Mancha and 'quixotically' exemplifies what the real life of a character of the 'Colloquies,' of a Glición or a Eusebio, would be like]"; see his *Personajes y temas del Quijote* (Madrid: Taurus, 1975), 219–20.

41. Johnson, *Don Quixote,* 64–65.

flects the growing division between professionals and humanists, stemming in part from the clash between neo-Platonism and neo-Aristotelian aesthetics, which focused outward toward external reality.[42]

Don Diego soon makes his rational preferences known. After hearing about Don Quixote's recently published tale of chivalry, he reveals his distaste for literature based on the Aristotelian distinction between fiction and history, replacing the fictive chivalric narratives with Don Quixote's "real" adventures:

> ¡Bendito sea el cielo!, que con esa historia, que vuesa merced dice que está impresa, de sus altas y verdaderas caballerías, se habrán puesto en olvido las innumerables de los fingidos caballeros andantes, de que estaba lleno el mundo, tan en daño de las buenas costumbres y tan en perjuicio y descrédito de las buenas historias.

> ["Blessed be Heaven! By means of this history of your noble and genuine chivalrous deeds, which you say has been printed, the countless stories of fictitious knights-errant with which the world is filled, so much to the injury of morality and the prejudice and discredit of good histories, will have been driven into oblivion.] (II.16)

Don Diego's impassioned critique of fiction is brought home by his son Lorenzo's choice of vocation: against the father's wishes, the young man has preferred poetry to law. Moreover, Don Diego's seemingly moral concern that the humanities remain a source of ethical conduct is undercut by his keen interest in his son's obtaining a good post:

> Los seis [años] ha estado en Salamanca, aprendiendo las lenguas latina y griega; y cuando quise que pasase a estudiar otras ciencias, halléle tan embebido en la de la poesía, si es que se puede llamar ciencia, que no es posible hacerle arrostrar la de las leyes, que yo quisiera que estudiara, ni de la reina de todas, la teología. Quisiera yo que fuera corona de su linaje, *pues vivimos en siglo donde nuestros reyes premian altamente las virtuosas y buenas letras*; porque letras sin virtud son perlas en el muladar.

> [For six years he has been at Salamanca studying Latin and Greek. When I wished him to turn to the study of other subjects I found him so wrapped up in the science of poetry, if that can be called a

42. El Saffar, "Sex and the Single Hidalgo," 78, n. 4.

science, that he will have nothing to do with law, which I wished him to study, or with theology, queen of them all. I would like him to be an honor to his family, *as we live in a time when our kings liberally reward the study of virtuous and worthy letters*; for otherwise learning is a pearl on a dunghill.] (II.16; emphasis added)

Don Quixote immediately challenges this patriarchal imperative. His response to Don Diego offers a defense of poetry and the vernacular tongue as well as an exhortation to parents to love and support their children. In a sense, Don Quixote here becomes an A-father, assuming parental authority when he lectures both father and son. Yet his madness—evinced once more in the episode with the lions, where he names himself the Knight of the Lions—disallows any oedipal effect on the Miranda family. When Don Quixote first meets them, the son's own position is that of the mirror stage: still closely identified with his mother, he has neither rejected the father nor bowed to his counsel. Don Quixote's intervention, rather than contributing to the Symbolic order, instead works against it. As he compares his own "studies" of knight-errantry to the "science" of poetry, his final Imaginary solution—that Lorenzo join the ranks of the knights-errant—offers no resolution to the family romance. Despite his lucid moments, Don Quixote fails to mediate between the Imaginary and the Symbolic because he continues to hold to his vision of the Same.

But this vision begins to cloud through the adventures that follow. Critics have remarked Don Quixote's waning imagination in part II; Arthur Efron, for example, points out that the knight assumes a passive role as "his apparent opposition to the ways of his world increasingly becomes unthreatening entertainment."[43] Ruth El Saffar sees the episodes as raising the question of reality, with Don Quixote preferring to "hold fast to his illusions, since to give them up would mean relinquishing his invented identity."[44] The knight's passivity prefigures his entry into the world of the Symbolic. As part II gathers meaning with part I its retroactive point of reference, Don Quixote is no longer unsettling as an Imaginary "ideal ego." Instead, he depends more and more on the others around him.

As he continues on his journey, these others present ever fewer

43. Arthur Efron, *"Don Quixote" and the Dulcineated World* (Austin: University of Texas Press, 1971), 17.
44. El Saffar, *Beyond Fiction*, 92.

obstacles to his madness, thereby unwittingly contributing to his sanity.[45] After leaving the Knight of the Green Coat, Don Quixote is joined on the road by a *bachiller* and a licentiate whose own inconsequential disagreement over the importance of the art of fencing is finally resolved in a duel arbitrated by the knight. Not coincidentally, it is this licentiate's cousin—a "famoso estudiante y muy aficionado a leer libros de caballerías [famous scholar very much given to reading books of chivalry]" (II.22)—who serves Don Quixote as guide to the Cave of Montesinos, the most imaginative locus of part II:

> En el camino preguntó don Quijote al primo de qué género y calidad eran sus ejercicios, su profesión y estudios; a lo que él respondió que su profesión era ser humanista; sus ejercicios y estudios, componer libros para dar a la estampa, todos de gran provecho y no menos entretenimiento para la república.

> [On the way Don Quixote asked the cousin about the nature of his pursuits, avocations, and studies, to which the cousin replied that he was by profession a humanist, and that his pursuits and studies were writing books for the press, all of great utility and no less entertainment to the nation.] (II.22)

Despite his Horatian intentions, the cousin discloses his unoriginality and lack of serious scholarship; his inept literary efforts at *imitatio* result in unwitting parodies of Ovid and Polydore Vergil. Instead of questioning Don Quixote's good sense on his descent into the cave, the cousin looks forward to the knight's report, hoping to include the knight's sightings in his version of Ovid's *Metamorphoses*: "Suplico a vuesa merced, señor don Quijote, que mire bien y especule con cien ojos lo que hay allá dentro; quizá habrá cosas que las ponga yo en el libro de mis *Transformaciones*" ["I beg you, Señor Don Quixote," said the guide, "observe carefully and examine with a hundred eyes everything within. Perhaps there may be some things for me to put into my book of *Transformations*"] (II.22).

When Don Quixote is pulled from the cave, rather than doubt the knight's adventures, the cousin participates vicariously in their narrative and staunchly defends their veracity: "¿Pues había de mentir el señor don Quijote, que, aunque quisiera, no ha tenido lugar para componer e imaginar tanto millón de mentiras? [Would Señor Don Quixote lie? Why, even if he wanted to, he has not had the time to

45. See Anne J. Cruz, "Don Quixote's Disappearing Act: Structural Unity and Character Transformation in *Don Quixote*," *Indiana Journal of Hispanic Literatures* 1 (Fall 1992): 83–99.

imagine and put together such a host of lies]" (II.23). As a humanist, the cousin recognizes the need for truth in Don Quixote's discourse, yet his facile endeavors are misdirected; his *méconnaissance* disallows him to realize that he is "seeing" into the cave through the knight's own gaze.

In the text's critique of yet another letrado, the cousin's willingness to believe in Don Quixote's adventures in the cave serves as counterpoint to the turn of events at the duke's castle, where the knight's adventures will be conjured up by the duke and duchess. But Don Quixote's increasing passivity is not due to the others' having become like him; rather, he is becoming more and more like *them*. Upon his final confrontation with an A-father, when he again comes under the gaze of Sansón Carrasco—this time as the Knight of the White Moon—Don Quixote moves from ideal ego to ego ideal; that is, from the Imaginary to the Symbolic. Following Jacques-Alain Miller, Slavoj Žižek explains: "The relation between imaginary and symbolic identification . . . is . . . that between 'constituted' and 'constitutive' identification; to put it simply, imaginary identification is identification with the image in which we appear likeable to ourselves, with the image representing 'what we would like to be,' and symbolic identification, identification with the very place *from where* we are being observed, *from where* we look at ourselves so that we appear to ourselves likeable, worthy of love."[46] The shift is indicated in the novel by the knight's doubling experiences and by the narrative's retroversion. His arrival in Barcelona serves to anchor the knight in the historical moment, as Luis Murillo has nicely phrased it, "on the stage of history, the city, and the sea."[47]

After his arrival Don Quixote is paraded around town with his name written on his back; literally read by others, he finds himself being duplicated in the printshop's edition of Avellaneda's second part. Geographically he has traveled as far as he can go, and his trajectory has come to a standstill. Indeed, he is at land's end when he encounters Sansón Carrasco in his guise as the Knight of the White Moon, whose invitation to fight recalls Don Quixote's first meeting with him as Knight of the Mirrors:

> Vengo a contender contigo y a probar la fuerza de tus brazos, en razón de hacerte conocer y confesar que mi dama, sea quien fuere, es sin comparación más hermosa que tu Dulcinea del Toboso . . . y

---

46. Slavoj Žižek, *The Sublime Object of Ideology* (London: Verso, 1989), 105.
47. Murillo, *A Critical Introduction*, 176.

si tú peleares y yo te venciere, no quiero otra satisfación sino que dejando las armas y absteniéndote de buscar aventuras, te recojas y retires a tu lugar por tiempo de un año.

[I come to do battle with you and prove the might of your arm, in order to make you acknowledge and confess that my lady, whoever she may be, is incomparably fairer than your Dulcinea del Toboso. ... If you fight and I vanquish you, I demand no other satisfaction than that, laying aside your arms and abstaining from your search for adventures, you withdraw and go to your village for the space of a year. (II.64)

This time, however, Sansón Carrasco wins. The battle, staged in the presence of the viceroy of Catalonia, ensures Don Quixote's return to his village, even as the Knight of the White Moon grants Dulcinea's superior beauty: "Viva, viva en su entereza la fama de la hermosura de la señora Dulcinea del Toboso; que sólo me contento con que el gran don Quijote se retire a su lugar un año, o hasta el tiempo que por mí le fuere mandado [Long live the fame of the lady Dulcinea's beauty; all I require is that the great Don Quixote retire to his own home for a year, or for so long a time as I shall determine]" (II.64). Carrasco's second pseudonym, that of the feminine, reflective moon, emerges here as an image of the female realm that remains despite the Symbolic order, for in vanquishing Don Quixote, Carrasco concedes defeat to the knight's most central Imaginary stance. But in giving in to Don Quixote's demand, he effectively robs the narrative of its impetus, as the knight has no other reason for continuing his quest. Thus, the moon also points to the Law's impenetrability; Carrasco's knightly name, despite its feminine contours, is that of the father, the reiterative *lunas* of his earlier guise recovered in the seeming wholeness of one white moon. Don Quixote can no longer see himself reflected, even fragmentarily, in the moon's opacity; he is, instead, vulnerable to Carrasco's gaze, the agency from which his image will now be determined.

It is at this point that the narrative doubles back on itself, tying up the loose ends of various subplots: the tale of Ana Félix and her transvestite lover not only ends happily but also resolves the earlier travails of the *morisco* Ricote. And on leaving Barcelona, Don Quixote meets with Tosilos, who briefly relates the final outcome of the doña Rodríguez episode. Divested of its desire, the narrative now proceeds in a linear fashion, retracing Don Quixote's steps. The knight's retrogression into his past is carried out without his previous illusions; he has become symbolically identified with the paternal gaze. It is in this sense that he is being "seen" by others: he identifies himself from the place from which he is being observed. Where he once stood his ground before a herd of bulls, he is now overrun in the dark by swine. Most significant, his forced arrival at the duke's castle, arranged yet again by Sansón Carrasco, where he witnesses Altisidora's feigned funeral and resurrection, lacks the hilarity and humiliation associated with his first visit. Only his return to the grove where the actors dressed as shepherds celebrated a false Arcadia seems to inspire a new illusion. But, as we shall see, his efforts at forging a new Imaginary identity are subverted by the others, who willingly subscribe to the fiction.

Don Quixote's return to his village is thus marked by his increasing identification with the gaze of the Other. Shortly before arriving at the village, he negates Alvaro Tarfe's version of Don Quixote only to become its double, as Tarfe notes when asked to declare that he has never seen the knight before, "puesto que cause admiración ver dos don Quijotes y dos Sanchos a un mismo tiempo, tan conformes en los nombres como diferentes en las acciones [though it amazes me to find two Don Quixotes and two Sancho Panzas at once, as much alike in name as different in action]" (II.72). The knight's attempts to remedy this split self by assuming the persona of a fictive shepherd are now welcomed by the priest and Sansón Carrasco, who hope that this new madness will deter him. Although the episode parallels the knighting ceremony in part I, where the hidalgo emerges as Don Quixote, the naming process here is preempted from Don Quixote's imaginative versions of pastoral names such as Quijotiz, Carrascón, Curambro, and Pancino by Sansón Carrasco's materialist determination that feminine names be assigned from published pastoral novels, easily purchased in the marketplace.

Don Quixote's efforts to return to the Imaginary are therefore thwarted by the others; his new persona, his names, even his desires have been coopted. Only the two women, alienated from patriarchal discourse, understand his entrapment, as they warn him of the hardships real shepherds face: "¿Y podrá vuestra merced pasar en el campo las siestas del verano, los serenos del invierno, el aullido de los lobos? No, por cierto; que este es ejercicio y oficio de hombres robustos, curtidos y criados para tal ministerio casi desde las fajas y mantillas. [And . . . will your worship be able to stand the hot afternoons of summer and the night air of winter and the howling of the wolves out in the fields? Certainly not. That's a life and a business for hardy men, bred and seasoned to such work almost from the time they were in diapers]" (II.73). The conflict, however, lies not between reality and fiction but between patriarchal law and Don Quixote's resistance. By pandering to the knight's ideal ego, the Other ensures the former's conversion to ego ideal. Don Quixote may enact a new form of madness, but symbolically he is now identified with the patriarchal gaze of the father.

Thus, the interplay between Imaginary and Symbolic identification, Žižek tells us, allows for the subject's integration into a given sociosymbolic field.[48] Yet in *Don Quixote* this field constitutes a historical moment of crisis, aptly illustrated by the "world upside-down" topos. Don Quixote flees from his own sociohistorical locus only to be thrust back into the conflictive atmosphere of seventeenth-century Spain; his homecoming finds the Other expropriating his place. If, as José Antonio Maravall has suggested, such a reversal stems from a society in flux and disorder, then the Law's assuming Don Quixote's role is manifestly a conservative gesture, one compelling either reaction or protest.[49]

Cervantes's criticism of the letrados points to his frustration and concern over Spain's lack of moral and intellectual leadership, as well as to his wariness of all systems of knowledge.[50] This critique is ironically achieved by the letrados' success in controlling both the narrative thrust and Don Quixote's fate. Checked by its doubling back on itself, the narrative ending elides any possibility of continued circularity. Yet such a critique, read in tandem with the Lacanian systems of signification, raises questions of linguistic and, therefore, cultural determinism. By positing the Symbolic as interpreting the Imaginary, Lacan himself valorizes the former at the expense of the latter—a valorization that results in his diagnosing the Imaginary as psychosis. But the drive to build systems of signification, Ragland-Sullivan states, "is itself based on the structural lack in being." Sublimation is the "over-all price" that we, as human beings, "pay for sanity."[51] Through Don Quixote's encounters with his A-fathers, Cervantes problematizes the cultural issues of authority, knowledge, and moral order, even while admitting to the impossibility of a return to a mythical Golden Age.[52]

48. Žižek, *The Sublime Object*, 110.

49. Maravall thus challenges a Bakhtinian reading of the text, as he views this *mundo al revés* a product not of the marginalized, popular counterculture but of traditional society. José Antonio Maravall, *La cultura del Barroco* (Barcelona: Ariel, 1981), 315–16.

50. This issue has been eloquently addressed by Alban Forcione in the conclusion to his *Cervantes, Aristotle, and the 'Persiles'* (Princeton: Princeton University Press, 1970), 339–48, in which he nonetheless ultimately asserts Cervantes's faith in humanity.

51. Ragland-Sullivan, *Lacan and Philosophy*, 272–73.

52. Remarking on the similarities between *Don Quixote* and Cervantes's so-called romance

Don Quixote's inability to reject the figures of authority, despite his resistance, prevents his psychotic discourse from foreclosing the signifier of death and separation. The narrative's final emphasis on temporality reinscribes the condition of the Symbolic; the course of Don Quixote's life, like all things human, cannot be arrested. The knight's fears of being remembered as mad impel him to leave some proof of his sanity, and so, willing his death and repudiating his previous mad state, he renames himself Alonso Quijano "el bueno." Yet at the novel's end, Sansón Carrasco vies with Cide Hamete for the last word: the narrative closes not with Sancho's laments, or the tears of the niece and the housekeeper, or with the new epitaphs written in Don Quixote's honor, but with a pedestrian *décima* written by Carrasco. The knight's ultimate remembrance follows the letrado's law: the epitaph's last line, "morir cuerdo y vivir loco [dying lucid and living mad]," anticipates, prejudges, and supplants Don Quixote's Imaginary with his final entrance into the Symbolic.

Persiles y Sigismunda, Anthony Cascardi considers it part of a global paradigm of "rationalization." If, according to Cascardi, the *Persiles* pays the price of idealization for its progressiveness, it is also true that *Don Quixote* must carry the burden of critical belief in Cervantes's aspiration to moral authority; see Anthony J. Cascardi, "Reason and Romance: An Essay on Cervantes's *Persiles*," *MLN* 106 (1991): 279–93.

6

The Whole Body of Fable
with All of Its Members: Cervantes,
Pinciano, Freud

Mary Malcolm Gaylord

Whatsoever thy hand findeth to do, do it with thy might.
—Ecclesiastes 9:10

No question has vexed readers of *Don Quixote* more than the matter of its author's intentions. Did Cervantes mean simply to burlesque knight-errantry, to cut its madness definitively down? Or did he think to immortalize chivalry, confirming with an imposing literary monument its immense symbolic power? Whatever we choose to affirm by way of an answer, we can locate the genesis of our critical perplexities in the work of the novelist himself. From the pages of the part I prologue, where a personified author, stymied at the moment of saying what he means to say in the book he is presenting, gratefully lets a "friend" read out the sum of his intentions, we are led into the textual labyrinth of a plot in which declared aims proliferate, collide with one another, even work against themselves. My premise in this essay is that Cervantes's novel foregrounds intentions—his own, Don Quixote's, those of a whole host of other characters—not in order to tease us into deciphering his own "true" authorial purpose but rather to dramatize the difficulties inherent in all intending and meaning. In his exposure of the contradictions at the core of orthodox plotting, Cervantes not only foreshadows the Freudian account of a masochistic contest between repressing consciousness and intractable unconscious but anticipates ironically Freud's linking of the work of repression to the idea of civilization itself.[1]

1. Sigmund Freud, *Civilization and Its Discontents*, trans. and ed. James Strachey (New York: Norton, 1961).

In chapter 43 of the 1605 *Quixote*, Cervantes exposes the special embarrassments occasioned by our attempts to handle our fondest intentions in narrative. During a nocturnal lull in the heady rhythm of encounters in the inn, Maritornes and the innkeeper's daughter lure Don Quixote into a conversation that becomes a physical and discursive trap. This episode—in which the knight responds to an entreaty from these two "semidoncellas" (semidamsels) with the vainglorious proffering of his heroic extremity, only to find himself caught in a bind—literally fuses the body of the hero/victim with the shape of his story. In Cervantes's tale, the body of the man becomes the parodic figure of *fábula* or argument; Don Quixote passes corporeally through the stages traditionally prescribed for plot construction. Through its identification of the knight's body with the "cuerpo de fábula entero con todos sus miembros [whole body of fable with all of its members]"—the body which the canon of Toledo prescribes as the ideal fictional anatomy of the prose epic (I.47)—this episode makes one set of members and dismemberments into figures for the other, and finally shows both physical and textual bodies simultaneously held together and torn apart by the violent, contradictory, mythic forces of desire.

Knowing that Don Quixote is keeping mounted, armed guard outside the inn, Maritornes and her friend decide to "pasar un poco el tiempo oyéndole sus disparates [pass the time for a while by listening to his nonsense]" (I.43) and choose a hole in the wall of the hayloft (*pajar*) as the vantage point from which to witness, and potentially to participate in, his vigil. The knight, at first unaware that he has a real audience, happens to be addressing a lover's monologue to his absent Dulcinea. But the mere request, uttered in a woman's voice, that he approach the "window" where the young women have positioned themselves calls up to his ready imagination the thought that the castle keeper's daughter is continuing her enamored pursuit of his own person, begun during his earlier stay there (I.16). Chastity naturally requires that he urge the "fermosa señora [beauteous lady]" to withdraw; yet such is his good will toward his imagined admirer that he offers to deliver anything she might ask, other than love.[2] The exaggerated overreach of this heroic volunteering immediately elicits a matching gesture from Maritornes, who steps forward and thrusts herself with evident relish into the game of which she has

2. See Jacques Lezra, "Icarus Reading: Trope, Trauma, and Event in Shakespeare, Cervantes, and Descartes" (Ph.D. diss., Yale University, 1990), 139ff. Lezra's canny reading of Cervantes's chapter 43 sees this "otra cosa" offered by the knight as a key to the entire series of linguistic transformations which make up this episode, that he uses as an emblem of Cervantes's narrative strategy in *Don Quixote* (see his chap. 3).

hitherto been an amused but silent observer. Reminding the knight of the danger the damsel's compromised situation poses, Maritornes utters the fateful request. To his "Pues ¿qué ha menester, discreta dueña, vuestra señora [What then is it, discreet duenna, that your lady requires]?" she replies: "Sola una de vuestras hermosas manos . . . por poder deshogar con ella el gran deseo que a este agujero la ha traído, tan a peligro de su honor, que si su señor padre la hubiera sentido, la menor tajada della fuera la oreja [Only one of your beautiful hands . . . so as to be able to relieve with it the great desire that has brought her/it to this hole, at such great peril to her honor, that if my lord her father should sense her/it, the least part of her to be sliced off would be her ear]" (I.43).

Whether or not he grasps the cultivated ambiguity with which the duenna's discourse threatens to burst—the double sense of "si su señor padre la hubiera sentido" (which means simultaneously "sensed," "heard," and "touched"), for example, suggesting that the father's vigilance could also involve incest[3]—Don Quixote walks straight through the discursive opening Maritornes has provided for him, offering not only his hand but his entire person as the daughter's protector against the imagined excesses of paternal wrath. That Don Quixote has, in fact, caught Maritornes' sly suggestion of the concupiscence latent in the father's desire to punish his daughter seems clear from his own voyeuristic imaginings of the hypothetical offense and from the violent punishment he in turn promises the punisher: "¡Ya quisiera yo ver eso! . . . Pero él se guardará bien deso, si ya no quiere hacer el más desastrado fin que padre hizo en el mundo, por haber puesto las manos en los delicados miembros de su enamorada hija [Now I'd like to see that! . . . But he had better watch out, unless he wants to come to the most disastrous end that ever a father came to in this world, on account of having laid his hands on the delicate members of his lovesick daughter]" (I.43).

Sure by now that she has hooked her victim, Maritornes scurries off to get Sancho's donkey's halter to tie him up. By the time she returns, Don Quixote has managed to get to his feet on Rocinante's saddle and, straining toward the "ventana enrejada donde se imaginaba estar la ferida doncella [grate-covered window where he imagined the heartsore damsel to be]" (I.43), prepares to surrender her his hand. It comes, of course, with an accompanying speech:

Tomad, señora, esa mano, o, por mejor decir, ese verdugo de los malhechores del mundo; tomad esa mano, digo, a quien no ha

3. A point also noted by Lezra, "Icarus Reading," 138.

tocado otra de mujer alguna, ni aun la de aquella que tiene entera
posesión de todo mi cuerpo. No os la doy para que la beséis, sino
para que miréis la contextura de sus nervios, la trabazón de sus
músculos, la anchura y espaciosidad de sus venas; de donde sacaréis
qué tal debe de ser la fuerza del brazo que tal mano tiene.

[Take, my lady, this hand, or rather this scourge of the evildoers
of the world; take this hand, I say, from one who has never touched
the hand of any other woman, not even that of the one who has
entire possession of my whole body. I give it to you not so that you
may kiss it, but so that you may contemplate the texture of its
sinews, the network of its muscles, the breadth and spaciousness
of its veins; from whence you may gather just what must be the
strength of the arm that has such a hand.] (I.43)[4]

In no time at all, Maritornes has caught his hand in the donkey's
halter and secured it to the hayloft door. As the slipknot around his
wrist tightens, Quixote's hand is pulled so far through the hole in
the wall that first his hand and then, as though obeying the suggestion
of his own words, his whole arm is drawn inside.

The story, however, does not end when the knot is tied. While the
knight finds some consolation in the thought that "de la paciencia y
quietud de Rocinante bien se podía esperar que estaría sin moverse
un siglo entero [judging from Rocinante's patience and calm one could
easily suppose that he would stand there without moving for a
hundred years]" (I.43), he knows this amounts to a confession of his
paralysis. Deciding that he has for a second time fallen prey to some
enchantment in the very "castle" where he had earlier suffered humiliation, he berates himself for reentering the same place and prays
for some benevolent intervention. It is not, of course, the arrival of
another, "wiser" enchanter but that of another horse, whose sniffing
pricks up the patient Rocinante's drooping ears—"como, en fin, era
de carne, aunque parecía de leño [for though he seemed like a bump
on a log, he was, after all, made of flesh]"—and moves him out from
under "su estirado señor [his stretched-out master]," that brings the
latter finally to excruciating torment.

Don Quixote's fate, though only a half-fall, is infinitely worse than
a straightforward plunge to earth:

4. To translate "la fuerza del brazo que tal mano tiene" as "the hand that has such an
arm" would eliminate a delicious ambiguity present in the original Spanish. The freedom
Castilian syntax gives to sentence order means that the passage could either claim that the
arm has (i.e., owns, controls) the hand, or that the hand has the arm. The issue of which
member is in charge quickly becomes central in this chapter.

Resbalando de la silla, dieran con él en el suelo, a no quedar colgado del brazo; cosa que le causó tanto dolor, que creyó, o que la muñeca le cortaban, o que el brazo se le arrancaba; porque él quedó tan cerca del suelo, que con los estremos de las puntas de los pies besaba la tierra, que era en su perjuicio, porque, como sentía lo poco que le faltaba para poner las plantas en la tierra, fatigábase y estirábase cuanto podía por alcanzar el suelo.

[Slipping from the saddle, his feet would have landed him on the ground, had he not been hanging by his arm, a fact which caused him such pain that he thought that either his wrist was being severed or his arm was being yanked out, for he found himself so near the ground, that with the tips of his toes he was kissing the earth, which was a great disadvantage to him, for since he could feel how little he lacked in order to be able to set his feet on the soil, he strained and stretched as far as he could to reach the ground.] (I.43)

The impossible broken fall, holding him just short of reaching the ground, brings him instead to authentic extremes of torture,

bien así como los que están en el tormento de la garrucha, puestos a toca, no toca, que ellos mesmos son causa de acrecentar su dolor, con el ahinco que ponen en estirarse, engañados de la esperanza que se les representa, que con poco más que se estiren llegarán al suelo.

[just as those who are suffering the pulley torture, and are made to touch yet not to touch, so that they themselves are the cause of their own pain, with the energy they put into stretching themselves, fooled by the hope they glimpse, that with just a bit more stretching they will reach the ground.] (I.43)

Clearly the mischievous girls are not alone in enjoying a joke at the knight's expense. Even on its surface the scene is a pinnacle of Cervantes's parodic art. After the insistence with which the body in question has been presented as a virtual wreck, shriveled by age, fantasy, fasting, battering and misapplied home remedies, the subject's vanity about his strong and sinewy hand can only appear ridiculous. The episode is, moreover, a triumph of irony. Proffering to the "ladies" a hand that is "verdugo de los malhechores del mundo [scourge of the evildoers of the world]," he inserts that member into a literal noose, and is himself left physically hanging. We have, then, a classic case of the counterproductivity of intentions, and particularly the vainglorious counterproductivity of heroic intentions: a fall of pride, a punisher punished, a hangman hanged.[5]

But if the don's ultimate grotesque suspension frustrates his production of specifically chivalric significance, it nonetheless succeeds (in spite of him) in relocating the entire episode to the realm of mythic drama. The symbolic figure he cuts is not the one he would have chosen—that of a proud sentinel of civilization—but instead that of a man caught in the self-torment of human desire. In a crude, makeshift version of the pulley torture, with his feet straining to "kiss" the ground, the knight joins victims of counterproductive desires, like Tantalus, and those afflicted with physical conditions such as dropsy (accumulation of fluid in the body that is caused by and in turn causes extreme thirst) or the moral maladies of greed and lust. The would-be agent of exemplary punishments, as the oxymoronic designation "su estirado señor" makes painfully clear, becomes the victim of his own intent; as victim he becomes in turn the paradoxical agent of his own excruciating torture, and his hopeful imagination of a solution serves as the mechanism that keeps him bound in apparently unending, and at the same time grotesquely eroticized, anguish. Golden Age philosophers and poets relished the paradoxes presented by frantic desires such as these, desires by definition incapable of satisfying themselves, which instead leave the afflicted person ever more ravaged, as the application of apparent remedies only succeeds in multiplying the painful symptoms, and symptoms in turn increase the desire for a cure that continues to lie always beyond reach.

Another feature that works to intensify the story's mythic overtones is the way it places the knight in immediate physical proximity, even contiguity, with his "steed." Throughout the episode, up until the animal's fateful unwanted (and unwonted) move, the man is quite

5. Sebastián de Covarrubias Horozco's definition already promises trouble for would-be *verdugos* such as Don Quixote. According to his 1611 *Tesoro de la lengua castellana o española* (Madrid: Turner, 1979), *verdugo* is "el ministro de justicia que ejecuta las penas de muerte, mutilación de miembro, açote, verguença, tormento. . . . Este fué siempre oficio infame [the minister of justice who executes sentences of death, mutilation of body members, lashes, shaming, torture. . . . This has always been an infamous profession]." Covarrubias goes on to report that the Romans made executioners literally marginal by obliging them to live on the outskirts of the city. Finally, he records the traditional military euphemism for *verdugo*: "Por honestar este nombre, le llaman *maestro de altas obras,* porque el ahorcar y descabeçar y dar tratos de cuerda, se haze en alto, porque todos lo vean [To make this name more respectable, they call him *Master of High Works,* because hangings and beheadings and pulley tortures are done in high places, so that everyone can see them]" (1001–1002; emphasis added). Don Quixote, apparently untroubled by the questionable flavor of the epithet he has conferred on himself, proceeds unwittingly to act out simultaneously its high letter and its dubious spirit.

literally connected to the beast. Astride Rocinante, Quixote replicates one of western culture's standard representations—the knight on horseback—of the control of reason and virtue over instinct and the passions. The Manchegan's own favorite symbolic equestrian figure is Saint George, whose jousts in Zaragoza are the original destination of his third sally, and whose effigy he celebrates in chapter 58 of part II in "la fingida Arcadia [the make-believe Arcadia]." But here, when Don Quixote stretches the literal point of symbolic uprightness, taking it into his head not simply to sit but to *stand* on Rocinante's back, the risky redundancy of his pose undoes him. The beast beneath literally pulls the ground out from under him, leaving him still tied, in any case, to the animal world in the form of the donkey's halter and the hayloft.

Though perilous and sometimes imperiled, contiguity with the beast seems nonetheless to be an inescapable human condition, the inevitable "end" of every adventure, dictated by unconscious drives when not by conscious will.[6] Indeed, another even more suspicious mythic shape lurks in Don Quixote's equestrian pose. By insisting on his inseparability from his steed (he repeatedly urges that the venerable beast be treated as though he were his master's own person), Quixote virtually turns the union of himself and Rocinante into an image of the centaur. For sixteenth-century Christian recyclers of pagan myth, such as Juan Pérez de Moya, the centaurs' upright human faces and warriors' shields conceal the bestiality of what lies below and behind them: "Al principio parecen humanos, y su[s] fines son bestiales [At the beginning they seem human, but their ends are beastly]."[7] With the pregnant ambiguity of the fabled creatures' "ends," pointing to two kinds of extremes—bodily extremities, or backsides, and the "ends" of purposes, goals, and consequences—the Golden Age mythographer makes anatomical description do double duty as narrative teleology: the centaurs make formidable adversaries because, behind their deceptively human faces, they hide beastly "ends," projects anatomically doomed by their placement with the inferior (or posterior) sexual and digestive organs to incarnate "extremes" of moral degradation.

6. So the narrator repeatedly reminds us throughout the two parts of the novel, as, for example, in the conclusion of the "barco encantado [enchanted boat]" adventure: "Volvieron a sus bestias, y a ser bestias, don Quijote y Sancho, y este fin tuvo la aventura del encantado barco [Don Quixote and Sancho went back to their beasts, and to being beasts, and this was the end of the adventure of the enchanted boat]" (II.29).

7. Juan Pérez de Moya, *Philosophia secreta*, ed. E. Gómez Baqueiro (Madrid: Compañía Iberoamericana de Publicaciones, 1928), 245v.

As it fuses together into one body the human rider and the beast, the shadow of the centaur in Cervantes's episode presses the suggestion that the struggle with the Beast Below (or Behind) is also a struggle with the Beast Within. Don Quixote's emphatic rhetorical appeals to his own moral anatomy teeter on a symbolic line that separates the man-body from the beast-body, the superior from the inferior members. Despite the fact that the word *mano* is repeated three times in the offertory discourse, we are left wondering exactly what member he is actually proffering. From the high ground of allegorical periphrasis ("verdugo de los malhechores del mundo [scourge of the evildoers of the world]"), the speaker moves onto the shiftier terrain of ambivalent negations about the hand's real activities: the hand he extends for a *non*-embrace has *never* been touched by any woman, *not even* the one who enjoys "entera posesión de todo mi cuerpo [complete possession of my whole body]"; and it is offered *not* to be kissed but merely to be admired. After the loaded ambivalence of this (non)offer, the overblown anatomical close-up that follows deepens our sense that the hand is a synecdochic stand-in, a part for a whole—but indeed what part, and for what whole? Nerves, musculature, veins ("la contextura de sus nervios, la trabazón de sus músculos, la anchura y espaciosidad de sus venas [the texture of its sinews, the network of its muscles, the breadth and spaciousness of its veins]") reach in comic disproportion beyond the part in question, as the knight begs his supposed admirers to imagine the strength of what (he mentions "la fuerza del brazo [the strength of the arm]") the hand is connected to.

But whether Don Quixote realizes it or not, such an invitation to remember what hands are connected to is slippery business. He would surely be much more reluctant to endorse other substitutions that the allegorical self-portraiture concentrated in his hand encourages. Maritornes's parody of the lovesick damsel's desires has already hinted at the "extremes" to which these substitutions might lead. Her friend wants to hold one of the beautiful members, she explains, "por poder des[a]hogar con *ella* el gran deseo que a este agujero *la* ha traído [in order to relieve with her/it the great desire that has brought her/ it to this hole]" (emphasis added).[8] I engage in a bit of critical malice here in order to put into bolder relief just what sort of part the hand

---

8. Jacques Lezra sees a number of ambiguities latent in Maritornes's curious choice of the verb *deshogar* ("Icarus Reading," 135–36). For an illuminating reading of the way erotic architecture stands in for the female body, and the way this venerable literary convention anticipates Freud's work on dreams, see Márquez Villanueva's analysis of "El celoso extremeño" in "Erasmo y Cervantes, una vez más," *Cervantes* 4 (1984): 125.

is being asked to play. It is, of course, a blatantly erotic role, one that might easily have been assigned to another member of the "corps." For all her lack of culture, Maritornes has a real way with pronouns. Her evocation of a female lover who wants to vent on another feminine someone or something ("ella"), literally "la mano," the desire that has brought "her" ("la"— but which one, the lover or the hand?) to the window simultaneously assigns the desire in question ("el . . . deseo que a este agujero *la* ha traído [the . . . desire that has brought *her* to the window]" [emphasis added]) to the daughter and to the hand. This double reference means that the violence Maritornes predicts will ensue from this tryst—which will very likely result in either dismembering or dishonoring "ella" or "la"—also takes on the doubly threatening form of deflowering (of the daughter) and castration (of her protector).[9]

But to what "end" do the narrator and his surrogate, the self-portrayer, describe, or ascribe, the bigger-than-life hand? Despite the semantic and syntactic traps into which he keeps falling, Don Quixote remains faithful to the idea that he is indeed proffering a member representative of his higher humanity; and he raises it vaingloriously to a position where it can enjoy its superiority over lower members (even over his head!), and over the beast on which he stands. Joaquín Casalduero takes the knight at his heroic word, finding in his latinizing descripion of the sinewy *mano* "a strongly sculptural value," by implication a kind of Renaissance monument to manly strength.[10] Within the lexicon of the novel, "la anchura y espaciosidad de sus venas [the breadth and spaciousness of its veins]," hovering between anatomy and geography, resonates with other Cervantine evocations of sweeping symbolic landscapes—military and literary—where heroes are permitted to range freely.[11] But while Don Quixote can contemplate with vainglorious complacency this uplifting version of his own epic enlargement, he unwittingly reinforces another, less lofty perspective on the conspicuous member's graphically detailed swelling. By having him aim its muscles, veins, and nerves, aroused in

9. The pronouns of the rest of her speech are, to be sure, just as shifty as the earlier ones—"tan a peligro de su honor, que si su señor padre *la* hubiera sentido, la menor tajada *della* fuera la oreja [at such great peril to her honor, that if my lord her father had sensed it/her, the least part of her to be sliced off would be her ear]" (I.43; emphasis added)—conveying the doubly obscene suggestion that the father would experience and respond to the intruding hand.

10. Joaquín Casalduero, *Sentido y forma del "Quijote"* (Madrid: Insula, 1975), 183.

11. For example, the "largo y espacioso campo por donde sin empacho alguno pudiese correr la pluma [wide and spacious field over which the pen might run free]" of the "escritura desatada [unleashed writing]" of the epic in prose according to the canon of Toledo (I.47).

direct response to expressions of female desire, toward their fateful destination in a *pajar*, the narrator (with the cheerful complicity of Maritornes) multiplies obscene suggestions that run from the trivializing to the animal, and finally to the frustrated but still guilty eroticism of masturbation.[12] The route of synecdoche has led, then, not from part to glorious whole but around, or back, to another, much more questionable part.[13]

If we have by now begun to suspect what "lending" such a "hand" may possibly entail, we can perhaps watch with less astonishment as Don Quixote acts out precisely the sort of action he has volunteered to punish: with a heroic "member" rendered impotent by a slipknot, he is made to perform a grotesque, and prodigiously long, penetration of the "hole" behind which he "senses" the two semidamsels. Not only does Don Quixote fail as the scourge of evildoers, but he actually becomes, half actively, half passively, an offender and is caught in flagrante delicto. And not only is he caught; he is appointed to castigate his own transgression by having his member, in its capacity as hand, the controlling arm of heroic will, punish its own suspect impulse in the guise of *membrum virile*, locus of his imperfectly repressed sexual instinct.[14] The episode's finishing touch is to tie his hand with a donkey's harness, binding the hero's body even at its uppermost extreme to a token of bestiality, so that when Rocinante unexpectedly awakens to the call of his own nature, pulling the (animal) ground out from underneath his raised humanity, the hand's owner is still harnessed to what Pérez de Moya might have called his "beastly ends." While the horses presumably act out, according to nature, the

12. Covarrubias, who gives a number of animal assocations for *paja* ("comida de bestias" ["straw" or "food for animals"]) and *pajar* (hayloft), and who lists expressions that link straw with valuelessness and insubstantiality ("No monta una paja [It's not worth a straw]"; "a lumbre de pajas, por lo poco que dura [by the light of a straw, because it burns so quickly]"; or even irresponsibility ("No dormirse en las pajas, no descuidarse ['Don't fall asleep in the hay,' meaning 'Don't fall asleep on the job']"), does not register the common usage "hacerse una paja" (make oneself a straw, that is, masturbate)" (*Tesoro*, 844). José Luis Alonso Hernández registers the appearance of *pajar* meaning "mouth" in the apocryphal *Quijote* of Avellaneda in his own *Léxico del marginalismo del siglo de oro* (Salamanca: Universidad de Salamanca, 1977), 572.

13. I am indebted to Inés Azar for the observation of a double synecdoche at work here— a part for a part—with doubly dismembering results.

14. Francisco Márquez Villanueva has called to my attention the presence of *mano*, with the meaning of "male genital," in the glossary of *Floresta de poesías eróticas del siglo de oro*, ed. Pierre Alzieu, Robert Jammes, and Yvan Lissorgues (Toulouse-Le Mirail: France-Ibérie Recherche, 1975), 343. On Don Quixote's sexuality, see Louis Combet, *Cervantes ou les incertitudes du désir* (Lyons: Presses Universitaires de Lyons, 1980); Carroll Johnson, *Madness and Lust: A Psychoanalytic Approach to Don Quixote* (Berkeley: University of California Press, 1983); and Maurice Molho, *Cervantes: Raíces folklóricas* (Madrid: Gredos, 1976).

erotic promise which the episode has already uttered, denied, and grotesquely counterfeited, poor Don Quixote hangs suspended in pain, reduced to bellowing like a bull, yet soon to be "elevated" by the girls' makeshift pulley to the status of the self-tormenting victims of myth.

Yet even this version of the episode's unsettling, suspenseful finale as symbolic enactment of timeless myths of self-subverting and self-contradicting desire is not the whole story. For its tail end is also a tale end. The second part of chapter 43 tells not only a story, but the story of the *writing* of that story. In this sense the episode resembles much of the rest of the novel: its "actions" are chiefly words or discourse, and Don Quixote's principal "deed" is none other than to write aloud the text of his heroic identity. It is no accident, therefore, that Don Quixote should proffer that extremity which is symbolically linked to deeds and to their discursive transformation into history, the member responsible for wielding both sword and pen. And the episode that turns on the proffering of a hand dramatizes not only the heroic, virile gesture in itself but also the gesturer's double role as writer of his own story, as writer of the story of that gesture. It insists throughout on the hand's double agency as doer and as writer, or at least on its owner's desire to exercise that agency, guiding with his upright intentions the double movements of his heroic arm. So it should not surprise us to find that double design figuring in the narrative detail, figured *literally* into the warp and woof of Cervantes's authorial design.[15] And in chapter 43 action and theoretical consideration do not merely tie in with each other: they are bound together, physically roped first into a slip noose, then in an untieable knot.

That knot belongs, on the literal level, to the rope with which Maritornes ties Don Quixote to the hayloft; yet knot and rope (cord, thread) are also, of course, favored figures since Aristotle for the work of plot construction, just as the body ("cuerpo de fábula entero [whole body of fable]") serves as the standard representation of harmonious poetic composition. *Enredos* and *desenlaces* rest on the notion of plotting as knotting: the thread of narrative or dramatic connections, stretched out in temporal sequence (prose itself in classical rhetoric is *oratio soluta*), is given form and intensity by the tensions that are brought to bear on the line. In the discussion of fabulation which

15. Lezra also considers bodies (Don Quixote's, the author's, woman's) as imperiled stand-ins for the integrity of narrative; see "Icarus Reading," 128, 141–43, 179. My own earlier readings of Cervantes's interest in heroic writing hands, notably his own, are found in Mary Gaylord Randel, "Cervantes' Portrait of the Artist," *Cervantes* 3 (1983): 83–102, and "Cervantes' Portraits and Literary Theory in the Text of Fiction," *Cervantes* 6 (1986): 57–80.

Cervantes knew best, El Pinciano's, knotting figures prominently: "La fábula se considera como cuerda y tiene ñudo y soltura, y tiene principio, medio y fin [The fable is like a rope and has a knot and an untying, and it has beginning, middle, and end]."[16] With the *cuerda* on the one hand, and its *ñudo y soltura* on the other, El Pinciano invokes the Aristotelian distinction between the enduring *essence* of fable (its "partes esenciales [essential parts]," including *imitación, agnición, verosimilitud* [imitation, anagnorisis, verisimilitude]) and its *accidents* (the "partes quantitivas" or temporal partitions). Yet the critical *ñudo* (*knot*) works to undermine the terms of the classical opposition, since it is at once a permanent physical feature of fable's rope and an event (the Spanish word signifies both the knot and its tying). The semantics of the principal metaphor for plot development thus suspends *fábula* in an unlocatable space—"De lo dicho consta q[ue] el ñudo no tiene lugar cierto, sino que él está embeuido en la fábula toda [From what has been said it is clear that the knot does not have one certain place but permeates the entire fable]" (84)—midway between essence and accident, between physical and temporal, static and dynamic.

This intermediate time-space—the space of *entre-tenimiento* (entertainment)—proves to be a conspicuously uncomfortable one, which the speakers in Pinciano's dialogue characterize with metaphors running from mild perturbation all the way to agony. *Fábula*'s Aristotelian beginning opens a story that progresses rapidly from discomfort to torture: "Comie[n]ça a apretar, y aprieta, y aprieta hasta y hasta q[ue] más no puede (assí como el q[ue] en el potro atormentan, q[ue], apretado assí, o confiessa o no confiessa, como quiera se le afloxa el garrote) [It begins to press, and it keeps pressing and presses still further until it can press no more (just as someone undergoing torture and pressed in this way either confesses or doesn't confess, as long as they loosen the garrote)]" (83–84). Yet it is the figure of the knot itself that pinpoints fable's teleology of self-torment: "Ñudo en la fábula se dize aq[ue]lla acción q[ue] va perturbándose más y más hasta el tiempo del afloxar, el qual se dize soltura [Knot in a fable is what we call that action that keeps distressing itself more and more until the moment of release, which we call the untying]" (84).

If the dialogue has relied heavily on the metaphor of the rope and its knots and/or knotting, it leans no less heavily here on the rhetorical figure of personification. And that figure raises a central issue: Just

16. Alonso López Pinciano, *Philosophía antigua poética* (Madrid: C.S.I.C., 1953), 2:83. Further references to this work are cited by page number in the text.

who is doing the tying, and who or what is being tied up in knots? Curiously enough, in this section of Pinciano's dialogue so much concerned with the effective structuring of fable, the figure of the *author* does not even make an appearance. The gripping story of torture by plotting involves only the fable and its action, the rope and its knots and knotting. The fable seems to succeed in its mission ("*El* [the plot] se comiença a añudar al principio y va procediendo siempre más y más hasta el tiempo de desañudar [*He* begins to tie himself up in knots at the beginning, and he keeps on doing it more and still more until the time of unknotting]" (84) to the extent that this "*él*" applies to *itself*, to its own *body*, a pressure that proceeds relentlessly to the point of a necessary release. By implication, literature's twin goals of instruction and delight are served as this male person inflicts upon himself (by design or by desire?) a series of excruciating, and at the same time conspicuously eroticized, torments. Earlier in this same dialogue, Pinciano's speakers addressed the way in which the principal action of the well-constructed epic or dramatic work is to be identified with a single figure, that of its male protagonist: "vn solo varón [a lone male]" (43). Such a fusing of the heroic agent with the action he heads gives the masculine personal pronoun of "*él* se comiença a añudar [*he* begins to tie himself up in knots]" an even more complex set of resonances. Rather than the fable/rope tying itself into an action/knot, we find the knot (*el ñudo*) tying itself. Or is it instead another *él*, the action's agent or protagonist, who is tying himself up in the knot? Just where in all of this agony is the author? Who will unbind the hero/action/knot? And who is, after all, to borrow Don Quixote's phrase, "el señor de la historia [the lord of the story]" (II.3)?

Pinciano's characters might have been surprised by such a discussion of the ambiguous nature of their theoretical tropes. Cervantes, I think, would not; nor, of course, would Freud. The paradoxes of the plot's and the hero's tying up and eventual release are precisely the ones that shape the grotesque twists of chapter 43. In his foregrounding of the mad knight's slip from lofty purpose into raging animal impotence, Cervantes reads out ironically El Pinciano's apparent lack of concern with the role of the author. Aspiring to tell, with his words and with his body, *his* story, History, the classic tale of heroic agency, Don Quixote finds himself tied up by the very rope that represents figuratively his own moral and aesthetic authority. Suspended in helpless impotence, he calls in vain on all of the imagined guarantors of his discursive authority—Amadís's sword, a needy world suffering in his absence, Dulcinea, his loyal squire, the wise enchanters. Yet he is left to incarnate instead the ideal order's inversion, as the control he tries to impose on his discourse dissolves into the braying of a bull. And in the final stage of his agony, where Cervantes transforms Pinciano's garrote into the pulley's gruesome scheme, the knight acts out in a composite dramatic emblem the ultimate logical consequences of the narrative binds he himself has tied. The garrote's force logically could come only from some external source, whereas the pulley's victim is made to share responsibility for his own torment. The episode makes it painfully clear that such binds of the self are always double binds. It reads out the profoundly ironic vision that Don Quixote's master narrative— which is, after all, the proto-narrative of male mastery—is ultimately and exquisitely counterproductive, in multiple radical senses, not the least of which is to make the Virtuous Knight simultaneously impotent and a rapist.[17]

But what of Cervantes's own role in handling the ropes of an episode in which Vladimir Nabokov found evidence of "appalling" authorial cruelty?[18] What power is there, indeed, in the "real" author's demonstration of his protagonist's authorial impotence, of narrative ties that turn out to be double binds of the self, of virtuous intentions that are fated to enact the unconscious transgressive impulses they vainly claim to negate? The torture of Don Quixote's textual body is surely, in Cervantes's uncanny presentation of his character as surrogate author, yet another instance of self-torture, of an authorial hangman hanging himself. But of course beyond Don Quixote's unwitting complicity in the representation of the self-inflicted torments of authorship, chapter 43 has another surrogate author, one whose counterfeit of the master story's "origin" in feminine distress in fact sets the episode's events in motion, in the person of none other than Maritornes. Maritornes is barely half a damsel, a stand-in for the protected and/or ravished "maiden," figure of anti-idealism, and the voice here and elsewhere of the female desire Don Quixote's plot represses as unsuccessfully as it does his own. It is this mischievous figure who, half purposefully, half forgetfully, clearly has her hands on the ropes, tying and untying all the critical knots in grotesque parody of Pinciano's observation that the untying of plots gives the

17. Lezra offers a different reading of the tortured body of fable as representation of "the way in which a certain phenomenalization . . . of the interaction between two rhetorical modes can rack the text, drawing it apart" ("Icarus Reading," 145). See Lezra also for an astute account of the exchange between Don Quixote and the *cuadrilleros* (men on horseback) who arrive at the inn and unwittingly contribute to the knight's distress (147).

18. Vladimir Nabokov, *Lectures on Don Quixote*, ed. Fredson Bowers (New York: Harcourt, Brace, Jovanovich, 1983).

greatest delight "quando humanas manos lo obran [when human hands do the work]" (87). In this fable's painfully long-overdue dénouement, it is Maritornes who remembers, who quite literally remembers, the hero. And finally it is she, as female surrogate of authorial (anti)authority, who, literally and figuratively, cuts him down, severing the tortured thread that has held him suspended in the agony of his desire, thereby both subverting the heroic designs of the master narrative and at the same time temporarily releasing him—body, fable, and all—from his own story's impossible binds.

Like Don Quixote's handy anatomical exemplum, Cervantes's story as I have been reading it—as the story of writing (his)tory, of knotting and plotting, of (prot)agonizing and authoring— involves a series of substitutions which have the hand synecdochically standing in for something other than itself. In the first instance the hand stands in for the body of its owner, who, as would-be heroic protagonist and author, in turn stands in for a host of other heroes and authors, among them the narrator of the framework. At the same time, the man's body stands in, metonymically, for a body of another order, El Pinciano's and the canon of Toledo's body of fable. The tale's principal figure is a composite one, a metaphor or synecdoche that keeps two, or even more, of its terms visible as an essential feature of its work of signification. When Don Quixote underlines the link between the hand and "la fuerza del brazo que tal mano tiene [the strength of the arm that has such a hand]," he determines that in his story the hand will serve not simply to replace the body (et alia), but rather to represent that one preeminent member in its relationship to the body. And the story thereby becomes the story of the hand's role as would-be protagonist of the story.

Yet this tale of a part that is insistently engaged in reminding us that it belongs to a whole ("cuerpo . . . entero con todos sus miembros [whole body . . . with all of its members]") continually founders on the shoals of its own synecdochic structure. As the text focuses attention on the member-body connection, it multiplies questions about the nature, "real" and imagined, of that connection. Does the hand play the part of an extremity, subordinate to the body, rightfully its servant and instrument? Or does the hand, raised above the head, assume the physical and moral superiority of the highest human features and faculties with a view to guiding the body, directing and controlling its movements? Even the language with which Don Quixote assigns the part of heroic protagonist to his uplifted member— not to mention the subsequent interventions of Maritornes, Rocinante, and the narrator—leaves nagging questions about what part after all is involved, about which member is about to get into the act, and about just what the act is to be. And if the ambiguously virile member is indeed a sexual organ, pertaining to the lower end of human moral anatomy, its role as controlling protagonist would replace the promise of punishment for evildoers with nothing less than the overturning of the social order.

As a structural figure that presents a part proposing to lead or control a whole, the hand-over-body of chapter 43 fosters, as we have seen, a rich series of metonymic displacements: hand is to body as head is to body, as man is to beast, as mind is to matter, as actor is to history, as author is to story, as intention is to instrument— and as meaning is to figure. In these ideal arrangements, according to which the role of each part in service to the whole is determined by its position on the Great Scale of Being, man's superior faculties preside over his baser parts, legislating their subordination in service to his (and the whole's) higher ends. For Aristotle and his Scholastic followers in Golden Age Spain, this paradigm incarnated nothing less than the order of nature and was, naturally, used as a blueprint not only to structure the body politic from household to empire but also to describe (or prescribe) the structure of knowledge and experience. And that structure simultaneously informs the very structure of consciousness, which in turn is a sort of consciousness of the structure in question, that is, an awareness of the rule of mind over matter.[19]

It is, of course, this same structure that governs the orthodox understanding of the function of metaphor and allegory on which Don Quixote rests both his discourse and the literal, physical weight of his hand and body. The traditional view of metaphor also subordinates sensory experience to intellection, the physical to the abstract, body to mind. Aristotle, whose formulations in the area of language cast as long a shadow as his political ideas, recommends to the poet that "the greatest thing by far is to be a master of metaphors . . . since a good metaphor implies an intuitive perception of the similarity in dissimilars."[20] Good metaphors, that is to say, capture and fix an authoritative apprehension of the natural order of the world. Allegory, unfolding as the temporal extension of a metaphor and thereby dependent on the structure of an "initial troping proposition," does

19. Joel Fineman, describing allegory and the desire that animates it as a movement in the direction of the original apprehensions that underlie conventional systems of tropes, sees this straining back toward the origins of literature and language as pre-Freudian. See his essay "The Structure of Allegorical Desire," in *Allegory and Representation*, ed. S. J. Greenblatt (Baltimore: Johns Hopkins University Press, 1981), 26–60.

20. Aristotle, *Poetics* 1459A, 5–6, quoted ibid., 54.

the same—or strives to. Joel Fineman argues that allegory is born of "allegorical desire" (actually the desire *for* allegory) and that its movement obeys this desire: "Like the [Freudian] dreamwork, [it] enacts a wish that determines its progress." And since allegory is "always a hierarchizing mode, indicative of timeless order," its movement inevitably reveals a nostalgic investment in the power of its own structures, and in the power of structure itself.[21] Inherent in Don Quixote's wish to offer his hand and himself *not* as presence but as representation—as a real-life metaphor that logically extends itself into allegory—is a devotion to the hierarchical structure he wants his own physical and rhetorical figure to incarnate.

Yet, in Cervantes's hands, neither Don Quixote nor the traditional signifying project of which he so earnestly desires to be a part is destined to succeed. While classical notions of metaphor and (allegorical or symbolic) plot come down to the principle that both ought to *serve understanding*—that is, they ought to be subordinated to authorial purpose, which in turn ought to reflect the "true," "natural" order of things— Cervantes makes of Don Quixote's "troping position" a very precarious form of "under-standing" (the horse is *under* the man, but the man is *under* the loft window, *under* a serving girl, *under* a donkey's harness). As that "understanding" spins itself out in narrative, not only is Don Quixote un-horsed, but the whole epistemological ground (the comforting order of man over beast, mind over matter, and so on) is pulled out from under him, leaving him and the lifework he aims to write suspended in the agony of his frustrated allegorical desire. Cervantes's apprehension of the perils of runaway metaphor and allegory anticipates Francisco Cascales's complaints (or echoes Quintilian's) about Góngora's poetic language: too many tropes lead to allegory, and allegory leads to enigma. To Cascales, the only point of such hopeless tangles of tropes is to torture human understanding: "Sólo sirven de dar garrote al entendimiento."[22]

But Cervantes is much closer to the humor of El Pinciano's theoretical *tertulia* than to the self-righteousness of the *Cartas filológicas*. He is also much closer to Freud.[23] The traditional definitions of con-

---

21. Fineman, "The Structure of Allegorical Desire," 26, 32. The similarity between allegory and Freudian dream work is explored exhaustively by Diana de Armas Wilson in the chapter on allegory in her *Allegories of Love: Cervantes's Persiles and Sigismunda* (Princeton: Princeton University Press, 1991).

22. Francisco Cascales, *Cartas filológicas*, ed. Juan García Soriano (Madrid: Espasa-Calpe, Clásicos Castellanos, 1959), 1:219, 195. Quintilian is cited in "The Structure of Allegorical Desire," Fineman, 30.

23. Stephen J. Greenblatt's essay on issues of self and identity that arise in the historical

sciousness and understanding that I have been invoking are, it goes
without saying, conscious understandings in a pre-Freudian sense.
By letting Don Quixote act out the master plot's full potential for self-
torture, Cervantes presses that classic formula relentlessly, all the way
to its most painful extremes. In the hanging figure of the knight, he
literally dangles before us the titillating self-punishment to be found
at the heart of moral and aesthetic gratification. And in Don Quixote's
grotesque double self-bind, he offers an arresting Golden Age emblem
of civilization's tragicomic struggle with its discontents.

---

case of Martin Guerre, and the way in which they anticipate the later Freudian model of
self, sounds an important challenge to readers of pre-Freudian and particularly Renaissance
literature. See his "Psychoanalysis and Renaissance Culture," in *Literary Theory/Renaissance
Texts*, ed. Patricia Parker and David Quint (Baltimore: Johns Hopkins University Press, 1986),
210–24. Peter Brooks, whose account of the Freudian master plot in *Reading for the Plot: Design
and Intention in Narrative* (New York: Vintage Books, 1985) bases itself largely on later works,
urges in a subsequent article, "The Idea of a Psychoanalytic Literary Criticism," *Critical Inquiry*
13 (1987): 334–87, the importance of psychoanalysis as "a particularly insistent and demanding
intertext" for reading in general, one that "both confirms and complicates our understanding
of how the mind reformulates the real, how it constructs the necessary fictions by which we
dream, desire, interpret, indeed by which we constitute ourselves as human subjects" (348).
Brooks maintains that "the detour through psychoanalysis forces the critic to respond to the
erotics of form, that is, to an engagement with the psychic investments of rhetoric, the
dramas of desire played out in tropes" (348). While I obviously accept the notion that immense
intertextual potential can arise from mergers of psychoanalytic and formalist readings, I want
to note that in the case of this study it is not psychoanalysis that has forced me to respond
to the erotics of form but rather the force of the erotics of form, approached through rhetoric
and poetics, that has led me toward a psychoanalytic reading.

7

Sancho's Jokework

George A. Shipley

—Tal modo de contar [la historia] ni dejarla, jamás se podrá ver ni habrá visto en toda la vida, aunque no esperaba yo otra cosa de tu buen discurso.

—Miguel de Cervantes

Chapter 20 of *Don Quixote*, part I, is Sancho Panza's chapter. In it Sancho is mentioned fifty-three times, his master but thirty-nine. The point of the chapter is discovered by attending to Sancho, to what he says and does, and to the narrator's way of treating him. The often reluctant fellow traveler wrests the initiative from his guide for the first time in these pages and dances out, awkwardly, a series of stumbling variations on the theme of *aprieto*: together with his companion and the narrator, Sancho draws repeatedly from a cluster of leading terms that have to do with binds, with getting into, bearing up against, and working out of squeezes.

An Introduction, a Succession of Excesses, Order Restored

The proceedings that so favor this vocabulary of constraint form a whole, apparently comic in shape, divisible into four acts and a coda. The first of these is a scenic introduction. In a dry wasteland, past midnight, Sancho and Don Quixote are pushed by thirst and induced by the sound of cascading water to enter a pastoral pleasance that at once springs a nasty surprise. A terrifying thump ... thump ... thumping, creaking, menacing sound issues from within the torrent, paralyzing the human actors, whose reactions for the remainder of the night will be greatly inhibited substitutes for the movements they

135

would undertake were it day. Don Quixote verbalizes heroically and prepares to move forward. Sancho sobs, discourses windily in favor of falling back, then takes his defense into his own hands, literally: "Cuando apretaba las cinchas al caballo, bonitamente y sin ser sentido, ató con el cabestro de su asno ambos pies a Rocinante . . . [While he tightened the horse's girths, quite nicely and without being noticed, he tied Rocinante's legs together with the halter of his ass]." Achieving this impasse, Sancho triumphs "quite nicely" over the hazards of space: he will not be left behind; he will not be moved toward the dreadful pounding. Sancho squeezes his master's leg and "quedó abrazado con el muslo izquierdo de su amo, sin osarse apartar dél un dedo; tal era el *miedo* que tenía a los golpes, que todavía alternativamente sonaban [he stood embracing his master's left thigh, without daring to move a finger's width away, so afraid was he of the blows that continued to resound regularly]."

His next act is Sancho's principal undertaking of the night, the matter of containing time, which (as might be expected in a "true history") proves less tractable. Don Quixote rules out sleep as a resort for the night. Sancho proposes a substitute refuge: he will kill the time by filling it with stories.[1] Unfortunately both for them and for lovers of crafted narrative, Sancho's choice is inept and his narration worse. We can be thankful that the narrative is interrupted when but five of Lope Ruiz's three hundred goats have been transported over the swollen river, that is, long before the tale can realize its full plodding, unimaginative excess. Accounting for this clumsy story is my object in the present study. Sancho's tale, as I maintain, is *humorous* and *comic*; most important, it is a *joke*, within the definitions Sigmund Freud assigned to those words in *Jokes and Their Relation to the Unconscious*. The material Miguel de Cervantes puts before us is superior, I think, to the examples Freud adduces and analyzes. My discussion demonstrates the value of the text for testing Freud's hypotheses, although that is a secondary consequence of what is primarily an attempt to show that Freud's categories and investigatory techniques elucidate moments of chapter 20 that are at once nonsensical and yet drenched in meaning and order.

When his story, though incomplete, is finished and Sancho returns to an awareness of real time, he feels pressed to extemporize a third

1. In "A Prologue and Afterword for an Inquiry into *Don Quixote*, Part I, Chapter 20," in *Studies in Honor of Elias Rivers*, ed. Bruno M. Damiani and Ruth El Saffar (Potomac, Md.: Scripta Humanistica, 1989), 169–83, I apply Kenneth Burke's *Philosophy of Literary Form* (Berkeley: University of California Press, 1973) to this chapter and Sancho's hope of using literature for purposes of therapy and prophylaxis.

act in response to a new and urgent need and desire. "Bonitamente y sin rumor alguno [quite nicely and without a single sound]," says the narrator, he drops his pants about his ankles (thereby achieving parity with Rocinante) in order to "hacer lo que otro no pudiera hacer por él [do what no one else could do for him]." To state this with more truth and less decorum than the narrator provides, Sancho then has the shit scared out of him. Hours later, when it dawns on Sancho and Don Quixote that the latter's imagination and the former's fear have made fools of them both, they erupt with uncontainable laughter, one after the other and over and over again. The narrator describes Sancho's "evidentes señales de querer reventar [clear signs of wanting to explode]" in terms that echo the recent tension and helpless explosion at the other end of Sancho's alimentary canal. This eruption of laughter is the fourth act, and from it issues the fifth, or coda, in much the same way that the awful pounding rose out of the pleasant cascade: Sancho's mirth devolves into a mocking repetition of his master's grandiloquent declamation hours earlier, when the slapping mill paddles first sounded challenging. Don Quixote corrects this, Sancho's last and most offensive excess with one—or rather two—of his own: he strikes two killing blows with his crude lanzón, off target, of course, and then he pounds his subordinate back into his proper place—or thinks he does—with as many assertions of his own superiority as several conventional notions of authority provide him. Now, let us give the second in this series of acts the special attention it merits.

SANCHO'S ESCAPE: FROM NIGHTMARE TO DAYDREAM

"Realmente no pasa nada," says Joaquín González Muela of this chapter, "es la primera aventura sin aventura [Really nothing happens; it is the first adventure without adventure]."[2] If we classify the episode according to standards derived from chivalric and other heroic literature, this comment can stand. Viewed from another angle, the action here, or what passes for action, is remarkable. As if to gainsay González Muela, the very verb *pasar* and related forms appear in this chapter with attention-catching frequency. Offering themselves as a clue to guide us, fifteen of the twenty-four instances of the use of the

2. Joaquín González Muela, "La aventura de los batanes," *Insula* 18, Supplement (1963): 15.

pasar family are compressed into the brief extension of Sancho's story of the passage of goats across a river.

Much as dreams are thought to be reworkings of the still energized residue of recent experience which, in forms more or less distorted, make possible gratifying fulfillment of unpronounceable wishes, Sancho's tale reformulates (if incompletely and unsatisfactorily) the dismaying detritus of his long day into a midnight daydream capable, if it goes well, of displacing his nightmarish current reality from the focus of his awareness. An inventory of his story's arresting features reveals how together they amount to so many systematic transformations of the narrator's present and recent experience.[3]

Sancho, so intent on "killing time," chooses a prolongable tale, and distends its every element, beginning with its prologue. His reduplication of each bit of material conforms so slavishly to the narrative conventions of the folktale that it strikes Don Quixote as unacceptably mannered: "Dilo seguidamente [Tell it straightforwardly]," he urges. Sancho feels protected by traditional ways of telling, especially as these promote time wasting in a story that, unabridged, says Don Quixote, would go on for two days.

Sancho's protagonist, Lope Ruiz, like his narrator, is caught in a double bind. He cannot retreat or advance. Before him, as before Sancho, stretches an unfathomable water barrier, and Lope is increasingly pressured from the rear by the approaching Torralba. He enjoys, however, two advantages that are denied Sancho: he knows how he got into this press, and he sees how to get out of it. The essentially visual story makes mention seven times of seeing (and choosing not to see) before its premature end restores the clairvoyant narrator's blindness.[4] The first of these is Sancho's description of his tale's antagonist, who appears so vivid in his imagination that "parece que

---

3. I depend on hypotheses elaborated by Sigmund Freud in *The Interpretation of Dreams*, vols. 4 and 5 of *The Standard Edition of the Complete Psychological Works of Sigmund Freud*, ed. and trans. James Strachey, 24 vols. (London: Hogarth Press, 1953–74), broadened to comprehend jokes (*der Witz*), humor, and the comic in *Jokes and Their Relation to the Unconscious*, vol. 8 of the *Standard Edition* (New York: W. W. Norton, 1963), hereafter cited in the text as *Jokes* with page number, and lucidly distilled in the *Introductory Lectures on Psychoanalysis*, vols. 15 and 16 of the *Standard Edition* (London: Hogarth Press, 1963).

4. Kenneth Burke, *Philosophy of Literary Form*, 17, tells us that in literature as in dreams we attempt to convert our debts into assets. Sancho, disconcerted by the blackness of the night, bathes his story in sunlight, and endows his protagonist with the virtue of willful blindness to his alluring seductress, whose unworthiness is clear even for her to see: "*Por no verla*, se quiso ausentar de aquella tierra e irse donde *sus ojos no la viesen jamás*. La Torralba, que *se vio* desdeñada del Lope, luego le quiso bien [*So that he would not see her*, he attempted to leave that land and go where *his eyes would never again see her*. Torralba, *seeing* herself disdained by Lope, then loved/wanted him]" (emphasis added).

ahora la veo [it seems I can see her now]" as surely as he can almost
see his master in the dark. The winsome object of Lope's affection
was a nicely rounded shepherdess, according to Sancho's report; but,
the teller singularizes her disturbingly, calling her unmanageable and
somewhat manly ("zahareña, y tiraba algo a hombruna"), "porque
tenía unos pocos de bigotes, que parece que ahora la veo [for she had
a bit of a moustache, which it seems to me I can see now]." We need
only to visualize the narrator's own scene, in which he stands embracing Don Quixote in conversation and with both arms, to grasp
the decidedly untraditional source and significance of the moustache
that tickles Sancho's fancy and intrudes into his folk story. The comparability of Don Quixote and Torralba, and of Sancho and Lope, is
suggested further by the names Sancho assigns his players: Lope,
like Sancho, is a salt-of-the-earth bisyllable; Torralba and Quixote are
make-believe arcane composite trisyllables.

As Torralba is Quixote-like, but with a difference, Lope Ruiz is a
manifest improvement on Sancho. He is high-minded, competent,
resourceful, prudent, and decisive; he deserves better than he gets.
The history of his soured love is remarkably undetailed at the very
point where a crafter more skilled than Sancho would focus and
reward our attention. The story moves to that focal point predictably:
first, Lope loved Torralba; second, time passed; third, and remarkable
but unremarked, Lope's love was transformed into hate. Sancho
chooses not to detail the matter—it was the devil's work: "El diablo,
que no duerme y que todo lo añasca, hizo de manera que el amor
que el pastor tenía a la pastora se volviese en omecillo y mala voluntad
[The devil, who never sleeps and fouls up everything, caused the
shepherd's love for the shepherdess to become hate and bad will]."
Lope is innocent and injured. The devil, like Don Quixote a sleepless
meddler, tempted Torralba (who in her hairy way also is a likeness
of Don Quixote) into unspecified jealousy-causing excesses "tales que
pasaban de la raya y llegaban a lo *vedado* [such that they *went beyond*
the bounds and landed up in *improprieties*]" (emphasis added).

The punning and devious patterning of language here alerts us to
the presence of disguised intrigue, partly beyond Sancho's conscious
awareness, certainly beyond Don Quixote's. Torralba has crossed the
border of respectability, repeatedly. Lope, the image of respectability,
gathers in his goats and backs away toward a more honorable borderline: "para *pasarse* a los reinos de Portugal [to *cross over* into the
kingdom of Portugal]" (emphasis added). His withdrawal represents
a passage to safety from sexual insult and toward a refuge for Lope
and his flock in a *vedado*, a preserve, of a more honorable kind than

Torralba offers. But when Lope reaches the crossing, he finds it flooded: impasse. He is briefly at a loss. Seeing herself scorned, Torralba loves Lope, or more exactly wants Lope, more than ever before: "Le quiso bien, más que nunca le había querido [She loved/wanted him more than she had ever before loved/wanted him]." She pursues him with the intention, we suspect, of coaxing him back to *probar el vado*, "test the water," in the erotic sense these words carry in folk expressions.[5]

Do I judge Torralba harshly? Has she experienced a change of heart, or is she deceitful? Don Quixote thinks she exhibits the generic fickleness of women, and he dismisses her with a misogynist bromide. Sancho, to this point so prone to draw out every detail, withholds information we need to have elaborated ("que yo no me quiero meter ahora en averigualloo [for I don't intend to get into proving it now]"), censoring his account of Torralba's fall and stepping back ("sólo diré que dicen que . . . [I will say only that they say that]") from the action he recounted initially with vivid particulars, right down to the facial hair. But Sancho's censor lets slip enough evidence to convey the suggestion of Torralba's perversity in forms that leave little room for doubt. Because she is unshod and carries a staff, one might mistake her for a lovesick shepherdess, and perhaps one reborn, a discalced penitent supported by a humble pilgrim's crook (*bordón*). But her knapsack contains, "según es fama [as is notorious]," a fragment of mirror, a comb, and some cosmetics, evidence of the vain and erotic self-concern that kept her from embracing Lope's proffered love. Far from discarding these tokens of her past, she hoards them to the exclusion of a pilgrim's devotional relics and also the staples of pastoral life, which plump Sancho might have been expected to include in his inventory, had he regarded Torralba as better than a vamp.

Sancho chooses not to sketch Torralba's truancy, past or present. It is enough that the manly and unmanageable lass fell in with bad company. Given his lady's unspeakable devilish embroglios and unmentionable border violations, Lope must hate after having loved. It does not seem to occur to Sancho that both the dissolute mustachioed lady and the sleepless devil with whom she is entangled are degraded representations of the man he is presently holding in his arms. Nor does Don Quixote suspect how much Sancho has made his own, their

5. For example, when in a ballad La Cava attempts to bend the sexual probing of King Rodrigo: "La Cava, como discreta, / en risa lo había echado: / —Pienso que burla tu alteza / o quiere probar el vado [Cava, being clever, / laughed off [Rodrigo's overtures]: / 'I think Your Highness mocks me / or wishes to test the water']."

own, the folk story someone once told him and that he now is passing on, he claims, in time-honored fashion.[6]

When Sancho first pleads for a hasty retreat from the threatening waters, his master replies stiffly: "Que no se ha de decir por mí, ahora ni en ningún tiempo, que *lágrimas y ruegos* me apartaron de hacer lo que debía a estilo de caballero [It shall not be said of me, now or ever, that *tears and complaints* moved me from my knightly duty]" (emphasis added). Sancho achieves a self-serving inversion of this honorable sentiment in his story when Lope, stalled by a river as engulfing as Sancho's cascade is percussive, seeks to avoid confrontation with his dishonorable temptress "porque *veía* que la Torralba venía ya muy cerca, y le había de dar mucha pesadumbre con sus *ruegos y lágrimas* [because he *saw* Torralba approaching, who would weigh on him with her *complaints and tears*]" (emphasis added). While projecting onto Torralba his own clinging vulnerability, Sancho arms Lope appropriately with Don Quixote's uprightness. Acting in a way that is ethically exemplary and economically pragmatic, the goatherd takes care to gather his flock and plan for their future together; then he sees to their transport across the river. Lope makes the best of a bad situation; if and when Torralba arrives, he can save his honor and a steadily increasing fraction of his flock by floating to the far bank and interrupting the emigration there, at the expense of the unevacuated remnant.

That is just what happens, of course, and the cost of Lope's honor is great. Torralba interrupts the orderly proceeding, or rather Don Quixote intrudes disruptively into the story, and two hundred and ninety-five goats are sacrificed because of Torralba's untimely appearance, or more exactly because of Don Quixote's failure to honor his part of the story contract.[7] Lope and his fortunate few are freed of Torralba at last and forever; and Sancho is true to his contracted word "porque así como yo pregunté a vuestra merced que me dijese cuántas cabras habían pasado, y me respondió que no sabía, en aquel mesmo instante se me fue a mí de la memoria cuanto me quedaba

6. For discerning words on folklore in Sancho's story, see Mac E. Barrick's essay "The Form and Function of Folktales in *Don Quijote*," *Journal of Medieval and Renaissance Studies* 6 (1976): 101–38, esp. 131–37. Barrick thinks Sancho's tale noteworthy partly because Cervantes captures there a "natural" folk-story recitation (137). We see there is reason to qualify that view and to reject Sancho's claim that he is but another conservative link in a popular narrative chain.

7. Sancho's contract is oral, of course: "Tenga vuestra merced cuenta en las cabras que el pescador va pasando, porque si se pierde una de la memoria, se acabará el cuento [Keep count of the goats that the fisherman ferries across, for if a single one is lost from memory, the story will be finished]."

por decir, y a fe que era de mucha virtud y contento [because as soon as I asked you to tell me how many goats had crossed, and you answered that you did not know, in that very instant everything I had yet to say flew from my memory, and I swear it was all good and satisfying stuff]."

Torralba cannot trespass this time to satisfy her desire; she is left to the devil's devices. As for Don Quixote, when he is asked how many goats had crossed, he replies angrily: "Yo ¿qué diablos sé? [I, what *the devil* do I know?]" (emphasis added). The devoted lover of stories will remain forever perplexed and bedeviled by this interrupted affair. The frustrations of Don Quixote and of Torralba are somehow analogous, as are the costly victories that Sancho and Lope score at the expense of their outwitted consorts. Lope sacrifices most of his flock; Sancho must soon undergo a distressing evacuation of his own.

SANCHO'S TALE: HUMOR, THE COMIC, AND THE JOKE

Editors' footnotes and commentaries on chapter 20 record that "este cuento 'de nunca acabar' pertenece a la tradición oral y folklórica universal [this endless tale belongs to the universal oral and folklore tradition]" (244), or something similar. This is so, but the pertinence has little explanatory power. The likeness between Sancho's tale and folk analogues in fact scarcely extends beyond or below a few shared structural motifs. Despite his disclaimer, Sancho's tale is very much Sancho's. Sancho names his characters significantly; he provides them with a history and a cloak of mystery, secret motives and vivid particulars (a mustache, a bit of mirror, and so on). All of this detail springs to his lips less from inherited texts than from memory and imagination ruminating on recent experience. Sancho's assigning of the work of counting goats to the receiver of the story is not traditional; it is a devious innovation of capital and scarcely remarked importance.[8] Amid this technical reworking, and especially the thematic grounding of the story in Sancho's recent experience, the folk forms and Sancho's claim of membership in the guild of conservative folk narrators amount to little more than a disguise for legitimizing what

8. Barrick, "Form and Function," 134, comments perceptively on this technical adjustment. One could say that Sancho conscripts Don Quixote and assigns him the role of silent partner and coproducer of the tale; in so doing he makes his subordinate responsible, along with the narrator, for its outcome or lack thereof.

really is going on in a story that is at heart expressive of the narrator's resentment of his companion.

Freud accords humor, which he defines narrowly, slight attention in his book on jokes. He addresses the matter in the seventh and last (but for one brief) section of his seventh and final chapter, there viewing it as a species of the comic. He treats the broader field of the comic more generously; its study fills the rest of that chapter. The preceding chapters deal at length with the techniques and purposes of jokes, their mechanisms and motives, and their relation to dreams and to the unconscious. Freud's translator, James Strachey, has as much difficulty putting into English his author's key term, *der Witz*, as Don Quixote has labeling Sancho's story "una de las más nuevas consejas, cuento o historia, que nadie pudo pensar [one of the most novel tales, stories or histories ever thought up by anyone]." Students of both of these texts will find that the two are mutually illuminating, despite their infelicities of definition.

Humor

Depending on what focus we as readers adopt, Sancho's story reveals either a humorous function (so long as we regard it as its narrator's undertaking), a comic mechanism (if we take it the way Don Quixote and most readers receive it), or (if we dare peek beneath the cloak, as only readers are able to do, to see what *realmente pasa*, what is really happening) an aggressive joke more ingeniously elaborated than any Freud examines.

Let us proceed in this exploration from mechanisms of lesser to greater complexity. Humor, "the most easily satisfied among the species of the comic" (*Jokes* 229), is pleasure obtained simply by suppressing distressing affects, already in preparation, and substituting itself for them. As a defensive process, indeed "the highest of these," comparable to displacement, it is a "psychical correlative of the flight reflex," and it performs "the task of preventing the generation of unpleasure from internal sources" (*Jokes* 233). When the noisy cascade appears to promise Sancho a new pummeling of his sore body, and thereby reawakens his accumulating anxiety, his immediate response is appropriate and natural: "Bien podemos torcer el camino y desviarnos del peligro [We can easily turn off this road and turn away from the danger]." Sancho's flight reflex is finely tuned; but his master's authority and the disorienting darkness block its work. So the story of Lope Ruiz and Torralba becomes the benign substitute to ease anxiety by converting an awful pounding into the comparably regular but belittled and even soothing problem of the goat ferry.

"Repetition makes the story comic" here, as in one Freud recalls from Mark Twain (*Jokes* 231); but the *humorous* pleasure, such as it is, arises from our sympathetic understanding of Sancho's effort at suppressing the affects generated within him in response to a thundering reality that will not cede its tenacious claim on his awareness. As long as we hold to Freud's definition of humor, we are led to conclude about the story of Lope and Torralba that neither Don Quixote nor Sancho nor the reader derives significant humorous pleasure from it. The repetitive mechanism promises its narrator pleasure and relief by competing successfully with his distressing affects: it offers itself as a replacement. The interruption after five crossings, however (in contrast with forty-six repetitions in Twain's story) breaks the promise before the narrator can effect a significant savings and conversion of distress.

The diversion proves unavailing, wanting in humorous pleasure; hence Don Quixote's and Sancho's contradictory reactions once their cooperative narrative effort has ceased. Don Quixote, intrepid and impatient, squeezes his nag toward the source of adventure. Sancho, losing patience in another form, proceeds to squeeze out of his backside a fecal surrogate for his fear. The reader's laughter rises not out of Sancho's attempt at humor, incomplete and interrupted, but from Cervantes's comic achievement, which is complete though it culminates in interruption.

The Comic

The broad and complex field of the comic, in which humor occupies a corner, encompasses several additional species, among which the naive might be thought one that fits Sancho. Like other forms of the comic, the naive arises in the remarks and actions of another, a "second person," in whom a "first person" discovers what is comic. The first person may intensify this comic thing, naive or not, by telling it to a "third person," or receiver, who adds nothing to it (*Jokes* 181). The naive comic occurs most frequently "in children, and is then carried over to uneducated adults, whom we may regard as childish" (*Jokes* 182). Don Quixote (but not he alone) often regards his companion in this way; patronizing condescension drips from his lips when he praises Sancho's narrative and narration. Sancho has his moments of simplicity, to be sure; for past performances, and for his comportment this night and subsequently, he lives crowned in many readers' recollection as one of the literary types of the naive.

At this early point in part I, Sancho's rounded figure and simple ways appear to fit comfortably within another category, which Freud thinks of (but does not label) as the comic of character. That is the sort that elicits "a pleasurable sense of the superiority we feel in relation to [one who] in comparison with ourselves . . . makes too great an expenditure on his bodily functions and too little on his mental ones" (*Jokes* 195). Indeed that is Sancho, but only up to a point; and this episode, which gives good evidence of Sancho's comic character, also illustrates a distinction Freud draws, as if with Sancho in mind, between the comic grounded in traits of character and the comic that inheres in a situation.

A considerable portion of the pleasure readers get from chapter 20 comes from their perception of the childlike nature of Sancho's response to the novel midnight scene. You and I might have reacted in much the way Sancho does had we found ourselves, when we were very young, in this situation. This concession is useful on two counts. It amounts to a recognition that Sancho's behavior is that of a child, childlike, and not merely childish; and it suggests that our laughter is produced partly by the situation that puts the comic character to the test. Laughable Sancho finds himself unnerved by a provocation that draws several primitive reactions out of him in succession. One of these is the story of Lope Ruiz, who finds himself provoked in a situation similar to Sancho's.

Sancho reproduces his own scene in distorted, highlighted miniature, and as we listen to his protagonist come to grips with his dilemma, we smile and perhaps we laugh, well before Don Quixote interrupts the narrative. This pleasure, which we must distinguish from that other caused by the subsequent interruption, is not the consequence of a judgment of our superiority over Lope. We confess we would want to act, not when we were young but today, in Lope's situation pretty much as he acts. Lope is not risible; he is admirable. We laugh because of the nature of his bind: "We are here extracting the comic from the relation of human beings to the often overpowerful external world" (*Jokes* 196).

The act of comparison that Freud maintains is indispensable for the generation of comic pleasure contrasts in this instance not inside and outside perspectives (Lope's expenditure in the tale and our calculation of our own outside) but before and after: the expectation of the high-minded Lope, who is determined to get away from it all, runs up against the flood-bound Lope's discovery that his clean gesture of renunciation and renewal at the river bank must be enacted three hundred times, losing through mechanization its honorable simplicity and its efficiency. Superior and unaccountable forces unleashed in the external world force Lope (as others force Sancho) into an indecisive tactic of withdrawal, as constrained as Sancho's impasse which prevents him from moving to and fro, where vacillation—back and forth over the flood—provides evidence of decisive and virtuous character (while the immobilized Sancho marshalls in his imagination resources for his own defense and, as we shall see, for offense).

A small paradox arises from within Sancho's story, cautioning us not to laugh off the story as simply comic. We are amused by Sancho and his way of confronting a comic situation, but we do not laugh at Lope and his way. Out of his fear Sancho has created a character who bears up with dignity against indignities behind him and before him, against Torralba's unmanageable infidelity and the incontestable indifference of the flooded external world. To create a worthy character out of himself (and not out of folklore) in such circumstances is a telling indication that Sancho Panza contains more within him than failed humor, the typical traits of a comic character—and constricting bowels.

The Joke

Don Quixote's enthusiasm for literature and its criticism exceeds his judgment. We do not accept all of his assessments. His analysis of Sancho's story assumes the narrator's naïveté; the pleasure he is prepared to receive is the sort produced by the naive, which both depends on and nourishes a sense of the beholder's superiority. By limiting his expectations (and inducing readers to limit our own), Don Quixote cuts himself (and many readers) off from truths I propose we now consider.

Sancho's story is at heart a bad joke. It is a joke Don Quixote misses, a joke on Don Quixote, disguised technically so that the censoring authority of the story's third person, its receiver, will not take offense and suppress thoughts that ought not to be uttered. At the moment when the comic story is interrupted, to the everlasting frustration of its receiver, the joke is in fact made and finished and ready for the appreciation of Cervantes's receivers, his readers. The unconventional ending is beyond the comprehension of Don Quixote, who proves once again to be a poor judge of the relation of literary forms to the rest of his reality. Taking up our places alongside Don Quixote as virtual third persons, let us consider what eluded him, which is Sancho's jokework and the pleasure we imagine Sancho derived from it. We learn that Sancho's joke works unusually, radiating implications from its second person that contaminate his third person. We are led to conclude that Sancho's story is a bad joke in the therapeutic sense that Sancho as joke maker gets little pleasure from it, derives little relief and satisfaction from his expenditure of words, and so must have recourse finally to other mechanisms for venting his anxiety.

"Where argument tries to draw the hearer's criticism over on to its side," Freud claims, "the joke endeavors to push the criticism out of sight" (*Jokes* 133). Sancho begins his defense against the obscure and noisy enemy by arguing at remarkable length with his protector.[9] He reasons explicitly and critically against Don Quixote's enterprise, maintaining that flight from the scene is appropriate and honorable. But that reasoning and allied arguments fail to win the receiver over to Sancho's side. With a donkey's halter Sancho secures a stay of execution and then tells an endless comic story that—we are now ready to see—conceals within it, pushed out of sight, similar and additional criticism that Sancho could never speak straightforwardly.

The comic and jokes operate in fundamentally different ways. One discovers the comic in a second person, where it is begotten, not made; a third person, unnecessary to the making, partakes of the comic by means of empathy and comparison. As Freud explains in economic metaphors, one puts oneself into the mental process of the second person (of Lope at the bank, for example) and calculates the difference of expenditure between oneself and the other in meeting the demands of the situation. The savings effected from one's comparison with the second person is "the economy in expenditure which we discharge by laughing" (*Jokes* 186–87). Jokes, by contrast, do not promote empathy. The second person (Torralba in the present ex-pample) is rather the object of an attack staged by the first person, to whom the joke occurs and who does not discover the joke in the second but instead makes a joke of the second, and invites a third person to share the profit of this expenditure. The joke, Freud concluded from his evidence, is always tendentious.

There is no necessary relation between the comic and the joke,

---

9. Sancho's weepy and windy discourse is his longest to this point. Howard Mancing gives "this extraordinary passage," Sancho's "most sophisticated and rhetorical speech," the attention it merits, and counts Sancho's words for us, in *The Chivalric World of "Don Quijote": Style, Structure, and Narrative Technique* (Columbia: University of Missouri Press, 1982), 72–78. The squire's third-longest discourse is the story of Lope Ruiz and Torralba. The coincidence of two of the three longest in this chapter is compelling evidence of its importance in the representation of Sancho Panza.

though frequently they are found together. Not uncommonly a joke makes use of the comic as a mask or facade to "dazzle the examining eye" (*Jokes* 106), attracting attention away from the locus of tendentious thoughts and concealing even the suspicion that something forbidden is being concocted. This comic pretense is present in Sancho's tale, and we have uncovered part of its mechanics of diversion; we have studied a mask without knowing it was that. Our analysis and readers' recollections generally have tended to gather at the extremes of the tale: at the river bank, where Lope confronts the comic situation, and at the taxingly overwrought beginning of the tale. What lies between is easily slighted in memory and interpretation. How many readers recall the story (which Sancho claims he is merely drawing from the familiar stores of the community's common memory) well enough to pass it on? How many recall even the lovers' names? Sancho draws our attention away from the cause of their falling out, simply asserting that Torralba misbehaved and that the community and Lope rejected her. He draws back also from analyzing the contents of Torralba's knapsack, after seeding prejudicial evidence in it, and leaves her defamed ("según malas lenguas [according to gossip]," "según es fama [as is commonly known]"), her case closed to further inquiry. Just what is it that Sancho, short-circuiting our curiosity and his own story, chooses not to get into? After such a deliberate opening, why does the narrator undertake a breathless rush to the river bank, where so little will transpire?

We have seen already that Lope Ruiz is a representation of Sancho Panza. The former's rejection of his fickle beloved and his narrator's haste to reach and cross the watery frontier put a comic face on Sancho's longing to flee his own present scene and to legitimize his flight. Sancho has attempted self-justification in his first lengthy and argumentive discourse, and what comes out is slimy casuistry: "Aquí *no nos vee* nadie, bien podemos torcer el camino [*Nobody can see us here, we can easily turn back*]" (emphasis added). In the story's revision of this argument, Lope does not "torcer el camino": virtuous and buttressed by his community and our third-person empathy, he pushes in bright daylight directly for the border of respectability. Lope straightens out the knotted defensiveness Sancho has demonstrated in thought, word, and deed.

Sancho's identification with Lope, the intimate companionship of Sancho and Don Quixote, and the shattered intimacy of Lope and Torralba inevitably invite our recognition of the fourth relation of likeness among these four beings. I touched on this earlier: Torralba is Don

Quixote.[10] She is manly, mustachioed, and incorrigible; what is more, she has the name for the job. Alonso Quijano crafted his own name by pretentious (and potentially ridiculous) appropriation of the name of a piece of armor for protecting a knight's manliness.[11] Sancho, provoked to create a femme fatale who fascinates and betrays his alter ego Lope, gives her a name formed from nouns of feminine gender that represent spatial and temporal defenses against his acute anxiety: *torre* and *alba*. The exposed Sancho longs for nothing more than a shield against the noisy night fiend, and what protection is close to hand? Only that self-proclaimed tower of strength to which he now clings like ivy to the wall. (Perhaps the image of a *torre albarrana*—a term for a bulwark built into fortified walls—has sprung to vulnerable Sancho's mind.) What other protection does Sancho desire so intensely that he lies in order to summon it? Dawn, which he has heard Don Quixote personify and embellish as a companionable feminine consort whose reassuring laugh will signal the end of this emergency.[12] Anxious Sancho, who has heard his first eloquent arguments glance off his master's armor and feels time, measured by the dreadful pounding, grinding oh so slowly, condenses his resentment of his indifferent protectors (an im-mobilized knight and a dilatory daybreak) into the hybrid name and being of Torralba, who stumbles under the burden she is made to carry. She conducts her affairs not with Dawn's radiant purity but lewdly, and proves so unworthy of that new and true tower of respect-ability Lope Ruiz that, always grasping after him, she is forever denied his redemptive embrace.

The composition of Torralba's name exemplifies the duplicity of speech that Freud regarded as a distinguishing characteristic of jokes (*Jokes* 171).[13] The name's principal significance, however, results from

10. The four are two pairs, and the two ways of pairing them represent the common senses of the term *alter ego*: (1) Sancho and Don Quixote are inseparable friends, constant companions, and (2) Sancho in Lope and Don Quixote in Torralba show another side of themselves, a complementary self.

11. Alonso devotes a week to crafting a composite name (his surname root *quix-* plus the augmentative suffix *-ote*) that elevated his new self into comparability with the Spanish Lancelot (*lanza[r]* plus *-ote*). The latter's name flaunts his phallic assertiveness; the former's protects its bearer's inadequacy under cover.

12. Moments before Sancho names Torralba, Don Quixote vows to wait through the night "*a que ría el alba, aunque yo llore lo que ella tardare en venir* [until dawn laughs, though I may weep all the while *she* delays her coming]" (emphasis added). Sancho and Don Quixote, locked in embrace, reverse the valence that dawn's arrival has in the lyric *albas*, where early light interrupts truant lovers' precious moments of bliss.

13. This duplicity corresponds rigorously to the work of condensation that produces neo-logisms in dreams; see on this point Freud's *Interpretation of Dreams*, 330.

its role as the signal of a comprehensive process of displacement of meanings through which Sancho finds it possible to tell a story that is duplicitous not in the antagonist's name alone but *grosso modo*.

Representation by the opposite is Sancho's master strategy, as it is often in jokes and oftener still in dreams (*Jokes* 173–74). The knight who is no knight to his squire is made into a lady who is no lady to her suitor. The knight professed to be chaste and faithful to Dulcinea, to his code, and to his squire; the lady is wanton, devil-may-care, habitually trespassing. As for Sancho and his other self, the former is afraid to leave his master and feels ashamed of his fear, while his opposite number, Lope, is the competent master of his fate whose flight signifies and preserves his honor. Torralba has degraded her love and lost Lope's regard by doing the devil's work; similarly Sancho's intimate companion, whom he is at present embracing, would abandon him to consort with a heavy-breathing dark invader, and so would earn his friend's resentment. There is an element of revenge as well as of displacement (for the purpose of disguise) in the teller's switching the center of attention from the deformed Don Quixote that is Torralba to the improved Sancho that is Lope Ruiz. Lope/Sancho is the hero by virtue of his divorce from Torralba/Don Quixote; scandalized by her conduct, he breaks off a relationship with a companion who has encumbered his honor, goodness, and prosperity. He knows how to act, and when he flies, we are induced to follow, in sympathy, to the river bank, and to share concern for his double bind. We are satisfied that he has left his lady/master behind to be punished by gossip and to struggle, unshod, against the double presumption of guilt and hypocrisy.

An overly systematic representation by opposition might give Sancho away to his censor. A lucid set of equivalents could be read as irony and would risk giving its receiver its message to understand. Sancho sees to it, as joke makers must, that his story is sufficiently distorted to resist easy deciphering. The required distortion is achieved first in the joke's comic facade. Initially Sancho draws attention away from the relationship of Lope and Torralba by gathering attention to himself as narrator. He tells a traditional tale in the traditional way, he avers; but he is so deliberately mannered a narrator that the narration itself captures Don Quixote's attention and ours. We might not suspect that anything devious could be masked behind such ineptitude, but it happens that Sancho is gaining strategic advantage from this start, "distracting attention by putting forward something in the joke's form of expression which catches it, so that in the meantime the liberation of the inhibitory cathexis and its discharge may be completed without interruption" (*Jokes* 152). These wrinkles in the fabric of the narrative and the unkempt narrator's awkwardness are enough to dissuade an impatient, inattentive receiver (Don Quixote or his reader) from suspecting that there could be design and significance in certain omissions that appear to rob the tale, once it has got under way—of motivational profundity. The first such omission is Sancho's refusal to detail the cause of the degeneration of Lope's love into hate and rejection. Sancho masks the cause but simultaneously flags the omission with censorious references to gossip, Lope's grounds for jealousy, and Torralba's unspecified transgressions. There follows a related ellipsis when the teller condemns Torralba, by allusion, and refuses to spend (implicitly to waste) the time required to weigh the incriminating erotic evidence she carries like a weight of guilt in "unas alforjas al cuello [a knapsack about her neck]."

The comic facade's finale most cleverly disguises and serves the joke's hidden interests. It displaces the receiver's attention, and ours, further from the story's main matter onto the surprising and untidy denouement with its easy (though incomplete) discharge of seemingly innocent, comic laughter. Concerning the process of displacement in general, Freud notes: "Its essence lies in the diversion of the train of thought, the displacement of the psychical emphasis on to a topic other than the opening one" (*Jokes* 51). Freud's term for this particular kind of distraction, the kind that anticipates and assists the joke by means of an accessory comic discharge, is piercingly appropriate: "The comic is here operating exactly like a bribing fore-pleasure" (*Jokes* 152–53). The illegitimacy and aggressiveness connoted by "bribing" are appropriately ascribed to the joke, which is tendentious by nature, and to joke work, which is a devious undertaking often facilitated under cover of the comic.

Bribing the receiver is no secondary consideration of a joke, to be accomplished adequately by comic pleasure alone. A joke, Freud holds, is essentially an attenuated and socialized form of brutal hostility which, by suppressing unruly impulses and angry feelings, functions as a tolerable form of invective for enlisting the cooperation of a third person against a common other (*Jokes* 103). "A joke will allow us to exploit something ridiculous in our enemy which we could not, on account of obstacles in the way, bring forward openly or consciously. . . . It will further bribe the hearer with its yield of pleasure into taking sides with us without any very close investigation." The joke, so understood, is Janus-like and two-faced (*Jokes* 214 and passim); it is directed to appeasing the receiver's consciousness, which nonetheless may be stumped by what it takes to be nonsense, while on another level it appeals to the unconscious. There its sense is completed in such a way as to give pleasure without surrendering to rational understanding and criticism, except perhaps after analysis. Sancho's joke work conforms to this model of double-dealing and roundabout exploitative ridicule. But in this instance the joke maker works with a highly unusual double motive for masking from consciousness the significance of his protagonist's rejection of his admirer. His double motive finally hobbles Sancho; it is directly linked to the failure of Sancho's story. I mean the failure for Sancho, of course; that charge cannot be redirected toward the author who makes of his teller's failings such a hilarious success story.

Let us now complete the discovery of Sancho's tendentiousness and the contradictions raised in its expression. By means of allusions, ellipses, and the diversion of attention to the finale, Sancho attacks his tale's female lead and shields his deed from inspection. Torralba is discredited and morally isolated, and the story's receiver is commissioned to assist in the symbolic savaging: Don Quixote acquiesces in the disparagement of Torralba and even broadens the attack by charging her with generic inferiority ("Esa es natural condición de mujeres [That is the natural condition of women]"). The "true identity" of Torralba goes without saying; the third person cannot be permitted an awareness of his identification with the harlot he has demeaned. The story moves on to the river bank, but this central point of the joke remains incomprehensible to Don Quixote, hidden beneath his shallow understanding of Torralba's character.

It is normal for a joke to work without calling on its receiver's rational awareness. What is unusual in Sancho's joke is the relation the teller establishes between his second person (his object, Torralba) and the third (his receiver), and consequently between the third and the first (the teller). There exist many witty stories in which the teller jokes about an "us." Freud's Jewish jokes are of this kind, punishing with ridicule a part of "us" that "we" own up to. More common and often less discomforting to "our" sense of superiority are the jokes "we" tell about "them": WASP jokes about Catholics, or about Jews, say, and many less aggressive characterizations of diverse others. Far less common and more hazardous to "us" are jokes that an exclusively defined "we" (in the extreme, you and I alone, the minimum complement required to undertake a conspiracy or to tell a joke) tell about "you." When the joke's object is defined not as different from "our" kind but rather as of the same kind as the receiver, the bond thereby asserted between the receiver and the object puts the bond linking the teller and the receiver (on which the existence of the joke depends) to the maximum test. Equally tested in these rare instances is the tolerance of the receiver, who is faced with the teller's assertion that the target of their aggressive cooperation is none other than that same receiver of the joke. The claim is paradoxical: the first person needs an unattainable measure of cooperation in order to claim that the first and third are a "we" while conforming the second and third into a ridiculous "them."

This unusually personal and alienating claim is the one Sancho creates by telling a joke to Don Quixote about Don Quixote. Sancho takes appropriate measures to protect himself and his working relation to his third person: he distorts, he omits, but first of all he claims that his tale is not his at all but "ours" in the most impersonal and comprehensive sense, a folktale passed down from our kind and passed along among our kind. Sancho implies he is merely a link in a chain of transmitters; Don Quixote as receiver becomes another link, whereupon they become effectively alike. This impersonalizing ruse fools Don Quixote, who therefore sees nothing personal, nothing of himself, in Torralba. She is, her mustache notwithstanding, just another one of "them," a fickle female.

Sancho's identification of Don Quixote with Torralba, disguised in these several ways, is hostile in the extreme: Don Quixote's sex is altered, his values are prostituted, he is isolated and abandoned, he is made laughable. This attack, launched parabolically, sails over Don Quixote's head; but later in this same chapter Sancho scores a hit to Don Quixote's nose with another, foul-smelling missile, and later yet another hit to his ears with his greatly offensive mimicking words of mockery. Don Quixote hits back, on his squire's shoulders and with punishing verbal blows to the ears. Beneath this apparent comedy a tense joking relationship between Sancho and Don Quixote persists, manifested indirectly but with sufficient pattern to permit its discovery and study.

Sancho cannot contain his aggressive feelings; he expresses them—but not to Don Quixote—in his joke. He formulates them in a second way, more directly, in the ending of his story, in what amounts to a second paradox. The story ends prematurely, to the frustration of Don Quixote, and the cause of his frustration is none other than Don Quixote himself. Sancho assigns him a simple accounting role and gives him fair warning of its significance. The teller punishes his inattentive receiver and coauthor for his irresponsibility in allowing the count to fail. As Lope shows his superiority over Torralba, so does Sancho show his over Don Quixote: he mocks his master's memory lapse and, what is meaner, he claims for the untold tale and for himself "mucha virtud y contento [much virtue and satisfaction]." Torralba and Don Quixote are sentenced to remain forever and comparably frustrated, *desvirtuados, descontentos.*

If readers have wondered why Sancho drew this story from his bag rather than a more prolix piece of folklore, the answer is now evident: Sancho chose and refashioned his tale for the purpose of symbolic humiliation of his master, whom he makes his target both within the story and in his way of telling the story. "Simple" Sancho finds the means to punish his master twice over, remotely by representing him in the form of the discredited Magdalen Torralba and directly by promising and then withholding Don Quixote's favorite gratification, the pleasure of literature. In revealing its pointlessness, Sancho's story achieves its point and completes its work as a "take-in," a catch tale, one of those jokes that "give the person who tells them a certain amount of pleasure in misleading and annoying his hearer" (*Jokes* 138n.–139n.). In content and then again in nonsensical form the story serves interests that Sancho could not know fully and could not in any case declare to the companion he is symbolically mistreating— even as he hugs him—in payment for mistreatment received. Sancho has transposed the senseless pounding that is causing him such acute anxiety into the measured dignity of Lope Ruiz and the degradation of Torralba, which in its way amounts to a hostile pounding of Don Quixote.

IV

The Other's Story:
Interpolation
and Disruption

8

In Marcela's Case

Ruth Anthony El Saffar

If you want to know more about femininity, enquire from
your own experiences of life, or turn to the poets.

—Sigmund Freud, "Femininity"

The case of Marcela, a woman who declares her right to live beyond
the confines of the patriarchally constructed world into which she
was born, has stirred a storm of critical controversy, much of it surprisingly—or perhaps not so surprisingly—gender-inflected. In this
essay I explore some of the dimensions of the controversy that centers
on Marcela's role in *Don Quixote* before reflecting on issues of female
psychology that Marcela's presence in the novel invokes. I begin,
however, with a brief discussion of Marcela herself as she figures in
the interpolated tale that occupies chapters 12 through 14 of *Don
Quixote*, part I.

MARCELA

The first of five interpolated tales in *Don Quixote*, part I, the story
that involves Marcela so intensely draws those who want to know
more about her into a thicket as forbidding and impenetrable as that
into which she herself disappears. Like Gelasia of Cervantes's pastoral
romance *La Galatea*, Marcela is a woman who is loved but does not
love. In contrast to the "mujer esquiva [elusive woman]" of the Spanish *comedia*, Marcela succeeds in eluding the usual alternatives of
marriage or the convent prescribed for women of her social class.[1]

---

1. For a sense of how rare it was for a young maiden to escape from a marriage she sought
to avoid, see Melveena McKendrick's study of the *mujer esquiva* tradition in the Spanish
comedia in *Woman and Society in the Spanish Drama of the Golden Age* (Cambridge: Cambridge

Declaring her refusal to submit ("No gusto de sujetarme [I have no wish for subjugation]" [I.14]), Marcela justifies, on the grounds of her right to freedom, her rejection of all suitors, including the shepherd Grisóstomo, who has died for love of her. After her ringing speech in her own defense at his funeral, she returns to her preferred dwelling deep in the mountains, never to be heard from again.[2]

The rough sierras which Marcela makes her home are inhospitable to the men who enter them to seek her out. Drawn to a beauty that is at home only in the wilds, the men who desire Marcela meet, in the places where she lives, not her receptivity but their own madness and death. Any analysis of her case must take into account not only Marcela's refusal to mirror back the desire men express for her but also their desperate insistence that she do so. For Grisóstomo is not alone in desiring Marcela. The narrator describes a kind of bedlam in the mountains where she seeks freedom: "Aquí suspira un pastor, allí se queja otro; acullá se oyen amorosas canciones, acá desesperadas endechas [here one shepherd sighs; there another moans; from the distance you can hear songs of love; from near at hand dirges of despair]" (I.12). The number of men afflicted by desire for Marcela suggests that Grisóstomo represents only the most extreme case of a general cultural phenomenon.

Marcela thrives where madness, outlawry, desire, and rage, repressed in approved social discourse, find their home.[3] Her realm

---

University Press, 1974). The elusive woman, a favorite theme in Spanish theater, serves only to heighten the excitement of a drama that centers on the inevitability of the woman's eventual defeat.

2. Criticism on Marcela's speech divides fascinatingly along gender lines. Herman Iventosch is alone among male critics in reacting favorably to Marcela's claim for freedom. See his "Cervantes and Courtly Love: The Grisóstomo-Marcela Episode of *Don Quijote*," *PMLA* 89 (1974): 71. All other studies supporting Marcela are by women. Ann Wiltrout, for example, removes from Marcela all blame for Grisóstomo's death ("De ninguna manera se le puede culpar del desastroso fin de su enamorado [In no way can she be blamed for her suitor's disastrous end]"); see "Las mujeres del *Quijote*," *Anales cervantinos* 12 (1973): 169. Mary Mackey lauds Marcela for her rhetorical sophistication in her speech on freedom in "Rhetoric and Characterization in *Don Quijote*," *Hispanic Review* 42 (1974): 51–66, as does Elvira Macht de Vera, who praises the speech as a discourse on female freedom in "Indagación en los personajes de Cervantes: Marcela o la libertad," *Explicación de textos literarios* 31 (1984–85): 7. Adrienne Munich reads Marcela as an escape from a system designed to capture and silence women in "Notorious Signs, Feminist Criticism, and Literary Traditions," in *Making a Difference: Feminist Literary Criticism*, ed. Gayle Green and Coppelia Kahn (New York: Methuen, 1985), 138–59. Yvonne Jehensen sees Marcela's speech as undercutting all the conventional expectations, turning her from "an object of their [the male characters'] imagination" to "absolute subject," in "The Pastoral Episode in Cervantes' *Don Quijote*: Marcela Once Again," *Cervantes* 10 (1990): 26.

3. Part I of *Don Quixote* abounds in examples. In the sierras the shepherds clamor for Marcela (I.12); Grisóstomo commits suicide (I.14); Rocinante attemps a sexual encounter with some mares (I.15); galley slaves escape their chains (I.22); Cardenio lives as a savage (I.23);

proves dangerous and disorienting to the men who follow her there.[4] The exclusively female space Marcela occupies ("La conversación honesta de las zagalas destas aldeas me entretiene [I enjoy the modest company of the village shepherdesses]" [I.14]) and its implied harmony with nature ("Tienen mis deseos por término estas montañas, y si de aquí salen, es a contemplar la hermosura del cielo, pasos con que camina el alma a su morada primera [My desires are bounded by these mountains; and if they extend beyond them, it is to contemplate the beauty of the sky, a step by which the soul travels to its first abode]" [I.14]) have proved exasperating not only to shepherds desperate to gain access to Marcela but to critics as well.[5]

Don Quixote strips from the waist down and does somersaults to prove his love for Dulcinea (I.25); the curate imagines dressing as a damsel in distress (I.28); and the seduced and abandoned Dorotea, dressed as a man, kills the servant who tried to rape her as she pursues her false lover (I.28).

4. Many of the critics who condemn Marcela do so because of the disturbance her allure produces. See, for example, Peter Dunn, who notes: "We might say that for man to indulge his nostalgia for the state of nature is to desert the state of grace. Or, on a less purely theological plane, that those men and women who became shepherds and shepherdesses for the sake of love, abandoning their husbandry and social ties and duties, forgot the true relation of art to life," in "Two Classical Myths in Don Quijote," Renaissance and Reformation 9 (1972): 3–4; or Cesáreo Bandera: "Hay algo de Satánico, de auténticamente demoniaco en esa luminosa aparición de Marcela por encima de todos los concurrentes y como presidiendo con un gesto de suprema indiferencia la trágica escena del entierro de su víctima [There's something satanic, authentically demonic, in that luminous apparition of Marcela above all the spectators and as if presiding with a gesture of supreme indifference over the tragic scene of her victim's burial]," in Mimesis conflictiva (Madrid: Gredos, 1975): 95; or Harry Sieber: "Marcela finishes her speech and disappears into 'lo más cerrado de un monte que allí cerca estaba [the most enclosed part of a nearby wilderness].' The word cerrado also alludes to Marcela's closed mind and world, a world of madness," in "Society and Pastoral Vision in the Marcela-Grisóstomo Episode of Don Quijote," Estudios literarios de hispanistas norteamericanos dedicados a Helmut Hatzfeld, ed. José M. Solá-Solé et al. (Barcelona: Hispam, 1974), 194.

5. Renato Poggioli, for example, accusing Marcela of self-love, argues that Marcela "treats her far less carnal but no less profane passion as if it were a form of sacred love," in The Oaten Flute: Essays on Pastoral Poetry and the Pastoral Ideal (Cambridge: Harvard University Press, 1975), 174. Michael McGaha charges Marcela with insensitivity ("a modicum of humanity and respect for the man who killed himself out of love for her would surely have compelled her to keep silence") in "The Sources and Meaning of the Grisóstomo-Marcela Episode in the 1605 Quijote," Anales cervantinos 16 (1977): 34. Thomas Hart and Steven Randall also find Marcela lacking in charitable impulses in "Rhetoric and Persuasion in Marcela's Address to the Shepherds," Hispanic Review 46 (1978): 292. They suggest that Marcela, in rejecting marriage, is rejecting society itself (290). Harry Sieber finds Marcela's move to the countryside destructive to humanity. He notes that "her refusal to place her social identity outside her pastoral role does not negate her responsibility and existence in history and society" in "Society and Pastoral Vision," 191. Carlos Varo impugns Marcela's supposed purity; comparing her with Virgil's Camila, he says: "Ambas tienen una estima excesivamente racionalizada y sospechosa de la virginidad [The two of them have an excessively rationalized and suspicious estimation of virginity]," in "Marcela y Grisóstomo," in Génesis y evolución del "Quijote" (Madrid: Ediciones Alcalá, 1986), 178. Javier Herrero sees her as an "instrument of the demon of love [who] charms and poisons his [Grisóstomo's] soul," in "Arcadia's Inferno: Cervantes' Attack on Pastoral," Bulletin of Hispanic Studies 55 (1978): 196.

Issues of sexual politics, as well as of deep psychological pain are clearly stirred in the image of a female figure who claims an autonomy that requires no support from men or from the social order. Pursuing Marcela's case means entering into a territory hedged around with silence and repression, as she opens us up into an area poorly described by classical psychoanalysis and avoided by the prescriptions that define feminine behavior. In order to approach Marcela and the deep-seated conflicts between men and women which her presence evokes, it is necessary to begin with an excursis into mythology.

ARCHETYPAL AFFILIATIONS

The archetypal perspective with which I begin this inquiry into the nature of Marcela is intended to reveal a psychic pattern that has a history deeper than that of the particular individual. To insist on Marcela's individuality or pathology would be to miss the echoes of her character type present in figures already outlined in Greek and Roman mythology.[6] The Marcela who prefers the "conversación honesta de las zagalas," like the Grisóstomo who experiences a psychic dismemberment by inner wild beasts when Marcela rejects him, have counterparts in the figures of Diana and Actaeon as Ovid portrayed them in book 3 of the *Metamorphoses*. In Ovid's telling, Actaeon on the hunt strays into the area where Diana is bathing with her nymphs. Infuriated by his uninvited gaze, Diana flings water in his face. Where the drops fall, horns emerge, and soon Actaeon has been transformed into a stag whom his hounds attack. Both Cervantes and Ovid dis-

---

6. A criticism often made of archetypal psychology is that in its recourse to mythology it supposes eternal personality types that are impervious to the shaping factors of personal history and the impact of time, place, and economic and social factors. My references to Artemis and the Great Mother are intended to show a conditioning that is a response to the pervasive impact of father god and sky god rule on the lives of women and on the patterns of female response. Studies by Robert Graves, *The Greek Myths* (Middlesex, England: Penguin Books, 1961); Charlene Spretnak, *Lost Goddesses of Early Greece* (Boston: Beacon Press, 1984); Jane Ellen Harrison, *Myths of Greece and Rome* (London: Ernest Benn, 1927); and Marija Gimbutas, *The Goddesses and Gods of Old Europe: Myths and Cult Images* (Berkeley: University of California Press, 1989), suggest that the images of gods and goddesses recorded in Greek mythology already reflected the usurpation of goddess-worshiping cultures by the Zeus-centered Indo-Europeans. Thus, patterns such as those described by Hera or Persephone or Artemis are patterns that reflect on patriarchal structures of the psyche. They are therefore, these gods and goddesses, images of our pathologies, drawn in terms that embrace not just the individual but the culture as a whole. The gods, as Carl Jung has noted, "have become diseases"; see "Commentary on the 'Secret of the Golden Flower,' " in *Alchemical Studies: The Collected Works of C. G. Jung*, ed. Herbert Read, Michael Fordham, and Gerhard Adler (New York: Pantheon, 1953–79), 13:37.

guise the murderous nature of the desired woman by linking the lovers' deaths to their own destructive qualities. The Greek goddess Artemis from whom Diana descends, however, much more obviously combines attributes of beauty with an active desire to kill. It is worth exploring in a little more detail the characteristics of Artemis because a sense of her complexity sheds light on what has so confounded critics when approaching Marcela.

Artemis, goddess of the moon and twin of the sun god Apollo, is associated with hunting, chastity and childbirth. Only a few hours old, Artemis helped her mother, Leto, give birth to her twin brother, Apollo. Although the moon goddess herself remained fiercely virgin, the stories of her infancy made her the patroness of midwives in the popular imagination. That "strange, disquieting savagery" that Karl Kerenyi finds in Artemis has to do with her role not only in helping but also in killing women in childbirth.[7] In the Homeric hymn to her, Artemis' bloodlust is even more evident. While presenting Artemis as capable of enjoying with Apollo "the grass country," Delphi, where she goes and "arranges a chorus of Graces and Muses," the poet also shows her at home "in the wind on mountain-tops," where "she darts in and out everywhere . . . killing all kinds of animals."[8] Artemis, like Diana, clearly has a dual aspect that involves death as well as beauty.

Cervantes's Marcela, who appears as "una maravillosa visión [a marvellous vision]" (I.14) atop the very peak at the bottom of which lies Grisóstomo's dead body, belongs to the same constellation of psychic energies that informed the Greek conception of Artemis and Ovid's depiction of Diana. Like her Greek and Roman antecedents, Marcela represents a dual goddess whose beauty is associated with death. Her very name, as Dominique Reyre points out in her onomastic study of *Don Quixote*, supports the "pastora homicida [homicidal shepherdess]" (I.13) epithet the shepherds have attached to her.[9]

Marcela's coldheartedness has received ample commentary. Echoing the condemnation of the goatherds, Grisóstomo's friend Ambrosio asks, when Marcela appears at the funeral, "'¿Vienes a ver, por

7. Karl Kerenyi, *Goddesses of the Sun and Moon* (Dallas: Spring Publications, 1979), 42.

8. *The Homeric Hymns*, trans. Charles Boer (Dallas: Spring Publications, 1970), 4–5.

9. Associating the prefix *mar-* with the god of war, Mars, Dominique Reyre adds that "ce prénom est toujours porté par des femmes génératrices de conflit [this pronoun is always used for women who generate conflict]," in *Dictionnaire des noms des personnages du 'Don Quichotte' de Cervantes* (Paris: Editions Hispaniques, 1980), 91. Since Artemis is, among other things, a warrior goddess, the name that affiliates her female surrogate with Mars is especially appropriate.

ventura, ¡oh fiero basilisco destas montañas!, si con tu presencia vier-
ten sangre las heridas deste miserable a quien tu crueldad quitó la
vida? [Have you come here, perhaps, fiery basilisk of these mountains, to see if the wounds of this wretch, whom your cruelty killed,
will bleed at the sight of you?]" (I.14). Critics have tended, as I have
already noted, to follow suit in blaming Marcela for Grisostomo's
demise.

Only Peter Dunn and Herman Iventosch have noted the archetypal
underpinning of Marcela's characterization, Dunn relating her to
Diana-Hecate and Iventosch to Diana and the pastoral topos of freedom.[10] Unless Marcela is recognized as the expression of a pattern
long since familiar in depictions of female behavior, however, much
of the richness of her appearance gets lost in gender-based responses
that perpetuate the atmosphere of conflict that has long characterized
relations between men and women. Marcela's connections to the
moon goddess are surprisingly well developed, and are not simply
limited to her associations with beauty and death. To trace those
connections, it is necessary to amplify on images of Artemis present
in Greek sources. The huge statue of Artemis in the Temple of Diana
at Ephesus shows her with many breasts, as the mother who feeds
all, suggesting an early affiliation of Artemis with the Great Mother.
In this guise her triple nature—maiden, mother, and crone—corresponds with the three phases of the moon. In the time of Homer,
however, the more archaic aspects of Artemis' Great Mother characterization gave way to her more sisterly, virginal aspects.

Artemis' independence allies her with the Amazons. The stories of
the Amazons may hark back to a period of struggle between sky god
and earth goddess cults, as some have contended, or they may simply
reflect periods when the oppression of women or the inner feminine
provoked a retaliative movement in an effort to restore balance.[11]
Generally, as with the story of Achilles and Penthesilea, Diana and
Actaeon, or Artemis and Orion, the gendered battles for dominance

10. See Dunn, "Two Classical Myths," 4; and Iventosch, "Cervantes and Courtly Love,"
71. Two other critics have indicated an appreciation of Marcela's unearthly, non-novelistic
qualities. Edwin Williamson notes that "she fails to emerge either as a more plausible character herself, or one wholly absolved from the taint of pastoral artifice," in "Romance and
Realism in the Interpolated Stories of the *Quijote*," *Cervantes* 2 (1982): 49. Helena Percas de
Ponseti, without associating her with a particular goddess, sees Marcela as a transpersonal
character, "superhumana," in *Cervantes y su concepto del arte: Estudio crítico de algunos aspectos
y episodios del "Quijote"* (Madrid: Gredos, 1975): 129.
11. René Malamud says of the Amazon myth that it was "an 'answer' from the central
Mediterranean archetype of the Great Mother to the arrival of the Zeus-religion of the Indo-
European invaders"; see "The Amazon Problem," in *Facing the Gods*, ed. James Hillman
(Dallas: Spring Publications, 1980), 55.

that the Amazon archetype evokes end in the death of one partner or the other. In classical Greek and in western Christian re-evocations of the Amazons, it is the women who are generally depicted as either being defeated by or submitting to their male conquerors.[12] The important point for this study is that the defeat or submission of the goddess always entails a breakup of the original triplicity of her nature, dividing the maiden from the mother, the mother from the crone, and the "good" qualities from the "bad." Traces of the original unity can still be found, however, in the beauty-death amalgam that clings to the figure of Artemis. It is an amalgam much more clearly evident in non-European female goddesses such as Isis and Kali, who remain powerful as givers of both life and death. That Cervantes would include in *Don Quixote* a figure of female power who is not forced to submit suggests that he is introducing into his works a myth that counters the Christian orthodoxy that prevailed in his time.

To support the notion that throughout the pastoral episodes of which Marcela forms a part we are in the realm of the Great Mother, we have only to refer to chapter 11, which immediately precedes the Marcela-Grisóstomo episode. There Don Quixote delivers his Golden Age speech, which reveals him as enveloped in a fantasy of the all-good mother. Although he clearly yearns for a time before the era of father dominance, Don Quixote strips the Great Mother whom he evokes of her dark side. She is all-giving but not all-powerful. Like Dulcinea, Don Quixote's maiden version of the Great Mother, she retains only those qualities that are desirable and attractive to men.[13] The mother and the maiden whom Don Quixote extols bring only peace and satisfaction, having none of the terrifying attributes of Kali, or even Artemis.

An image symptomatic of the disturbed relations between the sexes that the presence of Marcela will later stir, the mother of Don Quixote's Golden Age fantasy bears a startling resemblance to the idealized image of the mother in the mother-son dyad to which Freud sometimes alludes in his own version of paradise lost. Don Quixote says of his picture of a bygone time of plenitude: "Todo era paz entonces,

12. Herodotus, in book 4 of *The Histories*, ed. Walter Blanco and Jennifer Tolbert Roberts (New York: W. W. Norton, 1992), 123–26, imagines a form of marriage between Scythian warriors, who move from their homeland and take up Amazonian nomadic ways, and their Amazon lovers. His is one of the few stories that seek to depict a relationship between Amazonian women and warrior men, and in it the men, in order to live with the women, leave their habitual ways and their society of origin.

13. Arthur Efron, in *Don Quixote and the Dulcineated World* (Austin: University of Texas Press, 1971), has been the most explicit among recent critics of *Don Quixote* in seeing in Dulcinea a figure that represents the life- and body-denying aspects of culture.

todo amistad, todo concordia [All was peace then, all amity, all con-cord]" (I.11). The mother, then, was still a virgin: "Aún no se había atrevido la pesada reja del corvo arado a abrir ni visitar las entrañas piadosas de nuestra primera madre [The crooked plough had not yet dared to force open and search the kindly bowels of our first mother with its heavy coulter]" (I.11). Her creative energy was turned entirely to the feeding and pleasure of her sons, to whom she was exclusively devoted: "Ella, sin ser forzada, ofrecía, por todas las partes de su fértil y espacioso seno, lo que pudiese hartar, sustentar y deleitar a los hijos que entonces la poseían [For without compulsion she yielded from every part of her fertile and broad bosom everything to satisfy, sustain, and delight the children who then possessed her]" (I.11).

Expressions of this yearning for the all-good mother appear again at the end of part I, when Don Quixote unfolds the fantasy of the Knight of the Lake. In that fantasy he imagines himself in a magical place, surrounded by beautiful women whose sole object is to gratify him. The tendency to split the feminine image into all-good and all-bad parts also becomes evident when Sancho fails to attach to Don Quixote's ethereal princess Dulcinea the split-off earthiness of an Aldonza Lorenzo, who knows how to salt pork and call in the hogs (I.25). In figures such as Maritornes, the innkeeper's wife, the Duch-ess, and Altisidora, Cervantes offers images of the dark, sexual, and sometimes cruel side of the feminine which Don Quixote seeks to expunge from his consciousness.

Further evidence of the splitting of the Great Mother archetype comes even later in part I, when Don Quixote witnesses a procession of penitents who carry a statue of the Virgin in mourning as they pray for rain. The whole landscape that is Don Quixote's purview has become a wasteland in the face of continuing efforts to depoten-tiate the Mother Goddess, to strip her of her relationship to sexuality, old age, and death, and to take her as a possession.[14] It is against all of that that Artemis as Marcela resists.

The fact that Marcela appears and disappears so mysteriously, leav-ing no trace, distinguishes her from most of the other characters in

14. Carolyn Merchant, in *The Death of Nature* (London: Wildwood House, 1985), has made the case that in the sixteenth century, western Europe entered into a paradigm crisis. The old agricultural order's earth-centered view of the universe was crumbling in the face of new technologies and the discovery of the New World. The construction of a paradigm appropriate to an intellectual, mobile, dominance-based order of being required the loss of attachment to animistic views that credited Mother Earth with powers to punish and withhold. See also my essay "In Praise of What Is Left Unsaid," *MLN* 103 (1988): 205–22, for a discussion of Don Quixote's Golden Age speech with respect to the loss of connection to the notion of Earth as mother.

the novel. Her speech, however rhetorically complete, also lacks the quality of feeling that would align her as a character among characters.[15] Other hints deepen the sense that, through Marcela, Cervantes was invoking Artemis, and beyond her the Great Mother. The goatherd Pedro, through whom the story of Marcela and Grisóstomo first comes to notice, tells his listeners that Marcela's mother died giving birth to her. From the very beginning death in childbirth is linked with Marcela. So also is beauty. Pedro insists that Marcela's mother's beauty was surpassed only by that of Marcela herself.

Peculiarly, unless we have the myth of Artemis and Apollo in the back of our minds, Pedro illustrates his notion of Marcela's mother's beauty by reference to the sun and moon. He says: "No parece sino que ahora la veo, con aquella cara que del un cabo tenía el sol y del otro la luna [I can just see her now, with that face of hers, the sun on one side, as you might say, and the moon on the other]" (I.12). The Artemis who combines the solar attributes of her twin, Apollo, with her own lunar qualities is surely hiding under the surface of this description, as is the Artemis of Bauron, whose priestesses inherited the clothes of women who died in childbirth.[16] Further underscoring the death-giving qualities of the moon goddess is the fact that Marcela's father, Guillermo, when deprived of the radiance of his wife's beauty, also dies. Much as Grisóstomo will later do, Guillermo lives when the woman with the sun and moon in her face shines on him, and he dies when it is eclipsed.

Already, with only this much detail, echoes of Artemis' disguised presence can be heard by the listener attuned for her. Further details show up like Freudian slips, pushing their way into the rustic narrator's accounting of Marcela and Grisóstomo through a series of lexical errors. Don Quixote's corrections highlight the errors, all of which call attention to elements constellated in the moon goddess in her triple aspect, that is, with the sun and the moon, life and death, and old age.

In the first case Pedro refers to solar or lunar eclipses, using the word *cris*, instead of *eclipse*; speaking of Grisóstomo's knowledge of astrology, he says "puntualmente nos decía el *cris* del sol y de la luna [for he could always give accurate notice of the *crisis* of the sun and moon]" (I.12; emphasis added). The darkening of the sun and the

---

15. Thomas Hart and Steven Randall, responding to Mary Mackey's study in praise of Marcela's speech, note that "the *ethos* projected by Marcela, far from disposing her audience to find her innocent, tends to confirm the charge that she is cruel and insensitive, a proud, cold creature incapable of sympathy with others," in "Rhetoric and Persuasion," 292.

16. Kerenyi, *Goddesses*, 42.

moon, associated with the death of Marcela's mother and with all kinds of disaster, is in fact *both* an eclipse and a crisis.

When Pedro goes on to confuse *estil* (summer) with *estéril* (sterility), Don Quixote again interrupts, slowing the narration to highlight another key aspect of the moon goddess—her ability to confer or withhold reproductivity. When the goddess of the moon was not properly worshiped, not only women but also land became barren. To refuse the goddess was to dam up the energies of life and death associated with her. Finally, the conflation of *sarna* (the itch) for *Sarra* (Sarah) brings to light the aging aspect of the moon goddess, who is still capable of reproduction. Sarah, as a mother goddess of the Abraham tribe, again takes us into the purview of Artemis' realm.[17] The "negative" aspects of the goddess include darkness (eclipse), death in birth (sterility), and birth in old age (Sarah). As these are repressed in the effort to reserve of the goddess only that which pleases and supports "man," they enter discourse by "mistake," in this case as the errors of an illiterate narrator. The Great Mother, who is autonomous, indifferent to the ego and its concerns, and deeply connected to all aspects of the life course, makes her appearance in Cervantes's novel through the beautiful, death-giving Marcela, to whom men in the wilderness cry out as an infant cries out to its mother.

Psychoanalytical Indagations

At this point discussion moves from an archetypal to a psychoanalytic base. In making this move I have two purposes in mind: to seek through the insights of classical psychoanalysis another avenue for understanding Marcela's case, and to look at the ways that psychoanalysis reveals its own embeddedness in the world view that seeks to repress the negative attributes of the Great Mother. In other words, I show, in this section, the degree to which the point of view that makes Marcela unintelligible to Grisóstomo and Don Quixote is built into classical psychoanalysis as well.

The oedipal phase of psychosexual development so privileged in Freudian psychology insists on the crucial role of the father in breaking the child's symbiosis with the mother. Although depicted retrospectively as idyllic, the child's early experiences with the mother

17. Much more has been passed down through the Hebrew tradition about Abraham than about his wife, Sarah. Yet it is well known that Sarah was, at the time of her marriage to Abraham, more powerful than he, an issue discussed by Barbara Walker in *The Woman's Encyclopedia of Myths and Secrets* (San Francisco: Harper and Row, 1983), 890.

were in fact recognized by Freud himself as full of pain and frustration.[18] The contradiction between the child's actual ambivalence and psychoanalysis's "bedrock" story of the boy's undying love for the mother has not gone unnoticed by Nicolas Abraham and Maria Torok, who suggest that the Oedipus complex is "a 'story' that the child 'tells' itself . . . in accordance with the contingencies of the cultural codes already in force."[19] According to them, the child's separation from the mother is part of an inevitable process, for which the threat of castration serves only as an excuse on the child's part to break away without hurting the mother.[20] Complications in the pre-oedipal nirvana have also been exposed by Melanie Klein, whose excavations into the realm of mother-infant relations have powerfully revealed the child's conflicting passions of love and hate, bliss and rage toward the mother on whom she or he is dependent.

By any psychoanalytic account, the realm of psyche over which the mother presides is clouded with passions so powerful and so destructive that they preclude the formation of a stable self-image. The true price of culture and entry into the father's realm, as Jacques Lacan has shown in his study of identity formation in the mirror stage, is the child's "castration" from the body and embrace of the mother. The notion propagated throughout psychoanalytic theory that culture, symbolization, representation, and law require the child's repudiation of the mother, however, has radically complicated the question of female psychology. The requirement that the little girl as well as the little boy reject the mother means that the girl who grows up to be a mother experiences her deepest relationship not with her

18. Although typically he left unexamined the assumption of warmth between mother and son in the pre-oedipal period, Freud did acknowledge, late in life, and after the death of his mother, that the mother-son dyad admitted of imperfections. In "Femininity" he writes: "It might be thought indeed that this first love-relation of the child's is doomed to dissolution . . . for these early object-cathexes are regularly ambivalent to a high degree. A powerful tendency to aggressiveness is always present beside a powerful love, and the more passionately a child loves its object the more sensitive does it become to disappointments and frustrations from that object; and in the end the love must succumb to the accumulated hostility"; see The Standard Edition of the Complete Psychological Works of Sigmund Freud, ed. and trans. James Strachey, 24 vols. (London: Hogarth Press, 1953–74), 22:124. Further references to the Standard Edition will be abbreviated SE, with volume and page number. While acknowledging that the feelings could be the same in a boy as in a girl, Freud insists, leading up to the crucial point of penis envy as that which produces the girl's rejection of the mother and turn toward the father, that none of the early pain is sufficient "to alienate him [the boy child] from the maternal object" (SE 22:124).

19. Nicolas Abraham and Maria Torok, "The Shell and the Kernel," trans. Nicholas Rand, Diacritics 9 (1979): 26.

20. For a good discussion of the work of Abraham and Torok, see Esther Rashkin, "Tools for a New Psychoanalytic Literary Criticism: The Work of Abraham and Torok," Diacritics 18 (1988): 31–52.

own mother but with the boy child who figures as her consolation for being socially and physiologically inferior.[21] Lacking a grounding in her own gender, she attains what little selfhood she can by projecting her ambitions onto her son, making inevitable his later need to reject her.

The autonomy that marks mature adult male behavior requires for its expression a corresponding forfeiture of autonomy by the "mature" woman, so that "normal" femininity entails a fall into passivity and envy which represses libido, hampers the development of the capacity for moral judgement, and restricts symbolic activity.[22] Indeed, the envy that captures the developing female child when, in the phallic period, she discovers her anatomical "inferiority" is resolved, according to Freud, only through motherhood, when the desire for a penis is sublimated in the birth of a (preferably male) child. Missing in the entire description of female psychosexual development is any reference to the transgenerational bonding of mother and daughter that would ground the girl in a way of being other than the masculine from which she is excluded. It is no wonder, given the silence surrounding the transmission of knowledge from the mother, that the girl would be understood, and would understand herself, as primordially lacking.

Also accruing to female psychology as it is rendered in classical psychoanalysis are attributions of narcissism. In "Femininity"[23] Freud makes a close association between femininity and narcissism which complements his 1925 paper "On Narcissism: An Introduction." In that essay Freud gives a description of the narcissistic woman that could well apply to Marcela: "Women, especially if they grow up with good looks, develop a certain self-contentment. . . . Strictly speaking, it is only themselves that such women love with an intensity com-

21. Freud writes in "Femininity," where he develops the notion of penis envy and its sublimation: "A mother is only brought unlimited satisfaction by her relation to a son; this is altogether the most perfect, the most free from ambivalence of all human relationships. A mother can transfer to her son the ambition which she has been obliged to suppress in herself, and she can expect from him the satisfaction of all that has been left over of her masculinity complex" (SE 22:133).

22. It is no wonder that in "Femininity" Freud presented apologetically his description of "normal" femininity. Lacking any notion of the feminine aspect of the godhead or of the goddess, he could not do any better than to describe woman according to the misogynistic tradition of the Hebrew and Christian fathers. See SE 22:126–35 for a set of female characteristics that varies in no way from that tradition.

23. Freud writes: "Thus, we attribute a larger amount of narcissism to femininity, which also affects women's choice of object, so that to be loved is a stronger need for them than to love" (SE 22:132).

parable to that of a man's love for them."[24] He goes on to add, however, that "such women have the greatest fascination for men. . . . For it seems very evident that another person's narcissism has a great attraction for those who have renounced part of their own narcissism and are in search of object-love."[25]

The generality arising out of Freud's exploration of male and female narcissistic patterns is that men's narcissism tends to be object-oriented while women's narcissism is self-oriented. Bela Grunberger, seeking to explain the divergence she endorses in the differentiation of male and female modes of seeking love, makes the point that in the pre-oedipal stage female children receive far less adequate mirroring than male children. She says: "We have every reason to believe that even the most loving, most maternal mother will be *ambivalent* toward her daughter."[26] It is the relative failure of the mother to provide narcissistic confirmation to her female child, according to Grunberger, that foments the particularly alluring narcissism of the beautiful woman, a narcissism that, because it seems so successful in its self-regard, awakens the envy of men, whose dominant source of narcissistic support comes not from themselves but from another.

Surely what is being discussed here is a psychoanalytic explanation for the problem that Marcela and Grisóstomo present in Cervantes's text. Marcela is a woman who stands for the zero-degree case of mother deprivation, her mother having died giving birth to her. According to the theory of female psychology elaborated in the Freudian mode by Grunberger and Janine Chasseguet-Smirgel, the little girl

24. Freud, "On Narcissism: An Introduction," *SE* 14:88–89.
25. Ibid, 89.
26. Bela Grunberger, "Outline for a Study of Narcissism in Female Sexuality," in *Female Sexuality: New Psychoanalytic Views*, ed. Janine Chasseguet-Smirgel (London: Maresfield Library, 1985), 72. The position taken by Grunberger is supported by Chasseguet-Smirgel, who attributes the mother-daughter sexual identity to the dissatisfaction inherent in their relationship: "Indeed, the relation between mother and daughter is handicapped from the start . . . This state is due to the sexual identity between mother and daughter"; see "Feminine Guilt and the Oedipus Complex," in Chasseguet-Smirgel, *Female Sexuality: New Psychoanalytic Views*, 98. Works by American theorists such as Nancy Chodorow, *The Reproduction of Mothering: Psychoanalysis and the Sociology of Gender* (Berkeley: University of California Press, 1978); Dorothy Dinnerstein, *The Mermaid and the Minotaur: Sexual Arrangements and Human Malaise* (New York: Harper Colophon Books, 1977); Adrienne Rich, *Of Woman Born: Motherhood as Experience and Institution* (New York: Norton, 1976); Carol Gilligan, *In a Different Voice: Psychological Theory and Women's Development* (Cambridge: Harvard University Press, 1982); and Kim Chernin, *The Hungry Self: Women, Eating, and Identity* (New York: Harper & Row, 1985), attribute the "reproduction of motherhood" to a bond between mother and daughter that remains, for better or for worse, unbroken. See Marianne Hirsch, *The Mother/ Daughter Plot: Narrative, Psychoanalysis, Feminism* (Bloomington: Indiana University Press, 1989), 125–61, for a more extended discussion of the subject.

who never had a mother would have had little support for her instinctual, pre-oedipal needs, and would have sought recourse in self-oriented narcissism to make up for the mirroring she lacked. She would have grown up, as Cervantes's story indicates Marcela did, with little support for her desire for instinctual gratification. She would have grown up, in other words, lacking desire for sexual experience and unable to return the love given her by others.

Everything in Cervantes's story of Marcela furthers the image of a woman closed in upon herself which Freud identified with female narcissism, and, in effect, with female object relations in general. The fact that Marcela was raised by a celibate uncle, a priest, emphasizes the degree to which the circulation of eros in Marcela's home came under the ban of repression. Like Don Quixote, himself a celibate uncle, the priest would have idealized a totally nonsexual femininity of the kind Marcela comes to embody.[27] The priest's own ambivalence about the marriage so many young men propose for his niece is sardonically alluded to when the narrator mentions the wealth the priest enjoys as long as Marcela remains single.[28] The uncle-priest clearly prospers from Marcela's aloofness, materially but also psychologically. Unlike more openly sexual or desirous women, she wants nothing from him.

All that is lacking—and this is a crucial point—for Marcela to make the passage into "normal" femininity, femininity rooted in her being *for* a man, is for Marcela to perceive her isolation as emptiness and to project onto a man (her uncle as father-substitute) the source of her completion. Marcela cannot make that change of object love from mother to father, however, because she presumably never made the first attachment, her mother having died. Here, however, hints from other parts of *Don Quixote* can come to our aid.

If we look at other mother-deprived women in the novel, in particular the cases of Don Quixote's niece, of Zoraida, and of Leandra, what emerges is the discovery that such mother-orphaned women

27. Carroll Johnson has pointed out the similarity between the household that Don Quixote escapes, one in which a celibate uncle lives with his marriageable niece, and the one Marcela leaves; see his *Madness and Lust: A Psychoanalytic Approach to "Don Quixote"* (Berkeley: University of California Press, 1983), 95.

28. The narrator says: "El, que a las derechas es buen cristiano, aunque quisiera casarla luego, así como la veía de edad, no quiso hacerlo sin su consentimiento, sin tener ojo a la ganancia y granjería que le ofrecía el tener la hacienda de la moza dilatando su casamiento [He was a good Christian and, though he would have liked to marry her off soon, since she was of age, would not do so without her consent. Not that he had an eye to the advantage or profit that he would get from managing the girl's estate by putting off her marriage]" (I.12).

are not in fact deprived of female care. Don Quixote's niece is looked after by a housekeeper, and Zoraida was raised by a Christian slave woman. We also learn that the girls raised by mother substitutes experience mothering by women much more radically "Other" to the cultures into which they were born than their own mothers would have been. The result is that the first love of the "motherless" girls is a woman very remote from the father's world. We know in the case of Zoraida that her attachment to her Christian nursemaid has caused her to reject her father's religion and values altogether. Through Zoraida, whose idea of Christianity is devotion to Mary, "la verdadera madre de dios [the true Mother of God]" (I.40), we sense that the underclass women who serve as nursemaids have a religion closer to the goddess than the women who have married into the official, patriarchal culture. It is the combination of sensitivity to mother-lack owing to her mother's death and love for a goddess-oriented slave woman that makes Zoraida especially vulnerable to the appeal of the archetype of the Great Mother. Leandra, whose substitute mothering is not revealed, also winds up misprizing her father's values and, like Zoraida, leaves his world permanently.

We can only conjecture, on the basis on these examples, that Marcela's preference for an all-female environment is not simply a matter of hardheartedness or lovelessness. It is also an expression of the deep split she experiences between the underclass women to whom she has formed an attachment and the upper-class male to whom she never turned for affection. If she does not turn to men for affection, it may be because she has found satisfaction for her needs in the women's world and in the goddess. It is only from the point of view of the men, after all, that the girl who chooses the mother world is represented as a traitor and a monster.

The woman who puts herself out of reach, though she appears to deviate from the norm, also serves that norm. Men like Don Quixote, the priest, and Grisóstomo, who are uncertain of their own potency, can fashion the woman who asks nothing of them according to their own fantasy needs. Don Quixote explains to Sancho: "¿Piensas tú que las Amarilis, las Filis . . . y otras tales de que los libros . . . están llenos fueron verdaderamente damas de carne y hueso? No . . . sino que las más se las fingen, por dar sujeto a sus versos, y porque los tengan por enamorados o por hombres que tienen valor para serlo [Do you think that the Amaryllises, the Phyllises . . . and all the rest that books . . . are so full of were really flesh-and-blood ladies? Not a bit of it. Most of them were invented to serve as subjects of verses, and so that the poets might be taken for lovers, or men capable of being so]" (I.25). So long as her power and sexuality are blocked from view, Marcela can represent for the priest, as Dulcinea does for Don Quixote, an idealized remembrance of a woman they are in fact afraid to approach. As maiden, she will be divested of both the sexuality and the rage that a figure such as Medusa or, in sixteenth- and seventeenth-century Europe, the witch would represent. Marcela, in her idealized form, bodies forth the image of the woman as phallus, fascinating in her narcissistic autonomy. Both Freud, with his identification of women with narcissism, and Lacan, with his emphasis on the role of woman as phallus, prepare the theoretical ground for seeing Marcela in her maiden aspect, not as a perversion but rather as normative.

Freud's giving centrality in his theories of psychosexual development to the Oedipus and castration complexes created immense difficulties when it came to explaining female development, as we have seen. Having made libido masculine and little girls "little men" through the phallic stage, he had then to explain why girls could change love object (from mother to father), erogenous zone (clitoris to vagina), sexual aim (homosexual to heterosexual), and libidinous drive (active to passive). Central to his explanation is the girl's discovery of her castration, which causes her to turn from her mother and seek in her father that which would make her whole. In the process the girl goes from identification to rivalry with her mother, and enters the social order as second-best and envious. She remains in her essentially crippled form, according to Maria Torok, out of fear of her mother's envy.[29] The fictitiousness of "normal femininity" as described by Freud is seen clearly by Lacan, who in a relatively early essay noted that "it is in order to be the phallus, that is, the signifier of the desire of the Other, that the woman will reject an essential part of her femininity, notably all its attributes through masquerade. It is for what she is not that she expects to be desired as well as loved."[30]

Torok also describes the illusory nature of the struggle for identification with or possession of the phallus that marks the failure of most heterosexual relationships. She attributes to an unsurmounted fear of the mother's powers the fetishization of the penis in both boys

29. To make her point, Torok paraphrases the story of penis envy the girl invents to reassure her mother: "Idealizing the penis, in order to envy it more, is reassuring you by showing you that this will never come between us, and that consequently I shall never be reunified, I shall never fulfill myself"; see Maria Torok, "The Significance of Penis Envy in Women," in Chausseguet-Smirgel, *Female Sexuality: New Psychoanalytic Views*, 141.

30. Jacques Lacan, "The Meaning of the Phallus," in *Feminine Sexuality: Jacques Lacan and the Ecole Freudienne*, ed. Juliet Mitchell and Jacqueline Rose (New York: Norton, 1985), 84.

and girls: "If at this stage a difference appears between the two sexes it is about the possession or nonpossession (one is just as illusory as the other) of the penis-thing and its varied symbolic significance."[31] The implication, very like the idea Luce Irigaray makes explicit, is that adult sexual relations, and the psychoanalysis that describes them, is caught in the anal stage of psychosexual development.[32] Denying the existence of a true sexual Other, according to Irigaray, Freud has to struggle hard theoretically to move the girl who is a "little man" into mature motherhood. Implicit in the presence of Marcela, however, is a sense that women are in fact always already Other, something Marcela would know if she had learned from her (unmentioned) nursemaid about the mother goddess, as Zoraida learned from hers. There would be in such women, furthermore, no sense of rivalry for the father's love, since the nursemaid would not claim him, and, in the case of the priest, he would have no interest in her, either. The girl would grow up in, and want to perpetuate, a female sense of herself for which psychoanalytic theory has no accounting.

Marcela seems to have a clear sense that to accept one of the many lovers who petition her uncle for her hand in marriage, she would have to be the wealth and beauty attributed to her, in rejection of her own experience of herself. Only by a mutually agreed overvaluation of externally visible attributes could Marcela and Grisóstomo form a couple. Marcela would have to identify with the "phallus"—her wealth and beauty. Then she would share with her suitors an overvaluation (fetishization) of attributes external to her. In an illusory process of mutual projection in which each is complicit in avoiding the deeper fear of the overpowering mother, she would appear to hold what he desires, and he would appear to have what she lacks. The game of phallic overvaluation is one that Marcela cannot play, however. Deeply embedded in the world of the mother substitute, and alienated from all desire for the father, she has from the beginning lacked the "lacks" that would inscribe her in culture. Her flourishing in a world other than the world of desire in which everyone else is caught exposes as fiction the arrangements of gender by which culture

31. Torok, "The Significance of Penis Envy," 169.
32. Irigaray discusses this idea at length in *Speculum of the Other Woman*, trans. Gillian Gill (Ithaca: Cornell University Press, 1985): "The specular conditions do not work in such a way as to allow a play of couples. . . . The castration of woman, penis-envy, hatred of the mother, the little girl's despisal and rejection of her sex/organ, the end of her (masculine) auto-erotism that results, the failure to explain the evolution of her anal erotism—except in terms of a 'stunted penis"—are all signs that the appropriation of the specular, or speculative, process/ trial is a victory for (so-called) masculine sexuality" (73).

perpetuates itself. Failing to mirror the Other's desire, she brings to light the very thing that culture, with its asymmetrical sexual roles, seeks to hide: the autonomous feminine that mythology represents in figures such as the Amazons, Artemis, and the Great Mother.

The patriarchal norm that relegates "mature" femininity to the woman's desire for a penis means that it is her "destiny" to relinquish the narcissism so characteristic of women and so irritating to men when she enters adulthood.[33] Now it is possible to understand the fury—both within and outside the text—that a case such as Marcela's awakens. Marcela remains, past the age-appropriate moment, in her "narcissism," which is to say, in her place of fullness that does not ask anything of a man. Doing so, she both refuses and comments on the norms of a culture that requires women to relinquish autonomy in order to support masculine identity. Marcela goes from beautiful damsel to "pastora homicida" in the eyes of her critics at the point when she makes clear her radical indifference to the social pressures that would make her responsible for Grisóstomo's death. What looks, from the standpoint of culture, like coldness and self-regard comes instead to be seen, from the underside of Freudian analysis, as an identification with the Great Mother who has no need of culture.

The phallus remains a signifier of difference, as Maria Torok has shown, only when the repressed fear of the all-powerful mother potentiates it. When the girl sees herself as a carrier of that Great Mother power, she identifies herself as belonging to a place, not at all sentimentalized, outside male-dominated cultural systems. By standing outside those structures, Marcela exposes their failure to incorporate her, and therefore the essential lack built into gender identities which perpetuates between men and women a false sense of mutual dependence.

Grisóstomo

What remains to be considered, now that we have looked at Marcela from the point of view of the archetype underlying her characteri-

---

33. Irigaray, commenting on Freud's essay "Femininity," says of the movement of woman from maiden to mother: "Everything is for the best: woman enters into the (re)production line with not the slightest desire to retain any auto-erotic satisfaction, any narcissism, any affirmation of her own will, any wish to capitalize upon her products. The work of gestation, of childbirth, of breast-feeding, of mothering, will be carried out with 'not directly sexual trends' but with 'aim-inhibited trends of an affectionate kind.' Her only payment will be the unconscious satisfaction of finally possessing (?) a penis-equivalent"; *Speculum*, 75.

zation and the psychoanalytic efforts to explain what led to her development, is Grisóstomo's part in the game of gender-identity formation so tragically played out between him and Marcela. What in Grisóstomo draws him to Marcela? The fact that Marcela attracts scores of men suggests that men still caught in the Oedipus complex are legion in the world Cervantes depicts.[34] They follow Marcela into the wilds in response to their own antisocial impulses. What they have not counted on discovering, however, is that although in pursuing Marcela they circumvent the world of the punitive father, they expose themselves in the process to the far more terrifying world of the pre-oedipal mother.

Grisóstomo's "canción desesperada [Song of Despair]," the only piece of his writing not buried with him in his grave, reveals the inner dismemberment he underwent as he experienced Marcela's refusal to desire his desire. The feelings of vulnerability, helplessness, and abandonment that Grisóstomo's suicide poem expresses expose the side of the boy's early experience with the mother which he has repressed in order to enter culture. Grisóstomo's poem, as Herman Iventosch correctly describes it, lends itself to psychological analysis, as it outlines "the story of a soul in torment in progress toward madness and self-destruction."[35]

The dismembering process that Grisóstomo is undergoing is announced at the beginning of his poem, where he promises not order but chaos: "Escucha, pues, y presta atento oido / no al concertado son, sino al ruido [Then listen, and lend your careful ear, / Not well-constructed tunes but howling sounds to hear]" (I.14). It is the sounds of beasts that will take over—"el rugir del león, del lobo fiero / el temeroso aullido, el silbo horrendo / de escamosa serpiente [the roar of the lion, the dreadful cries / Of the wild wolf, and the terrible hiss / Of the scaly serpent]" (I.14)—as the cultured young man reverts to his inchoate prehistory. The experience Grisóstomo recounts is one of being unheard: "Allí se esparcirán mis duras penas / en altos riscos y en profundos huecos . . . desnudas del contrato humano [my cries of pain fell unheard / against the steep cliffs and hollow depths . . . unclothed by any human contact]" (I.14). He experiences the negation of his very being: "Contra un temor de olvido no aprovecha / firme esperanza de dichosa suerte [Against fear of abandonment / fond hopes of a happy end hold no sway]" (I.14).

---

34. It is the thesis of Louis Combet's *Cervantes ou les incertitudes du désir* (Lyons: Presses universitaires de France, 1981) that men exhibiting masochistic tendencies and a failure to confront the father regularly appear in principal roles throughout Cervantes's works.
35. Iventosch, "Cervantes and Courtly Love," 69.

Grisóstomo's poem shows how vulnerable is the male who ideal-izes, by repression, a time before father when his early narcissistic needs were satisfied by his mother. The mother substitute he returns to for support, however, turns out to be an illusion. She is in fact Other, and radically indifferent to him. That indifference, which is a refusal to be his lack, shatters his fragile sense of autonomy. In Gri-sóstomo's poem feelings of exposure and vulnerability are repre-sented in images of hell and of wild beasts.

The inclination to follow a figure such as Marcela and invest her with the power to support and protect is born of a weakness the pursuer already feels vis-à-vis the social structure, as we have seen. The question then arises of what the story of Grisóstomo's life before Marcela can tell us about the young man's position in his society. On the surface Grisóstomo appears to have made a very good adjustment to the social norms of his community. We are told that he returned, after years of study in Salamanca, to play an active role in his village. He turned his knowledge of astrology and his ability to write verse to good use, advising the farmers when to sow what kind of crop, and writing songs for religious festivals. He was in fact so well in-tegrated into village life that no one could understand how he could suddenly leave everything to follow Marcela into the mountains.

A small, seldom commented-on bit of information, however, may give some hint of what provoked the sudden upsurge of lunar, an-tisocial energy within him. The text reveals—in one of those uncanny details that makes even the most minor of Cervantes's characters so psychologically rich—that Grisóstomo's father had died just around the time when Grisóstomo inexplicably reversed all his former be-havior to become a shepherd. The coincidence of the death of the father and the "birth" of Marcela suggests that Grisóstomo may well have long been inclined to the antisocial, pre-oedipal realm which his attraction to Marcela would imply. Perhaps the many years in Sala-manca and the interest in astrology and poetry hint at territories at odds with the values of the father culture. Grisóstomo's scrupulous turning of those interests to the communal good may have signaled less an active enthusiasm than an acquiescence to paternal pressures. Perhaps Grisóstomo chafed at having his gifts coerced into the pat-terns and practical demands of village life, but, like Cardenio, Persiles, and so many other Cervantine male characters, he dared not take head-on the figure of masculine authority in his life. In that case, Marcela would represent a freedom suddenly available to him now that he no longer has to submit to his father's law.

If we look from a psychological point of view at the relationships

Cervantes uses to describe Grisóstomo—that is, if we take the characters who surround Grisóstomo as images of his own psyche—we
could say that the death of the father has upset the precarious balance
of forces in Grisóstomo, leaving nothing to oppose the pressure of
antisocial desire in him represented by the figure of Marcela. In the
place where the father once stood as a restraining, socializing force
is the figure of Ambrosio, who, as Grisóstomo's alter ego, lacks the
power to check the Marcela (antisocial) impulses in him. As Grisóstomo's alter ego and rival, Ambrosio can only mimic, not contain,
his friend's desire. The nonhierarchical situation the Ambrosio-
Grisóstomo relation describes is the one on which René Girard and
Cesáreo Bandera focus in their discussions of mimesis and violence.[36]
It is the world abandoned by the father principle, a world ruled by
desire rather than law.

The story that follows Grisóstomo's "liberation" from the rule of
the father is not a happy one, in seeming confirmation of Freud's
insistence on the importance of the father in the formation of culture.
Out in the wilds, Grisóstomo finds Marcela to be a dazzling mirage
who leads him on, then darts away from his increasingly desperate
grasp. Like Anselmo, and later the desperate shepherds in Eugenio's
story of Leandra (I.51), Grisóstomo has no real notion of Marcela
except as an aspect of his need, desirable and hateful by turns as he
calculates her worth according to his state of inner coherence. Thrown
into the realm of the pre-oedipal, Grisóstomo flails about in a sea of
conflicting emotions that come to feel like Actaeon's hounds tearing
him apart.

The effort of classical psychoanalysis to explain as an inevitable
norm of culture that women find fulfillment only in the mothering
of sons—and by extension of their husbands—makes understandable
the reaction Marcela elicits among her critics. Post-Freudian considerations of the theory of psychosexual development such as those by
Lacan, Torok, and Irigaray, however, have unveiled the fictional,
illusion-driven nature of the gender roles instigated in patriarchal
culture. These later theories, in one way or another, point to a realm
of feminine power and autonomy which that culture seeks to repress.
The repressed mother realm, represented mythologically in the Amazons and in Artemis, emerges in Cervantes's *Don Quixote* through
the figure of Marcela, whose motherlessness paves the way psycho-

36. René Girard, *Violence and the Sacred*, trans. Patrick Gregory (Baltimore: Johns Hopkins
University Press, 1972); Bandera, *Mimesis*.

logically for her identification with the archetype of the Great Mother. My investigation is intended to reveal that Marcela is both a symptom of Grisóstomo's lack of a sense of identity and, furthermore an image of all that culture has rejected in its effort to foreclose the presence within it of female autonomy. It is as such a commentary—on our psychosexual cultural arrangements and on the limitations of cultural constructs— that Marcela's case is worth considering.

9

Against the Law:
Mad Lovers in *Don Quixote*

Carlos Feal

To Dr. Heinz Lichtenstein,
in memoriam

After freeing the galley slaves in chapter 22 of part I, Don Quixote, in Sancho's company, enters into the depths of the Sierra Morena. This site seems well chosen for the knight-errant, who, in liberating those imprisoned by the forces of justice, places himself at the margins of the law. Once in the sierra, Don Quixote comes across a valise, whose owner, Cardenio, later appears. The loss, if not abandonment, of this valise by its owner points to his profound alienation. In addition to money, the valise contains intimate writings and clothing. In effect, Cardenio loses everything he owns. His regression to a wild state, already initiated by his flight to nature, is then complete.

In Cardenio's memorandum book Don Quixote reads a sonnet with these lines: "¿Quién ordena / el terrible dolor que adoro y siento? [Who ordains / This penance that enthralls while it torments?]" (I.23). Cardenio adores his penance as much as his love; that is, he adores the penance that love procures for him. Although he subsequently claims not to know the cause of his ills, we can readily assume that he himself is their perpetrator. Following the sonnet is a letter, which Don Quixote also reads: "Lo que levantó tu hermosura han derribado tus obras; por ella entendí que eras ángel, y por ellas conozco que eres mujer. Quédate en paz, causadora de mi guerra [What your beauty raised up your deeds have laid low; the former induced me to believe you were an angel, the latter reveal to me that you are a woman. Peace be with you who have sent war to me]" (I.23). Cardenio's negative opinion of women in general, and not only of his

179

beloved Luscinda, manifests itself in this letter. No wonder, then, that Cardenio says to her, "Peace be with you," implicitly, "Leave me in peace." Peace, solitude, is precisely what Cardenio pursues. He wishes to keep Luscinda's deceit (*engaños*) hidden "porque tú no quedes arrepentida de lo que heciste y yo no tome venganza de lo que no deseo [so that you may not repent what you have done, nor I reap a revenge I would not have]" (I.23). Public knowledge of Cardenio's dishonor would oblige him to take revenge, something he does not wish to do.

Since Cardenio has abandoned society to take refuge in nature, his social preoccupations come as a surprise. He harbors a clear duplicity: if keeping his affront a secret matters so much, why does he mention it in a letter that he has recorded in his book? Furthermore, Cardenio loses his writings and never makes any attempt to find them; not once, in his speeches, does he refer to this loss. I suggest that Cardenio envisions an audience of readers, and it is to them, more than Luscinda, that he addresses his writings. This is the unconscious reason why he loses (abandons) his valise with his book in it: so that the world might know his sorrows and take pity on him in a massive projection of the pity he feels for himself. The valise is destined to be found by someone, a potential receptor of Cardenio's sufferings. He thus loses himself to be found in another; he empties himself to be filled by another.

Cardenio oscillates between his social preoccupations (the patriarchal world of honor and duty) and a maternal, natural world, where he can forget these concerns. The motherly character of the sierra is underscored by Cardenio's exact place of refuge: "Le hallamos metido en el hueco de un grueso y valiente alcornoque [We found him hiding in the hollow of a thick cork tree]," says the goatherd (I.23). In Lacanian terminology, Cardenio escapes the Symbolic order, founded on the Law of the Father, regressing to the level of the Imaginary, the dual mother-child relation, which precedes the appearance of the father and his law. As Ellie Ragland-Sullivan writes: "In Lacanian thought the residue of a child's development is the Imaginary as it asserts itself in adult life in relation to Symbolic order contracts, pacts and laws. But the Imaginary tends to subvert these laws, whether through innocuous irony or criminal acts.... Imaginary subversion of the Symbolic comes from a narcissistic drive toward an impossible fusion (a symbiotic Oneness)."[1] The mechanisms of psychosis are

1. Ellie Ragland-Sullivan, *Jacques Lacan and the Philosophy of Psychoanalysis* (Urbana: University of Illinois Press, 1986), 179.

unleashed, for Lacan, by what he calls foreclosure (the Freudian *Ver-werfung*), that is, the rejection of the Law or Name-of-the-Father with its accompanying threat of castration or separation from the mother. It is a case not of simple repression, as in neurosis, but of lack of integration into the unconscious (the Lacanian Other) of a fundamental signifier (castration, the phallus) and, therefore, a loss of the ability to symbolize. Psychosis, then, results from "the foreclosure of the Name-of-the-Father in the place of the Other and . . . the failure of the paternal metaphor."[2]

Yet, as we have seen, social concerns never cease to burden Cardenio, who, after all, is not a complete madman. The goatherd pointedly calls him "muy cortesana persona [a man of courtly breeding]" (I.23). Cardenio's adherence to the world of honor and manly values constitutes a desperate defense agains his fall into the Imaginary, that is, into madness. Only as a socially integrated being, subject to the Symbolic order, could Cardenio avoid his psychic disintegration. In his fits of madness, however, Cardenio cannot help projecting the image of the hated Fernando, his treacherous rival, onto the kind shepherds, who then fall victim to his furious attacks. Here again Lacan's words are appropriate: "What has not come to light in the Symbolic order, appears in the Real . . . by way of a hallucination."[3]

One cannot fail to note the similarity between Cardenio and Don Quixote. In his very madness, the knight-errant chooses a role that supposedly inserts him into the Symbolic—the masculine world of laws and chivalric codes, of phallic exploits—far from the confinement of home, with its intrusive and disquieting feminine presences (his housekeeper and his niece).[4] In order to escape from madness (absorption by the feminine or maternal), Don Quixote falls into madness, and, like Cardenio, he will charge against hallucinated enemies, remnants of the paternal metaphor.

2. Jacques Lacan, "On a Question Preliminary to Any Possible Treatment of Psychosis," in *Ecrits: A Selection*, trans. Alan Sheridan (New York: Norton, 1977), 215. Of course, psychosis may also be defined from the register of the Imaginary to which foreclosure of the Name-of-the-Father leads. John P. Muller says: "In psychotic development castration is foreclosed: the child remains in a dual, symbiotic union with the mother in which the child identifies with being the all-fulfilling object of the mother's desire"; see "Language, Psychosis, and the Subject in Lacan," in *Interpreting Lacan*, ed. Joseph H. Smith and William Kerrigan (New Haven: Yale University Press, 1983), 23.

3. Jacques Lacan, "Réponse au commentaire de Jean Hyppolite sur la 'Verneinung' de Freud," in *Ecrits* (Paris: Gallimard, 1966), 388-89.

4. Carroll B. Johnson writes: "Don Quixote's first plan of action involves simply escaping from his intolerable ménage to inhabit a fantasy world of knights and castles and giants"; see *Madness and Lust: A Psychoanalytical Approach to Don Quixote* (Berkeley: University of California Press, 1983), 200.

Chapter 23 ends with the encounter between the two madmen. Don Quixote embraces Cardenio "como si de luengos tiempos le hubiera conocido [as if he had known him for a long time]" (I.23). Cardenio is his alter ego, and vice versa.[5] Each madman functions as a mirror of the other, a mirror that also reveals ignored or buried aspects of the ego. It is his own shattered image that Cardenio tries to recompose and recognize in Don Quixote: "Puestas sus manos en los hombros de don Quijote, le estuvo mirando, como que quería ver si le conocía [Placing his hands on Don Quixote's shoulders, he stood gazing at him as if seeking to see whether he knew him]" (I.23).[6] Cardenio attempts to return to himself, to reincarnate the image of the gentleman that Don Quixote, unlike the shepherds, reflects back to him. For if Don Quixote is the Knight of the Mournful Countenance (Caballero de la Triste Figura), Cardenio is called the Roto de la Mala Figura (Ragged One of the Disreputable Countenance) (I.23). The gap to be bridged between them runs from the Ragged (or Broken) One to the knight or gentleman (*caballero*), that is, from what Cardenio is now to what he once was and can still be again.

Don Quixote incites the Ragged One to tell of his misfortune. For Cardenio, telling his story forms his defense against madness, a madness precluded by the very language he uses to structure his thoughts. In the words of Jacques Derrida, "Madness is in essence what cannot be said."[7] But Cardenio demands that, for the sake of brevity, no one interrupt his story. Such reasoning becomes suspicious when we later witness how the Ragged One, in narrating his life, delves into superfluous details. In fact the Ragged One identifies so completely with his own story that an interruption would destroy his efforts to reconstruct himself.[8] Any break would ruin the (narrative and

5. Edward Dudley writes: "The embrace signifies that Don Quijote has known Cardenio and Cardenio's condition in his own youth"; see "The Wild Man Goes Baroque," in *The Wild Man Within*, ed. Edward Dudley and Maximillian E. Novak (Pittsburgh: University of Pittsburgh Press, 1972), 130.

6. Joyce McDougall notes that "people who must constantly struggle to maintain their narcissistic homeostasis may do this in two different ways: they may keep a prudent distance from others felt to be a threat to their equilibrium, or, on the contrary, they may grasp onto others, displaying unquenchable need of the person chosen to reflect the image that is missing in the inner psychic world"; see *Plea for a Measure of Abnormality* (Madison, Conn.: International Universities Press, 1980), 303. Both attitudes may be observed in Cardenio.

7. Jacques Derrida, "Cogito et histoire de la folie," in *L'écriture et la différence* (Paris: Seuil, 1967), 68.

8. Stephen Gilman notes that "Cardenio is his story, and when it is interrupted, he interrupts himself"; see *The Novel According to Cervantes* (Berkeley: University of California Press, 1989), 159. Edward Dudley's comment is equally perceptive: "the very act of interrupting shatters Cardenio's narcissistic and masochistic mirror world"; see "Wild Man," 136.

psychic) assemblage of fragments, which are as carefully interlocked as the pieces of a puzzle.

Only in establishing contact with others through his story can Cardenio avoid madness; yet he must keep the others at a distance, never allowing them to erupt into the fictional world he commands as narrator. Instead, they must act as a benevolent mirror, a silent and empathic audience before whom Cardenio exhibits himself. Cardenio's story, then, serves not only as a protection against madness but also as a (fictional) expression of it.[9] Cardenio speaks, and by so doing (by articulating his case in linguistic form) proves that he is not mad, but he renders his audience mute. His story, encircled by silence, finally transforms itself into silence (the silence of madness), that is, alienation, suppression of the Other as an interlocutor. Even though he tells his story, Cardenio resists any intrusion into his autonomous world.

Cardenio and Luscinda—the story begins—loved each other since their childhood. Both his and her parents looked favorably on this relationship, but "por buenos respetos [for propriety's sake]" (I.24) Luscinda's father refused Cardenio entrance to his house as the pair grew up and their love deepened. Cardenio did not voice any complaint. Once distanced from his beloved, Cardenio initiated an epistolary relation with her, composing not only letters but also verses. Cardenio certainly suffers as a result of this separation, but, in line with the courtly love tradition, he feels pleasure in the midst of his sorrows.[10] Nonetheless, he recounts that, no longer able to endure his plight, he decided to ask Luscinda's father for her hand. The narration here diverges from the facts, as we later discover, for if Cardenio asks for the hand of his beloved, it is because she presses him to do so. The initiative is hers, not his.

Luscinda's father thanks the young suitor for his intentions, but claims that it befits the other father (Cardenio's) to make the request

---

9. Synthesizing Derrida's ideas, Shoshana Felman writes: "Madness, *inside of thought*, can only be evoked through fiction"; see "Madness and Philosophy or Literature's Reason," *Graphesis: Perspectives in Literature and Philosophy*, special issue of *Yale French Studies* 52 (1975): 219.

10. On the deleterious effects of this kind of love in Cervantes's work, see Javier Herrero, "Arcadia's Inferno: Cervantes' Attack on Pastoral," *Bulletin of Hispanic Studies* 55 (1978): 293, where he writes: "True love, for Cervantes as for the Christian humanists who were his masters, is the one which brings man joy of living and acceptance of this world; it is not the heretical emotion which pushes him to self-destruction and torture. As the novels which are closely linked with the Grisóstomo-Marcela episode show (the interpolated stories of Cardenio-Luscinda and Fernando-Dorotea), true love, for Cervantes, as for Erasmus, ends in marriage." It is not fortuitous that Cardenio reaches a pastoral world and thus resembles Grisóstomo, the lover who commits suicide.

for marriage. Cardenio agrees; yet before he can utter a word, his father hands him a recently received letter from Duke Ricardo, a grandee of Spain, calling upon Cardenio to enter his household as "compañero, no criado, de su hijo el mayor [the companion, not the servant, of his eldest son]" (I.24). Again, Cardenio shows himself to be compliant with respect to the father's word: "A mí mesmo me pareció mal si mi padre dejaba de cumplir lo que en ella [la carta] se le pedía [I felt it would be wrong of my father not to comply with the duke's request]" (I.24). But once in the duke's house, Cardenio develops a great bond of friendship with the younger son, Fernando, who, seeking to flee from Dorotea, a beautiful peasant whom he has seduced, one day proposes to go with Cardenio back to his hometown.

Cardenio rejoices at Fernando's plan, which will allow him to see Luscinda again. Cardenio, then, has not forgotten Luscinda; like a good courtly lover—or like Don Quixote, the chivalresque lover—he remains faithful to the "lady of his thoughts." If he now goes to see her, however, it is following in another's footsteps. Chance, either happy or unfortunate, always moves Cardenio, incapable as he is of designing his own course. We also note that neither the duke nor his older son seems to care about Cardenio's departure. It looks very much as if Cardenio could have avoided going to the duke's house simply by marrying Luscinda, without facing strong opposition from anyone.[11]

Cardenio gives further proof of his foolishness when he makes Luscinda attractive to Fernando by praising her qualities to him. One night he even takes Fernando to see her through a window of her house. Cardenio permits him to read his correspondence with Luscinda, since Fernando shows interest in it. The result of these actions is to be expected: Fernando falls in love with Luscinda. His passion for her increases the day he finds a letter from Luscinda asking Cardenio to request her hand in marriage. Curiously, instead of keeping this precious letter in a safe place, Cardenio has left it in a book, exposed to any intruder. But these are facts we learn only when Cardenio resumes his story in chapter 27; Cardenio does mention the book (*Amadís*) in chapter 24, but no connection is made yet between the book and the letter: "Acaeció, pues, que habiéndome pedido Luscinda un libro de caballerías en que leer, de quien era ella muy aficionada, que era el de *Amadís de Gaula* [One day Luscinda happened

---

11. Edward Dudley points out that "only by careful management does he [Cardenio] succeed in turning the golden situation toward disaster"; see "Wild Man," 135.

to ask me for a book of chivalry to read, *Amadís of Gaul*, of which she was very fond]" (I.24). At this moment Don Quixote cannot restrain himself and interrupts Cardenio, thus violating the condition necessary for the progression of the story.

Cardenio resents this interruption. Rather than continue his tale as Don Quixote exhorts him to do after this break, he has a strange reaction: "No se me puede quitar del pensamiento . . . que aquel bellaconazo del maestro Elisabat estaba amancebado con la reina Madásima [I cannot get rid of the idea . . . that that arrant knave Doctor Elisabat was not sleeping with Queen Madásima]" (I.25). How can we explain this outburst? We should take into account that *Amadís*, so admired by Don Quixote, contributes to Fernando's attraction to Luscinda, since that book contained her letter, "por quien quedó Luscinda en la opinión de don Fernando por una de las más discretas y avisadas mujeres de su tiempo [which led Don Fernando to look on Luscinda as one of the most discreet and prudent women of the day]" (I.27). *Amadís*, then, in Cardenio's disturbed mind becomes associated with Luscinda's infidelity, which he projects onto a character in the novel, Queen Madásima.[12] In the Queen, in turn, we can see a representative of the lascivious mother (as opposed to the pure one).[13] Both visions, rooted in childhood fantasies, manifest themselves through the clash between Cardenio and Don Quixote. Each of these two characters expresses the other's unconscious. In Lacanian terms, "the sender receives his own message back from the receiver in an inverted form."[14] Cardenio, resentful toward Luscinda—and, by extension, all women—unconsciously preserves an image of the pure mother, an image that he seeks desperately in the Sierra Morena. In his response, Don Quixote, by inverting Cardenio's message, reveals its unconscious meaning, the part that is unspoken or implicit in what he has just said. Cardenio in turn signals Don Quixote's unconscious, his repressed sexuality, which plainly emerges in chapter 16 when he embraces Maritornes in the middle of the night, mis-

12. Ruth El Saffar has made this point: "Clearly Cardenio's violence erupts as a result of his identification of Fernando and Luscinda with the two fictitious characters. And clearly Don Quixote defends Madásima's honor because he defends ladies' honor on principle, whether they be 'fictitious' or 'real' "; see *Distance and Control in "Don Quixote": A Study in Narrative Technique* (Chapel Hill: University of North Carolina Press, 1975), 60.

13. For a discussion of the split between the pure and the lascivious aspects of the mother, see Sigmund Freud, "A Special Type of Object Choice Made by Men," in *The Standard Edition of the Complete Psychological Works of Sigmund Freud*, ed. and trans. James Strachey, 24 vols. (London: Hogarth Press, 1953–74), 11: 165–75. Further references to the *Standard Edition* will be abbreviated *SE*, with volume and page number.

14. Jacques Lacan, "The Function and Field of Speech and Language in Psychoanalysis," in *Ecrits: A Selection*, 85.

taking her for the innkeeper's daughter. Of course, at bottom the madmen coincide, each reflecting the other's madness: the madness of rejecting that which strongly attracts them, thereby postponing indefinitely their encounter with a woman.

When Don Quixote awakens Cardenio's madness by interrupting him, Cardenio reciprocates by shattering Don Quixote's dream of feminine (or motherly) purity; he delights in confronting the knight-errant with the spectacle of female lust, which he thinks is responsible for his own grief and madness.[15] Don Quixote acts like a Cardenio not yet disillusioned about women, while Cardenio perversely enjoys disappointing his naive interlocutor, like an older brother vis-à-vis a younger one. Cardenio makes up for his pain by inflicting a similar one on another (on his alter ego). In so doing, he touches a sensitive chord in Don Quixote: "¡Estraño caso; que así volvió [Don Quijote] por ella [la reina Madásima] como si verdaderamente fuera su verdadera y natural señora! [Strange to say, he (Don Quixote) stood up for her (Queen Madásima) as if she were in earnest his true natural lady]" (I.24).

Cardenio, moreover, is not satisfied with hurling mere words: he also knocks down Don Quixote by throwing a stone at him. Both in word and in action, Cardenio once more rejects his own innocence, which Don Quixote personifies. Thus he, like Don Quixote, refuses to acknowledge his unconscious, which nonetheless reemerges in his last action in this chapter when he withdraws once again into his hiding place on the mountain. After his discharge of hatred and rage against his male rivals (he attacks not only Don Quixote but also Sancho and the goatherd), Cardenio recovers his "gentil sosiego [gentle composure]" (I.24) and retreats into the mountains, into the maternal (pure) world, without men, in which he would like to remain forever.

Undoubtedly, Cardenio's case history influences Don Quixote's subsequent behavior. He decides to do penance, claiming imitation of Amadís, who, when rejected by Oriana, withdrew to the Wretched Rock (Peña Pobre), changing his name to Beltenebros, and Roland,

---

15. Ruth El Saffar writes: "What Don Quixote sees yet does not want to see is that the virgin is an aspect of the mother"; see "In Praise of What Is Left Unsaid: Thoughts on Women and Lack in *Don Quixote*," *MLN* 103 (1988): 211. In the same article El Saffar comments on Don Quixote's Golden Age speech and his role as a protector of damsels in distress, saying, "as if, by preventing abductions, by stopping, symbolically, the father's intrusion on the mother-child dyad, Don Quixote could avert the Fall, could stop his painful experience of separation and individuation" (213).

whose madness was triggered by learning of Angelica's love for Medoro. Both Amadís and the mad Roland recall Cardenio's case.

Sancho cannot understand his master's behavior: "¿Qué causa tiene para volverse loco? ¿Qué dama le ha desdeñado, o qué señales ha hallado que le den a entender que la señora Dulcinea del Toboso ha hecho alguna niñería con moro o cristiano? [But what cause has your worship for going mad? What lady has rejected you, or what evidence have you found to prove that the lady Dulcinea del Toboso has been trifling with Moor or Christian?]" (I.25). Don Quixote answers that there is a point in doing something for no reason at all. The reason for his unreason is clear, however: it is the reason of the unconscious, the repressed, which, as we have seen, Cardenio has compelled Don Quixote to face.[16] The knight-errant now dares to confront his fears, to fantasize what he has been denying: woman's dishonesty. Don Quixote, then, decides to write a letter to Dulcinea. If the answer is the one he hopes for, his madness will be ended; if not, he will become completely mad: "Seré loco de veras, y, siéndolo, no sentiré nada [I shall become mad in earnest. Being so, I shall suffer no more]" (I.25). In his madness Don Quixote would, like Cardenio, penetrate a natural, unconscious world. The madness Don Quixote imagines cannot be distinguished from plenitude; in complete alienation he seeks to escape from the alienating world of consciousness, the ego, and language, from all inner divisions and their accompanying grief.

Like Cardenio, Don Quixote looks for receptors of his misfortunes who can take pity on him: "¡Oh vosotras, napeas y dríadas . . . que me ayudéis a lamentar mi desventura, o, a lo menos, no os canséis de oílla! [Oh, ye wood nymphs and dryads . . . help me to lament my hard fate or at least weary not at listening to it!]" (I.25). Here mockery and truth become inseparable from each other. Thus Don Quixote speaks of his "imaginados celos [imaginary jealousy]" (I.25), and the narrator correspondingly introduces Don Quixote's monologue in these terms: "Comenzó a decir en voz alta, como si estuviera sin juicio [He exclaimed in a loud voice as though he were out of his senses]" (I.25). Don Quixote therefore performs a role—that of the rejected

---

16. Richard Rorty writes: "What is novel in Freud's view of the unconscious is his claim that our unconscious selves are not dumb, sullen, lurching brutes, but rather the intellectual peers of our conscious selves, possible conversational partners for those selves. As [Philip] Rieff puts it, 'Freud democratized genius by giving everyone a creative unconscious' "; see "Freud and Moral Reflection," in *Pragmatism's Freud: The Moral Disposition of Psychoanalysis*, ed. Joseph H. Smith and William Kerrigan (Baltimore: Johns Hopkins University Press, 1986), 7.

lover, the madman—and is also aware of putting on an act. Despite this awareness, he tells Sancho: "Quiérote hacer sabidor de que todas estas cosas que hago no son de burlas, sino muy de veras [I would have you know that all these things I am doing are not in jest, but very much in earnest]" (I.25). Feigned pain and jealousy become real inasmuch as they obey a profound unconscious motivation. Like Cardenio, Don Quixote builds an imaginary story through which deep psychic structures are revealed, as they are through fiction in general.[17]

Yet, interestingly, the mad knight can choose from a variety of fictional roles, while the characters of traditional narrative (for example, Boccaccio's *Decameron* or the picaresque or chivalric mode) do not have this option. Whereas they depend on a single role (miser, jealous lover, knight-errant, whatever it may be), Don Quixote, as Américo Castro has remarked, has the freedom to change roles and to question them all.[18] Cervantes's invention of the modern novel grows precisely out of this intuition of a true self beneath the roles one may perform. But one should also point out that the madness constitutes the limit—a human one, and not only quixotic—of that very freedom. For, as Lacan points out, "not only can man's being not be understood without madness, it would not be man's being if it did not bear madness within itself as the limit of his freedom."[19] Here, the madman (Don Quixote or Cardenio) becomes a human paradigm in his ability to feign a story (a truth) and to designate the limit where, in relinquishing freedom, one may totally (and not only temporally) be transformed into another. For both Don Quixote and Cardenio, this danger is present in the possibility of their never abandoning the Sierra Morena, that is, never abandoning the world of madness.

Before Sancho leaves with his master's letter to Dulcinea, Don Quixote in fact refers to the place he now inhabits as the "laberinto de Perseo [labyrinth of Perseus]" (I.25). Martín de Riquer, in his edition of *Don Quixote*, annotates this unique expression as "an error of Cer-

---

17. Peter Brooks has noted that "we constitute ourselves as human subjects in part through our fictions, and therefore the study of human fiction-making and the study of psychic process are convergent activities and superimposable forms of analysis"; see "The Idea of a Psychoanalytic Literary Criticism," *The Trial(s) of Psychoanalysis*, special issue of *Critical Inquiry* 13 (1987): 341.

18. Américo Castro writes, "Seemingly bound to a myth, Don Quixote negates and surpasses all myths, since in the final analysis he manipulates them as he pleases"; see "Los prólogos al *Quijote*," in *Hacia Cervantes* (Madrid: Taurus, 1957), 225.

19. Lacan, "On a Question," 215.

vantes, who should have written Theseus."[20] The revised John
Ormsby translation reads: "the labyrinth of Theseus." We cannot be
certain, however, that Cervantes made an error. Even if he did, it
would still be legitimate to wonder why. In a 1989 article Joan Ramón
Resina states: "Perseus' mention ceases to look inappropriate when
we consider that Don Quixote, in the midst of the labyrinth, necessarily identifies with the classic hero and that his feat, as in the archetypal myth, will consist in decapitating the monster: the giant
Pandafilando de la Fosca Vista, of course, but also the seduction of
madness, the fixing of the subject by the look reflected in the void,
in the labyrinth of the inner self."[21] I agree with Resina and add a
few data in support of his interpretation. Perseus kills the Gorgon
Medusa, who petrifies anyone who looks at her. We owe to Freud a
classic essay on Medusa's head. He connects the horror at the sight
of this figure with the castration anxiety (decapitation = castration)
that the male experiences when he first views the female genitals
(essentially the mother's). At the same time, Freud explains, the
snakes on Medusa's head, though frightening in themselves, contribute toward mitigating the horror, since they replace the penis.
Also, the male spectator, who becomes stiff with terror, thus defends
himself against the threat of castration, "for becoming stiff means an
erection. . . . He is still in possession of a penis, and the stiffening
reassures him of the fact."[22]

Freud's remarks here are representative of his thought concerning
the pre-oedipal mother, whose powerful and terrifying aspects, once
they are hinted at, need to be downplayed.[23] Deviating somewhat
from my Freudian-Lacanian model, I therefore turn to other authors
more attuned to the sounds of matriarchal language. Thus, for example, Erich Neumann writes: "The petrifying gaze of Medusa belongs to the province of the Terrible Great Goddess, for to be rigid
is to be dead. . . . The Gorgon is the counterpart of the life womb; she

20. Miguel de Cervantes, Don Quijote de la Mancha, ed. Martín de Riquer, 2 vols., 7th ed.
(Barcelona: Juventud, 1971), 249.
21. Joan Ramón Resina, "Medusa en el laberinto: Locura y textualidad en el Quijote," MLN
104 (1989): 301.
22. Sigmund Freud, "Medusa's Head," SE 18:273.
23. Madelon Sprengnether has dealt extensively with this subject. Using precisely the
story of Medusa as a metaphor for Freud's attitude, Sprengnether affirms: "It seems in
Freud's writing that the preoedipal mother, like Medusa, cannot be looked at directly. At
the same time, she exercises a fatal kind of attraction that inspires in him a multitude of
defensive strategies"; see The Spectral Mother: Freud, Feminism, and Psychoanalysis (Ithaca:
Cornell University Press, 1990), 6.

is the womb of death or the night sun."[24] The allusion to the Gorgon would, then, reinforce the negativity of the labyrinth as a maternal prison. What Resina calls "the seduction of madness" is indeed the seduction by the mother imago that leads to madness. The motherly character of the Sierra Morena becomes patent in the conclusion of Don Quixote's letter to Dulcinea: "Fecha en las entrañas de Sierra Morena [Done in the heart/womb of the Sierra Morena]" (I.25). Moreover, Don Quixote bares himself like an infant in front of Sancho to carry out his penance: "Y desnudándose con toda priesa los calzones, quedó en carnes y en pañales [Hastily pulling off his breeches, he stripped himself to his skin and his shirt]" (I.25).

In the chapter that follows, the depths or womb of the Sierra Morena receive a negative connotation in the verses written by the hidalgo: "entrañas duras [harsh womb]" (I.26). The harsh Mother Nature finds correspondence in the unreceptive Dulcinea, or vice versa, proof that both images (mother and loved one) are in fact intertwined. Therefore, the Sierra transforms itself into "hell" (I.25) not only in connection with a Minotaur (that of Theseus' labyrinth, as Javier Herrero claims) but also in its implicit association with the terrible Gorgon, whom, along with her sisters, Neumann refers to as the "uroboric symbols of what we might justly call 'the Infernal Feminine.' "[25]

Philip E. Slater interprets the Perseus myth in terms similar to Neumann's: "Like other heroes he [Perseus] attacks and kills the representative of the Evil Mother."[26] But Slater adds an interesting dimension by noting that "in this case the emphasis is placed on what we might call, with only partial inappropriateness, castration. To do so is not to make some automatic equation: decapitation = castration. . . . Castration is used here in the more general sense of 'unsexing': the mother and the sexual aspect are separated."[27] Slater, then, seems to imply that Medusa, instead of inspiring fear because of her castrated appearance, evokes the phallic (evil) mother of infancy, who must be castrated (unsexed or disempowered). In this light the parallel between Perseus and Don Quixote increases, given the knight-errant's effort to deprive mother (woman) of all sexual connotations

24. Erich Neumann, *The Great Mother: An Analysis of the Archetype*, trans. Ralph Manheim (New York: Pantheon Books, 1963), 166.

25. See Javier Herrero, "Sierra Morena as Labyrinth: From Wildness to Christian Knighthood," in *Critical Essays on Cervantes*, ed. Ruth El Saffar (Boston: G. K. Hall, 1986), 70; and Erich Neumann, *The Origins and History of Consciousness*, trans. R. F. C. Hull (Princeton: Princeton University Press, 1970), 214.

26. Philip E. Slater, *The Glory of Hera: Greek Mythology and the Greek Family* (Boston: Beacon Press, 1968), 309.

27. Ibid, 309–10.

(an endeavor prolonged by other masculine characters in the novel). Yet in Dulcinea's enchantment, that is, in the conversion of the ideal lady into a rustic peasant, we clearly witness a return of the repressed.

Finally, the myth of Perseus can also accommodate the subsequent development of the story when Dorotea, the woman seduced by Fernando, invents the giant Pandafilando de la Fosca Vista (a projection of Fernando himself), from whom Don Quixote must free her. Likewise, Perseus, after killing the Medusa, liberates Andromeda from a horrible monster. Neumann writes in this respect: "This monster has been sent by Poseidon, who is referred to as the 'Medusa's lover' and is, as ruler of the ocean, himself the monster. He is the Terrible Father, and since he is the Medusa's lover, he is clearly related to the Great Mother as her invincible phallic consort."[28] All the essential motifs in the legend of the hero are, then, condensed in the myth of Perseus, whose modern descendant is Don Quixote.[29]

When Cardenio resumes his story in chapter 27, we once again witness his great resistance to marriage. Undoubtedly he fears the realization of his desire, as if requesting Luscinda's hand would constitute a sort of violation. Cardenio dares not speak to his father in regard to this matter, anticipating paternal opposition even though there is no (conscious) reason to expect it. In Cardenio, then, desire and law (as represented by the father) clash in a deep, insurmountable manner. The oedipal root of this contradictory relation has been expounded by Lacan, whose ideas on this point Jean Laplanche and J.-B. Pontalis summarize thus: "The Oedipus complex is not reducible to an actual situation— the actual influence exerted by the parental couple over the child. Its efficacity derives from the fact that it brings into play a proscriptive agency (the prohibition against incest) which bars the way to naturally sought satisfaction and forms an indissoluble link between *wish* and *law*."[30] In this respect Cardenio's initial words are of interest: "A esta Luscinda amé, quise y adoré desde mis tiernos y primeros años [This Luscinda I loved, worshiped, and adored from my earliest and tenderest years]" (I.24). Sexual desire here is directed toward an object that was previously qualified as innocent, childish. Cardenio is afraid of destroying the purity with his adult sexuality,

28. Neumann, *Origins*, 216.
29. Curiously enough, the Perseus and knight-errant figures are often fused in Victorian representations of the Andromeda myth, as Adrienne Munich has shown in *Andromeda's Chains: Gender and Interpretation in Victorian Literature and Art* (New York: Columbia University Press, 1989); see esp. the plates at 17, 20, 44.
30. Jean Laplanche and J.-B. Pontalis, *The Language of Psycho-Analysis*, trans. Donald Nicholson-Smith (New York: Norton, 1973), 286.

as well as of destroying the father figure, which interposes itself between him and the object of his desire. One cannot fail to note the extent of his submission to other men, whom he perceives as superiors. Cardenio yields with docility before Luscinda's father, his own father, the duke, and Fernando. Over and over he curbs his wishes, the intensity of which may be inferred from the strength of his defenses.

When he confesses his fears to Fernando, the solution comes quickly: "A todo esto me respondió don Fernando que él se encargaba de hablar a mi padre y hacer con él que hablase al de Luscinda [To all this Don Fernando answered that he would take upon himself to speak to my father and persuade him to speak to Luscinda's father]" (I.27). Fernando acts as Cardenio's emissary, the representative of the phallic potency that Cardenio refuses to embody or of the desire that he fails to assume. Yet, in a treacherous move, Fernando requests Luscinda's hand for himself, to which her father unhesitatingly agrees.

Fernando distances Cardenio from the arena of his exploits. Having decided to buy some horses, he sends Cardenio to the duke's house to request the necessary funds. Once more Cardenio offers no objection. In fact, Cardenio obeys his inner law, that of his violent superego. The dictates of others support his rigorous conscience. Ironically, what now strengthens Cardenio's superego is not the Law of the Father, from which moral conscience originates, but the desire of the disrespectful Fernando. And, though Cardenio was destined to be "the companion, not the servant" of the duke's elder son, he makes himself into the servant of the younger son, that is, the servant of a wish (not a law) in opposition to his own wish. In other words, it is significantly a second son, a *segundón*, who finally embodies the power of the law for Cardenio. In submitting to Fernando, then, Cardenio obeys a man not destined to accede to the dukedom, the paternal title, a man who correspondingly acts in defiance of the law, following his instincts. This case is exemplary in that it points to the instinctual roots of what masquerades as law; in this regard we should also recall the docility of the father figure when faced with Fernando's powerful desire. A whole range of accommodations seems possible between fathers and sons, the *segundones* often having at their disposal a wider margin of freedom, inasmuch as they do not identify so rigidly with their fathers and are not perceived to be as great a threat to their fathers as are firstborn sons. Cardenio, of course, is incapable of reaching a similar degree of adaptation to paternal dictates, which, when not strictly followed, plunge him into madness. Escaping from the Terrible Father, he finds the Terrible Mother, rather than the good, pure mother he seeks. Fleeing into the reign of pure mothers proves as sterile as rejecting lascivious mothers to embrace instead—as does Don Quixote—the masculine world of rivalries in the name of the ideal woman (the pure mother again).

On the day of her wedding to Fernando, Luscinda informs Cardenio of her intention to stab herself with a dagger hidden in her bosom unless the marriage is stopped. Cardenio sneaks into Luscinda's house, and, concealed behind two tapestries, he witnesses the ceremony. What Cardenio secretly observes may be assimilated to a primal scene; like a child, he feels excluded from that scene in which he nevertheless would like to take part by replacing one or the other of the two parent surrogates. Before his audience in the sierra, Cardenio incriminates himself in exposing what he considers his cowardice and foolishness. He did not dare to emerge from his hiding place and say as he now does: "¡Ah traidor don Fernando, robador de mi gloria, muerte de mi vida! ¿Qué quieres? ¿Qué pretendes? Considera que no puedes cristianamente llegar al fin de tus deseos, porque Luscinda es mi esposa, y yo soy su marido [O, treacherous Don Fernando, robber of my glory, death of my life! What are you seeking? Remember that you cannot as a Christian attain the object of your wishes, for Luscinda is my bride and I am her husband]" (I.27). Cardenio seems to imply that he took part in a secret marriage with Luscinda, though it is not certain that this marriage reached consummation, as Edward Dudley and Javier Herrero would have us believe.[31] Thus Cardenio says, after recounting his last farewell to Luscinda: "A lo que más se estendía mi desenvoltura era a tomarle, casi por fuerza, una de sus bellas y blancas manos, y llegarla a mi boca, según daba lugar la estrecheza de una baja reja que nos dividía [The utmost extent of my boldness was to take, almost by force, one of her fair white hands and carry it to my lips, as well as the closeness of the low grating that separated us allowed me]" (I.27).[32]

---

31. See Dudley, "Wild Man," 133, and Herrero, "Sierra Morena," 75. On the subject of Luscinda's relation to Cardenio, see also Francisco Márquez Villanueva, who writes: "The secret marriage 'by present words' continued to be legitimate in literature, even though it had lost its validity after Trent. . . . The promise that binds Cardenio and Luscinda may also be considered a marriage 'by future words' (palabras de futuro) (that is, consented but postponed)"; see Personajes y temas del "Quijote" (Madrid: Taurus, 1975), 32.

32. Herrero dismisses these words as "the expression of a gentleman talking about his lady"; see "Sierra Morena," 75. Yet this gentleman often refers to his lady in very harsh terms. The proofs Herrero adduces in support of his opinion are doubtful to me. For example: "Cardenio can enter her [Luscinda's] house, when she is forced to marry don Fernando, because ['I knew all its entrances and exits very well']"; see "Sierra Morena," 75. Let us not

To the ritual question from the priest whether she will take Fernando for her husband, Luscinda surprisingly answers: "Sí quiero [I will]" (I.27). For the afflicted Cardenio, this answer revives all the pain and frustration of the child who watches or imagines the primal scene. As Freud indicates, such a scene does not always amount to a memory: "So far as my experience hitherto goes, these scenes from infancy are not reproduced during the treatment as recollections, they are the products of construction."[33] What matters in Cardenio's case is that his (supposed) rejection by Luscinda and her (supposed) attraction to another man takes the form of a primal scene. It is significant that, of the many roles Cardenio could adopt in his situation, he chooses precisely this one: the role of the voyeur (the child) who observes in hiding the scene of a sexual encounter. Here, this scene constitutes a way of recreating (remembering) figuratively an infantile past.[34] In the story of "The Curious Impertinent," Anselmo—another Cardenio—himself produces all the elements of the scene by fostering the attraction between his wife, Camila, and his intimate friend, Lotario. The contrivance allows Anselmo to gaze through the keyhole at the spectacle offered by this pair. On one level, Anselmo hopes the two actors will not confirm his fears. But on another level, that of his self-confessed obsessive madness, Anselmo needs to reconstruct the position of dependency and rejection in order to stimulate his desire.

After agreeing to be Fernando's wife, Luscinda falls fainting into her mother's arms. In Luscinda's bodice her mother discovers a note, which Fernando begins to read. At this moment Cardenio abandons the spectacle, despite the obvious fact that it has not yet ended. His mind has already forged an interpretation along the lines of the classic primal scene and his own unconcious need. He can only turn away from the events that contradict the expected meaning.

Dorotea's appearance in the sierra introduces another narrative voice. Like Cardenio, she too will tell of her misfortune: the story of her surrender to Fernando. To conquer Dorotea, Fernando resorts to a secret marriage, an illicit practice at that time.[35] She dispels her

---

forget that Luscinda and Cardenio had known each other since childhood and that he had had access to her house for a long time. I return to this subject later in this essay.

33. Sigmund Freud, *From the History of an Infantile Neurosis, SE* 17:50–51.

34. Following Freud, Ned Lukacher presents his position on this matter: "We have situated the notion of the primal scene in the interval between memory and imagination, between historical knowledge and metaphorical construction, between philosophical truth and the free play of interpretation"; see *Primal Scenes: Literature, Philosophy, Psychoanalysis* (Ithaca: Cornell University Press, 1986), 275.

35. Marcel Bataillon writes: "We do not have any reason to believe that Cervantes longs

resistance with this argument (among others): "Y si quiero con des-
denes despedille, en término le veo que, no usando el que debe, usará
el de la fuerza, y vendré a quedar deshonrada y sin disculpa de la
culpa que me podía dar el que no supiere cuán sin ella he venido a
este punto [If I strive to repel him by scorn, I can see that, fair means
failing, he is in a mood to use force, and I shall be left dishonored
and with no way of proving my innocence to those who cannot know
how innocently I find myself in this position]" (I.28). Dorotea fan-
tasizes a possible rape, which could, however, be interpreted (to her
dishonor) wrongly, as if it were something wished by her and not
only by him. In order not to be judged groundlessly as compliant,
she finds reason to comply. She consents lest someone believe that
she consented.

Finally, Dorotea explains to her listeners (Cardenio among them)
what happened the day of Fernando and Luscinda's wedding, thus
filling the gaps in Cardenio's narration. In the letter hidden in her
bosom, Luscinda revealed that she had accepted Fernando as a husband only out of obedience to her parents, and that she intended to
kill herself after the wedding. If, as Dudley affirms, Don Quixote,
vis-à-vis Cardenio, "anticipates the twentieth-century analyst who
begins the cure by having the patient tell his story," we could add
that Dorotea prolongs this beneficial role by replacing the story of the
disturbed youth with a truer one.[36]

The intrigue is finally resolved in Juan Palomeque's inn, where
miraculously all parties coincide. Dorotea pities Luscinda "¿Qué mal
sentís, señora mía? Mirad si es alguno de quien las mujeres suelen
tener uso y experiencia de curarle; que de mi parte os ofrezco una
buena voluntad de servircs [What are you suffering from, señora? . . .
If it should be anything women are familiar with and know how to
relieve, I offer you my services with all my heart]" (I.36). Here we
note the alliance (the assimiliation, in the last analysis) of the two
women. Fernando keeps his arms around Luscinda, while Dorotea

---

in petto for the freedom previous to the Council [of Trent], a freedom that was condemned
by the best minds of the century, be they Catholic or heterodox"; see "Cervantes y el
'matrimonio cristiano,' " Varia lección de clásicos españoles (Madrid: Gredos, 1964), 254.

36. See Dudley, "Wild Man," 132. Commenting on the role of story in psychoanalysis,
Roy Schafer notes that "people going through psychoanalysis—analysands—tell the analyst
about themselves and others in the past and present. In making interpretations, the analyst
retells these stories. In the retelling, certain features are accentuated while others are placed
in parentheses; certain features are related to others in new ways for the first time; some
features are developed further, perhaps at great length. . . . The end product of this inter-
weaving of texts is a radically new, jointly authored work or way of working"; see "Narration
in Psychoanalytic Dialogue," On Narrative, special issue of Critical Inquiry 7 (1980): 35–36.

also holds her; thus the seducer asserts his grip on the two women, inseparable as they are from each other.

Dorotea appeals to Fernando's Christian morals: "Si . . . tú eres tan cristiano como caballero, ¿por qué por tantos rodeos dilatas de hacerme venturosa en los fines, como me heciste en los principios? [If you are a Christian as you are a gentleman, why do you with such subterfuges put off making me as happy in the end as you did at first?]" (I.36). Being a gentleman is not enough; Dorotea cannot ignore what Aminta in Tirso's *Trickster of Seville* offers as irrefutable truth: "La desvergüenza en España / se ha hecho caballería [Shameless impudence has become a mark of nobility in Spain]."[37] She further challenges blood nobility when she remarks to Fernando: "Cuanto más, que la verdadera nobleza consiste en la virtud [Reflect, moreover, that true nobility consists in virtue]" (I.36).

Fernando's acceptance of Dorotea and the simultaneous liberation of Luscinda allows the reunion of the original couples.[38] When Fernando releases Luscinda, she starts to fall down, but at this moment Cardenio supports her in his arms. "Estos brazos . . . ahora te reciben, y otro tiempo te recibieron, cuando la fortuna quiso que pudiese llamarte mía [These arms . . . now receive you, and received you before, when fortune permitted me to call you mine]," he exclaims (I.36). Herrero adduces these words as definitive proof that Luscinda is not a virgin.[39] In reflecting on this point I realize that, in my critical discussion with Herrero (and Dudley), I am uncannily reproducing the exchange between Don Quixote and Cardenio on Queen Madásima's purity (or lack thereof). Did Cervantes intend to trick the readers by making them the equals of his literary characters? And should we therefore conclude that Luscinda, like the mother imago she em-

---

37. Tirso de Molina, *El Burlador de Sevilla*, ed. Américo Castro, 8th ed. (Madrid: Espasa-Calpe, 1967), 3.131–32. Regarding Cervantes's criticism of the nobility (*caballería*) of his time, I cite these words by the late Stephen Gilman in his posthumous work: "When Sansón Carrasco informs Don Quijote and Sancho that 'those who are most given to reading [Part I]' are 'pages' and that 'there are no lordly antechambers where one can't find a copy of *Don Quijote*' (II.4), he implies that these mischievous inferiors understood very well Cervantes's muted criticism of the pseudogreatness of the *caballeros* (knights of the court) and grandees of the time"; see *The Novel According to Cervantes* (Berkeley: University of California Press, 1989), 43–44.

38. Ruth El Saffar notes that "when the fourth figure—the female alter ego—manages to bring herself into the consciousness of the male contenders, as Dorotea does, she will provide the means by which destruction can be avoided and harmony restored"; see *Beyond Fiction: The Recovery of the Feminine in the Novels of Cervantes* (Berkeley: University of California Press, 1984), 67. The idea of a fourth saving figure, who dissolves the tensions caused by the triangle, appears as a major thesis in this book by El Saffar.

39. Herrero, "Sierra Morena," 76.

bodies, is perceived (at least through masculine subjectivity) as both pure and impure?

Now for the first time Cardenio can separate his beloved from the image of the lascivious mother, which he has projected insistently on her: the image of the mother engaged with the father in a traumatic primal scene. Hidden behind Fernando, Cardenio can witness a scene that runs counter to the one he believed he had observed at Fernando and Luscinda's wedding. Luscinda's forced acceptance of the amorous rival gives way to her rejection of the hated intruder. On gaining release from Fernando, she herself proceeds to embrace Cardenio "sin tener en cuenta a ningún honesto respeto [heedless of all considerations of decorum]" (I.36). These actions corroborate the assimilation of Luscinda and Dorotea. The latter, like Luscinda, gave proofs of loyalty to a man; Luscinda, like Dorotea, eschews decorum to give free rein to physical expression of her love.

On the masculine side, Fernando and Cardenio also come to resemble each other. Cardenio dares to assume his desire (previously represented by Fernando). Fernando, in turn, reveals a conception of women in harmony with Cardenio's. Thus he says to Dorotea: "Pues la misma ocasión y fuerza que me movió para acetaros por mía, esa misma me impelió para procurar no ser vuestro [For the same cause and force that drove me to make you mine impelled me to struggle against being yours]" (I.36). That is, Dorotea inspires fear in Fernando, since she easily surrendered her alluring beauty. Joaquín Casalduero reaches a different interpretation: "Don Fernando explains his vacillation and downfall; the occasion and force that moved him toward Dorotea impelled him to abandon her. Driven by his lust, man is unable to stop."[40] But Casalduero cannot explain why the lustful Fernando, who flees from Dorotea, is willing to marry Luscinda, thus putting an end to his life as a Don Juan. These lines from "The Curious Impertinent" support my interpretation: "Que estas añadiduras trae consigo la maldad de la mujer mala: que pierde el crédito de su honra con el mesmo a quien se entregó rogada y persuadida, y cree que con mayor facilidad se entrega a otros [For the erring woman's sin brings this further penalty with it, that her honor is distrusted even by the man to whose overtures and persuasions she has yielded. He believes her to surrender more easily to others]" (I.34). Therefore, Fernando also shares in the idealism of the world around him, a spurious idealism that has in Don Quixote its highest exponent. Indeed, this is a Dulcineated world, as Arthur Efron has

---

40. Joaquín Casalduero, *Sentido y forma del "Quijote,"* 3d ed. (Madrid: Insula, 1970), 162.

called it. "Dulcineism," writes Efron, "is thus a name for the broadest effects of acculturation. . . . It involves a drastic idealization of sexuality."[41]

Dorotea must give exceptional proof of fidelity to Fernando for him to wish to marry her.[42] She should, then, come close to the model presented by Luscinda, who is not without reason the object of Fernando's devotion. Let us remember that Fernando feels attracted to Luscinda when he reads the letter that she addresses to Cardenio in which she asks him to demand her hand from her father, "si quisiéredes sacarme desta deuda [amorosa] sin ejecutarme en la honra [if you desire to relieve me of this (amorous) obligation without cost to my honor]" (I.27). Dorotea, in contrast, does not ask a man to request her in marriage; she hands herself over with cost to her honor—that honor so prized by a gentleman. The difference between the two women, however, is more apparent than real. By contracting a secret marriage, Luscinda, like Dorotea, has defied patriarchal law (as well as the law of the church). Unable to tell her story, Luscinda, of course, cannot assume Dorotea's prominent role; but everything we know about her demonstrates that, contrary to Fernando's expectations, she is not lacking in initiative.[43]

In short, to the union of the two couples must be added the union (or reconciliation) of the two men on the one hand and of the two women on the other. In psychological terms, the two stories become fused: Cardenio-Fernando marries Luscinda-Dorotea. The happy denouement contrasts with the tragic outcome of other similar stories in *Don Quixote*, part I: Marcela-Grisóstomo, "The Curious Impertinent," Leandra. In all these cases harmony is impeded by a binary opposition: either inaccessible purity (Efron's Dulcineated world) or lust (the world of Maritornes). An obvious link connects these two worlds and makes for easy transitions from one to the other. In this light the happy ending becomes an ideal—the ideal of an author (both skeptical and compassionate) who ultimately removes his afflicted

41. Arthur Efron, *Don Quixote and the Dulcineated World* (Austin: University of Texas Press, 1971), 11–12.

42. Márquez Villanueva states: "We cannot see Cervantes's attitude toward the sexual aspect of love as puritan at all. Not that he is willing to legitimate it literarily or ideologically in the same manner as a libertine, a feminist or a present-day Freudian. Dorotea does not represent any concession to free love nor any form of unbounded sexuality"; see *Personajes*, 63. We can only guess that free love and unbounded (*desatada*) sexuality should be reserved for libertines, feminists, and present-day Freudians, a most curious grouping that some of us might find a bit annoying.

43. I do not share Márquez Villanueva's opinion that Luscinda "has been conceived as a mere extension of Cardenio's character"; see *Personajes*, 55.

creatures from the danger of extremes.[44] Precarious as this ideal may appear, its worth (deserved or not) is underlined by all present in the inn, since "cuando se cumplen las fuertes leyes del gusto, como en ello no intervenga pecado, no debe de ser culpado el que las sigue [when the strong laws of pleasure assert themselves, so long as there is no mixture of sin in it, he who follows them is not to be blamed]" (I.36). The laws of pleasure or desire, *leyes del gusto*, finally assert themselves, though not in defiance of the Law of the Father. The fusion of Fernando and Cardenio reflects the conciliation of the two opposites, blind desire and blind submission to law (to the Terrible Father), which the two men respectively incarnate. In parallel fashion, the two women show a new face to their lovers: Luscinda ceases to be a forbidden object for Cardenio once she becomes dissociated from the image of the mother (a mother both pure and lascivious), and Dorotea also loses her threatening character for the lustful Fernando. Like the Terrible Father, the Terrible Mother has been dethroned; consequently the women relinquish the traits that made them terrifying to the men in the first place.

44. Gilman objects to this finale: "Once they have come to the end of their insane, foolish and lascivious stories, Cardenio and Dorotea are ready to be transported from that labyrinth to the impromptu stage of the inn, where they find the happy ending they do not deserve"; see *The Novel*, 180. Surprisingly, he remains silent about Fernando, the worst culprit of all.

10

Curious Reflex, Cruel Reflections: The Case for Impertinence

Eduardo González

> *"And if curiosity be not enough,* Messer Leonardo?" she said
> slowly, an unwonted fire in her eyes; "if something further,
> a profounder feeling, were needed to lay bare the cavern's
> last and greatest treasure?" And she turned toward him a
> smile he had never seen before . . .
>
> —Dmitri Merezhkovsky, *The Romance of Leonardo da Vinci*

In homage to surrealism, let us begin with five simultaneous Dul-
cineas faceted around a politely hidden phallus (Fig. 1), a mouth
sealed by a famous smile, a cavern, and a treasure—a dowry perhaps. The convergence of polygamous elements (such as five circling
brides for the imagination) and the monogamous yet polymorphous
model (Francesco del Giocondo's wife posing as Leonardo's gnostic
womanmate) plus some untold chthonic mysteries bespeaks old
psychoanalysis, its early fondness for peering into those dark dwellings from which Platonists had once fled, garments ablaze with
sacred fear.

In the same spirit of ceremonial turmoil, a fivefold stripping Dulcinea next to a smiling womb may suggest the psychoanalytic belief
that no one marries just in a single pair, and that it should always
prove hard, if not impossible, to break up the premarital affair carried
out between one's unweaned self and its own treasured likeness.
Hence, to the cavern's nameless womb (and to the birth of seduction
from its depths) we could add Leonardo's mystic infatuation with
his own younger semblance, and (more remotely) with the likeness
borne to him by the smiling face of his crib mother, Caterina, his

Figure 1. Marcel Duchamp, *Dulcinée*, 1911. Philadelphia Museum of Art: Louise and Walter Arensberg Collection.

biological mother as well, which he found drawn on the Mona Lisa's lips.[1]

MONOGAMY/HYSTEROGAMY

Moving along such plastic/specular descent lines, our composite view of Anselmo's impertinent curiosity considers two parallel notions of weddedness and severance holding hands across the borderline between exogamy and incest. In the one form, marriage attains a sacred glow and a notorious talent for enduring wretchedness as it steals the fire it needs to survive and to generate lawful births from vestiges of maternal incest. Such might be Anselmo's core predicament if starkly rendered in Freudian terms. For instance, by stressing severance one may see how a species of *divorce* surrounds marriage at both ends of the plot of "The Curious Impertinent." Divorce would come with the fact of *having to part with*, or in the inherent act of severance that may correspond to the tightest marriage bond. Proof of some insoluble consent to the facilitations of severance offers itself as a token of the basic renunciatory and sacrificial economy of marriage: of having to part with a portion of wealth, with tokens of bodily integrity, with a good deal of autonomy, and with a peculiar measure of negotiable freedom. In Anselmo's case, the ordeal of divorcing Lotario carves a weird statue out of the solid rock of their fabled friendship, out of their double and well-attuned image of reciprocal independence, such as their mutual sporting, their parallel hunting and dallying with beasts and women.

1. Commenting on the evolution of scientific curiosity, Hans Blumenberg interprets "the darkness confronting Leonardo at the entrance of the cave" as "an index of natural concealment, which, however, is no longer respected as something intended by nature"; see *The Legitimacy of the Modern Age*, trans. Robert M. Wallace (Cambridge: MIT Press, 1983), 364. Much earlier, the Russian émigré and visionary Nietzschean Dmitri Merezhkovsky, whose novel *The Romance of Leonardo da Vinci* became Freud's favorite source for Leonardo as genius and narcissist, had shown the painter standing before the cave's mouth "like a magician pronouncing an incantation, one of his mystic tales," and had attributed to the occasion the birth of the newly minted maternal smile in the mirror of Mona Lisa's semblance; see *The Romance of Leonardo da Vinci*, trans. Herbert Trench (New York: Washington Square Press, 1963), 441. By contrast, Blumenberg would locate the face-to-face between Leonardo and the cave "alongside Petrarch's letter on the ascent of Mont Ventoux," so as to best appreciate "the independence and matter-of-fact quality that curiosity has acquired [in Leonardo] and the way in which its reservations and its hesitation have been humanized." Thus, in Blumenberg's view, Leonardo's *Madonna of the Rocks* "no longer has anything in common with Petrarch's falling back on Augustine's *Confessions*" (364). Blumenberg's philosophical history of *curiositas* deals with Freud and Leonardo in "The Integration into Anthropology: Feuerbach and Freud," in *Legitimacy*, 437–53.

The other form of severance that concerns us in this psychoanalytic reading of the "Curioso" places cross-generational incest next to the homoerotic embedding of Anselmo's spying syndrome inside Lotario's steadfast friendship. Being more speculative perhaps than both Anselmo's love for roving manliness and his hell-bent search for the flawed woman (and mother) in Camila, this other kind of severance propels the wife (and daughter) into the foreground, just as it hints darkly at the now obliterated figure of her father (whom we might find in the magical world of Ariosto's learned sage and ultrabachelor, the savage hermit who, after living all his life "solo e selvaggio," buys himself a wife and makes a daughter at the age of one hundred twenty-eight).

We must deal with an ingrown set of childhood bondings mirrored forth in conjugal crisis. In the foreground, standing on the gazing point, Anselmo (though it could well have been Lotario) acts the incest-haunted spouse. In the background, near the vanishing point, Camila (with Leonela's sinister help) embodies a certain crying need to execute (as in a dance number) divorce in the face of conjugal sickness. Hence, the lost embodiment of incest (the omnipotent and vanished mother) comes forth to shadow and to haunt the spoused issue (her son) in the *histrionics/hysterics* of unfaithfulness and severance staged by incest repetition through the acting wife's figure, held in vicarious and voyeuristic shape inside her husband's imagining gaze.

When, in the story's longest scene, Camila offers a hysterical show for the benefit of both Anselmo and Lotario, she performs the wife as a mirror of spouse hysteria. Her performance stages the "illness" (*Unbehagen, malestar*) which stands for the turbulent joining of (and mutual resistance between) body and soul, the somatic and the psychic. So sketched, hysteria registers the impact of an enforced yoking, a shotgun wedding between flesh and symptom; it represents the oldest among psychoanalysis's successive but never annulled marriages. The hysteric or specular (the mirroring and mirrored) body is viewed here as a compact, as a nexus of pain and bliss usually rising from a woman's bisexual depths, from her innermost erotogenic biography, but which in Anselmo's case gives us a *plaque*, a photo negative, a dogtag of his likeness to an otherwise quite unknowable mother.

Our psychoanalytic curiosity cannot let go of two unavailable persons: the bride's father and the groom's mother. We call the object constructed by means of such curiosity a *hysterogamy* because it entails the union and constant rumble between male and female, between flesh and soul, bachelor and spouse, and, foremost, between the adult child and some buried but still festering parental corpse.

As such notions may suggest, in traditional psychoanalytic terms the "Curioso" should lie in between a case history on hysteria and a juicy soap opera (as best represented in Freud's *Dora* monograph). This hermeneutic stream (with *curiositas* as its nymph muse) drains into the glassy waters of a specular hole and a mirrored woman's body: "To construct her identity, a subject retains—from everything that makes up her life—scenarios in which her body is at stake: not her entire body, but certain of its movements, states, or positions. These manifestations have characterized her body in the empirical course of events, to be sure; but after the cathexis in question, they survive in what henceforth takes the value of symptom."[2] We see in the "Curioso's" main specular instances (in Camila's grand mise-en-scène, in Anselmo's acts of spying, and in his own and Lotario's bumping into a nocturnal visitor to Leonela's chamber) a spectral bondedness, a shadow image of the marriage bond itself, in which the origination of the hysterical body as a depicted woman knots itself with the man's embodiment, with his spying hunk's shape as voyeurist spouse or plain *regardeur* (and hence as a crude version of the artist's propelling curiosity).[3] A body knotted and shared, registered in disgust, rapture, and pain. Typically:

> just as the delusion about genital filthiness is being established, just as disgust is being actualized, every experience of jouissance is locked onto the urethral and (especially) the oral erotogenic zones. Every sexual experience is precipitated onto these places in the body, in that register of jouissance, so as to exorcise any experience of anguish that might be felt as a sort of disaggregation of these erotogenic zones. . . . From this viewpoint, a hysteric (male or female) suffers not from a lack of body, but from an omnipresence of body. (Ménard 103–4)

2. Monique David-Ménard, *Hysteria from Freud to Lacan: Body and Language in Psychoanalysis*, trans. Catherine Porter (Ithaca: Cornell University Press, 1989), 40, hereafter cited as Ménard.
3. Among the meanings of "hunk" offered by the *Oxford English Dictionary* as derived from Dutch, the following seem to reflect Freud's sense of umbilical curiosity (in the uncanny, or *Unheimlich*) toward the sought-after, perhaps inherently lost home of children: "*honk* goal, home in a game; of Frisian origin: . . . 'house, place of refuge or safe abode' . . . 'corner, nook, retreat, home in a game' "; perhaps related to the *curiositas* value attached to "hunker," as in "squatting" for a variety of creatural urges, among which impertinence seems to occupy a proverbial place.

Freed from "energistic metaphors" and the "prepsychoanalytic opposition between the psychical and the somatic" (Ménard 177), a new hysteronomy may emerge in kinship with corresponding modes of omnipresent meaningfulness at play in current intertextual approaches to narrative.

In order to illustrate such an approach in conjunction with the subject of *curiositas*, I have brought together Cervantes and Duchamp, mediated by some scissored clips from various commentaries on two of the latter's most famous artworks, known in English as: *The Bride Stripped Bare by Her Bachelors, Even* (1915–23; fig. 2) and *Givens: 1st the Waterfall / 2nd the Illuminating Gas* (1946–66; fig. 6, detail). For the most part, the Cervantes-Duchamp partition/connection has been framed inside two textual boxes (figs. 3 and 4), which the reader may inspect at his or her leisure. These boxes provide an alternate (self-sufficient though fragmented) and somewhat cryptic museum exhibit on the topic of curiosity, they aspire to pictorial status but obviously fail to achieve it, and instead may resemble the residual stuff deposited by Duchamp in his own *Green* and *White* boxes (see fig. 7 from *The Green Box*), in which he left a teasing commentary on his artwork.[4]

The specular marriage between curiosity and hysteria finds a place in Duchamp's sequence linking *The Bride* (viewed first) with the voyeurist tunneling of sight into the *Givens*, or *Etant donnés* (viewed last). As placed in Philadelphia's Museum of Art, the two artworks offer a symbolic passage through hysteronomy: *The Bride* (or *Great Glass*) appears like a transparent (and released) afterimage of Plato's cave, the kind of originary enclosure of mimetic bondage to which the visitor to the Arensberg Collection is led as he or she moves to the old Spanish door, through whose peepholes the cavern (with its female tokens) would restore itself to sight (figs. 5 and 6). Bracketed by Cervantes and Duchamp, Leonardo's cavern and Plato's cave bring us face-to-face with the alpha and omega of curiosity and perverse enclosure, back to the womb of representation in which Luce Irigaray (discussing Plato's *Hysteria*) locates what she calls *speculogamie*, or *auto-*

---

4. The Cervantes-Duchamp material (figs. 3 and 4) has been edited from the following texts: Octavio Paz, *Marcel Duchamp: Appearance Stripped Bare*, trans. Rachel Phillips and Donald Gardner (New York: Seaver Books, 1978); Arturo Schwarz, *La mariée mise à nu chez Marcel Duchamp, Même*, trans. Anne-Marie Sauzeau-Boetti (Paris, 1974); John Golding, *Marcel Duchamp, "The Bride Stripped by Its Bachelors, Even"* (New York, 1972); Craig E. Adcock, *Marcel Duchamp's Notes from the "Large Glass": An N-Dimensional Analysis* (Ann Arbor: UMI Research Press, 1983); John J. Winkler, *Auctor & Actor: A Narratological Reading of Apuleius's "The Golden Ass"* (Berkeley: University of California Press, 1985); Robert Graves's translation of *The Golden Ass* (New York: Noonday Press, 1951); and Blumenberg, *Legitimacy*.

Figure 2. Marcel Duchamp, *The Bride Stripped Bare by Her Bachelors, Even*, c. 1915. Philadelphia Museum of Art: Bequest of Katherine S. Dreier.

Portrait (Dulcinea) 1911title essentialelement against "retinal" ["retiano"] art visual tactile [i.e. dulci-née/dulci-mea] [Large Glass (will get) him away from the physicality of olfactory art] [[embedded transparent interacting planes build up the images large symbolic phallus]] this period closes with Coffee Mill [Breton: "a mechanical and cynical interpretation of the phenomenon of love" Phare de la Mariée; lighthouse, revolving horizontal light, the mill, vertical, molinos de viento] Dulcinée, "simultaneist" painting/[sic: birth/rivalry (simultas) simul-née] vision of a stripping in five stages the woman keeps her hat on like the Bride in the Large Glass In 1926, The Large Glass shattered while in transit [dio a Tomás uno de estos que llaman hechizos . . . estas bebidas o comidas amatorias . . . membrillo ("especie de manzana muy dulce") . . . imaginóse el desdichado que era todo hecho de vidrio] the scratched surface of the large Glass is like the scarred body of a war veteran [—Señores, yo soy el Licenciado Vidriera, pero no el que solía: soy ahora el Licenciado Rueda. . . . Esto dijo y se fue a Flandes, donde la vida que había comenzado a eternizar por las letras la acabó de eternizar por las armas] the cracks "brought the work back into the world" [Duchamp] the restoration involved enclosing the original work between two sheets of heavier plate glass and the whole was encased in a new metal frame[es una operación circular: comienza en el Motor-Deseo de la Novia y termina en ella/an unbridgeable separation between feminine and masculine/the inferiority of the males/a herd, rather than polyandry] LOS NUEVE MOLDES MACHOS the males are molds machotes suits them admirably [empty suits inflated by the illuminating gas that is their life's breath] Between the Nine Malic Molds and the Sieve is the Chariot also known as the Sleigh [the Mill is set in motion by a waterfall. It is invisible] Swinging to and fro, the Chariot recites endless litanies: "Slow life Vicious circle Onanism" These litanies are the bachelors' theme [the Chocolate Grinder the center of the bachelors' realm continuous gyratory movement "principle of spontaneity" "the bachelor grinds his own chocolate himself" A chocolate that "comes from one knows not where"] LOS TESTIGOS OCULISTAS figuras geométricas que recuerdan a las de la óptica los testigos que presencian los milagros al voyeur de la pornografía [the upper half is the bride's domain HANGED FEMALE the Bride is an apparatus (the look stains the virgin goddess wishes to be stained) FRESH WINDOW guillotine Widow French jargon] Of all interpretations psychoanalytical most tempting easiest [onanism destruction (or glorification) Virgin Mother castration retention anal symptoms self-destruction] the bachelor his virility intact husband disperses it becomes feminine seen [by] former comrades [as] traitor adolescent's terror of woman fascinated revulsion her hidden sexual organs][La Diosa es] [[un mito que se refiere al carácter cíclico del tiempo]]

Figure 3. Box: Vidriera on the Grand Verre.

THE GODDESS SEEMED TO BE STRIDING TOWARDS YOU AS YOU ENTERED *in Latin patristic literature curiositas anti-Gnostic aspect* BEHIND THE GODDESS WAS A CAVERN, ITS ENTRANCE CARPETED IN MOSS, GRASS, FALLEN LEAVES AND BRUSHWOOD naked girl stretched on a kind of bed or pyre of branches and leaves her head almost completely covered by the blond mass of her hair *[Elle est alongée sur un lit de brindilles et de feuilles sèches. Dans une pose provocante et exhibitionniste* WITH SHRUBS AND CREEPERS GROWING HERE AND THERE her legs open and slightly bent *ses jambes écartées découvrent son sexe imberbe* cruza una puertecilla y penetra *le visiteur s'y trouvera devant une vieille porte de grange* Una verdadera puerta condenada brick portal topped by an arch worm-eaten remendada y cerrada por un tosco travesaño The old door used in *Etant donnés* one time courtyard Cadaqués la vieja puerta traída de España cemented firmly into its brick archway THE BACK WAS A HIGHLY POLISHED SLAB WHICH MIRRORED HER SHOULDERS *curiositas became the dominant trait of a character type polypragmosyne [officious, busyness, meddling; [a bastard Mnemosyne]]* Diana enormous occupies center attention Acteon off center APPLES AND GRAPES SO EXQUISITELY CARVED YOU FANCIED YOURSELF IN MID-AUGUST waterfall tumbles down rock small lake AND WHEN YOU LOOKED DOWN AT THE RIVULET THE GODDESS'S FOOTPRINTS THE TANGLE OF BRANCHES THE FACE OF ACTEON PEEPING EAGERLY descubre dos agujeritos a la altura de los ojos lucecita parpadea in the brilliant light the hand grasping a small gas lamp inmóvil día de fines de verano *Curiosity seeks no longer what is admirable and wonderful in the cosmos but strange peculiar can only be gaped at il sera émerveillé par une scéne* [que no es fácil (he is not likely to) que olvide (to forget) jamás] *d'une rare beauté qui unit la perfection réaliste d'un trompe-l'oeil à une mise en scéne irrationelle et irréelle Comme dans un roman de science fiction, le mur du fond de la grange disparaît d'un coup et fait place à* OUT, ALREADY HALF-TRANSFORMED INTO A STAG *Augustine [mistake he sees in] curiositas [unreflectiveness] use of reason denial debt of gratitude [for being created]* como Diana a través de Acteón se envidia a sí misma [desea verse a sí misma] and the reflection of foliage in it [un deseo que implica ser vista por otro] and then Acteon [seen] el cuerpo esencial de Diana es invisible también *concupiscentia oculorum [distinguishes itself] naive delight in the senses its indifference [qualities of the beautiful/the pleasant] it enjoys not its objects but rather itself* [lo que ve Acteón apariencia/encarnación momentánea] or rather a stone simulacrum of Acteón [its curious gaze directed] goddess [ambiguous bilocation] ET IN SAXO SIMUL ET IN FONTE [but who is the agent here who views Acteon's gaze? *you: "You will think" (putabis), "you would think" (putes), and at the climax "if you bent forward and looked into the fountain, you would believe (si fontem ... pronus aspexeris, credes)*] Diana Janus' double/Janus and Diana divinidades circulares/dobles/el fin es el principio/anverso es el reverso/dioses reflexivos/van de sí mismos a sí mismos **[el lugar sagrado es la diosa]** del voyeurismo a la videncia

Figure 4. Box: Paz, Schwarz, Blumenberg, Winkler, Adcock, etc., December 8, 1990.

Figure 5. Marcel Duchamp, door of *Etant donnés*, 1946–66. Philadelphia Museum of Art: Gift of the Cassandra Foundation.

Figure 6. Marcel Duchamp, detail, *Etant donnés: La chute d'eau; le gaz d'éclairage.*

gamie spéculaire, the nuptial and bachelor apparatus harnessing masculine curiosity to the allegory of (the) woman as naked truth, enwombed in proper darkness or else emergent from a peep show of fire and shadows.[5] Having to divorce his old and very own narcissist buddy, Irigaray's single allegorical man (made up of all the men chained inside Plato's cave) offers as barter an old dream of parthenogenesis in exchange for a vanishing gift as he marries himself (in her) near the echo of a jumbled hysteroid phrase: "Ce sexe qui n'en [*rien sinon*] est pas un [*curieux*] [That sex which is not (*nothing if not*) one (*a curious one*)]."

THE BACHELOR APPARATUS: A TYPONOMY

Freud had difficulty tolerating extraneousness. His relationship with the psyche as an object of knowledge implies a regulation of curiosity in the face of chaotic meaningfulness. In allegorical terms Freud practices husbandry on the psyche while being madly attracted by its untamed wildness; he is a married Lothario who leads a double life as the seductive lover of his own spouse. It is Freud the husband, then, rather than the impertinent lover who would dismiss this rash of typos:

> Eran solteros, mozos de una misma edad y de unas mismas costumbres; todo lo cual era bastante causa a que los dos con recípoca [*sic*] amistad se correspondiesen...

> Calló en diciendo esto el virtuoso y prudente Loratorio [*sic*], y Anselmo quedó tan confuso y pensativo que por un buen espacio no pudo responder palabra. [Prudent and virtuous Loratorio (*sic*) fell silent upon thus speaking, and Anselmo is turn remained so confused and thought-bound that, for a good stretch of time, he was unable to utter a word.]

> ... sino asegúrate que Loratorio [*sic*] te estima... [but instead be assured that Loratorio (*sic*) holds you in high esteem...]

> ¿Qué es lo que quieres hacer con esta daga? ¿Quieres por ventura quitarle [*sic*] la vida o quitársela a Lotario? [What do you want to do with that dagger? Do you by any chance want to take (*sic*: "his,"

5. Luce Irigaray, *Speculum de l'autre femme* (Paris: Minuit, 1974), 367.

"its," whereas it should read "quitarte," i.e., "your") life or to take
it away from Lotario?][6]

For a good husband shall avoid impertinence, excessive intercourse,
too hard a push on the knowledge drive. But a good lover may stop
at nothing: on herself, on himself, on all loving means and motions
Eros rides hard and with unbridled fancy. The husband is a system,
lovers are machines. Consider the following business in written love
messages: "Un innamorato scrive una lettera alla sua amata. Riduce
i suoi sentimenti alle lettere dell'alfabeto, scrive parole. Compra un
francobollo, infila la lettera nella buca dell'istituzione statale Posta [A
lover writes a letter to his beloved. Renders his feelings in the letters
of the alphabet, writes words. Buys a stamp, drops the letter in the
mailbox of the state postal service]." (Fingers, keyboard, tongue on
francobollo [stamp], horizontal slot: lovers are machines fed by error.)
Error (and typos) may follow the script of a neo-dadaist melodrama.
Thus the post office (la posta) "sells the letters to a paper factory.
This paper factory pulps the letters and manufactures notepaper from
the pulp. The lover buys two sheets of such notepaper and writes
more than he did the first time, since he has received no reply."[7] It
seems as if eager bachelors should deposit their letters directly with
Lady Celestina, leaving post office slots for well-trained husbands.

The post, *la posta*, is a false goddess, or rather a goddess in place
of an office, who pulps *macera* and excretes blank paper like a brutal
machine, a cannibal mother, Great Mistress of erotic pets. She wears
a huge belt, she drives sex-fed/sex- starved males on a journey to
nowhere:

> Just as a huntsman will pursue a hare
> O'er hill and dale, in weather cold or fair;
> The captured hare is worthless in his sight;
> He only hastens after things in flight.

6. I found these typos in the Martín de Riquer edition of *Don Quijote de la Mancha* (Barcelona:
Talleres tipográficos Ariel, 1958).

7. Harald Szeemann, "Le macchine celibi," in *Le macchine celibi/The Bachelor Machines* (New
York: Rizzoli International, 1975), 9. The exhibition *The Bachelor Machines* toured Europe in
1974–75. The central and motivating object of the exhibition was Marcel Duchamp's *Mariée
mise à nu par ses célibataires, Méme*, 1915–23, Philadelphia Museum of Art, Louise and Walter
Arensberg Collection. The exhibition's male-specific (nowadays "gazing") focus on tinkering
and curiosity may be situated between Gilles Deleuze's formula "The unconscious is an
orphan, an atheist and a bachelor" (Szeemann, *Le macchine*, 19) and Michel Carrouges's
diagnosis "A bachelor machine is a fantastic image that transforms love into a technique of
death" (Szeeman, *Le macchine*, 21).

So writes Montaigne quoting *Orlando Furioso* on the huntsman's perpetual motion.[8] As lovers, men evince a wild desire ("desir forcené") for what eludes them ("aprés ce qui nous fuit").[9] Animallike, machinelike, human beings geared in maleness would seem to track universal desire from a primal reflex action to a final overcoming of both satiety and exhaustion in a sort of relentless *mechanotony*. From erection to apparatus, from reflex to contraption, male desire orbits Mother Earth from dawn to dusk, shifting from animal to machine, from son to sun, from nomad to satellite.

Montaigne's ethical conception of male friendship unites harmonious wills ("convenance des volontez") unburdened by sex. His men/friends should not suffer from vestigial animal symptoms (such as a downward reflex curiosity) or from the corresponding libidinal huntsman's frantic boredom and territorial nomadism. In contrast with a conception of friendship such as unalloyed spirituality, sexual love is a mestizo, a hybrid that entails a mixture of (female) care with cure. Sex-tainted love blends and seasons, as in Catullus's: Car nous sommes connus aussi de la déesse / Qui mêle à ses soucis une douce amertume. [For we are not unknown to the goddess / Who mingles a sweet bitterness with her cares]."[10] Voluptuous Venus mingles bitterness with sweet cares, her cures have a lingering taste of torture. Because of her, "venereal" (that is, erotic, *venerienne*) friendship carries a female taint all the way up to marriage, which in terms of Claude Lévi-Strauss's well-known culinary triangle might be deemed an *affaire metaculinaire*.[11]

Where a Caribbean Montaigne might have spoken of juice and salsa (of *condimento* and *papaya*), the original one from Bordeaux speaks of a man's marriage as something of a mixed affair, part commerce part entrapment: "As for marriage, for one thing it is a bargain to which only the entrance is free—its continuance being constrained and forced, depending otherwise than on our will—and a bargain ordinarily made for other ends. For another, there supervene a thousand

8. Ariosto's *Orlando Furioso* 10.7, as rendered in Michel de Montaigne's "Of Friendship" (1.28), in *The Complete Essays of Montaigne*, trans. Donald M. Frame (Stanford: Stanford University Press, 1965), 137; all English quotations are from this edition and are cited in the text.

9. Michel de Montaigne, "De l'amitié," chap. 28 of *Oeuvres complètes*, ed. Maurice Rat (Paris: Pléiade, 1962), 184.

10. Montaigne quotes from Catullus: "Neque enim est dea nescia nostri / Quae dulcem curis miscet amaritiem" (*Oeuvres complètes*, 184).

11. See Claude Lévi-Strauss, "A Short Treatise on Culinary Anthropology," in *Introduction to a Science of Mythology*, vol. 3, *The Origins of Table Manners*, trans. John and Doreen Weightman (New York: Harper and Row, 1979), 474–95.

foreign tangles to unravel, enough to break the thread and trouble
the course of a lively affection; whereas in friendship there are no
dealings or business except with itself." ("Of Friendship" 137–38). In
what it has of a perennial transaction, marriage leaves behind a hybrid
record, a paper trail full of errors and potentially marred with typos,
like unattributable emotional slips, documents punctuated by the
slang and gossip of tribal negotiations. Thus regarded, man's exo-
gamous nest resembles a ragtag muse, next to whom the soul of
unspotted friendship remains more inwardly endogamous than that
of any stale bachelor—and as such quite male and pure.

All those enforced, pregnant after-dinner silences between Lotario
and Camila (coupled with her aria-like soliloquy and sham depiction
of self-injury) should be seen against the light of such virile purity
(or as a counterscene staged on Montaigne's ingrained notion of wom-
en's paucity of spiritual conviviality):

> The ordinary capacity of women is inadequate for that communion
> and fellowship which is the nurse of this sacred bond [nourrisse de
> cette saincte couture]; nor does their soul seem firm enough to
> endure the strain of so tight and durable a knot. And indeed, but
> for that, if such a relationship, free and voluntary, could be built
> up, in which not only would the souls have this complete enjoyment
> [cette entiere jouyssance], but the bodies would also share in the
> alliance, so that the entire man would be engaged, it is certain that
> the resulting friendship would be fuller and more complete. But
> this sex [women's] in no instance has yet succeeded in attaining it,
> and by the common agreement of the ancient schools is excluded
> from it. ("Of Friendship" 138)

A virile friendship, such as the one between Montaigne and Etienne
de la Boétie, may generate letters, a certain traffic, a whole dossier;
it may even be perpetuated by means of a private gift from the dying
friend to his survivor: "Moy qu'il laissa, d'une si amoureuse recom-
mandation, la mort entre les dents, par son testament, héritier de sa
bibliothéque et de ses papiers [I, to whom in his will, with such loving
recommendation, with death in his throat, he [Etienne de la Boétie]
bequeathed his library and his papers]" ("Of Friendship" 136).

Accordingly, a double bequeathing of papers facilitates the reading
of the "Curioso" (in mixed [female] company, such as Dorotea's). In
the first bequest, a traveler's apparent neglect leaves behind a "maleta
olvidada con . . . libros y . . . papeles [a suitcase left behind with . . .
books and . . . papers]," containing those "ocho pliegos escritos de

mano [eight hand-written sheets]" ("de tan buena letra [in such a good handwriting]") which the busy canon would want to copy ("trasladar"), provided that what is written in them pleases him ("si la novela me contenta").[12]

Being an advocate of "repúblicas bien concertadas [well-ordered republics]" and proper entertainment (397), the canón should profit from the work of such an absentminded itinerant writer and unfit carrier, or from the abandoned work of a *cartero sin cartera*, a courier-in-spite-of-himself, and a writer by hand only. As a result of such backhanded bequeathing, the novelist's text (in its own confinement to the innkeeper's care) obtains curious postage. In not being carried to print, the eight- sheet *novela* is stamped like an undelivered message, an open letter available for copying, handling, or spoken delivery (as in the framing fiction of a fireside reading in Henry James's "Turn of the Screw").

The second bequest offers a riveting picture of a man's desperate will and compulsion to deliver a message, to cast his last word in the mold of an open letter broken by death in midsentence, as in Anselmo's: "Un necio e impertinente deseo me quitó la vida. Si las nuevas de mi muerte llegaren a los oídos de Camila, sepa que yo la perdono, porque no estaba ella obligada a hacer milagros, ni yo tenía necesidad de querer que ella los hiciese; y pues yo fui el fabricador de mi deshonra, no hay para qué [A foolish and impertinent desire took away my life. If news of my death were to reach Camila's ears, she should know that I forgive her, for she was in no need to perform miracles, nor did I have any need to have her perform them; and since I was the contriver of my own dishonor, there is no need to]" (445). Anselmo writes this message in extremis, with his body stretched out, half in bed and half over the writing desk, just as he will be found by the landlord: "Y hallóle tendido boca abajo, la mitad del cuerpo en la cama y la otra mitad sobre el bufete, sobre el cual estaba, con el papel escrito y abierto, y él tenía aún la pluma en la mano [And he found him stretched face down, his body half in bed and the other half over the writing desk, on which he lay, with the paper written and unfolded, as he still held the pen in his hand]" (445).

Anselmo's death tableau allows us to sketch two intersecting psychoanalytic perspectives on the "Curioso": one textual-intensive, the

---

12. Miguel de Cervantes Saavedra, *El ingenioso hidalgo Don Quijote de la Mancha*, ed. Luis Andrés Murillo (Madrid: Clásicos Castalia, 1978), 1:398. Unless otherwise noted, all quotations are from this edition and are cited in the text by page.

other audio-visual or specular. The two perspectives may correspond to a *postal* (textual-intensive) mode and a *hysteric* (aural-specular) mode. On the one hand, we would have the random and virtually centerless processing of messages, such as happens in the flow of modern information; on the other, the concentric emanation, the magical issuing of ancestral mysteries from a primal core, from a navel oracle. Whereas the postal mode delivers the message but does not read it, the hysteric-oracular mode rehearses the endless birth of personal meaningfulness uncannily unveiled, in sound and image, as a reiteration of the mimicry of death.

Anselmo's last posture unveils a painterly remnant of his ill-spent energies. In terms of Duchamp's aesthetics in rejection of the *tactile* feeding of the retina, Anselmo's death elongation betwixt bed and desk represents a gesture in oil, a visual pun dabbed on repressed attitudes and contortions of pain and desire, as if such grotesque transparencies of a body's vying for dual location were a desperate way of alluding to some unseen sexual obscenity, such as the one Anselmo craves in Camila's eventual surrender to Lotario's verbal and physical onslaught. In ritual and theatrical terms, the "Curioso" depicts the relentless increase of Camila's feeding Anselmo's programmatic greed to know and exhaust the truth, as she blossoms into histrionic extravagance in her one-woo-man show and lures Lotario's own extant curiosity into absorption and eventual death.

As a textual-intensive apparatus, the postal perspective bisects the stage of hysteria with the agencies of parody. The apparatus's laughter lies beneath Camila's furious simulation of injury and her fake suicide. If taken further toward the realm of Bertolt Brecht's *Verfremdungseffekt* and Duchamp's abstract glass paintings, hysteric eventfulness may move a final step into mimetic prosthesis and the body uncanny: "The hysteric symptom is construed as a mysterious and spectacular mechanism when one abandons the attempt to specify the coordinates of the terrain on which it originates" (Ménard 48). In other words, when the nonempirical ubiquitousness (omnipresence) of the hysteric body is deprived of its ultra- or multidimensionality, a countereffect, a mechanical up-and-down of lower parts into higher parts (as in symptoms of *astasia-abasia*) might take over, and then we would have something like the bachelor apparatus.[13]

13. In Michel Carrouges's influential *Les machines célibataires* (1954), the bachelor apparatus is constrained in its basic features by the original model of partitioned upper and lower halves as found in Duchamp's *Large Glass* (see fig. 2). As is the case with Freud's model for the psyche, an *Apparat* regulates passage through a high and low topography (Szeemann, *Le macchine*, 5–6). In hysteria, such vertical partition, instead of just collapsing, folds over,

In the "Curioso," the apparatus implants itself here and there, in random and sequential fashion. Its most trivial, ready-made, and (in the computer age) perhaps endangered species is the typo. Octavio Paz defines Duchamp's *Readymades* as "anonymous objects that the artist's gratuitous gesture, the mere fact of choosing them, converts into works of art," adding that "this gesture does away with the notion of art object," and that the "essence of the act is contradiction." For Paz, a *Readymade* (fig. 7) "is the plastic equivalent of the pun."[14] In parallel fashion, typos lie on the page like flies on a tablecloth; they are an unwanted litter, a spontaneous generation of foundlings. Some (like "recípoca" for "recíproca" ["recifewcal" for "reciprocal"]) seem the product of a typographic devil, an imp of the perverse. Other typos (such as "Loratorio" for "Lotario") may set in motion the bachelors' grinding wit or chocolate factory.

By dint of such wit, a typographic flaw may become a *typogram*, a postal message (fig. 7). Viewed as a factory of typographic debris, the apparatus acts like a gossipy bug or impish virus. For instance, it should follow from the existence of "repúblicas bien concertadas" (as the canon might wish) that a friendship such as that between Anselmo and Lotario ought to move on like clockwork (like a mechanical version of Montaigne's "convenance des volontez"). Thus: "Andaban tan a una de sus voluntades, que no había concertado reloj que así lo anduviese [They went about so much of a piece with their wills that no well-set clock could match their pace]" (327). Timepieces and clockwork soon suggest a host of other concerted routines and schedules—and that essential bureaucratic evidence of public concert, the postal system.

As opposed to the ancestral, magic-bound call of the specular mode, the postal mode winds up the "Curioso" and sends it forward like a toy, on to a future it pretends to read in text- intensive fashion. The postal mode is *typonomic*; it looks at words and phrases through a magnifying glass: "cOncerTAdo Reloj" shows jumbled signs of L[otar]io, just as later on the sonnet pen name of "Cloris" gives hints of CamiLa-LOtaRIo, as a simple Scrabble play most obviously rendered in the game of the "cuatro eses" and the "abecé entero" mentioned by Leonela.

For instance, if one takes "vana" as the tailor-made adjective for "curiosidad" ("vana e impertinente" [338]), and insists on a gender

---

whereupon symptoms migrate from lower to higher body areas, episodically disturbing the body's regular deployment of erogeny and need.

14. Paz, *Appearance Stripped Bare*, 21–22.

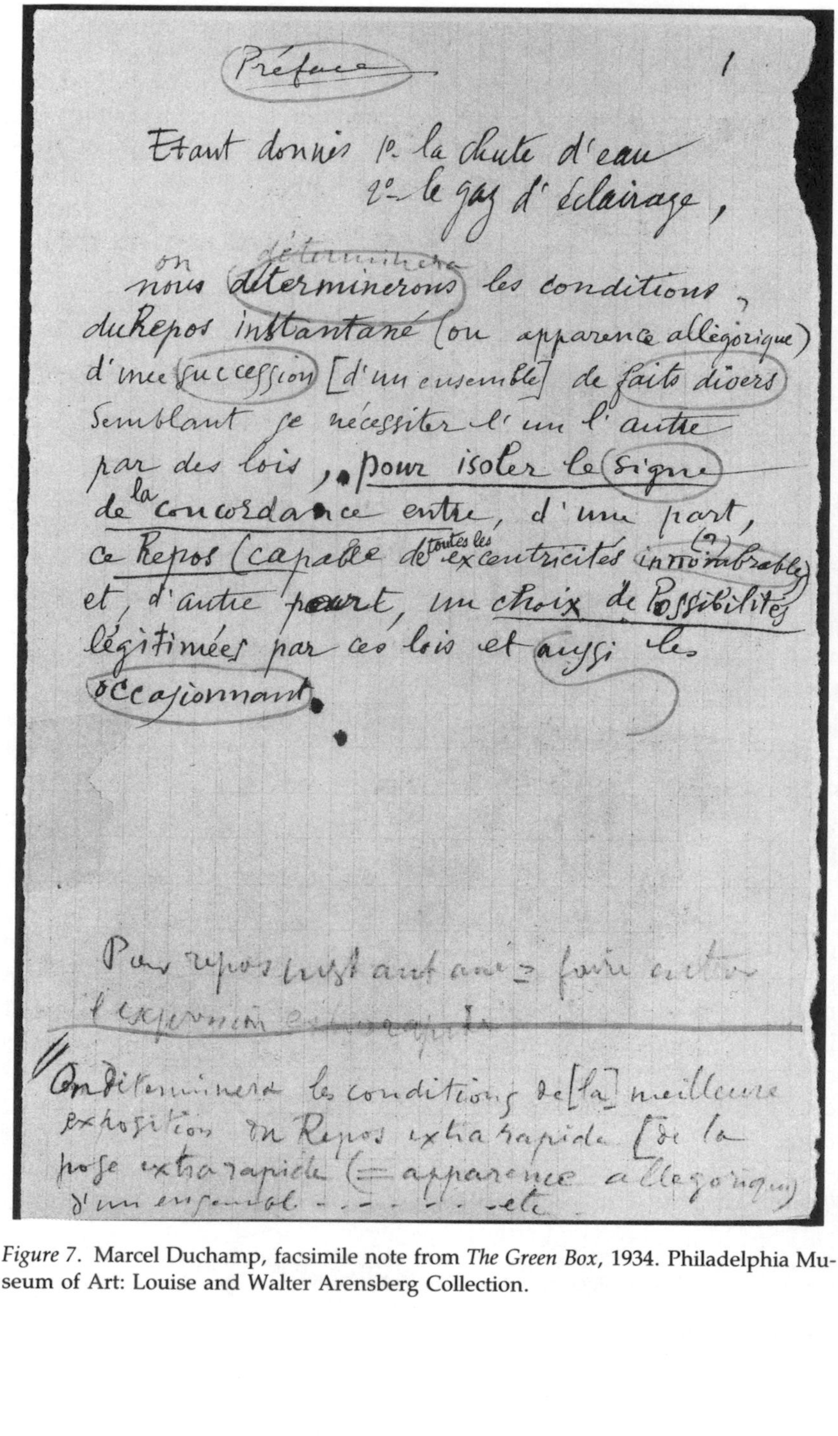
Préface 1

Etant donnés 1° la chute d'eau
2° le gaz d'éclairage,

on déterminera
nous déterminerons les conditions
du Repos instantané (ou apparence allégorique)
d'une succession [d'un ensemble] de faits divers
semblant se nécessiter l'un l'autre
par des lois, pour isoler le signe
de la concordance entre, d'une part,
ce Repos (capable de toutes les excentricités innombrables)
et, d'autre part, un choix de Possibilités
légitimées par ces lois et aussi les
occasionnant.

Pour repos instantané = faire entrer
l'expression extra-rapide

// On déterminera les conditions de [la] meilleure
exposition du Repos extra rapide [de la
pose extra rapide (= apparence allégorique)
d'un ensemble . . . . . etc

Figure 7. Marcel Duchamp, facsimile note from *The Green Box*, 1934. Philadelphia Museum of Art: Louise and Walter Arensberg Collection.

view of the coupled adjectives, "vana" could then disclose its root *v*-prefix as a proverbial signifier of femaleness in a misogynist key, just as Thomas Pynchon does in his novel *V.*, in which the eternal feminine punctuates itself into a cloning reality of vanishing *v*-words generated and chased by masculine consciousness into infinity. In such a fashion the two sonnets inscribed in the "Curioso" would enclose a postal syllabarium for a typogram punctuated in *v* ("va/voy, renovado/envía, Vuelve/vuelvo, verme/verme, olvido/vida, verse, navega/vía").

Having the postal system as its basic model, typonomy may grasp time as a virtual commodity linking all sorts of clocks (biological, sexual, and so forth). Thus, with a homophonic "[h]orario" (and *rato*) embedded in the typo "L[*ora*]to[*rio*]," a double sexual/reproductive scheduling frequency ticks into place in the early reference to "sosegada ya la frecuencia" (328), which marks the dwindling reiteration of visits by Lotario to Anselmo's house, until a "concierto" is reached between Anselmo and Lotario on having such meetings limited to "dos días a la semana y las fiestas [twice a week and holy days]" (328). But the phrase may refer (by parody rather than mere analytic habit) to a tacit conjugal settlement between the new spouses touching on the routines of coition and birth control.

Under whichever label (either "postal" or "typonomic"), this kind of reading toys around with what it perceives as the increasing commodification of time. The textual-intensive mode takes any sort of enchantment or magical prestige out of the remedial, oracular, or charismatic experience of time, or from any broadly ceremonial use of the time factor to influence, impress, forecast, cure, improve, charm, or harm anyone. As such, the textual-intensive method may preserve the oracular and hermeneutic thickness (and occasional grossness) of narrative discourse, but just in order to transport such crystallized syllabic treasures into an ensemble of figural objects evasively and teasingly linked to writing. Duchamp's phrase "Il n'y a pas de solution parce qu'il n'y a pas de problème [There is no solution because there is no problem]" can be easily misconstrued as signifying a certain dadaist indifference toward content as such, or cynicism regarding enigmas bound in some inward shape. But, as it turns out, the solution (itself always shifting with age and perspective) gives shape to the problem. The solution changes as the problem migrates back and forth between a string of words and a cluster of figures.

Looking inward, in the "Curioso," Anselmo implants a lethal problem in Lotario's soul, as he creates a secret and with it a virtual construct, part human being, part animated thing:

... un deseo tan extraño y tan fuera del uso común de otros, que yo me maravillo de mí mismo, y me culpo y me riño a solas, y procuro callarlo y encubrirlo de mis propios pensamientos; y así me ha sido posible salir con este secreto como si de industria procurara decillo a todo el mundo. Y pues que, en efeto, él ha de salir a plaza, quiero que sea en la del archivo de tu secreto.

[so strange a desire and so far removed from the common ways of others, that I marvel at myself, and blame myself, and fight with myself alone, and try to quiet it and to conceal it from my own thoughts; and thus, it has been possible for me to come out with this secret as if by industry I wanted to tell it to everyone. And since, indeed, it (él, = "he") must go forth to the square, I wish it to be inside the archive of your own secret]. (402)

Together with the repeated attitudes of *suspensión* and *turbación* (and their cognates *suspenso, suspensa, turbada,* and so on), the "Curioso" tempts us into linking the "él" type (the thing- and personlike "secreto," the secreted poison sealed into a portable archive) with Leonela's secretarial virus ("que el ser ella secretario de nuestros tratos me ha puesto un freno en la boca [that her being secretary of our dealings has placed a bridle in my mouth]," as Camila declares to Lotario [427–28]). The "Curioso" tempts us into further linkages and jumbled etymologies as if they were lead type (*archivo, arkhâios, arkhêion*) lying in a drawer under dust, promiscuously confusing the archaic with the powerful, in the manner of a contract between psychoanalytic cunning and mythmaking.

But there is no real secret in the "Curioso," that is to say, not one whose moral implications the story would not already have known or unsealed. The best that psychoanalysis can do is to say that the secret always lies in someone, *engramed* in a noun body and thus by force *fathered*. The father secret descends the narrative ladder of social hierarchies, it moves downward from persons endowed with names (such as Anselmo and Lotario) to Leonela's nameless lover (whose secret consists in his not bearing a name, a label that could support, underwrite, weigh in, or lend talent to a deeper genealogical mark). This nameless intruder, this stud of the night and proletariat in the toil of escaping identity, is stamped by Leonela as a "mancebo bien nacido [a well-born youth]" (351). Besides such iridescent irony, what remains in such final curiosity amounts to a mark of ghostliness, a minimalist but shocking proof of maleness exuded in darkness by Lotario and Anselmo.

Leonela's ultrabachelor night visitor may stand for what Stephen

Greenblatt refers to in his study of Martin Guerre as "the successful insertion of one individual into the identity of another." If, as Greenblatt asserts, the textuality of Renaissance identity marks property, the intruding *mancebo* lacks (and therefore critically lures onto himself) those threshold signs (borne by a proper name) that would bind him to "proprietary rights" and to "a place in an increasingly mobile social world"; the *mancebo*'s intrusions punctuate those substantive rights that, according to Greenblatt, "seem more an historical condition that enables the development of psychoanalysis than a psychic condition that psychoanalysis itself can adequately explain."[15] With such an incidental and opportune John Doe (or an Italo-crypto-Hispanic stud carefully and timely secreted into anonymity), the psychoanalytic appropriation of the "Curioso" may rest its case.

Conclusion: The Taste of Truth

Lotario concludes his brilliant oratorical piece against "vain and impertinent curiosity" (Saint Augustine's "vana et curiosa cupiditas") on a consubstantial note. He reminds Anselmo that both husband and wife come from Adam and Adam's rib, so the divine sacrament of matrimony miraculously rules that "dos diferentes personas sean una misma carne [two different persons may be one and the same flesh]" (411), and that "la carne de la esposa sea una mesma con la del esposo [the wife's flesh be the same with the husband's]" (411), whereby a husband would himself suffer injury if his wife were injured, more so when he himself may have caused her peril. Unmoved by such consubstantial notions, Anselmo responds with his own analogical equivalent of a shared (and gendered) substance as he diagnoses his own species of cognitive greed as a woman's eating disorder:

Has de considerar que yo padezco ahora la enfermedad que suelen tener algunas mujeres, que se les antoja comer tierra, yeso, carbón y otras cosas peores, aun asquerosas para mirarse, cuando más para comerse.

[You must consider that I now suffer the same illness that ails some

15. Stephen Greenblatt, "Psychoanalysis and Renaissance Culture," in *Learning to Curse: Essays in Early Modern Culture* (New York: Routledge, 1990), 191, 141.

women, who fancy eating soil, chalk, coal, and worse things, even those loathsome to look at, and more so to eat.] (411–12)[16]

As Caroline Walker Bynum has so richly illustrated, from paradise to Eucharist Christian intergender conduits run full of all species of food, invested with the ambiguous powers of a polymorphous controlled substance.[17] To speak of food in traditional Christian idioms seems to imply the inextricably gendered nature of a divine presence and body permeated with woman-specific feelings, talents, and needs otherwise dogmatically banished from the focal maleness of the Judeo-Christian deity.

At its nearest point from Cervantes, the "Curioso's" literary ancestry begins on a note of evil ingestiveness: "O esecrabile Avarizia, o ingorda [O execrable avarice, o gross (greed)]" (*Orlando Furioso* 43.i). In the world of Ariosto's Mantuan knight, women are drawn toward such feminine, fattened names by their own mirrored cravings. In the "Curioso" the womanly-filthy and omnivorous Anselmo (that "most deliciously deceived of men") prescribes to Lotario a change in seductive tactics from "palabras" to "obras"; for Anselmo the time has come to tempt Camila with gold and to fatten her with jewels ("que compréis joyas con que cebarla" [314]), with the same glittering food and "malvagio stimulo [wicked lure]" of "le belle gemme [those lovely jewels]" with which Rinaldo breaks Melissa's chaste fasting in the *Orlando*.

Thus, Ariosto's Rinaldo plays his own (wife's) seducing bachelor in a magical collapsing of male roles from which the "Curioso" seems to abstain, unless prompted by psychoanalytic play. Yet the merging or collapsing of male roles may still prevail in the "Curioso's" plot, perhaps embodied in the third, unnamed presence cast by Leonela's night lover in between Anselmo and Lotario. We may imagine a shift from the illusions of magic to the deictic (or pointing, as in "I" or "you") ambiguities of psychic anxiety. In Ariosto's archaic layers of Mantuan sorcery, the experimental bride moves not to a monastery but to the palace of that falcon-chasing "cavallier giovene, ricco e bello [young, rich, and beautiful gentleman]," all too briefly and devastatingly impersonated by curious Rinaldo. What is left of a *macchina celibe* in Ariosto is a puppet show, as if activated by the drop of a

16. Luis Murillo points out that Anselmo's words might allude to a type of hysteria ("cierto tipo de histerismo") or to the cravings of pregnancy ("los antojos del embarazo"); see *Don Quijote*, 1:412, n. 22.

17. Caroline Walker Bynum, *Holy Feast and Holy Fast: The Religious Significance of Food to Medieval Women* (Berkeley: University of California Press, 1987), passim.

coin, in which each husband (and bachelor at heart) takes the goblet, and with mouth still agape, spills it on his chest with an involuntary wink at Freud's hermeneutic arts.

One might conclude that Anselmo's brand of moral vampirism and lethal impertinence deserves a taste of the sublime sadism declared in Lou Andreas-Salomé's tribute to memory: "I am eternally faithful to memories." To this tribute she added: "I will never be faithful to men" (Ménard 187). One may also conclude that, as an all too busy masochist, the curious and impertinent man seems someone who mourns wrongly, as if not knowing that he mourns (or for whom and with whom he should share his present mourning). In the end, one may repeat Anselmo's stubbornness in trying to carve from the "Curioso's" layered body nothing if not a few all too obvious psychoanalytic templates. Therefore, if Anselmo's unconscious and perverse desires seem to resonate the most as gestures of self-punishment, my own search for arcane etiologies and hidden motives in his drama should prove as impertinent as his proverbial male malady, unless I choose to be as unfaithful to the "Curioso" as Andreas-Salomé claimed she would remain un/bound to/from men. Still, with her in mind, rather than being faithful to memories only (like a madly self-aware Don Quixote) and hence mainly to the past and the ability to mourn, the critic- analyst may assume that art objects (such as stories) project themselves into the future, as if into their own still unfathomed yet ever so actual past.

Besides such reversal of time arrows, psychoanalysis may confirm what tradition and doctrine already know: that the question of truth (its subject and object) in the "Curioso" appears forever biased in a way in which (a) man is fixed as a hostage to curiosity, as a man whose jailer he himself remains in masochistic reflection, a reflection so disfigured as when a woman may result in [Wo]man. in a sole woman embedded in a man, as a surrounding, enveloping presence which he otherwise would rather keep in a cage—or suck into a bottle. A museum exhibit of this most curious and empowering male bias is offered in the last three boxes (figs. 8, 9, and 10) appended to this essay as a contribution to the peculiar intertextual legacy of exemplary fiction that runs from Boccaccio through Cervantes into Henry James.[18]

Little truly new or profound can be said about curiosity as one

18. Figure 8 quotes the opening paragraph from Henry James's novella *In the Cage*. Figure 9 mixes another passage from the novella with Leon Edel's commentary in *Henry James: The Treacherous Years, 895–1901* (New York: Avon Books, 1978), 248. and with Morton Dauwen Zabel's introduction to *In the Cage and Other Tales* (New York: W. W.

It had occurred to her early that in her position—that of a young person
spending, in framed and wired confinement, the life of a guinea-pig or a
magpie—she should know a great many persons without their recognising
the acquaintance. That made it an emotion the more lively—though
singularly rare and always, even then, with opportunity still very much
smothered—to see any one come in whom she knew outside, as she called
it, any one who could add anything to the meanness of her function. Her
function was to sit there with two young men—the other telegraphist and
the counter-clerk; to mind the "sounder," which was always going, to dole
out stamps and postal-orders, weigh letters, answer stupid questions, give
difficult change and, more than anything else, count words as numberless
as the sands of the sea, the words of the telegrams thrust, from morning to
night, through the gap left in the high lattice, across the encumbered shelf
that her forearm ached with rubbing. This transparent screen fenced out or
fenced in, according to the side of the narrow counter on which the human
lot was cast, the duskiest corner of a shop pervaded not a little, in winter,
by the poison of perpetual gas, and at all times by the presence of hams,
cheese, dried fish, soap, varnish, paraffin and other solids and fluids that
she came to know perfectly by their smells without consenting to know
them by their names.

Figure 8. Box: Henry James, *In the Cage.*

emerges from the intertextual legacy rehearsed in this essay—little
beyond my noting that, as a figure of art and a theme of wisdom,
curiosity blames women. It makes them victims of greed and revenge
even as it bestows on them an infinite measure of potency which men
seem not to want to possess unless previously beheld as corporeally
animating femaleness.

Norton, 1958), 6–7. Figure 10 excerpts from Jacques Derrida, *The Post Card: From Socrates
to Freud and Beyond*, trans. Alan Bass (Chicago: University of Chicago Press, 1977), 229–
30.

The barrier that divided the little post-and-telegraph-office from the grocery was a frail structure [sic: grocería(!) / fragilidad / virginidad] of wood and wire; but the social, the professional separation was a gulf that fortune, by a stroke quite remarkable, had spared her the necessity of contributing at all publicly to bridge. . . . *She is curious . . . we know the girl only as a troubled observer, using her inductive and deductive capacities to satisfy an insatiable curiosity about her environment. . . . [. . . during his attentive exploration of London . . ("the habit and the interest of walking the streets") . . .] his "eyes greatly open" and his "mind curious" ("mystic solicitation, urgent appeal") . . . in those days of the 1890s before the spread of the telephone system, the telegram was a means of quick communication . . . the local postal-telegraph office, usually installed in a convenient grocer's shop. . . . The cage-girl's notions of the world are derived in part from romantic novels; the telegrams handed in through the high aperture of her cage become a part of the fictional furnishings of her mind. . . . It was in such a shop [so he tells us in his preface] the "spark" of his tale, kindled by the "wonderment" . . . about the "confined and cramped and yet considerably tutored young officials of either sex" who were "made so free, intellectually, of a range of experience otherwise quite closed to them" [[the "caged telegraphist," "a proper little monument"]] a "focus of divination," "her quite definitely winged intelligence; just as the catastrophe, just as the solution, depend[ed] on her winged wit"* [sic: dependent, wigged, i.e. H. G. Wells's Griffin, Samson as Delilah, etc.]

Figure 9. Box: Henry James, Leon Edel, M. D. Zabel, *In the Cage.*

. . . and you asked me: is it true that men can have children until their death.....[*4 August 1979*].....imagine a book of testamentary sentences (strophes, cartouches), the last words of a whole collection of guys before their suicide........................The post card would be full of secret dedications, collective murders, embezzlings of funds, tight transactions with poker face, impasse or blank check, and I make flowers, and I "*self-address*," as they say, optical money orders, and I call myself so that it answers busy and afterward have the communication gratis, with which I offer myself bargain alliances, poisoned strokes of the syringe............................., the *carte* will be full of inaudible murmurs, of deformed names, displaced events, real catastrophes [*Un necio e impertinente deseo me quitó la vida. Si las nuevas de mi muerte llegaren a los oídos de Camila*] . . . ["Dícese que aunque se vio viuda, no quiso salir del monesterio [*sic*], ni, menos, hacer profesión de monja...].......mad exchangers, abortion right in the confessional....[. . . , hasta que, no de allí a muchos días, le vinieron nuevas de que Lotario había muerto en una batalla que en aquel tiempo dio monsiur de Lautrec al . . . "]...., a breathless information, absolutely forbidden sufferings, and the virgin who traverses everything with a love song, our oldest game......[*9 August 1979*] . . . she is a new one, very beautiful, she comes regularly and earlier. As she is only a replacement. . . . I give her money each time (a telegram, a certified letter, etc.) . . . to myself I call her Nemesis..

Figure 10. Box: Jacques Derrida, *The Post Card*.

11

"The Captive's Tale": Race, Text, Gender

Paul Julian Smith

"*Amexi,* cristiano, *ámexi.*"
—*Don Quixote*

My aim in this essay is to reread "The Captive's Tale" (*Don Quixote* I.39–42) in light of the work of the gay theorist and activist Guy Hocquenghem.[1] In his major work *Homosexual Desire*, Hocquenghem draws a distinction between vertical and horizontal paradigms of social interaction. As we shall see, these paradigms engage a series of binary oppositions: closed/open; planned/random; temporal/spatial. I maintain that these oppositions are interrogated by Cervantes's text, which sets in motion characters such as the renegade and the captive himself, who refuse to be confined to one side or the other. The main question I ask is whether it is possible to draw out of Cervantes's text a male alternative to the patriarchal, hierarchical order, an alternative that may perhaps be identified with a desublimated homosexuality.[2] The problem of sexual preference, however, is inseparable from that of sexual difference. I therefore also attempt a new reading of the women in the text, one that does not draw on Hocquenghem's theories of a "desiring machine" among men.

When Zoraida, as yet unnamed, is asked by Dorotea to share the

---

1. This essay serves as a supplement to the final volume of my trilogy, *Representing the Other: "Race," Text, and Gender in Spanish and Spanish American Narrative* (Oxford: Oxford University Press, 1991), which does not treat Cervantes. I thank the editors of this volume for their many helpful comments and meticulous attention to detail.

2. For a study of homosocial bonding in another text by Cervantes, see Diana de Armas Wilson's " 'Passing the Love of Women': The Intertextuality of 'El curioso impertinente,' " *Cervantes* 7 (1987): 9–28.

227

Christian women's lodgings in the inn, she makes no verbal reply,
but inclines her head with hands joined (I.37). Draped or masked by
veil and robe, the woman of color is initially, at least, deprived of
language and can speak only through her body. She is silent, infan-
tilized, and triply marginalized—through "race," religion, and gender. How is the critic to make her speak, or, rather, to interrogate
the conditions of her exclusion from discourse? The answer would
seem to lie in a "symptomatic reading" of the kind that, for Gayatri
Spivak, is the greatest contribution French feminism has made to
critical theory.[3] I am inevitably dependent here on María Antonia
Garcés's pioneering analysis of the veiled woman in "The Captive's
Tale."[4] Like Garcés, I hope to interweave Zoraida's story with the
narratives of psychoanalysis, as well as to attempt to unravel those
knots in the text in which "race," text, and gender (ethnicity, textuality, and sexuality) are most closely intertwined. I argue for a shift
in the reading of "The Captive's Tale" from a vertical paradigm of
filiation or patrimony to a horizontal model of contingency or contiguity. Following Hocquenghem, I suggest that the former is a phallic
mode and the latter an anal one.

As the captive begins his narration, there is a sense of a hermetically
sealed male society which frequently recurs during the course of his
story. The founding moment is one of patrimony, of the division of
the father's wealth among the three male children (I.39). Avatars of
the father appear in the pages that follow, in which Cervantes seems
to take pleasure in ringing the changes on all possible forms of male
relation: fathers, sons, and brothers cede to uncles, fathers-in-law,
and even a would-be godfather. This reproduction of patriarchal relations (transmission of the father's name and capital) is so hermetic
as to exclude women almost entirely: not only does the captive's
family have no mother but neither, for that matter, does Zoraida's.
By the time of the final anagnorisis, when the captive is recognized
by his brother once more, almost no women remain in the family:
the brother's wife has also died, leaving behind only the dowry that
will ensure the brothers' future prosperity (I.41). As Garcés notes,
Zoraida serves the traditional role of object of exchange between men:
it is her exclusion from the patriarchal system that is the precondition
for the functioning of that system.[5] Exiled outside history (from the

3. Gayatri Chakravorty Spivak, *In Other Worlds: Essays in Cultural Politics* (New York:
Methuen, 1987), 149.

4. María Antonia Garcés, "Zoraida's Veil: 'The Other Scene' of 'The Captive's Tale,' "
Revista de estudios hispánicos 22 (1989): 65–98.

5. Ibid., 77.

men's time of filiation and generation), Zoraida is confined to a woman's time of circularity and monumentality (of movement from man to man and of idealized aestheticism).[6]

But Zoraida is also the embodiment of capitalization, both libidinal and economic: when they are threatened by the French pirates, the captive fears lest Zoraida lose the "most precious jewel" of her virginity (I.41). As in Michel Foucault's icon of the "pierres sonnantes,"[7] it is in the mute language of the body (the precious enigmas of feminine sexuality) that woman speaks and takes on value. It is significant that Zoraida is introduced in the captive's narration through the synecdoche of the "white hand" which drops money from a slitlike window to the prisoner (I.40). The woman of color is thus reduced to the (white) same, a homogeneous female beauty which must constantly reproduce (reflect) itself but can have no basis in the real. When Zoraida's veil falls each of the white women believes her to be even more beautiful than her companion (I.37). As in Barthesian catachresis,[8] female beauty refers to an origin that is itself a fiction, that can have no autonomous existence in or for itself. Where woman is concerned, even "racial" difference, elsewhere held to be so determining, cannot be permitted to trouble this mirror effect.

Initially the division between "races" is as hermetic as that between genders. The difference between Christian and Muslim is a binary divide at once ethical and epistemological: that between truth and falsehood. North Africa is thus the mirror of European production,[9] its duplicity and treachery the inverse of the Christian captive's loyalty and true faith. But, as we have already seen, the ethnic mirror also reproduces certain patriarchal structures unchanged, most particularly the silent erasure of the maternal function, as conspicuously absent in Algiers as in León. At one point Zoraida's father curses the moment when he engendered her; but even here there is no mention of a mother (I.41).

It is Zoraida herself who warns the captive not to trust her fellow Moors (I.40); and the juxtaposition of gender and "race" in a single subject thus muddies the paradigm that at first seemed so clearly hierarchical. For woman's falsehood is also proverbial; indeed, the name of the shore on which Zoraida's father is abandoned (La Cava Rumía) is said to mean "false Christian woman" (I.41). As a Christian

6. See Julia Kristeva, "Women's Time," trans. Alice Jardine and Harry Blake, in *The Kristeva Reader*, ed. Toril Moi (New York: Columbia University Press, 1986), 187–213.
7. Michel Foucault, *La volonté de savoir* (Paris: Gallimard, 1976), 101–2.
8. Roland Barthes, *S/Z* (Paris: Seuil, 1970), 40–41.
9. See Jean Baudrillard, *Le miroir de la production* (Tournai: Casterman, 1973).

convert, Zoraida is at once true and false, faithful to her new religion and its cult of the Virgin, and faithless to the father whom she so cleverly deceives. Garcés notes the disagreement among critics as to whether Zoraida is coldly manipulative or passionately devoted.[10] But I would agree that it seems fruitless to speculate on what her motivations might be. Rather she embodies a number of disparate and indeed irreconcilable moments: of Christian truth as opposed to Muslim error; of feminine falsehood as opposed to male truth; and perhaps (as I argue in my conclusion) of womanly self-assertion, independent of male values. As in Jacques Derrida's *Spurs*, truth is here an "effect of the veil,"[11] called into being by a feminine disguise which serves the purposes of both modesty and coquetry.

North Africa, then, is the space of the mirror in the twin senses of reproduction and inversion. It is a phantom, carnival space in which even patriarchy may be parodied, at least for a moment: when he tries to drown himself, Zoraida's father is fished from the sea and held upside down by his Christian kidnappers, a symbolic inversion of a figure of authority (I.41). What is more, there are a number of marginal subjects in the narrative other than Zoraida who refuse to be assigned to one side or the other of the paradigm. Most disturbing is the Murcian renegade, who serves as intermediary between the two cultures, translating Zoraida's notes to the captive and, later, her conversations with her father (I.40, 41). The renegade collects signatures which will guarantee his good faith on his return to Spain; and we are told at the end of the tale that he returns to the Christian group or "gremio" through the offices of the Inquisition (I.41). But his very existence suggests duplicity or deviance, the possibility of treacherous translation. Far from guaranteeing good faith, the signatures collected by renegades may be counterfeit: as Derrida suggests, the very fact that a signature can be repeated means that it is subject to unauthorized reproduction.[12]

The renegade moves with relative freedom between Christian and Muslim lands: like the pirates who prey on Mediterranean shipping, or the people of the Spanish village where the captive lands who are "accustomed" to Moorish dress (I.41), the renegade is a marginal creature, defined by the frontier or the space between two cultures. In the discussion that follows, I suggest that the logic of the renegade

10. Garcés, "Zoraida's Veil," 90, n. 3.

11. Jacques Derrida, *Eperons/Spurs* (Chicago: University of Chicago Press, 1979), 58.

12. Jacques Derrida, "Signature événement contexte," in *Marges de la philosophie* (Paris: Minuit, 1972), 365–93.

is based on contiguity and contingency rather than filation and heredity, that is, on space rather than time. Freed from the obligations imposed by the oedipal reproduction of the family (the orderly succession of generations), he or she is open to continuing chance encounters in the present.

Most significant here is the passing reference to the renegade, described as a "pampered youth" ("regalado garzón"), implying perverse (nonreproductive) sexual practices "in the Moorish manner" (I.40). The betrayal of nation and religion are here combined with a rejection of the compulsory heterosexuality enforced in the Christian territories. In the pleasure dome of the Orient, even the nefarious vice may speak, at least for a moment. While heterosexual desire circles around the same (transmission of capital, reproduction of male genealogy), homosexual desire opens out onto the Other (cultural, religious, "racial"). The captive wonders at the lack of patronymics among the Turks: while the tyranny of men over women is undiminished in Algiers (Zoraida fears her father will stone her to death in a pit or a well), the fact of cultural difference introduces a certain interference into patriarchy, into the necessary process of filiation. The juxtaposition of different cultures ensures that certain practices held to be natural or universal (such as the transmission of the name of the father) are relativized, denaturalized.

The marginality of the renegade, then, suggests a trouble in reproduction, in the twin senses of generation and representation. It does so in two areas: language and space (text and territory). I argue in my conclusion that both of these are related to a certain homosexual desire, as (in Hocquenghem's phrase) "être à l'étranger" ("belonging to the foreigner" and/or "being in a foreign country").[13] We have seen that the mirror mechanisms of patriarchy and Eurocentrism are disrupted to some extent by the marginal or parasitic movement of the renegade. And as the narrative progresses, the binary of same and other comes under increasing pressure. Thus, having been told that Christians are true and Muslims false, we learn that Christian captives, once released, cannot be trusted to return and redeem their fellow prisoners (I.40). Zoraida, too, soon discovers that there is conflict and difference among Christians when the Spaniards are taken prisoner by the French pirates (I.41). But, what is more, the narrator acknowledges that Muslims are also subject to differentiation: the Moors go in mortal fear of the Turks,

13. Guy Hocquenghem, *La beauté du métis* (Paris: Ramsay, 1979), 10.

to whom they are subject (I.41). Even Spanish *moriscos* are subdivided into different species, such as the *tagarinos* or Moors from Aragón (I.41). The Other is thus different from itself, intermittently deidealized and historicized.

This stress on material specificity is particularly true of language. Much has been written on Cervantes's insertion of (sometimes inaccurate) Arabic words and phrases into his Castilian text. These serve to some extent as "reality effects": it is their very superfluity to the development of the narrative that lends them the appearance of direct testimony to the real. But it does not seem to have been noticed how often these loan words are proper names: thus *juma* is Friday (I.40), *nizarani* is Christian (I.41), and *lela Marién*, the only phrase in Zoraida's letter which the renegade does not translate, is the Virgin Mary (I.40). By choosing not to give the Spanish equivalents for these terms, Cervantes seems to be insisting here on the material specificity of the other language, on the extent to which it is enmeshed in cultural practice. Onomastics reveal the arbitrary nature of language which is normally repressed (the process by which the random becomes conventional). Elsewhere the captive reproduces the use of prefixes characteristic of Semitic languages and infrequent in Romance: a *t* distinguishes the interrogative from the imperative, as in *tameji* ("are you going?") and *ameji* ("go!") (I.41). It is of little importance whether these words (variously emended by modern editors) are correct or not. They reveal nonetheless that language is based on a network of differences both internal and external; and that meaning is produced both within and between cultures. The insertion of a single consonant here marks the insistence of the letter[14] with a vengeance, the persistence of language as the producer of cultural identity.

But, once more, this linguistic territorialization is under threat: there exists a *koiné* or lingua franca which is neither one thing nor the other, a "bastard language" which undermines authorized cultural patrimony and facilitates improper intercourse between Moor and Christian (I.41). Like the "pampered youth" or the lost patronymic, the lingua franca suggests a trouble in reproduction which is at once cultural and sexual. When the binaries dissolve (when the hierarchies crumble), then fixed oedipal territory gives way to an unstable border country of multiple and polymorphous desire. The family triangle

14. Jacques Lacan, "L'instance de la lettre dans l'inconscient ou la raison depuis Freud," in *Ecrits* (Paris: Seuil, 1966), 2:249–89.

cedes to the autonomous and anarchic libido of Freud's early work.[15] It is at this point, then, that language gives way to space, text to territory.

The captive's story alternates between internal and external spaces. Thus the Spanish fortress breached by the Moors suggests those fragile boundaries that protect Christians from the chaos of the outside (I.39); and the Algerian prisons and houses that confine hostages and women, respectively, suggest the internal space of conservation, capitalization. Inversely, the father's garden in which the captive and Zoraida engage in coded conversation is a liminal space between the public and the private, at once outside and enclosed. As Garcés suggests, the internal space is thus coded as the feminine, private sphere.[16] But I would suggest that it is also anal: that space in which precious matter is stored up and released as gift or reward. This duality is acknowledged in Zoraida's kerchief: extended on a cane from the tiny opening of her father's fortresslike home, it repeatedly releases money to the waiting captive. At one point it is said to be "pregnant," and to "give birth" to its monetary progeny (I.40). Here womb and anus (child and money) coincide. Zoraida's jewel casket, the tiny space enclosing precious metals, also suggests that internal moment of conservation which Freud identifies with anal sublimation, and which Hocquenghem claims as the necessary precondition for the ownership of property.[17]

But if, under patriarchy anal desire is sublimated, diverted into social or financial investment, then phallic competition is ubiquitous and overtly symbolized. Men are constantly engaged in murderous combat (Christian against Moor, captive against pirate), and thus risk castration. When Arabs betray a Christian knight, they decapitate him (I.39); when pirates attack the captive's ship, they cut down its mast (I.41); the daring exploits of Cervantes, mentioned as a hostage in his own text (I.40), leave him vulnerable to impalement by his Moorish masters. For Hocquenghem such obsessive phallic competition is characteristic of a society in which sublimated homosexual desire is the basis of the great social machines: "Every man possesses a phallus which guarantees him a social role; every man has an anus which is truly his own." To desublimate homosexual desire would thus be to challenge "vertical" phallic hierarchy and to promote "hor-

15. See Guy Hocquenghem, *Homosexual Desire*, trans. Daniella Dangoor (London: Allison and Busby, 1978), 63.

16. Garcés, "Zoraida's Veil," 86.

17. Hocquenghem, *Homosexual Desire* 84.

izontal" or anal grouping: "The anus's group mode is an annular one, a circle which is open to an infinity of directions . . . [and] causes the social of the phallic hierarchy to collapse."[18]

As a narrative of time (of filiation or genealogy), "The Captive's Tale" tends to reinforce the masculine prestige of a rigorously sublimated homosexuality: exclusive relations between men serve only to reproduce patriarchal structures. As a narrative of space (of contingency or contiguity), "The Captive's Tale" tends to subvert phallic hierarchy: the transmission of the male line is subject to diversion and deviation, an "infinity of directions." Here "desvío" is the key word. The tale of the captive properly begins with his drifting away from his home ship on the alien vessel he has boarded at Lepanto (I.39); the boat on which he and Zoraida make their escape from Algiers drifts uncontrollably back toward the African coast (I.41); in the final scene at the inn, the captive communicates his presence to his brother "through indirection" ("por rodeos") and remains himself out of the way ("desviado") while the priest tells his story on his behalf (I.42). Although this last scene is deliberately staged by the captive, his career until then has been based on random encounters or contingencies, of which the meeting of the two brothers at the inn is only the most emphatic. Outside the oedipalized hierarchy of the Christian family, there exists no formal structure except that of multiple chance encounters in the present, an interminable sequence of events that Hocquenghem baptizes (after Gilles Deleuze and Félix Guattari) the "desiring machine." Once more the Muslim land serves as that utopian space in which the subject abandons control (desublimates the anal): the captive loses his inheritance, and the treasure chest is swallowed up by the sea (I.41). Like the pampered youth, the captive qua captive both "belongs to the foreigner" and "is in a foreign country." His encounter with the Other frees him from the bonds of filiation which bind him in Spain.

As the narrative ends, the phallic order seems complete once more: the captive will return to see his father before the latter dies (I.42). And with the imminent conversion of Zoraida/María, religious hermeticism is also complete. The women are secluded ("recogidas") in their room, guarded by Don Quixote. But they are awakened by a muleteer who compares himself in a song to Palinurus, the Virgilian helmsman who will never reach his destination, never achieve a decent burial. In spite of the closure of "The Captive's Tale," the nar-

18. Ibid., 83, 97.

rative thus at once opens out again, becomes subject to deviation and deferral.

I would suggest, then, that "The Captive's Tale" be read as a narrative of deterritorialization. The love for, or of, the foreigner (of Zoraida, of the captive) is emblematic of the fact that desire is multiple and eludes confinement within the fixed frontiers of the great social machines. We have seen that when gender intersects with "ethnic" difference, the conventional paradigms suffer interference: the Moorish woman beloved of the Christian man embodies truth, falsehood, and a certain self-affirmation (the oscillation between those terms). If we move with Hocquenghem, however, from a model of society based on phallic competition (on hierarchy and filiation) to one based on anal grouping (on contingency and contiguity), we must abandon the "molar" conception of the individual (the literary character) as unified whole and adopt a "molecular" model of the subject as inevitably fragmented and diffused.[19] In their fluidity and virtuality (their migration from one side of the "ethnic" paradigm to another), Zoraida/María, the captive, and the renegade are thus emblematic of a model of human identity which is no less material for its provisionality: as Hocquenghem remarks, we must acknowledge the position from which we speak; but that position is mobile, shifting.[20] Their fluctuating role within the logic of the text suggests, finally, that we cannot elude those determinants (such as "race" and gender) which go to make up our subject position; but neither are we confined to them or imprisoned by them. If the characters themselves remain captives of "race" and gender, they also point the way to a reexamination of those terms as they emerge into language and take on historical specificity.

19. Ibid., 58.
20. Guy Hocquenghem, *L'après-Mai des faunes: Volutions* (Paris: Grasset, 1974), 197.

V

The Mother's Story: Incorporation and Abjection

12

Cervantes and
the "Terrible Mothers"

Maurice Molho

No se cerraron sus ojos
cuando vió los cuernos cerca,
pero las madres terribles
levantaron la cabeza.

—Federico García Lorca,
  "Llanto por Ignacio
  Sánchez Mejías"

We can find in Cervantes a large group of iron-willed and over-whelming women whom I designate in this essay "Terrible Mothers." These are the same mothers who "raised their heads" when the bull gored the bullfighter in Federico García Lorca's poem "Llanto por Ignacio Sánchez Mejías." They are the bull-mothers who dominate men of diminished virility. The likelihood that a mother of this type dwelt in Cervantes's unconscious can be revealed by a close look at something as simple as his name. Why did Cervantes call himself Miguel de Cervantes Saavedra? There is much to suggest that, when he so denominated himself, he revealed a deep aversion to the ma-ternal, whose power he sought to evade. I propose here that the official and canonized name Miguel de Cervantes Saavedra is a cru-cible for erasure and repression, a crucible that contains further depths of unsuspected meaning.

Saavedra occupies the place in Cervantes's name conventionally reserved in Spanish for the mother's surname. Yet Saavedra is not the name of Cervantes's mother. As I argue in the discussion that follows, the substitute name Saavedra, while it displaces the mother, also reveals the power and virility that are associated with her in

Cervantes. In order to interrogate a subject so rife with parental fantasies, I take as a limiting factor the parameters of the name itself. Cervantes is the name of the father. It carries association with the deer. Yet the name offers a curious ambiguity: the deer is symbolic of wisdom and prudence; but the name is also insulting because of its reference to horns, which derive from equivalents such as Kuernalla, Kuklillo, Zervante.[1] The prudence of the deer (positive theme) and his horns (negative theme) coexist, then, in the same personal context.

This signifying chain would equate Cervantes, son of a cuckold and heir to horns (according to the symbolic reading of the name), with any of the provincial dignitaries of "The Wonder Show" ("El retablo de las maravillas"), all of them symbolic cuckolds like Cervantes himself. In the Cervantes family, in contrast to what happens to the foolish provincial dignitaries, horns and prudence are inseparable. The symbolic paternal horns direct us to the figure and character of Cervantes's actual mother, Leonor Cortinas. In Cervantine onomastics, Leonor(a) represents, by its own etymology, a leonine woman, associated with the zodiacal sign of the lion, symbol of light and power. For example, we have Leonarda in *The Cave of Salamanca*, Leonela in "The Curious Impertinent," and Leonora in the "The Jealous Extremaduran"—all of them strong and bold, and most of the time of violent and irascible temper. One should remember that, unlike to the Isabel who, in the first version of "The Jealous Extremaduran," ends up succumbing to the amorous wooing of Loaysa, the Leonora of the second version strongly resists her would-be lover to the point of exhausting his strength. At the end of the amorous struggle she remains, in Cervantes's word, "victorious," her unfulfilled lover asleep at her side. Leonora's victory is appropriate to a woman as strong and courageous as her name suggests. This is the way Cervantes's mother, Leonor Cortinas, most likely represented herself to her family—at least to some of her family—if one reads her name for what it is: as a nucleus of fantastic-symbolic meaning.

As for Leonor's second name, Cortinas, it means, according to Sebastián de Covarrubias's *Tesoro de la lengua castellana*, "the linens that cover the bed." These are familiar domestic objects that adorn what they conceal. This concealing of the name Cortinas allows itself, in turn, to be concealed—or better, masked—by Saavedra, the name

1. See Sebastián de Covarrubias Horozco, *Tesoro de la lengua castellana o española* (1611; reprint, Madrid: Ediciones Turner, 1977); see also Gonzalo Correas, *Vocabulario de refranes y frases proverbiales* (1627), ed. Louis Combet (Bordeaux: Feret et Fils, 1967), 707.

Cervantes chose to put in the place where Cortinas would normally have appeared.

The problem of genealogy in Cervantes has been made more difficult because many critics, especially before the 1966 publication of Américo Castro's *Cervantes y los casticismos españoles*, wanted to persuade themselves that Miguel de Cervantes had to have had an illustrious genealogy—one that could be traced to the ancient kings of León, or at least to the ancestry of Cardinal Juan de Cervantes, who served in the Court of Ferdinand and Isabella. Such wishful fabrications reproduce with variants those that were carried out by families of modest means (as was the case of the Cervantes family) throughout the sixteenth and seventeenth centuries in Spain. At a time when lineage was everything, families such as Cervantes's prided themselves on imagined glorious ancestries, and so the name Saavedra was probably born of multiple attempts to construct a genealogical novel founded on imaginary bloodlines. In that way everyone was able to create a "false chronicle" of his own family, one that could then be engraved in the collective memory with themes and plots composed of fantasy.

Those who have asked themselves about the Saavedra tacked onto Cervantes's name have vacillated between taking it as a genealogical reality, however incredible, and as a literary construct.[2] In fact, the problem posed by the name Saavedra is that which the construction of any name poses. The materials that restore memory, either individual or collective, do not function unless they integrate themselves into the fantastic construction which in the final analysis is what produces the name. The genealogical novel locked into the name Miguel de Cervantes has at its base the erasure of the maternal surname. Everything begins, then, with a disavowal (*Verneinung*) of the mother.

If we accept the hypothesis of Fernández de Navarrete that to con-

2. Thus Louis Combet identifies Sa(y)avedra with characters of the heroic tradition, balladric or novelesque. He also refers to a certain Gonzalo Cervantes Saavedra, originally of Córdoba, who appears in the *Galatea*; see *Cervantes ou les incertitudes du désir* (Lyons: Presses Universitaires de Lyons, 1980), 533ff. Luis Astrana Marín associates the name Saavedra with a family from Seville: that of Juana de Cervantes, who was abbess of Santa Paula in 1590. This is a positivist stance that omits the fantastic Saavedras who appear throughout literature and especially in Cervantes; see *Vida ejemplar y heroica de Miguel de Cervantes Saavedra, con mil documentos hasta ahora inéditos y numerosas ilustraciones y grabados de época*, 7 vols. (Madrid: Reus, 1948–57), 1:17ff. A genealogy in which a Saavedra appears who is completely fantastic and imaginary was proposed in 1815 by Fernández de Navarrete, suggesting that there is no contradiction between reality and fantasy, that fantasy is born of a reality which shapes it; see Dominique Reyre, *Dictionnaire des noms de personnages du "Don Quichotte"* (Paris: Serie Collection Thèses Mémorires et Travaux 1980), 136–37.

struct a name is really to mythologize it, Cervantes would have borrowed the name Saavedra from a historical-imaginary genealogy. In one such genealogy there appears, in fact, a certain Juan Arias de Saavedra, father of a hypothetical great-grandmother who married Diego de Cervantes, *comendador* of the Order of Santiago. Needless to say, the great-grandmother is as fictitious as her father, and they both have little function other than introducing the military theme in the genealogical novel. The names and occupations, however, allow for the substitution of Saavedra for Cortinas, a substitution that allows weapons to usurp the place of the mother.

In 1569 Cervantes adduced the name Saavedra to solicit a "purity of blood" report before going to Rome in the retinue of Cardinal Acquaviva. Saavedra is also the name he used to designate the captive soldier who is a thinly disguised version of himself in *Don Quixote*, "un soldado español llamado tal de Saavedra [a Spanish soldier known as de Saavedra]" (I.40). Similarly, in the *Tratos de Argel*, Cervantes uses the name Sayavedra to designate an exemplary soldier. The name, then, appears closely associated with the military theme.[3] Saavedra is the name that Cervantes would later give his daughter Isabel. To what representation of maternity, then, does the substitution of Saavedra for Cortinas correspond?

One should observe that although Saavedra obliterates the patronym of the mother, it fails to eliminate the corporeal mother, who remains present under the name that signifies her. The name change serves only to transform her, imposing on her, without altering her femininity, unknown traits and attributes. In other words, a surname symbolic of weapons and a military career must necessarily represent a supervirile woman who, looked at under the maternal aspect, can be nothing other than a phallic mother, that is to say, a mother with virile attributes that confer upon her a powerful, domineering vocation. We are left, through the grafting of the substitute name Saavedra, with the image of a woman who, however much she maintains her feminine stature, never stops flaunting her weapons—those swords that mark her femininity with the contradictory sign of the phallus.

The ambiguous mother is now signified by the military theme linked to the name Saavedra, yet this theme is itself ambiguous because

3. The fact that the name Saavedra appears in a petition relative to a "purity of blood" report could signify that it connoted, in addition to the military theme, the old Christian theme. In such a case, Saavedra could be something like a nominal mask designed to hide stains on the heritage; see Rosa Rossi, *Escuchar a Cervantes: Un ensayo biográfico* (Valladolid: Ambito Ediciones, 1988), 91–101.

Sa(y)avedra contains within it the word *saya* (skirt), a woman's garment, which works to counter the military connotations of the name.[4] We must also remember that Lorca's bull, alluded to at the beginning of this essay, also contains contradictory images. From the paleolithic throughout the Mediterranean mythological period, the bull, crowned with its heraldic crest composed of the half-moon, is a lunar and feminine symbol. Given the castrating potential of this maternal symbol, it is not surprising that the phallic mother would be represented in signs that highlight both her feminine and her military nature. A corollary of the phallic mother is the impotent man, who appears in many Cervantine texts. Like the mother, he is often marked by ambiguous gender indicators.

DISAVOWING THE MOTHER

The disavowal (*Verneinung*) of the mother occurs at least once in the work of Cervantes, and in that case it appears implicated in the theme of witchcraft. The rejected mother appears in the figure of Montiela in "The Colloquy of the Dogs." It is well known that the problematic aspect of the "Colloquy," and of "The Deceitful Marriage" with which it is associated, consists in discovering whether or not the dogs of the Hospital of Valladolid actually spoke in the presence of Ensign Campuzano as he lay sweating his fourteen treatments for syphilis. Speech is a human, not an animal, phenomenon. Is a dog that speaks a dog? Or is it something else? A man, perhaps, in the form of a dog?[5]

The central episode of 'The Colloquy of the Dogs" is articulated in the meeting of the dog Berganza and the witch Cañizares in Montilla. Cañizares reveals to Berganza that he was born not a dog but a man, and that his mother was a witch, a famous disciple of the renowned Camacha. Being pregnant, Montiela (the dogs' "mother") was assisted in her delivery by Camacha, who later confessed that, out of jealousy or envy, she changed the two boys into dogs, but that under the right conditions they would recover their human form.

---

4. With the root *saya-*, Sayavedra includes the thematic vowel *-a*, which in Spanish is a sign of feminine grammatical gender.

5. On "The Deceitful Marriage" and "The Colloquy of the Dogs," see my introduction to the bilingual edition of this double novella, *Remarques sur le "Mariage trompeur" et "Colloque des chiens"* (Paris: Aubier-Flammarion, 1970), 11–97. See also my "Antroponimia i cinonimia del 'Casamiento engañoso' y 'Coloquio de los perros,' " in *Lenguaje, ideología y organización textual en las "Novelas ejemplares"* (Madrid: Universidad Complutense, 1983), 81–92.

Camacha's confessional statement has to be true, since one of the dogs (no one knows which one; perhaps a condensation of the two) appears reincarnated as the trickster-showman Chanfalla, who in "The Wonder Show" goes from village to village carting a marvelous play. Wherever he goes, he introduces himself as Montiel, the name of the witch's son: "Yo, señores míos, soy Montiel, el que trae el Retablo de las Maravillas [I, gentlemen, am Montiel, the one who brings "The Wonder Show"]."[6]

If Berganza and Cipión are dogs, their speech is an inexplicable phenomenon, one that in all probability is nothing more than the delusion of a syphilitic soldier. It would be easier to explain their ability to speak if we knew they were men in the form of dogs, but that would mean accepting the possibility of witchcraft and the metamorphoses it purports to produce. Let us suppose, for the sake of the second hypothesis, that Montiela *was* a witch. About the father, we are told in passing that he must have been a certain good-for-nothing called Rodríguez: "que si no es con Rodríguez, el ganapán tu amigo, días ha que no tratas con otro [unless it was with your lover, that worthless Rodríguez, you have had nothing to do with anyone else]" (II.293). Is Camacha's declaration true or false? For the dogs, the criterion for answering this question is the credibility of the enigmatic five-line stanza that prophesies their resurrection. After examining all the possible readings of the stanza, Cipión opts to reject the prophecy and with it the hypothesis of his own humanity. It is this rejection of the prophecy that leads him to pronounce his ultimate denial of his mother: "La Camacha fué burladora falsa, y la Cañizares embustera, y la Montiela tonta, maliciosa y bellaca, con perdón sea dicho, si acaso es nuestra madre, de entrambos, o tuya; que yo no la quiero tener por madre [Camacha was a false trickster and Cañizares a liar, and Montiela was at once foolish, cunning, and malicious—if I may be pardoned for speaking that way of our mother, or rather of your mother, for I will not have her for mine]" (II.311).

Cipión's refusal is puzzling, since it is not possible to reject a mother who does not exist as a mother in the first place. This rejection, however, operates in the way described by Freud in his essay "Negation": "Negation is a way of taking cognizance of what is repressed; indeed, it is already a lifting of the repression, though not, of course,

6. Chanfalla identifies himself as Montiel in *El retablo de las maravillas*, ed. Eugenio Asensio (Madrid: Clásicos Castalia, 1970), 171. The "real" Montiel, the canine son of a witch, is a character in "Coloquio de Cipión y Berganza," in *Novelas ejemplares*, ed. Francisco Rodríguiz Marín, 2 vols. (Madrid: Espasa-Calpe, 1975), II.209–340. Subsequent references to the "Coloquio" will be cited in the text.

an acceptance of what is repressed."[7] Thus, by denying the mother, the dog actually recognizes her terrible maternity which nullifies the insignificant—infrapaternal—figure of the father (the lout Rodríguez). The mother here would seem to encompass both parental functions, mother and father, in virtue of her status as an ambiguous mother, both phallic and maternal.

It is her monstrous character that the dog (this time Berganza) contemplates with horror as the witch undresses. Berganza watches as Cañizares anoints herself with the unguent that permits her to enter into a catalepsy for the witch's sabbath. Unconscious and in a deathlike state, the naked witch presents to her canine "voyeur" a deformed and frightening figure: "Toda era notomía de huesos, cubiertos con una piel negra, vellosa y curtida; con la barriga, que era de badana, se cubría las partes deshonestas, y aun le colgaba hasta la mitad de los muslos [She was a skeleton covered with dark, hairy, shriveled skin; her belly was of parchment, covering her shameful parts and even hanging halfway down her thighs]" (II.305) In this description the genitals disappear behind a hanging belly that does not permit the identification of the exact nature of the "shameful parts," but nevertheless, by hanging "halfway down [the] thighs," the belly evokes a type of ambiguous sex that, by blurring the distinction between male and female organs, covers the maternal orifice with its enormity.

In their mutual rejection of the mother, the two dogs of the "Colloquy" become one. Even before Cipión's rejection of the mother, Berganza responds with disgust: "Quise morderla, por ver si volvía en sí, y no hallé parte en toda ella que el asco no me lo estorbase [I wanted to bite her to see if I could revive her, but could not find a single part of her that was not repulsive to me]" (II,305). Rejection, then, is followed by nausea, promoting a unique discourse continually founded on negativity. If rejection is in reality a recognition of that which is repressed by the intellect, terror and nausea are of a different nature: they concern the emotions rather than the intellect. After all, a nip is an inside-out kiss. Sharing the totality of the subject, intellect and emotion alternate. "With negation," writes Freud, we can see how "the intellectual function is separated from the affective process."[8] But in both cases the object is the same: accepting unpleasant

---

7. *The Standard Edition of the Complete Psychological Works of Sigmund Freud*, ed. and trans. James Strachey, 24 vols. (London: Hogarth Press, 1953–74), 19:235–36. Further references will be abbreviated *SE*, with volume and page number.

8. Ibid., 236.

representation without at the same time nullifying the repressive process. Although the attitudes of the two dogs appear divergent—intellectual refusal in the one, emotional refusal in the other—their motivations are the same: their constantly negative speech is an attempt to hide their similar filial affirmation of the embarrassing link that unites them with the witch. Both of them have her as their mother, and they repress the representation of the excessive mother, the one who lives in their unconscious as the substitute for a diabolical father. Independent of the real infrafather (that good-for-nothing Rodríguez), the materno-phallic witch transmits the virtues of the pact to the son. The gift of witchcraft persists in the only son, in that in human form Montiel is representative of the dual canine experience of Cipión and Berganza.

THE PHALLIC MOTHER: GENEALOGICAL NOTES ON "THE WONDER SHOW"

The image of the phallic mother and, more generally, of the dominating phallic woman is represented most clearly in "The Wonder Show" ("El retablo de las maravillas"), the play that Montiel brings to the villages of La Mancha and Andalusia. It is sufficient to reexamine the names of the characters in order to clarify and reveal the Cervantine problematic of a gendered dualism—an inverted pair. The condition that Montiel establishes as required in order to see the *retablo* of the wise Tontonelo is that the viewer be legitimate and of "pure blood," that is, without any traces of Jewish ancestry. This condition excludes bastards of either type—those of lineage and those of blood, of which only the first category interests us here. With the exception of the Señor Gobernador, who does not have a name, all the provincial dignitaries who make up the show's audience are specified by name and office: Pedro Capacho is a notary, Juan Castrado is the town councilor, and Benito Repollo is the mayor. All three names advertise the infravirility or impotence of those who possess them. In the name Capacho one recognizes the stem of the verb "*cap*-ar" (to castrate). Similarly, Castrado implies that the councilor and all his ancestry have suffered castration and that this prevents them from begetting legitimate children. Likewise, the name Repollo signifies a vegetable (cabbage) whose structure suggests the image of a womb. It is the suggestive shape of the *repollo* which in certain places has spawned the folkloric belief that children are born from cabbages.[9]

In comparison with the organic impotence inscribed in these names, let us now consider the corresponding status of the women. We may disregard Capacho because, according to what can be derived from his patronym, he has neither a wife nor descendants. In regard to Castrado and Repollo, however, it is important to observe that the onomastic symbolism of "The Wonder Show" utilizes the morphological structure of the language in order to contrast the sexes. In other words, it employs a commutation from -*o* to -*a* to mark the sexual opposition constitutive of the pair. Thus, since all the men of the Castrado line are named Castrado, through normal usage the women would be named by switching the -*o* ending to -*a*. Consequently, the daughter of Castrado would be Juana Castrada, a name that cannot signify castration, since women possess nothing that can be castrated. If a Castrado is a diminished man, a less-than man, then a Castrada must be a fully feminine woman, a complete woman, by definition. Juan Castrado is the son of Antón Castrado and of a woman who, if we make a qualitative leap, is not Castrada but something more on the scale of the sexual plenitude which covers the spectrum from femininity to the maximum virile superpower. Such in fact is the case of Castrado's mother, who by her very name—Juana Macha—announces herself as the prototype of the phallic woman.

Regarding the Repollo family, we know only the name of the daughter, a name obtained by the commutation of the mark of gender from Repoll-*o* to Repoll-*a*. Even though this commutation begets a morphologically feminine name, it continues to signify a supermasculine character with the mark of maximum virility. In addition to an innocent reading, the name Repolla admits other, more virulent interpretations; in the name Re-polla the prefix *re-* serves as an intensifier to the slang term for the penis: *polla* (prick). Teresa Repolla, therefore, is the morphological equivalent of the strictly lexical construction that produces Juana Macha; she is the *re-polla* or "superprick," the epitome of the phallic mother: Macha = *re-polla*. The caricatural nature of Cervantes's short comedy, then,

9. For more details and a bibliography, see my study of the "Retablo de las maravillas" in *Cervantes: raíces folklóricas* (Madrid: Gredos, 1976), 37–214, and esp. 176–87. The "Retablo" has inspired Rosa Rossi's "El lado cómico" in *Escuchar a Cervantes* 91–104, and pp. 73–88 of Lora Terracini's *Codici del silenzio: Le invarianti e le variabili dell'inganno* (Alessandria: Edizioni dell'Orso, 1988).

would have permitted giving body and name (it is all one) to the bull-mother *macha* or *re-polla*, whose dominating violence reduces the man to his irremediable infravirility.

Teresa Panza

It might seem strange to include Teresa Panza in the gallery of phallic mothers or bullfighting women. The ironic writing and distancing of *Don Quixote*, however, lets certain aspects of her character go unnoticed in the complex typological structure that creates them. Although Teresa Panza is not *sensu strictu* a phallic woman, she does possess traits characteristic of the dominating woman who overwhelms her husband with the weight of her authority. An attentive and partial reading reveals that behind the quick-witted country wife of Sancho Panza hides a terrible figure capable of inverting masculine virility.

As always, the onomastics say it all: "Cascajo se llamó mi padre; y a mí por ser vuestra mujer, me llaman Teresa Panza, que a buena razón me habrían de llamar Teresa Cascajo [My father's name was Cascajo; and as your wife I am called Teresa Panza, though by rights I should be called Teresa Cascajo]" (II.5). The surname of her husband is feminine: Panza. Yet, if we accept Teresa'a claim to her patronym, the name of the woman is masculine: Cascajo. This reversal of grammatical gender constitutes the inverted pair: the feminine for the man, and the masculine for the woman. Even apart from the fact that the name Panza evokes the carnivalesque figure of a glutton who is all *panza* (paunch) or roundness of belly, it also connotes a feminine silhouette. This phenomenon explains why, in a carnivalesque poem by Pedro de Padilla, the two mayors, Pero Pança and Sancho Repollo, are joined. Elsewhere I have tried to uncover the femininity of Sancho Panza, not only in his style of riding sidesaddle but also through his evocation, in the scuffles with Don Quixote regarding the disenchantment of Dulcinea, of historical ballads in which he identifies himself with Doña Sancha, the mother of the Infantes de Lara: "Aquí morirás, traidor / enemigo de doña Sancha [Here you will die, traitor / enemy of Doña Sancha]" (II.60).[10]

In contrast to Panza, a name suggestive of rotundity and softness, Teresa Cascajo carries a name that connotes stones and pebbles. Al-

10. Mauricio Molho, "Doña Sancha," in *Homenaje a José Manuel Blecua* (Madrid: Gredos, 1983), 443–48.

though it is associated with her "clodhopper" father, it continues to be hers because it is suited to the strong and rough, almost virile temperament of the female farmer. The Teresa Panza whom her husband evokes is by no means a model of suavity and affection:

> "Estaba diciendo entre mí que quisiera haber oído lo que vuesa merced aquí me ha dicho antes que me casara; que quizá dijera yo agora: 'El buey suelto bien se lame.' "
>
> "¿Tan mala es tu Teresa, Sancho?"—dijo don Quijote.
>
> "No es muy mala—respondió Sancho—pero no es muy buena; a lo menos, no es tan buena como yo quisiera."
>
> ["I was only telling myself that I would have liked to have heard before I was married what you said just now; in that case, I might be saying now: 'The ox that's loose licks himself well.' "
>
> "Is your Teresa as bad as all that, Sancho?" said Don Quijote.
>
> "She's not very bad," responded Sancho, "but she's not very good; or at least not as good as I would wish."] (II.22)

To what conduct or defects does Sancho allude with this clearly critical judgment? In both parts of *Don Quixote* we can assume, based on Sancho's criticism of his wife, that Teresa always serves, or almost always (with the exception of the ducal mocking and the letter from the duchess), as an instance of reality, repressive by definition. Unlike her husband, Teresa never loses sight of "el bien que [se ha de] sacar de las escuderías [the material gain which could come from (Sancho's) squirings]" (I.52). Upon Sancho's return from his first sally, Teresa's first question is about the ass, and then about gifts for the family: "¿Qué saboyana me traés a mí? ¿Qué zapaticos a vuestros hijos? [What garments have you brought for me? What shoes for the children?]" (I.52).

The same thing happens on Sancho's return from the second sally, which is more profitable than the first: "Dineros traigo, que es lo que importa, ganados por mi industria, y sin daño de nadie [I bring money with me, which is what matters, earned by my efforts and without harm to anyone]" (II.73). But his wife is not so scrupulous: "Traed vos dineros, mi buen marido"—dijo Teresa—"y sean ganados por aquí o por allí; que como quiera que los hayáis ganado, no habréis hecho usanza nueva en el mundo ['You just bring along the money, my good husband,' said Teresa, 'and whether you got it here or there, or by whatever means, you won't be introducing any new custom to the world']" (II.73).

Teresa's greediness is nothing but a mark of a repressive deprecation of her husband's clinging to the chivalric ideal: "Sólo te sabré decir, así de paso, que no hay cosa más gustosa en el mundo que ser un hombre honrado escudero de un caballero andante buscador de aventuras [All I will say in passing is that there is nothing more pleasant in the world than being a respected man, squire to a knight-errant who goes in search of adventures]" (I.52). Teresa works in her own way on Sancho, just as the priest and the barber work on Don Quixote, with the intention of debasing the poetic option that engenders the chivalric impulse in master and squire alike. This feminine repressiveness reaches its height in the debate in part II, chapter 5, between Sancho and Teresa about the opportunity of adventuring in search of islands to govern. The tension between the two characters continues to mount in proportion to Sancho's attempts to resist the repression. Teresa condemns all chivalric enterprises: "Viva la gallina, aunque sea con su pepita; vivid vos, y llévese el diablo cuantos gobiernos hay en el mundo; sin gobierno salistes del vientre de vuestra madre, sin gobierno habéis vivido hasta ahora [Long live the hen even though she may have her pip, long live you and may the devil take as many governorships as there are in the world; without a governorship you came out of your mother's womb, without a governorship you have lived until now]" (II.5).

Sancho responds to his wife's resistance by stating that the time will come for marrying Mari Sancha "tan altamente, que no la alcancen sino con llamarla señora [so high up on the social scale that no one will be able to come near her without calling her Lady]." Although Teresa continues to rail against all enterprises of knight-errantry, for Sancho, the chivalric desire to conquer islands has been changed into the ideal of courtly promotion. The marriage of the daughter will serve, then, according to the custom in noble houses, to negotiate titles and honors. Sancho's desire for social prominence provokes ire in Teresa: "Eso no, Sancho . . . casadla con su igual, que es lo más acertado [No, Sancho . . . marry her with her equal; that's the best way]." Sancho responds to this suggestion with mounting wrath: "Ven acá, bestia y mujer de Barrabás. . . . ¿Por qué quieres tú ahora, sin qué ni para qué, estorbarme que no case a mi hija con quien me dé nietos que se llamen *señoría*? [Come here, beast and wife of Barabbas. . . . What do you mean by trying to keep me from marrying my daughter to someone who'll give me grandchildren with noble lineage?]." Whereas the repressive stance of Teresa Panza consists of negating all social climbing, defending the idea that everyone should remain in his or her station, Sancho persists in his ambitions of heroic lordliness.

The argument is based on the radical inversion of functions: suddenly, "without any cause," Sancho assumes the kind of poetic discourse (speaking of adventures, islands, governments, heroic conquering, ennoblement, foundation of dynasties) until now associated with Don Quixote. In his customary speech the foolishly intelligent squire tends to employ a discourse deeply rooted in the quotidian. The Sanchescan discourse left vacant by the squire is taken up by Teresa in part II, chapter 5, and is used against Sancho, who at this point has assumed the role of Don Quixote. In other words, Sancho now occupies the place with respect to Teresa that don Quixote normally occupies with respect to him. From the instant when Sancho is converted into Don Quixote, the historic and squirelike discourse reverts to his wife, Teresa. The dialogue of Don Quixote and Sancho is now displaced by that of Sancho and Teresa. This latter dialogue is more authoritative and violent than the former one because Teresa behaves with a hard-heartedness—to my mind, characteristic of the terrible Cervantine maternity—unknown in Don Quixote.

This inversion of discourse is so radical that, throughout the whole debate, Sancho boasts of a rhetoric that is not customarily his, causing the translator to intervene twice in order to say that he considers this chapter apocryphal. In effect, such radical change is implausible and, therefore, unacceptable. Teresa's discourse, in fact, confirms the reservations of the translator. As she is about to conclude the debate, having abandoned any hope of convincing her husband, she quickly releases a Sanchescan malapropism which, like all the rest, is highly significant: "Haced lo que quisiéredes, y no me quebréis más la cabeza con vuestras arengas y retóricas. Y si estáis revuelto en hacer lo que decís . . . [Do what you want and don't give me a headache with your speeches and rhetoric. And if you have *revolved* to do what you say . . .]" (II.5).

How can one not recognize that the word Teresa has just blurted out is most accurate, most appropriate to the situation? In effect, Sancho *is* "revuelto," that is to say, topsy-turvy, thoroughly converted from farmer into gentleman, from the narrator of the story to a protagonist of poetry. He has become so different from the genuine Sancho that even the translator does not recognize him. Indeed, Sancho is so radically changed into Don Quixote that, instead of arguing for his side, he corrects, just as his master would do, Teresa's verbal blunder: "*Resuelto* has de decir, mujer, y no *revuelto* [Wife, you should say *resolved* and not *revolved*]." The poetic discourse which Sancho assumes in this chapter incapacitates him. Unable to resist the pressure of reality and dominate it, he is virtually reduced to impotence.

Teresa Panza, by contrast, who now assumes the particular and concrete presence of the story, is identified with the "reality principle," shown here by her wish to educate the children, to clothe them, and to supply the house with food and money. When Sancho promises to send her the money which is usually given to governors, Teresa Panza replies: "Enviad vos dinero . . . que yo os lo vestiré [a Sanchito] como un palmito [You send the money and I will dress him [Sanchito] up as fine as a palm branch]." Blinded by his dream of enrichment with money which will certainly be lent to him as governor, the delirious Sancho insists that he and Teresa are in accord: "En effecto, quedamos de acuerdo . . . de que ha de ser condesa nuestra hija [In effect, we are agreed that our daughter should be a countess]" (II.5). Once again we see that Sancho, unable to comprehend the reality of his circumstances, appears dominated throughout this episode by the fool's intelligence of Teresa, who, clinging to reality, drains his power from him. She will lose sight of it only when the perversity of the dukes captures her in the theater of the joke in which all is truth and all falsehood.

However much she overwhelms Sancho with her sense of reality, Teresa is no Juana Macha. Both women habitually express the desire to dominate, and each in her own way is a phallic woman. The difference between them is not of person nor even of character but only of literary genre. Juana Macha, out of the comic interlude tradition, is a caricature of the theater, a flat character with neither shadows nor subtleties. *Don Quixote*, however, being a novel, allows for a fuller development of character, so that each figure can be shown with a multiplicity of contradictory representations. Teresa Panza is a good example of such contradiction: she is a wise fool and, alternatively, a ridiculer of the foolish ravings of her husband.

THE INVERSE PAIR

A structural constant of the inverse pairs which we have been examining is that the feminine pole wins decisively, in weight, ardor, and power, over the masculine pole. I have considered Montiela and the worthless lout who passes as her lover; compared Juana Macha and the Señora Repolla, respectively, to the Castrado and Repollo families; and contrasted Teresa Panza's common sense to the stupidity of her husband. From the consistency of these examples we may infer that the examples of maternity in Cervantes can be assessed as "Terrible Mothers" to the degree to which they dominate fragile and impotent men with their phallic sexuality.

Nevertheless, it would be erroneous to reduce the Cervantine inverse pair to a formula

$$M < F$$

which, although it defines the respective relations of the referents, neglects the necessary internal equilibrium that safeguards the stability of the pair as an abstract binary structure. For this reason, the pair could be signified by means of a different equation:

$$\overset{(+)}{\underset{(-)}{M = F}}$$

in which the man (M) is negative in proportion to the woman's own positivity. The two poles of the pair can be considered equal in their inverse dynamism because the *minimum* of the masculine pole exactly equals the *maximum* of the feminine pole. The two contrary components of the pair are represented, then, as a conjunction of two contrary elements, as if the one had reverted into its opposite. This reversibility of each one of the two components of the pair makes it, ultimately, the projection of a general process of which the subject is at the same time representative, being likewise a reversible being who, moment by moment, is changed into its contrary.

A frequent argument raised by this inverse structure is one that opposes in the same being (the subject, the pair) the adverse modalities of activity and passivity. The active/passive polarity is nothing more than one of the forms which embodies the abstract opposition of the positivity and the negativity. In other words, the negativity of one of the elements of the pair implies its passivity compared to the activity of the necessarily positive opposite element. "The antithesis active-passive," writes Freud, "coalesces later with the antithesis masculine-feminine, which, until this has taken place, has no psychological meaning. The coupling of activity with masculinity and of passivity with femininity meets us, indeed, as a biological fact; but it is by no means so invariably complete and exclusive as we are inclined to assume."[11]

11. Sigmund Freud, "Instincts and Their Vicissitudes," in *Papers on Metapsychology*, SE 14:134.

One essential aspect of the Cervantine text is precisely that the conjunctions in question tend to disintegrate, and thus one entity—the masculine or the feminine—can revert to its contrary in order to institute the representation of a passive masculine compared with an active feminine and vice versa. The active femininity is that of the phallic woman: the witch, Juana Macha, Señora Repolla, or, in a more limited way, Teresa Panza.

The mechanical process that engenders the examples of maternity in Cervantes consists of the constituent elements of the pair inverting themselves: the man from active to passive, the woman from passive to active. Nevertheless, the man remains in the state of manhood while the woman, without ceasing to be woman, adopts her own active postures of phallic capacity. Consequently, the construction of the inverse pair occurs at the instant in which the subject (man or woman) is defined as an inverse being.

The inversion of the man from active to passive, and the same inversion of the woman from passive to active, is that which provokes the apparition of a pair in which the woman occupies the phallic pole and the man that of castration or impotence. Without an inversion of the very subject, the inverse pair is not established. In other words, the fantastic representation of an inverse pair, in which a phallic mother devours an insignificant man, implies on behalf of the subject—Cervantes or whichever leisurely reader ("desocupado lector") may identify with him—that he or she assume the pulsions inherent in a latent bisexuality, one that is effective only in fantastic scenarios.

The phallic mother is a feminine being who, with the phallus, possesses and devours the father. The devalued father is left to bear the burden of the Terrible Mother. To identify oneself with the mother, then—to *be* the mother—is at the same time to possess the father (active homosexuality) and to be possessed by him (passive homosexuality). The hybrid phallic mother accumulates, in her double physiology, the two inverse parental functions: mother and father, active mother and passive father. Is the witch not like this, with that double sex in the form of the belly that hangs halfway to her thighs, concealing/revealing the indecipherable private parts? How is it possible, then, to be the mother if not by rejecting her?

Translated from the Spanish by Joshua McKinney

13

"The Pretended Aunt": Misreading and the Scandal of the Missing Mothers

Mary S. Gossy

> Thus behind my Hispanism the Oedipus complex was hiding, the unconscious desire to possess the mother.
>
> —The Wolf-Man

"The Pretended Aunt" ("La tía fingida") is a scandalous little story, not in terms of its plot but in terms of its criticism.[1] Its subject matter is a seemingly obvious source of scandal since it involves an old, selfish procuress who, over and over again, sells the "virginity" of her supposed niece, not only insisting, into the bargain, that the young woman submit to painful surgical techniques that make it possible for her hymen to be torn repeatedly but also describing the process shamelessly and in great detail.

What has upset and scandalized scholars "for centuries"[2] is not so much the story's bawdiness as the possibility of its attribution to their father, Cervantes. Because the "Aunt" appears in a manuscript with two of the *Exemplary Novels*, and in the same handwriting as one of them, it causes a conflict in the relationships structuring literary at-

---

1. Miguel de Cervantes, "La tía fingida," in *Novelas ejemplares*, ed. Juan Bautista Avalle-Arce (Madrid: Castalia, 1987), 3:323–70. Further references are cited in the text; translations are my own. There is a bowdlerized English translation by Walter K. Kelly in *The Exemplary Novels of Miguel de Cervantes Saavedra, to which Are Added "El buscapié," or "The Serpent," and "La tía fingida," or "The Pretended Aunt"* (London: H. G. Bohn, 1855).

2. E. T. Aylward, *Cervantes: Pioneer and Plagiarist* (London: Tamesis Books, 1982), 13. My essay summarizes the critical obsession with the paternity of "The Pretended Aunt"; for an extended discussion, see Mary S. Gossy, *The Untold Story: Women and Theory in Golden Age Texts* (Ann Arbor: University of Michigan Press, 1989), 83–109.

tribution. If Cervantes did not write "The Pretended Aunt," then perhaps he did not write "Rinconete and Cortadillo" and "The Jealous Extremaduran," and has committed an offense like that of the unconscionable Avellaneda. If he *did* write those two stories, then the "bad" aunt has to be admitted with them into the family, to everyone's disgrace: the story, by general judgment, is not up to par stylistically, and the content of the Cervantine canon has been inscribed without it. To let it in is to disturb the hierarchy of the Cervantes family tree, to displace the critic-sons, and to terrify them with the displeasure of their author-father.

A paternity metaphor is well established in regard to the *Exemplary Novels*. Cervantes himself employs it in the prologue, and critics follow suit, referring to "The Pretended Aunt" with words and phrases such as "bastard," "padre legítimo," "hermanas carnales" "hija legítima," "legítimo autor," "hija," and "paternidad." The scandal of "The Pretended Aunt" is that of an illegitimate offspring: the object that brings to consciousness the ever-present but repressed question "Who is the father?" or, in the case of the critic, whose identity is determined, as if he were a child, by the author-father's name (Cervantist, Shakespearean), "Is my father (am I?) who I think he is, who I want him to be? Am I, then, legitimate or not?"[3] The word scandal comes from the Greek *skandalizo,* and "the basic concept is that of a physical block [*skandalon*] which impedes right progress or understanding and causes diversion into wrong courses, sin or error, or at least causes difficulty."[4]

In the hierarchical process of Cervantine scholarship "The Pretended Aunt" is a stumbling block. It trips up the orderly work of attribution and criticism. But in a larger sense, I suspect that not only Cervantists but many other critics as well have their "stumbling block," an element of the reading process that scandalizes the critic by making visible not—this time—the text's repressed content but rather the critic's. In other words, it is not the text but the critic who is the source of scandal. In the case of "The Pretended Aunt" the underlying oedipal structures of literary attribution are revealed in critics' preoccupation not with the question "What does the text say?" but rather with the question "Who is its (my) father?" The scandal is unavoidable (or so it seems), producing the inevitable point of slip-

---

3. Freud discusses the childhood fantasies behind these questions in "Family Romances," in *The Standard Edition of the Complete Psychological Works of Sigmund Freud,* ed. and trans. James Strachey, 24 vols. (London: Hogarth Press, 1953–74), 9:235–41.

4. *The Four Gospels and the Revelation,* trans. Richmond Lattimore (New York: Washington Square Press/Pocket Books, 1981), 269.

page that may duly be found in all critical writing: in this case not so much the untold as the misread.

"Misreadings and Slips of the Pen" is a chapter heading in *The Psychopathology of Everyday Life*.[5] When reading that book, I am often consoled by Freud's willingness to analyze his own slips, to confront the scandal of error and to know himself in it. I am aware of the meanings that elude his interpretive control—the seduction theory, the Dora case, and their attendant obfuscations—but I admire Freud's tenacity in exposing what he could, and the detail with which he explains often embarrassing movements of his unconscious. His analyses of his own parapraxes suggest that a shameful confrontation with scandal may not remedy it; that is, it will not restore lost honor or impute infallibility and omniscience, but it can help the critic-analyst to a greater understanding of the relationship between text and reader. So choosing Freud as my pretended father, and Cervantes as more of an uncle, I would like to turn to the scandal of my relationship with an aunt.

The fake aunt is named Claudia. She is, like Celestina's mentor Claudina, a hymen mender. She sells the fiction of virginity to men willing to pay to suspend their disbelief. Because I saw her function as hymen mender as preeminent, I was relieved when first researching etymologies for an essay on the text to discover that *claudo, -ere* means to close.[6] This explained the coincidence of the names Claudia and Claudina for members of the same occupation: hymen menders close up again that which has been opened. I remember seeing the verb *claudico, -are* nearby in the dictionary, but I discarded it: it means to limp or to be lame, to waver, to be defective or incomplete. I thought of the lame emperor, and of the obvious relationship between the names Claudius and Claudia. But *my* Claudia did not limp, so I opted for the other meaning and left the obvious one aside.

Two years later, while I was preparing notes for a graduate course I was teaching, I ran across the word *escándalo* in its only two appearances in "The Pretended Aunt." Grijalba, a duenna, uses it to try to avert the attentions of a band of serenading men who want Esperanza, the repeatable virgin, to come out and meet them:

---

5. Sigmund Freud, *The Psychopathology of Everyday Life*, in *Standard Edition*, vol. 6. Further page references are cited by page in the text. I use the terms "misreading" and "error" in their literal senses in Freud's work, that is, as parapraxes revealing the repressed of the reader, not of the text. In this my treatment differs epistemologically from poststructuralist discussions of misreading. I hope to engage them in a later essay.

6. Latin definitions are from Charlton T. Lewis and Charles Short, *Latin Dictionary* (1879; reprint, Oxford: Oxford University Press, 1962).

Señores, mi Señora Doña Claudia de Astudillo y Quiñones, suplica
a vuesa mercedes la reciba su merced tan señalada, que se vayan
a otra parte a dar esa música, por escusar el escándalo y mal egemplo
que se da a la vecindad, respecto de tener en su casa una sobrina
doncella, que es mi Señora Doña Esperanza de Torralba, Meneses
y Pacheco, y no le está bien a su profesión y estado que semejantes
cosas se hagan a su puerta; que de otra suerte, y por otro estilo, y
con menos escándalo, la podrá recibir de vuesa mercedes.

[Gentlemen, my lady madam Claudia de Astudillo y Quiñones asks
that you receive her esteemed courtesy, and please go somewhere
else to give this serenade, to avoid the scandal and bad example it
shows the neighborhood, because she has in her house a maiden
niece, who is my lady miss Esperanza de Torralba, Meneses y Pacheco, and it is not meet for her state and class that such things
should be done around her door; for she may receive you in another
way, and another style, and with less scandal.] (355)

In this quotation *escándalo* is the word that defines the public relationship between a gang of men and a woman, and since it necessarily
accompanies this relationship—Grijalba does not say "without scandal," just "with less"—it seemed crucial to me to define it more
clearly. I went to Covarrubias, who says that it means "en romance
tropieço, embaraço, estorvo, tropeçadero, trampa ["in Spanish obstacle, impediment, hindrance, stumbling place, pitfall]," and in Latin
"traditur a skanzo, claudico, quod obiectum offendiculum cogat claudicare et ad ruinam tendere [it is translated to *skanzo*, to limp, because
a stumbling block tends to lead to defectiveness and ruin]."[7]

For Covarrubias, *escándalo* is what trips you up, physically and
morally. That he would link the Greek root *skanzo* and the Latin
claudico suggested a functional relationship between Claudia, the procuress, and scandal. As go-between and hymen mender, Claudia is
the scandal that makes possible a relationship between the sexes that
is outside the positive morality of patriarchy but still participates in
its power structures and its exploitation of women's bodies. What is
a stumbling block to some is thus a stepping-stone to others.

In addition to scandal, the name Claudia also alludes to a faltering
or wavering, and to lameness. In this the name seems to me to be
related to Oedipus, both in terms of ambulatory metaphor and as the
avatar of a system of desire. As I mentioned earlier, the same oedipal
structures that produce Harold Bloom's "anxiety of influence" in

---

7. Sebastián de Covarrubias Horozco, *Tesoro de la lengua castellana o española* (1611; reprint,
Madrid: Ediciones Turner, 1977, 533b).

poets make for an anxiety of self-attribution in critics. For generations of Cervantists, "The Pretended Aunt" has pushed the unpleasant button of self-doubt. For me, a feminist critic who seeks to see around patriarchal structures and make legible what they have erased, Claudia has an analagous meaning. She is the mythical figure whose career in the text parallels that of a feminist critic. This faltering feminist is the one whose readings are hobbled by the unconscious imitation or residue of patriarchal critical structures. The process is not (as in Bloom's theory) that of a necessary forgetting of forebears so that one may rewrite them, not the repression of similarity, but rather the extinction of one's own difference, a pretense to inclusion in the system that seeks to silence one and a forgetting of solidarity with the other woman.[8] In the case of "The Pretended Aunt," my repression was not to forget Claudia but to imitate her. She sacrificed Esperanza for profit; as I will show in a moment, I sacrificed her for the sake of a happy ending—which amounts to the same thing.

My main misreading was not so much of *claudere* for *claudicare*[9] as of the final scene of Esperanza's erotic adventure. After the police, who have sneaked into Claudia's house, overhear her describing in great detail her illegal activities, they arrest her, Grijalba, and Esperanza and prepare to haul them off to jail. But the two students who have been eyeing Esperanza since the beginning of the story stage a rescue and save Esperanza from the law. Whether this fate is preferable to prison or not is hard to say, since "y queriendo el que la hubo quitado a la justicia gozarla aquella noche, el otro no lo quiso consentir, antes le amenazó de muerte si tal hiciese [the one who had taken her from the police wanted to enjoy her that night, but the other did not want to permit it, and instead threatened him with death if he should try such a thing]" (369). Under this threat of death, the would-be rapist comes up with an appropriately casuistic escape from his difficulty, and decides:

Ahora, pues, ya que vos no consentís que yo goce lo que tanto me ha costado, y que no quereis que por amiga me entregue en ella, a

---

8. I distinguish between this experience and that of "immasculation" as theorized by Judith Fetterley in *The Resisting Reader: A Feminist Approach to American Fiction* (Bloomington: Indiana University Press, 1978). According to Fetterley, immasculation is the process by which "as readers and teachers and scholars, women are taught to think as men, to identify with a male point of view, and to accept as normal and legitimate a male system of values, one of whose central positions is misogyny" (xx). The reading effect I describe here is an *unconscious* subversion of her own radical critical project which occurs in a reader who has already rejected immasculation or some other identification with an oppressor or oppressive system.

9. Lewis and Short, *Latin Dictionary*, find a coincidence of the meanings in the unattested form *clodo*.

lo menos no me podeis negar que, como a muger legítima, no me
la habeis, ni podeis, ni debeis quitar.

[Now then, since you won't let me enjoy that which has cost me
so much, and since you don't want me to take her as a lover, at
least you won't be able to deny that, as my legitimate wife you
wouldn't, couldn't, and shouldn't take her from me.] (369)

The rapist finds that marriage—that is, legitimacy—protects him and
his right to rape. I could not see this the first time I wrote about this
story. Despite the fact that I had scrutinized the text for months, I
misread the outcome, repeatedly understanding that it was not the
rapist but the protector who in the end marries Esperanza. I am well
acquainted with the historical, economic, and sociological work that
links the functions of rape and marriage, but for reasons I will soon
explain, I could not face them.

In Freudian terms this misreading qualifies as a parapraxis, and
one that bears some resemblance to the errors that Freud reports in
The Psychopathology of Everyday Life. Three of these mistakes, in academic publications, begin the chapter on errors. First Freud tells us
that he erroneously referred to Marburg (instead of Marbach) as Schill-
er's birthplace; called Hannibal's father Hasdrubal (his brother's
name) instead of Hamilcar; and confused the relationship of Zeus to
Kronos and Uranus (217–18). In a phrase that sends shivers of both
terror and relief down a scholar's spine, he says: "And how, too, did
I pass over these errors while I carefullly went through three sets of
proofs—as if I had been struck blind?" (218). Freud analyzes all three
errors and sees them as "derivatives of repressed thoughts connected
with my dead father" (219). The oedipal relationship is evident a page
before this confession in the phrase "struck blind," and boldly shows
how these structures invade scholarly writing. From these observa-
tions Freud derives the idea that "an unobserved error tak[es] the
place of an intentional concealment or repression (220)."

A further example of a philological misreading indicates how these
repressions perpetuate themselves. Freud includes an anecdote supplied by a Dr. Marcel Eibenschütz who, as a student, was working
on a little-known medieval text called Manuscript C, about which (O
lucky man!) there existed only one article, by Joseph Haupt. In his
essay Haupt reads the date on his *modern* copy of the medieval manuscript, "Anno Domini MDCCCL," as 1350, despite the fact that it
means 1850, the year when the copy was hand-transcribed from the
original by a nineteenth-century monk. Eibenschütz reads Haupt's

error as "his *wish* to be able to tell his readers as much as possible about the work he was discussing, and therefore also *to date Manuscript C.* This was the motive for the parapraxis" (112). But I am more interested in Dr. Eibenschütz's parapraxis than in Haupt's. "In the first place," he says "being an entire novice in the world of scholarship, I was completely dominated by Haupt's authority, and for a long time I read the date given in the subscription lying in front of me—which was perfectly clearly and correctly printed—as 1350 instead of 1850, just as Haupt had done" (112).

Freud's analysis of his own errors disputes Eibenschütz's notion that his mistake came from inexperience; rather, it is a sign of repression. Eibenschütz's awareness of his academic immaturity is more directly related to the fact that he felt "completely dominated by Haupt's authority." Adherence to authority here promotes error. Paradoxically, it is a mistake that leads to this truth—and not the mistake of the father so much as that of the son. In this quotation, too, one can see the immediate reflex of a critic-reader to establish a father-son relationship with academic authority. A man who can prove his legitimacy in the family can gain from submitting, whether his mind or his articles.

My mistaken reading of "The Pretended Aunt" overlooks the possibility of the coincidence of marriage and rape. In this regard, in terms of my place in the academic clan it is relevant to mention that I had been taught in graduate school that "The Pretended Aunt" has a happy ending, one intended to validate the "hope" of Esperanza and to confirm the punishment of Claudia. To have seen my error would have been to challenge—like Dr. Eibenschütz—a titan, a father, one of my professors during that curious stage of scholarly infancy, the two years spent taking classes, before exams, before the dissertation. As a Cervantist I claim descent from several brilliant men (not all of whom would or could acknowledge me). Nevertheless, my own need to claim this pedigree obfuscated the truth of the text.

It also erased the women who taught me. Thus, the result of these oedipal structures and their effects is, ultimately, to occlude the relationship with and desire for the mother: a difficult position for the feminist critic. Still, a mother does appear tangentially in this last example from *The Psychopathology of Everyday Life*. It is the only one in the chapter "The Forgetting of Foreign Words," and I found it caught my attention as a native English-speaker investigating misreadings of the Spanish in 'The Pretended Aunt." Here Freud is having a conversation with a young male friend about the rise of anti-Semitism in Europe, and the friend quotes Dido wishing vengeance

on Aeneas—"*Exoriar(e) ex nostris ossibus ultor*"—but he has trouble
with the quotation and rearranges the syntax so that he can do without
a word he cannot recall. Freud cheerfully supplies it, giving the quotation in its correct form: "*Exoriar(e)* aliquis *nostris ex ossibus ultor* [Let
someone arise from my bones as an avenger]" (9). The friend wants
to know why he forgot the indefinite pronoun, so he and Freud
embark on a voyage through his associations. First he divides *aliquis*
into two words, *a liquis*. Then he thinks of *reliquien* (relics), liquefying,
fluidity, fluid, followed by allusions to Saint Augustine and Saint
Januarius (whom Freud calls calendar saints), and finally the miracle
of the annual liquefaction of Januarius' blood at Naples. This brings
forth an association to the French occupation of that city, when the
liquefaction was delayed until a general insistently told the local priest
that he hoped it would occur as soon as possible, which it did. At
this point the man stalls in his associations, but when pressed by
Freud says:

> "Well then, I've suddenly thought of a lady from whom I might
> easily hear a piece of news that might be very awkward for both of
> us."
> "That her periods have stopped?"
> "How could you have guessed that?" (11)

It should be remembered that one of Covarrubias's synonyms for
escándalo is *embaraço*, similarly an obstacle or impediment, but also,
colloquially, a pregnancy. A woman's bleeding or lack of it is as
important here as it is in the question of Esperanza's virginity, which
is the narrative motive force of "The Pretended Aunt." The moral of
this anecdote is that a woman whose sexuality and reproduction ex-
ceed patriarchal control disrupts the orderly citation of the classics.
She always exists, but her identity and her own story are present
only as objects of exchange between male (or male-identified) interpreters; that economy uses her up.

What I think I have found in my errant understanding of "The
Pretended Aunt" is that, for a feminist—that is, for a radical critic
both within and without traditional systems—the misreading is the
product of the undertow of orthodoxy. It is what draws us back into
the conflicts apparent in the Freudian examples: a repression of murderous feelings toward the father, combined with a desire to be
claimed, or to claim oneself, as his son, all acted out over the body
of a woman—in other words, a function necessary to the continued
inclusion of the son in the orthodox hierarchy. This is the structure

that dominates criticism of "The Pretended Aunt." But for a critic who explicitly calls the right of the son and father into question, the misreading has the effect of undermining what I had hoped would be a radical analysis and dragging it back into line with phallocentric thinking. In a way this effect is parallel to what happens in the cases that Freud cites: the misreading places the reader back under the rule of the father. The problem is that when she erases the mother, the feminist critic erases herself, too.

In "Desire in Narrative" Teresa de Lauretis writes that "if the heroine of [Alfred Hitchcock's film] *Rebecca* is made to kill off the mother, it is not only because the rules of the drama and [Jurij] Lotman's "mythical mechanism" demand narrative closure; it is also because, like them, cinema works for Oedipus."[10] I do not know of any traditional narrative that does not somewhere depend for its motive force on a dead woman. In the case of *Rebecca*, I think of the heroine's own dead mother, briefly mentioned at the beginning of the film, rather than the title character. Like the second Mrs. de Winter's dead mother, the most invisible character in "The Pretended Aunt" is the invisible but necessary mother who left Esperanza on the church steps, where she was later found by Claudia. No critic has written about her because, like drama, myth, and narrative, critical writing, too, "works for Oedipus," that is, it works to erase the mother. "For this," says de Lauretis, "is the ultimate purpose of the myth, according to [Claude] Lévi-Strauss: to affirm, by the agency of narrative, the autochthonous origin of man."[11]

To stumble over the scandal that one tries to repress is to perform the Freudian slip. But the unconscious persistence of the oedipal is only a stumbling block to feminist and other radical criticisms while it remains unanalyzed; the interpreted scandal might be a faltering way of knowing mother differently. Maybe getting tripped up can provide the momentum to get over Oedipus.

10. Teresa de Lauretis, "Desire in Narrative," in *Alice Doesn't: Feminism, Semiotics, Cinema* (Bloomington: Indiana University Press, 1984), 153.
11. Claude Lévi-Strauss, *Structural Anthropology* (Garden City, N.Y.: Doubleday, 1967), 60; cited ibid., 156.

14

The Phantom of Montilla

Andrew Bush

> We perceived a still interior crypt...
>
> —Edgar Allan Poe

In the 1960s in France and shortly thereafter in the United States, students of literature found in Jacques Lacan a champion for a return to Freud—but not for a return of the repressed in Freud. Lacan's structural analysis of desire in his seminar on Poe's "Purloined Letter" and his network of the Imaginary, the Symbolic, and the Real in the development of the ego at the crux of the "mirror stage," to recall his two essays with the greatest influence on literary studies, both replay Freud's oedipal drama.[1] Yet there was a Freud before the Oedipus complex to whom Lacan did not return. But then neither did Freud. There has been renewed critical attention of late to Freud's abandoned "seduction theory," but this approach is hardly more helpful, I contend, if it elevates the father's real sexual abuse of the daughter, however widespread in Freud's Vienna and our neighborhoods, to

1. See Jacques Lacan, "Le séminaire sur 'La lettre volée' " [The seminar on "The Purloined Letter"] and "Le stade de miroir comme formateur de la fonction du Je" [The mirror stage as formative in the function of the I] in *Ecrits* (Paris: Seuil, 1966), 11–61, 93–100, respectively. Lacan's discussion of Poe led to a lengthy rebuttal by Jacques Derrida, "Le facteur de la verité," in *La carte postale, de Socrates à Freud et au-delà* (Paris: Flammarion, 1980), and subsequently to the engagement of American literary critics. Much of the relevant material has been collected in John P. Muller and William J. Richardson, eds., *The Purloined Poe: Lacan, Derrida and Psychoanalytic Reading* (Baltimore: Johns Hopkins University Press, 1988). Derrida's contribution to the debate has by no means been limited to the initial rejoinder, however; see especially the explicit references to Lacan's seminar in Derrida, "My Chances/Mes chances: A Rendezvous with Some Epicurean Stereophonies," in *Taking Chances: Derrida, Psychoanalysis, and Literature*, ed. Joseph H. Smith and William Kerrigan (Baltimore: Johns Hopkins University Press, 1984), 10–11. Note also that John T. Irwin has carried that debate into the realm of Hispanic letters in his essay "Mysteries We Reread, Mysteries of Rereading: Poe, Borges, and the Analytic Detective Story: Also Lacan, Derrida, Johnson," *MLN* 101 (1986): 1168–1215.

the status of a general psychic paradigm, alongside or in substitution for the son's unrealizable sexual desire for the mother. It is rather a return to an insistence on the particularity of any individual's trauma, to the consequent specificity of symptoms, and, finally, to a sustained analysis free of the predetermined conclusions of universalizing complexes—such as mark *Studies on Hysteria* which Freud undertook with Josef Breuer—which holds the greater promise for literary criticism.[2] Nicolas Abraham and Maria Torok, and now Torok's more recent collaborator, Nicholas Rand, have made that return.[3]

I offer an illustration to set the contrast, before elaborating on Abraham and Torok's theories of the Phantom and, to a lesser extent, the Crypt, which provide the basis for my discussion of "The Colloquy of the Dogs" ("El coloquio de los perros")[4] for this encounter between

2. Sigmund Freud and Josef Breuer, *Studies on Hysteria*, in vol. 2 of *The Standard Edition of the Complete Psychological Works of Sigmund Freud*, ed. James Strachey, trans. James Strachey et al., 24 vols. (London: Hogarth Press, 1953–74). Further references to the *Standard Edition* will be abbreviated *SE*, with volume and page number.

3. The work by Nicolas Abraham and Maria Torok collected in complete volumes includes: *Cryptonymie: Le verbier de l'Homme aux loups*, with an introduction by Jacques Derrida (Paris: Aubier-Flammarion, 1976); *L'écorce et le noyau* (Paris: Aubier-Flammarion, 1978); and *Le livre de Jonas* (Paris: Aubier-Flammarion, 1978), vols. 1–3 of the series Anasémies, respectively; and *Rhythmes, de l'oeuvre, de la traduction et de la psychanalyse*, with an afterword, "Paradictiques," by Torok and Nicolas Rand (Paris: Flammarion, 1985). Of these, only *Cryptonymie* is currently available in English, in the translation by Rand under the title *The Wolf Man's Magic Word: A Cryptonymy*, Theory and History of Literature 37 (Minneapolis: University of Minnesota Press, 1986). Several essays from *L'écorce et le noyau* have also been published in English translation by Rand. A complete two-volume edition in English translation published by the University of Chicago Press was not available at the time of this writing. For a complete bibliography of those English-language publications and a good general introduction to the work of Abraham and Torok, which includes further bibliographic information on other critical accounts of their work in English and French, see Esther Rashkin, "Tools for a New Psychoanalytic Criticism: The Work of Abraham and Torok," *Diacritics* (1988): 31–52. Much of Nicholas Rand's work in which he brings the psychoanalytic theories first developed by Abraham and Torok to bear directly on the study of literature is now collected in Nicholas Rand, *Le cryptage et la vie des oeuvres: Etude du secret dans les textes de Flaubert, Stendhal, Benjamin, Baudelaire, Stefan George, Edgar Poe, Francis Ponge, Heidegger et Freud* (Paris: Aubier, 1989). Several of these essays are also available in English, including the revised and augmented essay "The Political Truth of Heidegger's 'Logos': Hiding in Translation," *PMLA* 105 (1990): 436–47, where he points the way to the extension of these psychoanalytic concepts to the reading of philosophical texts and to political discussion.

In the area of Hispanic letters, the publication of *The Wolf Man's Magic Word* was the occasion for a *diálogo crítico* by Eduardo González, "INFORME: Sergei Pankeiev (alias *el hombre de los lobos*): Inmortal reiterado y por fin descubierto," as well as the only translation into Spanish, to my knowledge, of a text by Abraham and Torok: "Duelo *o* melancolía: Introyectar-incorporar," trans. Marina Pérez de Mendiola, *Revista de estudios hispánicos* 22 (1988): 109–25, and 93–107, respectively. I have also attempted to deploy Abraham and Torok's concept of cryptonymy in "The Riddled Text: Borges and Arenas," *MLN* 103 (1988): 374–97. See also my "Presentación" of the text by González and Pérez de Mendiola's translation, *Revista de estudios hispánicos* 22 (1988): 87–92.

4. I refer throughout to the Spanish text as published in Miguel de Cervantes, *Novelas*

Cervantes and psychoanalysis. To remain within the same textual milieu as Lacan's seminar, then, one may read Poe's "Cask of Amontillado," for example.[5] A certain gentleman plots revenge and establishes two rules: the victim must recognize the act of revenge for what it is, and the executioner must go unpunished. Thus he sets an elaborate trap. He lures his antagonist to his wine cellar with the promise of sampling an Amontillado, playing upon the latter's pretensions to connoisseurship; and there he shackles him within an obscure recess at the farthest extreme of the catacomb and walls him in.

Marie Bonaparte, one of Freud's early followers, easily assimilated the tale to the oedipal complex. For her the story recounts a wish fulfillment. The victim is the father, the executioner and narrator is the son, and the damp cavern in which they enact their deadly rivalry is a metaphor for the "mother cloaca": "Now the father's penis is finally captive and the phantasy wish to return to the womb, as to a once-experienced beatitude, is converted into a horrible phantasy of anguish and death." The violence of Bonaparte's own language accords ill, however, with her analytical conclusion: "The aggression released in Poe must have been extreme, when writing this story, to make it so convincing, despite its romantic trappings, and *to so completely stifle all visible affect* of remorse."[6]

Lacan can help address the discrepancy, not by dismantling the Oedipus triangle but by questioning Bonaparte's firm identification of the narrator as the subject. Lacan moves discussion from a conception of subjectivity that is bound to an isolate, unified self—the true "romantic trappings" that are as much a snare for Bonaparte, and perhaps for Freud, as for Poe—to a notion of a subject position filled successively by various individuals as the object of desire skids along a chain of signifiers. This theoretical change, along with the move away from Bonaparte's explicit project of analyzing the author through the work, which leads her to certain surmises about the narrator based on inferences from the life of Poe, permits a rereading of the oedipal allegory of "The Cask of Amontillado" in which the

ejemplares, ed. Fernando Gutiérrez (Madrid: Juventud, 1958), employing the English translations as they appear in Cervantes, *Exemplary Stories*, trans. C. A. Jones (Harmondworth: Penguin Books, 1972). Citations are indicated in the text by *Novelas* for the original and *Stories* for the translation, with page number.

5. Edgar Allan Poe, "The Cask of Amontillado," first published in 1846. I subsequently refer to the text as it appears in *The Complete Works of Edgar Allan Poe*, ed. James A. Harrison (New York: Thomas Y. Crowell, 1902), 167–75.

6. Marie Bonaparte, *The Life and Works of Edgar Allan Poe: A Psycho-Analytic Interpretation*, foreword by Sigmund Freud, trans. John Rodker (New York: Humanities Press, 1971), 509, 509–10; emphasis added.

narrator is no longer simply and uniquely the subject of wishes and desires. Considered as a tale of the very moment of the transition out of the mirror stage and into the Symbolic, this becomes the story of the imposition of the *Non-du-Père* (Name-of-the-Father),[7] quite literally the vanquishing of "Fortunato" by "Montresor." From this perspective the victim, Fortunato, shifts from the subject of the quest for the cask to the object that takes its place in the "still interior crypt or recess" (172) and the narrator takes up the role of the oedipal father: hence the apparent lack of affect or remorse. As the father figure, he does not repress his own desires; rather he suppresses the son with unassailable confidence in his right to do so. To this end, Montresor takes his proper task to be the education of his rival in the lessons of the castration complex by twice "knock[ing] off the neck of a bottle" (170) as they proceed through the catacombs, only to pronounce his paternal prohibition—modulated by the irony of the text as a twice-declared "Yes" (175)—and definitively shattering the illusion of wholeness by walling over the mirror likeness.

It needs to be underlined that, given a Lacanian understanding of subjectivity, cask, victim, and executioner may be taken to be one in this tale—which, the narrator stresses at the outset, is a question of words, not deeds: "The thousand injuries of Fortunato I had borne as I best could, but when he ventured upon insult I vowed revenge" (167). The insult, moreover, like the contents of the purloined letter, is never disclosed, in fact can never be disclosed for Lacan, though it remains universally legible without this or any text. For Lacan, as for Freud before him, the insult is the Real: the ubiquitous threat of castration that must disrupt the idyll of the Imaginary, reducing it to silence, just as it gives voice to the Symbolic:

> But to these words I hearkened in vain for a reply. I grew im-
> patient. I called aloud—
>   "Fortunato!"
> No answer. I called again—
>   "Fortunato!"

7. Lacan's concept of the *Nom-du-Père* literally signifies Name-of-the-Father (and is customarily translated thus) but functions simultaneously as a homophonic pun. *Non-du-Père* (No-of-the-Father). The concept has its place within the general economy of the oedipal complex, wherein, for Lacan, the repression (the No) that catapults the subject from the Imaginary into the Symbolic is promulgated as a paternal law ("Thou shalt not have thy mother") which imposes the father's will over the subject's desire. As the strained neutrality of "subject" makes clear even in this brief summary, any version of the Oedipus triangle and the associated castration complex is difficult to formulate coherently without explicit reference to a son and the consequent exclusion of daughters from psychic life

No answer still. I thrust a torch through the remaining aperture and let it fall within. There came forth in return only a jingling of the bells. My heart grew sick; it was the dampness of the catacombs that made it so. I hastened to make an end of my labor. (175)

Yet if the Lacanian analysis brings forth nuances in the text that Bonaparte passes over in haste I would also note that the labor does not in fact end. The narrator remains slighted, vengeful, ever unappeased. The silencing of Fortunato represents the defeat of Montresor, for a crucial condition of the plot is unsatisfied. Fortunato does not acknowledge the vengeance, and as a result the narrator must risk the fulfillment of the second condition as well—must risk retribution by confessing to a third party, the unnamed but explicit "You, who so well know the nature of my soul" (167), even after "half of a century" (175), the half century or so that separates, say, Freud's analysis of the Wolf Man from Abraham and Torok's effort to reopen the case, or more precisely to prove that it had never been closed.[8] To shift briefly, then, to an allegory of Abraham and Torok's "theory of readability," as Nicholas Rand aptly defines it,[9] the third is always the analyst, who finds a text before her on the couch, pleading to be heard. After all, if the voice is silenced, the bells continue to jingle: Fortunato is buried alive within the crypt.

Though I reserve a full textual analysis of Poe's tale, I offer here some further interpretive suggestions so as to highlight the contrasts between the work of Abraham and Torok and that of Lacan. Most generally, Abraham and Torok do not share the prejudice, inherited from Freud, that obliges the reduction of the text to some version of the Oedipus conflict, that is, to the rival subjectivity of men and the objectification of women. More specifically, they are explicitly opposed to the strict limitation of analysis imposed by Lacan's impenetrable bar between signifier and signified. An insult has generated the story: to leave that insult a cipher and its avatar, the cask, not even so much as an empty vessel, but rather a mere product of the Imaginary and so inarticulate, is to leave the morbidity of the tale unaddressed. Hence, against the stentorian pronouncement of the Nom-du-Père, Abraham and Torok constantly urge an *écoute profonde*,

8. The case history popularly referred to as the Wolf Man is Freud's "From the History of an Infantile Neurosis," *SE* 17:3–123, originally published in 1917. Abraham and Torok's revision of the case, *The Wolf Man's Magic Word: A Cryptonymy*, originally appeared just over half a century later, in 1976.

9. Nicolas Rand, "Translator's Introduction: Toward a Cryptonymy of Literature," in Abraham and Torok, *The Wolf Man's Magic Word*, esp. li–lii.

a deeper hearing: a *Ouïe-de-la-Mère*, I might say. I introduce this coinage—Ouïe-de-la-mère, the hearing (*ouïe*) but also the yes (*oui*) of the mother—in order to condense the most salient distinctions, for my present purposes, between the psychoanalytic theory of Abraham and Torok and the Lacanian Nom-du-Père (to reiterate: both Name- and No-of-the Father).[10] These might be enumerated as follows: an emphasis on hearing, especially on listening for the echoes of one language articulated in the disguise of another; an affirmation of the possibility of the discovery of meaning (a determinate, if not always verifiable, meaning); and a recuperation of the mother. The task of the analyst with regard to "The Cask of Amontillado," as Abraham and Torok might delineate it, would be to listen for the text of the insult, which must be constantly enunciated by the narrator, even if he cannot articulate it explicitly in the words of its original pronouncement.

One might begin the process of recuperation by rereading the Nom- du-Père, as I have already suggested, as a *nom de famille*, the surname or, more literally, name of (the patriarchal) family. The prior injuries mentioned in the opening gambit (even if these were understood in orthodox Freudian terms as a reference to symbolic enactments of castration), I take it, touched upon the person of the narrator; but the insult was addressed to the House of Montresor, in whose maligned name, I believe, the narrator exacts revenge. Abraham and Torok's concept of the Phantom, which is my central theoretical concern in the discussion of Cervantes's tale, permits just such a transgenerational analysis. The patient on the psychoanalytic couch presents symptoms whose point of origin does not lie in a personal trauma followed by the dynamic repression of the experience. Instead, the traumatic event was experienced by a family member in a preceding generation and considered so shameful that it was never spoken of thereafter. The patient, therefore, has never been conscious of the event and has not repressed it, and the investigation is marked by a peculiar lack of affect, since the patient in effect comes to join the analyst in the examination of the life of the pertinent forebears. Freud noted a similar and striking lack of affect in cases of melancholia, and in fact, Abraham and Torok's Phantom and the allied concept of the Crypt are related to their own clinical experience with melancholics.[11] Poe's setting in the family catacombs of the Montresors becomes the

10. For other discussions of the contrast, see Rashkin, "Tools," 45–46, and González, "INFORME," 124–25.

11. See Sigmund Freud, "Mourning and Melancholia," *SE* 14:239–58, and Abraham and

appropriate ground to listen for the insult that may indeed distinguish mourning from an interminable melancholia. And within that setting we find a scene of instruction:

> "These vaults," he said, "are extensive."
> "The Montresors," I replied, "were a great and numerous family."
> "I forget your arms."
> "A huge human foot d'or, in a field azure; the foot crushes a serpent rampant whose fangs are imbedded in the heel."
> "And the motto?"
> "*Nemo me impune laccessit.*" (171)

The narrator's use of the past tense, implying a faded glory, begs a question. But Fortunato's careless response is itself an insult and a reminiscence of *the* insult. His "forgetting," therefore, calls for a gloss: not repression, since he does not defend himself against the recollection of an injury received; nor the related Freudian terms of disavowal or denial; but perhaps a *Verwerfung*, a repudiation, a testimony thrown out of court, its credibility having been called into question.[12] It is as though Fortunato tells the narrator, "Your coat-of-arms cannot testify to the greatness of your family, least of all in your own generation."

To read the emblem and the accompanying motto is to read the insult, prying open the crypt of the text. Here I must content myself with a pair of leads, no more than the jingling of the bells. First, the

---

Torok's "Deuil *ou* mélancholie, Introjecter-incorporer" in Abraham and Torok, *L'écorce et le noyau*, 259–75, or Pérez de Mendiola, "Duelo *o* melancolía."

12. For a fine discussion of these and other Freudian terms, see the appropriate entries in Jean Laplanche and J.-B. Pontalis, *The Language of Psycho-Analysis*, trans. by Donald Nicholson-Smith (New York: Norton, 1973). It is important in the present context, however, to bear in mind Laplanche and Pontalis's consistent Lacanian bias, nowhere more evident than in their entry for *Verwerfung*, which appears under the heading of Lacan's translation "foreclusion" (*forclusion*) rather than the standard English "repudiation." The original term has its most significant use by Freud in the case of the Wolf Man, and Lacan's theoretical transposition, as Laplanche and Pontalis note, makes it the operative term for a conceptualization of psychosis; see esp. Jacques Lacan, "D'une question préliminaire à tout traitement possible de la psychose," in *Ecrits*, esp. 575–83. However the contribution to an understanding of psychosis may be assessed, the shift is tendentious, since it removes the relevant symptom from the realm in which it might be susceptible to decipherment. My gloss follows Abraham and Torok, *The Wolf Man's Magic Word* where they seek to demonstrate throughout that even the most recalcitrant texts may be made to yield the secret of their meaning. For a broader discussion of Laplanche and Pontalis's work which might serve to reequilibrate the Lacanian slant, see Nicolas Abraham, "L'écorce et le noyau," in Abraham and Torok, *L'écorce et le noyau*, 203–26, an essay that has appeared in English as "The Shell and the Kernel," translated by Nicolas Rand, *Diacritics* 9 (1979): 16–28.

coat-of-arms would reveal what the Lacanian prejudice of the Nom-du-Père would otherwise obscure: the biblical allusion to the eternal enmity between Eve and the serpent—"and between thy seed and her seed; it shall bruise thy head, and thou shall bruise his heel" (Genesis 3:15–16)—suggests that the resolution of the enigma rests not with the name of the father but with the childbearing mother. To this observation I add that the disputatious Latin epigram, pronounced anew between these Italian and French family names, between these translational synonyms Fortunato and Montresor, points the analysis toward the translinguistic orientation that is Abraham and Torok's customary if often astonishing milieu. The strife between their houses is analogous to the rivalry of sister Romance tongues for the literary legacy of their Latin matrix, though the canny text has hinted all along that the cryptic language may lie farther afield by its reference to another linguistic contender: the Spanish of Montilla. I now turn there to rejoin Cervantes.

The road to Montilla, to an analysis of the Cañizares episode of the "Coloquio," is paved, on his occasion, with Abraham and Torok's intentions, and so I interpose now a more comprehensive exposition of the Phantom, with some collateral remarks on its relation to the Crypt. I concentrate my attention on an overtly interdisciplinary essay by Nicolas Abraham, "The Phantom of Hamlet or the Sixth Act: Preceded by the Intermission of 'Truth' "—one text from a lifetime of work at the precarious crossroads where psychoanalysis, philosophy, and literature meet.[13]

I introduce this discussion with one further comparative reflection. In postulating his death drive as the basis of the repetition compulsion in *Beyond the Pleasure Principle* (SE 18:3–64), Freud had hoped to meet a theoretical challenge posed by clinical experience. Patients unable to remember all the material repressed in the unconscious, even with the stimulus of free associations, would repeat that material instead

---

13. Nicolas Abraham, "Le fantôme de Hamlet ou le sixième acte, précédé par L'entr'acte de la 'vérité,' " in Abraham and Torok, *L'écorce et le noyau*, 447–74. The essay, composed entirely in verse, has been rendered into English in a verse translation by Nicholas Rand as "The Phantom of Hamlet or The Sixth Act: Preceded by the Intermission of 'Truth,' " *Diacritics* 18 (1988): 2–19. See also Nicholas Rand, "Family Romance or Family History? Psychoanalysis and Dramatic Invention in Nicolas Abraham's 'The Phantom of Hamlet,' " which appears in the same issue of *Diacritics* 20–30. For other work that touches directly on literary texts, see Abraham and Torok, *Le livre de Jonas*; Abraham and Torok, *Rhythmes*; and Rand, *Le cryptage*. By way of introduction to the shift from Abraham and Torok's psychoanalytic investigations to literary study, see also the condensed remarks on Stendhal in Rand, "Translator's Introduction," lx–lxvi.

in the form of transference neuroses. Thus, Freud found his patients acting out on the analytic couch what he construed to be the otherwise irretrievable oedipal dramas of their childhood. It was their own clinical experience, however, that led Abraham and Torok to question the universal efficacy of that oedipal interpretation and to imagine that some of the bizarre effects they witnessed in analysis, and which Freud had denominated "uncanny," were not to be traced to infantile experiences at all. They came to propose that the sins of the fathers, when these are denied in the history of family life by means of a rigorous silence, are visited upon the sons, passing from unconscious to unconscious for literally untold generations. The symptoms may be varied, but in essence the maintenance of a family secret, unbeknownst to the bearers of its psychic burden, is a speech defect: the patient pronounces enigmas. Abraham and Torok's formulation of new metapsychological concepts, most prominent for my purposes here their revision of the Freudian death drive in the theory of the Phantom, allows for the elucidation of enigmas, including enigmatic literary texts.

Additional years in the clinic would prove that in theory and in practice, such analytic closure may be no more than a consummation devoutly to be wished. Uncanny patients disrupted the assimilation of melancholy to mourning proposed by Freud, and as Abraham and Torok listened ever more attentively to the voices from beyond the grave which would not rest in peace, they came to devote a seminar to the problem of the Phantom in the final year of Abraham's life. Yet the most daring exposition of the Phantom, or rather its critical reenactment, comes in Abraham's study of *Hamlet*. Had a patient-poem so perfect not existed, Abraham would have had to invent the first five acts, and not only the sixth with its prefatory "Intermission of 'Truth.' " Its history in relation to psychoanalysis, including the prior reflections of Freud, Ernest Jones, and Lacan, provides an implicit context in which to demonstrate the efficacy of the new metapsychological concept.[14] The prince had long been recognized as a model of melancholy. And, finally, Shakespeare offers Abraham a ghost in the role of the Phantom, which is to say that the anasemic figure is demetaphorized, finding its literal embodiment in the presence of King Hamlet *revenant*.

14. See Sigmund Freud, *The Interpretation of Dreams*, SE 4:263, n. 2; Ernest Jones, *Hamlet and Oedipus* (New York: Norton, 1976), along with Freud's approving remarks on Jones's work in Freud, "An Autobiographical Study," *SE* 20:63–64; and Jacques Lacan, "Desire and the Interpretation of Desire in *Hamlet*," trans. James Hulbert, ed. J.-A. Miller, *Yale French Studies* 55–56 (1977): 11–52.

The old king had borne a secret to the grave, the burden of a crime unconfessed and so unabsolved—a crime perpetrated by him rather than upon him: an easy supposition, since such is the customary literary situation of a soul in torment. But Abraham further supposes that the secret, while never consciously known to the prince, has nevertheless been transmitted to his unconscious. Prince Hamlet finds himself, therefore, in a contradictory state that Abraham refers to as "awareness-unawareness" (*science-nescience*).[15] This same state corresponds to a double and again self-contradictory task: on the one hand, to maintain the secret so as to guard the honor of the father, cost what it may to the psychic life of the son; and on the other, to reconstruct the history of the father from the gnomic fragments lodged in the unconscious of the son and so to bring the truth to the light of consciousness. Abraham of course aligns the analyst with the search for truth, indeed, for "one ultimate 'Truth' " (Abraham 1988, 3), and he brings forth Fortinbras in his "sixth act" to undertake that role, resuscitating the prince to undergo the therapeutic session. The adversary is the Ghost. The murdered king would keep his truth, his crime, concealed. Thus, recalling the language of T. S. Eliot's study of *Hamlet*,[16] Abraham claims: "The appearance of the Father's ghost at the start of the play objectifies [*objectiver*] the son's awareness-unawareness" (Abraham 1988, 3). But in transposing the Ghost of Shakespeare's drama as a Phantom, he quickly discovers a more malign purpose, at once a breakthrough in the metapsychological elaboration of the concept and an unprecedented literary interpretation. The Ghost has lied, Abraham asserts, or, more broadly stated, "A ghost returns to haunt with the intent of lying: its would-be 'revelations' are false by nature" (Abraham 1988, 3).

The details of the reconstruction of a prior history of King Hamlet, of the tainted duel that Abraham postulates between him and the royal father of young Fortinbras, and of the machinations of Polonius, revenging his homeland for the depredations of Denmark and Norway, need not detain me here. From that critical tour de force I draw on the concept of *science-nescience* as a revision of Freud's "negation" (see *SE* 19:235–39) to reconsider a different if contemporaneous enigma, a text likewise riddled by a "supernatural element" (Abraham 1988, 3): the Cañizares episode of Cervantes's "Colloquy of the Dogs."

15. Nicolas Abraham, "The Phantom of Hamlet," 3, subsequently cited as Abraham 1988 in text; and Abraham and Torok, *L'écorce et le noyau*, 449.

16. See Rand, "Family Romance," 22–23, and Jacqueline Rose's psychoanalytic rereading of Eliot's "*Hamlet*" (1919), "*Hamlet*—the 'Mona Lisa' of Literature," in *Sexuality in the Field of Vision* (London: Verso, 1986), 123–40.

"Así que la Camacha fue burladora falsa, y la Cañizares embustera, y la Montiela tonta, maliciosa y bellaca" [So Camacha was a false deceiver, and Cañizares a liar, and Montiela a foolish, malicious and wicked woman], comments Cipión in response to this portion of Berganza's narration, adding, "Con perdón sea dicho, si acaso es nuestra madre, de entrambos o tuya, *que yo no la quiero tener por madre* [Begging your pardon, if she is by any chance the mother of either of us both or just you, *for I certainly don't want her as a mother*]" (*Novelas* 490; *Stories* 239; emphasis added), before rendering the final word of his mock interpretation of Camacha's prophecy. More than contesting his denial—as does Freud when he asserts, "So it *is* his mother" (*SE* 19:235)—I wish to consider such questions as the Phantom may raise as a theoretical construct for the reading of the text.

"Awareness-unawareness of what?" asks Abraham of the haunted prince (Abraham 1988, 3), and this must ultimately be my interpretive burden with regard to Cipión's negation. But Abraham frames the task thus: "The tragedy's aim may now be stated more clearly: to spur the public to react unconsciously to the enigmas that remain and to backtrack [*cheminer à rebours*] towards an equally unstated yet no less imperative goal: breaking down the 'phantom' and eradicating its effect, the uneasy state of knowledge-nonknowledge responsible for the unconscious conflict and incongruous repetitions" (Abraham 1988, 3). Fascinating though it may be to speculate on the manner in which the Phantom of a work of art may come to haunt its public, including its analysts, I am not concerned here with the psyche of the readers of Cervantes's pages, either in his own time or now. Instead I observe that Cipión is already placed in the role of the reader within the text—the role that implicitly awaits Fortinbras at the end of Shakespeare's play and which Abraham makes explicit in his sixth act. I take Cipión's negation, therefore, as exemplary, though by no means isolated. The most comprehensive and illuminating exegesis of the "Colloquy," Alban Forcione's *Mystery of Lawlessness*, passes over Montiela in silence, begging the question of maternity: "But *which* witch is the mother?" as Diana de Armas Wilson enunciates it, adding: "Forcione consciously sets out to confound the two witches, reconstituting Cañizares, in her 'hideous vision of decay' as a 'parody' mother."[17] But even this penetrating critical reflection perpetuates the

---

17. Diana de Armas Wilson, review of Alban K. Forcione, *Cervantes and the Mystery of Lawlessness: A Study of "El casamiento engañoso y El coloquio de los perros"* (Princeton: Princeton University Press, 1984), *International Fiction Review* 13 (1986): 42.

confusion that it addresses—a confusion initiated by Cañizares herself. Which two witches? Were there not three?

Cañizares acts the part of the Phantom here, returning to haunt with the intent of lying. Her appearance is timed precisely to preclude Berganza's attempt to *examiner à rebours* when his master commands him to perform.

> "Volved, hijo Gavilán [Berganza], y con gentil agilidad y destreza deshaced los saltos que habéis hecho; pero ha de ser a devoción de la famosa hechicera que dicen que hubo en ese lugar." Apenas hubo dicho esto, cuando alza la voz la hospitalera . . .

> ["Come back, Gavilán Berganza), my boy, and go through again all those jumps you've done so nimbly and skillfully; but you must take your orders from the famous witch who they say came from this village." As soon as he had said this the hospitaler, who was an old woman . . . said. . . (*Novelas* 478; *Stories* 227).

To send *el perro sabio* back upon his own tracks, to pronounce, even as satiric *conjuro* (compare the preceding jibes [*Novelas* 477; *Stories* 226]), the name of the evil genius loci: Berganza is poised at the verge of a truth, his truth, "the final cause of so many lies, [which] is supremely *abominable* and as such is intolerable to the gaze" (Abraham 1988, 3–4; the emphasis is Abraham's with regard to *Hamlet*, but it corresponds to that of Forcione's study of the "Colloquy").

Cañizares imposes an obstruction: "¡Bellaco, charlatán, embaidor y hijo de puta [Scoundrel, charlatan, cheat and son of a whore]," she charges the drummer, "aquí no hay hechicera alguna! [there's no witch here]" (*Novelas* 478; *Stories* 227). This is elusive at best, treading nicely on the distinction between *hechicera* (sorceress) and *bruja* (witch). But her irate explanation constitutes a more significant repudiation—*Verwerfung*—than this transparent negation, and is itself the formative precursor of Cipión's *science-nescience*. For her subterfuge, of which his negation is but symptom and heir, consists of obfuscating the mother. "Si lo decís por la Camacha [If you were thinking of Camacha]," she continues, referring to the drummer's insinuation,

> ya ella pagó su pecado, y está donde Dios se sabe; si lo decís por mí, chocarrero, ni yo soy ni he sido hechicera en mi vida; y si he tenido fama de haberlo sido, merced a los testigos falsos, y a la ley del encaje, y al juez arrojadizo y mal informado, ya sabe todo el

mundo la vida que hago, en penitencia, no de los hechizos que no
hice, sino de otros muchos pecados, otros que como pecadora he
cometido.

[she has paid for her sins, and is God knows where; and if you
were thinking of me, you coarse lout, I am not and have never been
a witch in my life, and if I've ever had the reputation of being one,
thanks to false witnesses and an arbitrary law and to a hasty and
ill-informed judge, everyone knows the sort of life I lead, as penance
not for the sorcery I was never guilty of, but for the many other
different kinds of sins I've committed, like the sinner that I am.]
(*Novelas* 478; *Stories* 227).

She is herself already haunted as she transmits to Berganza and thence
to Cipión a secret not her own. Her twin acknowledgment of Camacha
and herself as the possible targets of the drummer's barb occludes
Montiela, whose voice, I suspect, speaks through her, usurping the
first-person singular, and which might be restituted by rendering the
final words, thus: "otros que como pecadora yo, *la Montiela*, he cometido [others which, sinner that I am, I, *Montiela*, have committed]."
Which witch, indeed, is the mother? Whose sins—nymph or witch,
hypocrite penitent or deceitful Phantom—are remembered in thy
orisons?

   In order to give a fuller theoretical account of such ventriloquism,
I would set the Phantom in a broader metapsychological context before undertaking to reread the prophecy that occasions Cipión's negation. Abraham offers an appropriate starting point in language
borrowed from literary study at the outset of his seminar "L'unité
duelle et ses vicissitudes" ("The Dual Unity and Its Vicissitudes") of
1974–75: "What is the concrete problem of analysis?" he asks, responding: "To transform symbols into metaphors."[18] Recalling that
for the Greeks, a symbol was a fragment, usually a shard, carried by
a soldier or other wanderer from home, which, when fitted with a
shard that stayed behind, constituted a token of recognition, Abraham
refers to the interrelated pieces, taken together, as metaphor. "So,
originally, any symbol is a metaphor. It is the repression of its metaphoric origin that makes the symbol" (Abraham and Torok 1978,
394). Abraham then further elaborates that the symbol is doubly rep-

---

18. Nicolas Abraham, "Notes du séminaire sur l'unité duelle et le fantôme" [Notes from
the Seminar on the Dual Unity and the Phantom] in Abraham and Torok, *L'écorce et le noyau*,
393; subsequent references to essays in this volume are cited in the text as Abraham and
Torok 1978, with page number. Translations are my own.

resentative: it is in metaphoric relation to the seme that has been repressed and also to the act of repression.

Abraham asks in the same introductory note to the seminar: "And where does metaphor come from?" (Abraham and Torok 1978, 394). His response, however, is hardly less than a condensed statement of his entire theoretical position with respect to the formation of subjectivity and the acquisition of language: "From the incorporation of the original unclenching [décramponnement], thus surmounted" (Abraham and Torok 1978, 394). It requires a substantial gloss.

Abraham and Torok are at special pains to define "incorporation" in contradistinction to "introjection" in their work on melancholy. Introjection is the very process by which the material satisfaction of desires becomes the figurative nourishment of language: "The passage from the mouth full of breast to the mouth full of words is effected through experiences of an empty mouth. To learn to fill the emptiness of the mouth with words that is a first paradigm for introjection."[19] Incorporation, in contrast, is a phantasm set in motion by a severe loss to the psyche in circumstances in which the subject nonetheless refuses to mourn; a magic act substitutes for the work of mourning, "accomplishing literally what has only a figurative meaning" (Abraham and Torok 1978, 261). And they provide a brief poetics: "One thus discovers two conjoined procedures in the magic of incorporation: *demetaphorization* (taking literally what should be understood figuratively) and *objectification* (that which is undergone is not a wound to the subject but rather the loss of an object)" (Abraham and Torok 1978, 261). In the explication of the origins of metaphor, an incorporation is said to have taken place by which an initial trauma is surmounted, though not healed. In making that final distinction I quote a further passage: *incorporer* "is to refuse to take into oneself the part of oneself that was invested in that which is lost, it is to refuse to know the true meaning of the loss, that which, upon knowing it, would make one different, in a word, it is to refuse its introjection. The phantasm of incorporation betrays a lacuna in the psyche, a gap at precisely the spot where an introjection should have taken place" (Abraham and Torok 1978, 261). In introjection the subject acknowledges loss and, however bereaved, recuperates the love invested in the lost object; the self is aggrandized as the subject learns, quite literally, to talk of the dear departed—whether the dead or the mother's breast, a sled named Rosebud or what you will—in the figures of speech that are our daily bread. Incorporation, it seems to

19. Nicolas Abraham and Maria Torok, "Deuil *ou* mélancholie," 260.

me, is Abraham and Torok's version of Freud's *Verwerfung*: not the Lacanian mechanism of the genesis of psychosis (foreclosure) but rather the psychic agency of melancholy. I stress the distinction again because Lacanian foreclosure is strictly illegible: a gap in sense and a senseless gap. Incorporations are enigmatic, but they remain symbolic; consequently, the original unity of the metaphor that subtends an incorporation may be recovered, however far the shard of sense may be thrown (ver-*werfen*, sym-*bolein*).

My gloss concludes with an elucidation of the trauma by which self and sense are thrown and fractured. In his seminar notes and elsewhere in his late writings, Abraham refers to that trauma, following the Hungarian psychoanalyst Imre Hermann, as "unclenching" (*décramponnement*).[20] According to this "myth-hypothesis" (Abraham and Torok 1978, 397), infant and mother constituted a primordial unity, a "*paido-mater*" (Abraham and Torok 1978, 396–97), as Abraham calls it, to suggest an analogue to the *andro-gyne*. The bipart unity is configured not as one might expect from Abraham's interest in the story of Jonah, for instance, as infant-within-mother but rather as infant-clinging-to-mother: the infant who, in Hermann's paleontological fantasy, gripped the mother's fur up until the universal catastrophe of the loss of long body hair—the loss, that is, of our grip on the mother. Setting aside Hermann's phylogenetic hypothesis, Abraham and Torok take up the notion of a utopian dual unity of mother-infant along with the filial instinct to reconstitute that paradise lost through various symbolic expressions of clinging, including that of a searching or even researching instinct. In this light the self is always the fragmentary remain of the dual unity. The integrity of the self is illusory. The in-dividual (*in-dividu*) is at best an "inseparable-separate" (*non-séparé-séparé*), marked by the cleavage of that loss: "a separation, internal to ourselves" (Abraham and Torok 1978, 397). To employ, then, the language of the preceding portion of this gloss, the self may be seen as a symbol, cast off from the prior metaphoric unit, the "infant-mother." And at the same time, "individual" is also but a metaphor for psychic integrity, whose internal fracture makes of the self a dual unity.

In sum: the filial instinct replaces eros as the life drive: to form *attachments* by a maturing capacity to introject, that is, to seek out and grasp on to figurative substitutions for the mother. These com-

---

20. See Nicolas Abraham, "L'enfant majuscule ou l'origine de la genèse" (The child with a capital C or the origin of genesis) and "Pour introduire l' 'instinct filial' " (To introduce the 'filial instinct'), both in Abraham and Torok, *L'écorce et le noyau*, 325–33 and 334–83, respectively.

pensatory metaphors, however, are founded on a deathly drive by which the child repeatedly and literally reenacts—compulsively, melancholically—the separation. The figures of self-aggrandizing, life-affirming introjections presuppose that the child has first become an individual self by incorporating the mother of the dual unity rather than recognizing her as lost.

This opposition of attachment-detachment is played out principally in the acquisition of language. "Verbal communication," Abraham states, "implies the impossible desire to cling [se cramponner] to the mother and at one and the same to detach oneself from her [s'en détacher]" (Abraham and Torok 1978, 420–21). If he asserts immediately thereafter that "language is always first of all an act of dematernalization" (Abraham and Torok 1978, 420), that is, apparently resolving the crossed impulses in favor of detachment, it is because he has conceived of the acquisition of language—already in his commentary to Jonas in 1957, no less than in the seminar of 1974—as the moment in which the child discovers a language that is not already pregnant with the unconscious of the mother.

In the seminar on the dual unity, Abraham illustrates the point by reference to the fort-da game of Freud's Beyond the Pleasure Principle (SE 18:14–17), which is to say in the context of the compulsion to repeat and the death drive.[21] Abraham situates the child verging on speech as living a stage in which he does not distinguish between the mother's conscious and her unconscious, such that the language that he is learning from her carries both her conscious meanings and her repressed desires. When Freud observes the boy throwing his toy and saying "o-o-o-o" (fort, "gone"), Abraham understands the game to indicate the moment when "these ends-of-mother" (bouts-de-mère), which is to say words, "are decentered from the person of the mother

21. In Freud's examination of the repetition of painful experiences which led him to propose the workings of a compulsion that overrides the demands of the pleasure principle (that is, that we seek pleasure and avoid pain), he put forth the example of an infant, in fact his grandson, who played a game in which he would throw a toy which was dutifully retrieved by Grandpa Sigmund. When he had launched the toy some distance, he would cry out "o-o-o," and when he received it anew he would exclaim "a-a-a." Freud inferred that these sounds were the infant's approximation of the German words fort (gone) and da (here), for which he received confirmation from the child's mother. He further observed not only that the child repeated the "painful" experience of losing his toy but also more significantly, that he repeated the same sounds—fort-da, gone-here—with respect to the far more painful disappearances of the mother in her normal comings and goings. This fort-da game was crucial in his formulation of the death instinct, and it is, moreover, the pretext from which Lacan departs in "Le stade de miroir"; more generally, the proper interpretation of Beyond the Pleasure Principle is the primary point of contention in the debate between Lacan and Derrida concerning the reading of Freud—and collaterally Poe (see note 1 for bibliographic information).

herself in order to designate objective events, that is [events] that are not grafted onto the mother's Unconscious" (Abraham and Torok 1978, 414). This allows the child to make some analytical surmises of his own about her repressions: "Strangely when the mother returns from a long absence, [the child] receives her with the words: '*Baby o-o-o-o*' (= baby gone) at the very moment that he is present (*da*). It is as though he were saying: 'When you say "o-o-o-o," Mommy, you're thinking "a-a." You have a problem with o-a' " (Abraham and Torok 1978, 416). Yet, while this important discrimination between the objective relation of words to things on the one hand and the mother's subjective correlation of words to unspoken desires on the other launches the child into the active use of speech, able now to communicate with a third person—his grandfather Sigmund, for instance—and so to enter into a language community, the mother's unconscious remains a part of his linguistic inheritance. What appears as detachment in fact masks an incorporation: the *bouts-de-mère* are swallowed alive, as it were, and in certain situations of psychic peril they—the repressed meanings of the mother—can speak through the child again. "Of course," Abraham remarks, "it is only in appearance that the child is unburdened of the parental Unconscious by speech, for it is precisely by the same apprenticeship of speech that he takes it [the parental Unconscious] up again on his own account in the mode of what I have called 'Phantom.' The maternal Unconscious is contained within the words of the child in the mode of the Phantom" (Abraham and Torok 1978, 415).

Having suggested that a Phantom is at large in the "Colloquy," and that she speaks lies with the intent of disguising "otros pecados [other sins]" of the mother, I may now begin to be more precise. The foregoing discussion of the dual unity suggests that the dogs may be embodying literally the figurative expression of the mother's unconscious. That they should remain under this spell, however, in an indefinitely protracted *cramponnement* (clinging) is indicative that the *dematernalization* accomplished through language has met with an obstruction. The Cañizares episode provides an explanation as to why the dogs have gained the power to speak, according to Berganza. In order to fathom that mystery, it still remains to inquire why they had previously been speechless.

Some structural considerations may initiate this inquiry. In this regard I remark that if the ghost of King Hamlet presents a felicitous *trouvaille* for the investigation of the Phantom, so too Cervantes's double novella, "The Deceitful Marriage" ("El casamiento engañoso") together with "The Colloquy of the Dogs," offers an appropriate occasion for taking up Abraham and Torok's "dual unity" and its vicissitudes.

It will be recalled, then, that Hermann's mythic configuration presented the dual unity as child-clinging-to-mother. Abraham and Torok refer more frequently to *inclusions*. Nor would one even need to depart from the context of a bioanalysis in the style of Hermann or Sandor Ferenczi to transpose the phylogenetic image of hairless man evolving from primate ancestors to an ontogenetic image of fetus inside mother as a foundational figure. The frame tale device structures the double novella as just such a dual unity, wherein the "Colloquy" is the inclusion carried by "The Deceitful Marriage," and whose development may be studied from conception to term, or, as the deathly repetition compulsion might suggest, to the failure to come to terms.

With a few final words of explanation about the crypt and its potential relation to the Phantom, I will be able to pursue the analysis of Cervantes's text. This crypt is a formation that arises within the ego when a subject may testify to the sins of a loved one and sacrifices psychic integrity to the end of maintaining the other's self-incriminating secret. To distinguish the crypt from the Phantom, I underline the act of witnessing. The Wolf Man actually saw a seduction scene between his father and his sister; consequently, he was consciously aware of the family dishonor before the twin circumstances of a drama internal and external to his psyche barred him from pronouncing his truth. Young Hamlet, by contrast, born the day of the treacherous duel between his father and King Fortinbras (Abraham 1988, 13), did not himself witness the scandalous event, nor was it ever communicated to him openly. Hence, he is not a cryptophore, as the Wolf Man was, but rather a subject haunted by a Phantom, objectified as his father's ghost. If the mother is a cryptophore, the bearer of someone else's secret, the language that she transmits to her child will be riddled not so much by her own unconscious desires as by the unpronounceable words (cryptonyms) that she buries within herself so as to safeguard the honor of that cherished other. Hence, Torok suggests: "The effects of haunting that thus constitute a disguise, raised to the second power, of the maternal cryptonyms (a further step in the evolution of the degree of 'lying') will consequently create an obstacle to the customary 'de-maternalizing' function of speech" (Abraham and Torok 1978, 422).

This is the complex situation of the "Colloquy." The mother is a cryptophore (a bearer of cryptonyms): call her Montiela—if Montiela is the mother, if indeed she exists at all as anything other than a variant of the toponym Montilla (*Novelas* 477; *Stories* 226), an empty placeholder invented by a deceitful Phantom to sunder, in appearance, the undivided dual unity of Cañizares-Camacha. She has penetrated the secret of her mentor only to be so thoroughly repudiated that Cervantes has extended the ban beyond certain unpronounceable words to subject her to utter silence. Unlike Cañizares, who narrates at length, and even Camacha, whose voice is recollected in the prophecy, the "Colloquy" bears no record of Montiela's speech. Instead, her language is *incorporated* in the form of the bizarre and gratuitous acts of the two dogs. Condemned to play at a diabolical game of charades, they are compelled to perform repeatedly the words that she cannot bring to light. And when Berganza returns, unwittingly and uncannily, to Montilla, the very site of the scandal so rigorously silenced, he evokes a Phantom, who issues forth in order to preserve the secret. Insofar as Cañizares's cell is itself a demetaphorized objectification of the crypt, that image reveals the presence of undeclared crimes. But the Phantom, it will be recalled, reveals only in spite of herself. Her purpose is to lie, in Cañizares's case doubly: she will lie down to enact the paralysis of the cryptonymic words ("leur état de 'paralysie' [their state of paralysis]," Abraham and Torok 1978, 422), cut off, as they are, from the coherence of the chain of signification.[22] And she will pronounce, or mispronounce, a prophecy that deceives the bearers of the mother tongue, diverting the dogs down the dead end of an inconsequential interpretation. A spectral emanation of the state of *science-nescience*, the Phantom does not appear except to lie near the truth. And so it is with Cañizares. She prophesies right enough. In theoretical terms she comes to warn that until Berganza and Cipión recover the "customary de-maternalizing function of speech," that is, until they learn to introject where they have been accustomed to incorporate, they will be beasts of their mother's burden.

Alban Forcione also remarks the paralysis of the text in the Cañizares episode, observing that "the narrative grinds to a halt" at the crypt—for him a grave.[23] It then becomes his interpretive project to train his gaze steadily upon this heart of darkness so as to rediscover

---

22. See Nicolas Abraham, "Notules sur le fantôme" in Abraham and Torok, *L'écorce et le noyau*, 421; this essay has been published in English as "Notes on the Phantom: A Complement to Freud's Metapsychology," trans. Nicholas Rand, *Critical Inquiry* 13 (1987): 287–92. The passage in question is cited and explicated by Torok in a contribution to "Notes du séminaire," in Abraham and Torok, *L'écorce et le noyau*, 431.

23. Forcione, *Cervantes and the Mystery of Lawlessness*, 59, 59–99.

the disrupted unity and set reading in motion again along the trajectory of Christian romance. But even his penetrating insight is deflected by Cañizares's textual cover-up, the "barriga, que era de badana, [que] se cubría las partes deshonestas [stomach which was like sheepskin and covered her dishonest parts]" (*Novelas* 486; *Stories* 236; translation modified). Diana de Armas Wilson's critical response to what she takes to be Forcione's complicity in this effacement of the female sex may then be understood to call into question the metaphor of humanist *vision* no less than the reaffirmation of humanist values. "Forcione himself notes Cervantes's curious association between the shameful birth of the dogs and the divine birth of Christ," she writes with respect to Camacha's prophecy, elucidated by Forcione as a double travesty of Virgil and the Magnificat, "but his focus on 'the mystery of lawlessness' has blinded him to Cervantes's focus on the mystery of birth."[24] The incarnation, parodied word made canine flesh, is the persistent phantasm of incorporation in the text, which blocks the reverse passage of introjection by which flesh might become word again. The critical challenge that Wilson poses—the "recovery of a different voice to find 'the words to say it' "[25]—alluding to the work of Ruth El Saffar,[26] would be met by accomplishing that introjection. To this purpose I would extend Wilson's deconstruction of vision by suggesting that Cervantes is in fact peculiarly *unfocused* in the "Colloquy"; hence its apparent "lawlessness." At the same time, I would reinforce her stress on voice by urging that the crux of the text, expressly overheard and underseen—"Yo oí y *casi* vi [I heard and *as good as* saw]," the Alférez tells the Licenciado as he introduces his manuscript of the dogs' colloquy at the close of "The Deceitful Marriage" (*Novelas* 440; *Stories* 191; emphasis added)—relates the mystery of birth to the birth of language.

At the earliest stage in Berganza's emergence from infancy to speech, and in an episode—the very first—that mirrors in anticipation Cañizares's interpellation of the dog, Cervantes plays out his own version of Freud's *fort-da* game.

Digo, pues, que mi amo me enseñó a llevar una espuerta en la boca y a defenderla de quien quitármela quisiese; enseñóme también la

24. Wilson, review of Forcione, 42.

25. Ibid., 43.

26. See Ruth El Saffar, *Beyond Fiction: The Recovery of the Feminine in the Novels of Cervantes* (Berkeley: University of California Press, 1984), as well as her *Cervantes, "El casamiento engañoso" and "El coloquio de los perros,"* Critical Guides to Spanish Texts 17 (London: Grant and Cutler, 1976).

casa de su amiga, y con esto se excusó la venida de su criada al
Matadero, porque yo le llevaba las madrugadas lo que él había
hurtado las noches. Y un día que, entre dos luces, iba yo diligente
a llevarle la porción, oí que me llamaban por mi nombre desde una
ventana; alcé los ojos y vi una moza hermosa en extremo; detúveme
un poco, y ella bajó a la puerta de la calle, y me tornó a llamar;
lleguéme a ella, como si fuera a ver lo que me quería, que no fue
otra cosa que quitarme lo que llevaba en la cesta y ponerme en su
lugar un chapín viejo. Entonces dije entre mí: 'La carne se ha ido
a la carne.' Díjome la moza en habiéndome quitado la carne: 'Andad.
Gavilán, o como os llamáis, y decid a Nicolás el Romo, vuestro amo,
que no se fíe de animales, y que del lobo, un pelo; y ése, de la
espuerta.' Bien pudiera yo volver a quitar lo que me quitó; pero no
quise, por no poner mi boca jifera y sucia en aquellas manos limpias
y blancas.

[I tell you, then, that my master taught me to carry a basket (*espuerta*)
in my mouth and to defend it from anyone who tried to take it from
me. He also showed me his mistress's house, and so avoided her
maid's having to come to the slaughter-house, for I would take to
her in the morning what he had stolen during the night. And one
day when, just at daybreak, I was duly going off to take her rations,
I heard my name being called from a window. I raised my eyes,
and saw a very beautiful girl. I stopped for a moment, and she came
down to the front door, and called me again. I went up to her, to
see what she wanted, and what she did was to take what I was
carrying in the basket and put in its place an old shoe. Then I said
to myself, "Flesh to flesh." When she had taken the meat, the girl
said to me, "Go on, Gavilán, or whatever you're called, and tell
your master, Nicholas the Flat-nosed, not to trust animals, and that
one must take from a miser anything one can get." I could easily
have got back what she took from me; but I didn't want to touch
those pure white hands with my dirty slaughter-house mouth. (*Novelas* 447–48; *Stories* 199)

In this encounter between beauty and the beast, Berganza receives a
seminal language lesson, by which he successfully assimilates
"aquella ciencia que llaman *tropelía*," as Cañizares will later say, "que
hace parecer una cosa por otra [that art they call *tropelía*, which makes
one thing appear to be another]" (*Novelas* 480; *Stories* 229). For beauty
performs a complex trope: a metaphoric substitution, heavily laden
with irony, of course, of *chapín* for *carne* (clog—C. A. Jones's "old

shoe"—for meat), which undoes a prior and unstated metaphor[27]—
Nicolás el Romo's meat in her basket—for her participation in an
implicit sexual triangle involving the butcher and his mistress, "o por
otra pendenzuela de celos, que nunca pude averiguar [or through
some other jealous quarrel that I could never get to the bottom of],"
in the words that Cañizares will apply to Montiela (*Novelas* 481; *Stories*
231). Berganza formulates his own baroque conceit on the antinomy
of *fort-da*: flesh is gone to flesh because flesh is all that's here. Con-
tented by this turn of phrase, he desists from the most literal of
incorporations—taking the meat into his mouth again—and instead
he introjects the words, bearing off the clog as a symbol of the fractured, and thus apparently illegible, metaphor. Cipión, an astute
reader, rightly understands this commercial loss as aesthetic gain and
offers his congratulations on the acquisition of language: "Hiciste muy
bien," he tells Berganza, "por ser prerrogativa de la hermosura que
siempre se la tenga respecto [You did quite right, for it's the prerog-
ative of beauty always to be respected]" (*Novelas* 448; *Stories* 199).

That judgment is repeated, if inverted, when beauty's place is supplied by abomination; Berganza avoids Cañizares's embraces and Cipión comments, "Bien hiciste; porque no es regalo, sino tormento, el
besar ni dejar besarse de una vieja [You were right, for it's no pleasure
but sheer torture to kiss or let yourself be kissed by an old woman]"
(*Novelas* 479; *Stories* 228). In this respect once again the two tales of
rivalry overlap; which is to say they are themselves rivals, competing
versions of a single scene, a primal scene or myth of origins: "Esto
que ahora te quiero contar," Berganza says, following Cipión's praise
for keeping his mouth closed, as it were, and eluding Cañizares's
kisses, "Te lo había de haber dicho al principio de mi cuento [What
I want to tell you now I ought to have said at the beginning of my
story]" (*Novelas* 479; *Stories* 228). As the repetition suggests, the introjection practiced at beauty's behest was incomplete. Indeed, in this
text, ultimately more graceless than lawless, the New Testament dic-
tum reverts to the prior disposition *sub lege*: one need listen to what
goes in rather than what comes out of the mouth; and what goes in,

27. I refer to Freud's *Ungeschehenmachung*, "undoing what has been done," a repetition in
reverse. See Sigmund Freud, "Inhibitions, Symptoms, and Anxiety," SE 20:77–175. His
remarks likening this ego defense to "negative magic" (119) are of course especially pertinent
to the Cañizares episode. It is in this light that I would interpret the drummer's command
to Berganza that leads to Cañizares's initial intervention as an *undoing*: "Volved, y deshaced
los saltos que habéis hecho" (*Novelas* 478), which I would read quite literally as: "Return,
and undo the leaps that you have done." Compare Jones's translation, "Come back, and go
through again all those jumps," in *Stories* 227.

by means of the phantasm of incorporation, are reified words. In the case of the deceit in the marketplace, Berganza's play on *carne* (meat) had proven so satisfying because it left in his mouth the taste, however adulterated and remote, of a magic word.

Carne is not itself a cryptonym. Were it so, it could not be pronounced, much less repeated, in the text. And as I have noted, Berganza does not actually incorporate the meat—neither the butcher's choice cut nor the *moza*'s hand. What he has learned from Nicolás to take into his mouth is the basket, *una espuerta*. "Y que del lobo, un pelo; y ése de la espuerta," the *moza* declares in the parody of proverbial speech that she fashions as a motto to her larceny. A premonition of the Phantom to come, she is both misleading and revealing. The deceit proffers an image for an oedipal reduction. The customary version of the *refrán*, meaning roughly "Take what you get," reads, "Del lobo, un pelo; y ése de la cola."[28] Transforming "cola" into "espuerta," like taking the dog's meat away, points the way to Freud's favorite allegory.[29] Whatever goes down or stands up again, to echo Camacha's prophecy, is a penis fretting over castration. The Phantom gleefully makes the interpretation of a castration complex available. "Go tell Nicholas, with his funny little nose, that he shouldn't trust too much to his beast; he shouldn't be trotting out his *feritas*. I can take what little he's got to offer and leave him with an empty receptacle—that is, metaphoric female genitalia—just where his meat was. In short, tell him he can go to hell in a handbasket."

But what if one were to listen to the word and not envision the image? The *moza*'s lie would then prove more revealing. *Espuerta* is a "gnome," embodying a "truncated knowledge ([truncated] by unawareness [*nescience*], one may assume)" (Abraham and Torok 1978, 421). To restore this butchered word—that is, the remaining shard or symbol of the sundered dual unity of a lost metaphor—it must be read as a lexical deformation of *espuela* (spur), as indeed it does reappear under a more transparent veil in the final shift from spirit to

28. José María Sbarbi records this version of the traditional proverb in *Diccionario de refranes, adagios, proverbios, modismos, locuciones y frases proverbials de la lengua española,* ed. Manuel José García (Madrid: Librería de los sucesores de Hernando, 1922), 1:530. As there is no strict equivalent of the proverb in English, Jones rendered the passage as it was transformed by the deceitful girl as: "One must take from a miser anything one can get"; see *Stories* 199. A literal version of the traditional proverb might read, "From the wolf, a hair; and that one from the tail"; and of the girl's parody, "From the wolf a hair; and that one from the basket [*espuerta*]."

29. Cipión and Berganza's remarks with respect to the word *cola* (tail) make it clear that they are perfectly well aware of its sexual connotation as a metaphor for "penis" (Latin for "tail"); see *Novelas* 462; *Stories* 212.

flesh at the close of the frame tale: "Vámonos al *Espolón* [Let's go off to the *Espolón*]" (*Novelas* 502; *Stories* 252; emphasis added). *Espuerta, espuela, espolón* (also "spur"): a trace, Jacques Derrida might say, but Abraham and Torok have demonstrated that amidst the mirage of seemingly infinite deferrals of meaning, there are cryptic words whose meaning may be fixed.[30]

Berganza's language lessons continue. He even pursues something of a formal education, gaining entrance to the Jesuit school by repeating his old trick with the *espuerta*: "Digo que los hijos de mi amo se dejaron un día un cartapacio en el patio y como [yo] estaba enseñado a llevar la esportilla del jifero mi amo, así del *vademécum* y fuime tras ellos [Anyway, I was saying that one day my master's sons left a satchel in the courtyard, where I was at the time; and as I was trained to carry the basket [*esportilla*] for my master the slaughterer, I got hold of the satchel and went off after them]" (*Novelas* 458, *Stories* 208–09). But despite his self-delusions, he is a recalcitrant pupil. Whether it is the Latin text, the hands and hats of the students, their lunches, or their grammars, transformed by barter into muffins and butter, Berganza's habit of taking things into his mouth proves incorrigible, and he is finally dismissed because his tendency to incorporation is interfering with the children's studies (*Novelas* 459–60; *Stories* 210).

Under Cañizares's tutelage, then, this habit reasserts itself. The proximity to the crypt and the threat of exposure to its contents divests the phantasm of incorporation of the benign aspect that it took on among schoolchildren, to appear instead as a demonic regressive force. Cañizares leaves him to watch over her inert body, like the faithful dogs of sepulchral monuments which Cipión had suggested he and Berganza take as their proper emblem (*Novelas* 444; *Stories* 195), as she makes for her witches' coven with the promise to fulfil his hunger for "las nuevas de lo que me quedaba por pasar hasta ser hombre [what I had to go through until I became a man]" (*Novelas* 486, *Stories* 235) while satisfying her own unrepressed desires. Finding himself faced with a Phantom—a "mala visión," or "ghost" as Jones had rendered the same words at the outset of the frame tale (*Novelas* 487; *Stories* 236), repeating the words previously cited from "The De-

---

30. For a discussion of the contrast between Abraham and Torok's work and Derrida's deconstruction, see Rand, "Translator's Introduction," lxvi–lxix. Derrida's own assessment of their work, "*Fors*: The Anglish Words of Nicolas Abraham and Maria Torok," appeared as a foreword to both the French and English editions of *Le verbier/The Wolf Man's Magic Word*, where it played an important role in bringing Abraham and Torok to the attention of a broader readership.

ceitful Marriage" (*Novelas* 429; *Stories* 181)—Berganza is unable to pa-
cify his specter with the resources of a more advanced semiotics, as
Peralta had done, "santiguándose [crossing himself]" and then troping the visible symptoms of Campuzano's malady as sexual innuendo:
"terciando allá la pica que arrastrando aquí la espada [trailing a pike
in Flanders, not dragging a sword along here]" (*Novelas* 429; *Stories*
181). Instead, the dog attempts a *cramponnement*, a clinging, but in
the mode of a demetaphorizing incorporation: he enacts literally what
should be understood figuratively. "Quise morderla," he relates to
Cipión, "por ver si volvía en sí, y no hallé parte en toda ella que el
asco no me lo estorbase; pero con todo esto, la así de un carcaño [I
wanted to bite her, to see if she would recover consciousness. I
couldn't find anywhere on her person where I could do it without
feeling revulsion, but all the same, I did grab her by the heel]" (*Novelas*
487; *Stories* 236). *Espuela*, "spur," by metonymy "heel": *carcaño* a me-
tathesis of *calcañar*. He seizes upon the rhyme of a cryptonym. He
incorporates a word. He reestablishes, as if by magic, the illusion of
the dual unity. Are you my mother?

If one listens to such rhymes, a different voice emerges from Camacha's prophecy. Where Forcione finds a grotesque lampoon of the
most canonical works of Cervantes's Christian humanism, Wilson
argues for an "agonistic, rather than, as Forcione would prefer, a
heuristic imitation of model texts," such that the prophecy participates
in a "truly Erasmian critique of the ideology of conquest," including,
she implies, the ideology of male sexual conquest.[31] Berganza's frantic
grip on Cañizares's heel gives evidence of more specific precursors.
Having found her Achilles heel, he recalls the Homeric template of
the *Aeneid*. And behind the Annunciation he reveals—repeating compulsively rather than remembering—the curse that the virgin birth
would miraculously redeem, the very curse, of course, to which Poe
had alluded in sealing his crypt and simultaneously marking the route
to its rediscovery: pain in childbearing and eternal enmity between
Eve and the serpent. Even the greatest works of culture are but *calcos*,
imitations. Not merely the tenpins of the dogs' mock allegorical interpretation but literature itself is subject to a process of recycling: if
Camacha's renegade prophecy is allegory, then it appears at first
glance as an allegory of reading, wherein meaning is ever receding
in a philological nightmare of distant intertexts walled over by surface
allusions.

Yet Abraham and Torok's "theory of readability," I stress once

31. Forcione, *Cervantes and the Mystery of Lawlessness*, 44–47; Wilson, review of Forcione, 42.

more, resists the *mise-en-abîme* of an indefinite deconstruction. The relations between the Castillian *carcaño* and the Latin substrate *calx* ("heel," and root of *carcañar-calcanar* and *calco* alike) encrypted in the text bespeak the urge that is the explicit purpose of the Cañizares episode, namely, to establish an affiliation to a matrix. Cervantes veils that impulse as an "anxiety of influence" in the prologue to the *Novelas ejemplares*.[32]

> Y es así, que yo soy el primero que he novelado en lengua castellana; que las muchas novelas que en ella andan impresas, todas son traducidas de lenguas extranjeras, y éstas son mías propias, no imitadas ni hurtadas. Mi ingenio las engendró y las parió mi pluma, y van creciendo en los brazos de la estampa.

> [And so it is that I am the first to write novellas (literally, "to have noveled") in Castillian; that the many novellas that circulate in print in that language are all translated from foreign tongues, and these are my own, neither imitated nor stolen. My wits have engendered them and my pen gave birth to them, and they are growing in the arms of the press.] ("Prólogo al lector," *Novelas* 9)[33]

Nevertheless, looking beyond Cervantes's all-too-easy victory over his contemporaries in Castilian, one detects the greater issue, already encountered in the struggles of Fortunato and Montresor, of the rivalry of Romance tongues for the Latin heritage. To be first among his countrymen would not in itself authenticate a claim to the legitimacy of Spanish as a vehicle for literature. And the skeptical Peralta presses the claims of Italian, attempting to foreclose the tale of Campuzano's deceitful marriage, by promoting Petrarch as a source of proverbial wisdom and citing a pair of verses from the *Trionfo d'amore* as a proper moral to that story. In this context, as Peralta notes against Cervantes's claim in the prologue, Castilian serves merely as a translation (*Novelas* 438; *Stories* 189). As in Poe's tale, here too prior injuries (syphilis, theft) may have been borne as best they could, but the insult of this implicit repudiation of his language—"el artificio . . . y la invención [the art . . . and the invention]" which Peralta is subsequently obliged to concede (*Novelas* 502; *Stories* 252)—leads to a bold response.

---

32. In a review of *The Wolf Man's Magic Word* in *Sub-Stance* 56 (1988): 99–102, I made some preliminary remarks on the situation of Abraham and Torok's work within the context of poststructuralist theory generally, including its special pertinence to Harold Bloom's theory of the anxiety of influence.

33. The prologue is not included in the C. A. Jones translation; hence this translation is my own.

The Alférez declares, be that as it may, he has not yet finished his story. The preceding novella, "The Deceitful Marriage," was no more than a pretext, and its Italianate background, moreover, cannot adequately prepare Peralta, nor "persona alguna" [any one else in the world]" (*Novelas* 441; *Stories* 190), for the marvelous tale to come. From the point of view of Peralta's foreclusion, of course, if Campuzano's insistence on the reality of his perception of the speaking dogs is not simply an elaborate lie, then it is only to be explained as the manifestation of a psychosis. But Abraham and Torok provide the theoretical ground on which to argue that the "Colloquy" is rather an incorporation. Introjection is eschewed—the words of, say, Boccaccio are not taken into the mouth—and a parodic repetition is enacted in its stead: a bite of the calx reattaches Spanish to Latin, but at the cost of replaying the primordial curse. And by that fall, the dogs regain the voice of their lost humanity and Cervantes reasserts the originality of Spanish as a literary language.

It would be possible to conjecture now about the "prehistory" of the family from Montilla "with the purpose of extrapolating *from the play*"—or in this case, from the text of Cervantes's double novella— "a fictive dramatic and psychological situation."[34] In my own speculations I imagine a mother and a daughter—a certain Carmen, known as Carmacha, and Carcañizares, to distinguish them from Cervantes's creations—who are rivals for the same man, or so, at least, is the mother's mistaken understanding. Social history makes it far more likely that the daughter was the victim of her father's violation than the willing protagonist of a female oedipal drama. And the daughter, for her part, recognizes no wrongdoing in herself to hide, although she comes to see her father's image damaged and her mother's love withdrawn in consequence. For in the terrible moment of anagnorisis the mother discovers the incest, and, misreading *his* seduction as *her*, that is, the daughter's, theft—"You stole my meat," she would have said, crudely—she indicts her daughter for biting the hand that feeds her: "¡Perra satánica! [Diabolical dog!]" and thereafter, in the most abrasive language possible, excoriating her daughter's undeveloped sex, her little Mount of Venus, or *montilla* (diminutive of *mons* or *monte*, "mount"), as the offending agent of the family's fall.

But as the pregnancy advances, the mother reverses herself. She can only suffer more if the shame is made known. She contrives to repudiate the birth, to deny the whole affair: "Yo encubriré este parto,

34. Rand, "Family Romance" 28.

y atiende tú a estar sana, y haz cuenta que esta tu desgracia queda sepultada en el mismo silencio [I will cover up this birth, and you give your mind to getting well. You can be sure that this misfortune of yours will be buried in silence]" (*Novelas* 481; *Stories* 230; translation modified). She opens a crypt within her daughter, burying there her curse along with the history of incest. The daughter bears a secret and a son, a bastard (*espurio*, another variation on *espuerta*), who will be haunted by the contents of the crypt. Or, indeed, the offspring might be twins, just as the pupils of La Camacha might be two. But I believe that Cañizares may well have been lying, that she was herself the mother of Cipión and Berganza, and that the projection of a double, the spectral Montiela, is repeated in my tale by a similar invention on the part of Carcañizares's son. He needs a name, too. Let it be a corruption of *camposanto*, since he embodies an unholy place of words buried alive: Campuzanto, for instance.

Child (or children) of a "perra satánica," in hallucinatory moments he will believe himself a dog, mouthing the grandmother's invective, even if he must butcher her words before incorporating the curse anew, hiding the *es-p(u)er-ta* in *per-(ra) s(a) tá (nica)*. This son will be condemned to reenact the whole of the cryptic drama, playing out the father's role as well. He will be a serpentine tempter, therefore, at once guardian and despoiler of the Tree of Knowledge, caught, that is, in the double bind of *science-nescience*. Aware, if unaware of the psychodrama of his forebears, he will live out repeated falls and banishments, attempting to surmount in this illusory way the real loss that was never introjected: the sundered dual unity of mother-daughter. He may even go so far as to seduce a woman who proves a thief, at the cost of mutilating his flesh by the chancre (*cancro*) of syphilis, a spirochete (*espiroqueta*), no less: driven unto death by the Phantom, if his therapy is to consist of nothing but negations, reenacting the rhymes (*carcaño, espuerta*) of the crypt.

With the perspicacity of Torok, the daring and dexterity of Abraham, and the obstinacy of Pierre Menard, I might elaborate such a tale as an intermission in the double novella, and write it in the prose of the Spanish Golden Age.

15

Berganza and the Abject:
The Desecration of the Mother

María Antonia Garcés

Si acaso es nuestra madre . . . yo no la quiero tener por
madre.

—Miguel de Cervantes, "El coloquio de los perros"

"The Colloquy of the Dogs" ("El coloquio de los perros") plunges the
reader into a monstrous universe that opens up to reveal the hideous
figure of an octopus.[1] Indeed, the *colas* or *rabos* (tentacles) of the
monster reappear throughout the novel, in the escalating images of
bestiality that haunt the "Colloquy." Originating in the delirious visions of Ensign Campuzano, who endures a "sweating" cure for his
bubas (pox) at the Hospital of the Resurrection in Valladolid, the colloquy is constructed around the figures of two talking dogs and the
sight of slaughtered cattle, dismembered sheep, savage "wolves," a
monkey, and an ass, among other animals.[2] These images are condensed in the phantasmatic[3] projection of the octopus, whose prolif-

---

1. A version of this essay was presented at Ruth El Saffar's panel "Cervantes and the
Unconscious," at the 1989 MLA Convention, Washington, D.C.

2. Miguel de Cervantes, "El casamiento engañoso" and "El coloquio de los perros," in
Novelas ejemplares, ed. Harry Sieber, 2 vols. (Madrid: Cátedra, 1981), 2:332–45. Further references to these works are from this edition and will be cited in the text. The translations
of "The Deceitful Marriage" and "The Colloquy of the Dogs," from C. E. Jones, *Cervantes:
Exemplary Stories* (London: Penguin Books, 1972), 181–252, have been slightly modified. *Bubas*
(pox) was the name given to syphilis because it produced many scabs on the face and head,
which forced the patient to cover them with bandages. See Sebastián de Covarrubias, *Tesoro
de la lengua castellana o española* (1611; reprint Madrid: Turner, 1979). For the treatment of
bubas in seventeenth-century Spain, see *Novelas ejemplares*, 2:282, n. 4.

3. I use the term *phantasy*—the French *fantasme* revived by psychoanalysis—and its correlative adjective *phantasmatic* when referring to a specific imaginary production related to
psychic realities, specifically to the phantasies that lie behind products of the unconscious
such as dreams, symptoms, acting out, repetitive behavior, and so on. In this sense the

erating tentacles metaphorically embrace the novella. But it is another image that crowns this bizarre representation of bestiality in "The Colloquy of the Dogs." In the center of the labyrinth stands the figure of the witch Cañizares, who oscillates between the animal and the human, depicting a monstrosity which exceeds that of the "asquero[o] . . . pulpo [hideous octopus]" of Cipión and Berganza's disquisitions.

It is precisely through this central nightmare that besets the dreamer(s)—both Campuzano and Berganza, and perhaps even Cervantes—that the "Colloquy" provides an intense elaboration on universal horror, one that explores the problematic question of the acquisition of language. I argue that the depiction of the witch Cañizares in terms of an apocalyptic female presence represents horror in its extreme manifestation, indeed constitutes a violent rejection of the maternal image, a desecration of maternity itself.

This horror that resists naming is significantly associated with female sexuality, as revealed by the sexual allusions of Cervantes's text, until recently elided by most critics.[4] Yet, the depiction of the witch Cañizares surpasses the traditional antagonistic image of woman as whore in order to posit the feminine as the abject. In her essay on abjection, Julia Kristeva reexamines the psychoanalytical status of the mother in order to propose that the abject is above all the ambiguous— namely, that which defies boundaries, "identity, system, order."[5]

---

subject's life as a whole seems to be shaped and ordered by what may be called a phantasmatic (*une fantasmatique*), which is not to be confused with the world of fantasy and imaginative activity in general. On phantasy, see Jean Laplanche and J.B. Pontalis, *The Language of Psychoanalysis* (London: Hogarth Press, 1983), 314–19.

4. Fernando de Toro-Garland highlights the timidity of the critics in regard to the sexual dimension of Cervantes's novellas; see "Aproximación a lo sexual en las *Novelas ejemplares* de Cervantes," in *Cervantes, su obra y su mundo*, Actas del Primer Congreso Internacional sobre Cervantes (Madrid: Edi, 1981), 365–70. Stating that sexual expression in "The Deceitful Marriage" and the "Colloquy" is quite explicit, the author, however, invalidates his own arguments by maintaining that "estas dos obritas [sic] . . . podrían subsistir si este elemento [el sexo] se eliminase [these two small works . . . could continue to exist if this element (the sexual) were eliminated]" (369). More recently Anthony Close has claimed that in "The Man of Glass" ("El licenciado Vidriera") and "The Colloquy of the Dogs," "faltan . . . los . . . temas consagrados de la tradición satírica: la mujer (o la sexualidad), la política, la religión [the consecrated themes of the satirical tradition: women (or sexuality), politics, religion, are missing]"; see "Algunas reflexiones sobre la sátira en Cervantes," *Nueva revista de filología hispánica* 38 (1990): 493–511. Mary Gossy, by contrast, advances the suggestion that the witch is "a powerful emblem of sexuality in Western consciousness," a fact that converts Cañizares, in the eyes of one of her (male) readers, into "an all-devouring womb"; see 'Marriage, Motherhood, and Deviance in *El casamiento engañoso/Coloquio de los perros*," in *The Untold Story: Women and Theory in Golden Age Texts* (Ann Arbor: University of Michigan Press, 1989), 57–82.

5. Julia Kristeva, *Powers of Horror: An Essay on Abjection*, trans. Leon S. Roudiez (New York: Columbia University Press, 1982), 4. Further references to this work will be abbreviated

Abjection is, therefore, the encounter with "something" radically strange, revolting, which epitomizes the threat of disintegration for the vacillating subject. As that uncanny "object" that functions as a magnet of identification, ensuring the advent of a subject for an object, the abject is intimately linked to the birth of language.[6]

THE CREATION OF A MONSTER

Alban Forcione has referred to "The Colloquy of the Dogs" as a "literary monstrosity, swollen and bursting" with narrative shapes, as if "saturation and narrative chaos" appeared to be its governing principle.[7] The ever-expanding character of the tale, with its endless digressions, have invited some critics to consider the image of the octopus as an appropriate analogy for the form of the story.[8] I suggest that the overflowing tendencies of the narrative, with its congestion of images and experiences, turn the "Colloquy" into a metaphor for uncontrollable and chaotic fertility. This terrifying fertility, epitomized by the invading tentacles of the octopus, is also incarnated by the greatest monstrosity of all, one lying at the imaginative vortex of the tale: the witch Cañizares.[9]

---

as *Powers* and cited by page in the text. My discussion specifically echoes Kristeva's theories on abjection, as formulated in *Powers of Horror* and other subsequently cited works.

6. See Julie Kristeva, "Freud and Love: Treatment and Its Discontents," in *Tales of Love*, trans. Leon Roudiez (New York: Columbia University Press, 1987), 21–56.

7. Alban K. Forcione, *Cervantes and the Mystery of Lawlessness: A Study of "El casamiento engañoso" and "El coloquio de los perros"* (Princeton: Princeton University Press, 1984), 22. Further references to this work will be abbreviated as *Cervantes* and cited by page in the text.

8. See, for instance, Joaquín Casalduero, *Sentido y forma de las "Novelas ejemplares,"* 2d ed., rev. (Madrid: Gredos, 1969), 242–44; and Forcione, *Cervantes*, 34. On the octopus's infinite tentacles as a metaphor for philosophical activity, see Michael Nerlich, "On the Philosophical Dimension of 'El casamiento engañoso' and 'El coloquio de los perros', in *Cervantes's 'Exemplary Novels' and the Adventure of Writing*, ed. Michael Nerlich and Nicholas Spadaccini (Minneapolis: Prisma Institute, 1989), 248–329.

9. For a fine study of the "Casamiento" and the "Coloquio," see Ruth El Saffar, *Cervantes's "El casamiento engañoso" and "El coloquio de los perros"* (London: Grant and Cutler, 1976). On the structure of the "Coloquio," see Alan Soons, "An Interpretation of the Form of 'El casamiento engañosoy Coloquio de los perros,' " *Anales Cervantinos* 9 (1961–62): 204–12; Oldrich Belic, "La estructura de 'El coloquio de los perros,' " *Philological* 4 (1966): 3–19; Felix Carrasco, " 'El coloquio de los perros': Veridicción y modelo narrativo," *Criticón* 35 (1986): 119–33; and Lelia Madrid, *Cervantes y Borges: La inversión de los signos* (Madrid: Editorial Pliegos, 1987), esp. 71–90. On the subtext of the "Colloquy," see Edward C. Riley, "Cervantes and the Cynics ('El licenciado vidriera' and 'El coloquio de los perros)," *Bulletin of Hispanic Studies* 53 (1976): 189–99; Anthony J. Cárdenas, "Berganza: Cervantes' Can[is] Domini," in *Cervantes and the Pastoral*, ed. José J. Labrador Herraiz and Juan Fernández Jiménez (Cleveland: Cleveland State University, 1986), 19–35; and Fred Abrams, "Cervantes' Berganza-Cipión Anagrams in 'El coloquio,' " *Journal of the American Name Society* 24 (1976): 325–26.

The Cañizares nightmare begins at the hospital of Montilla, at the point when the narrative is moving rapidly toward the climactic scene that will clarify the mystery of Berganza's origins and of his ability to speak. Arriving in Montilla as servant to a drummer boy, the dog understands language but is not endowed with the gift of speech. He acquires this human ability only after his fateful encounter with the witch. The uncanny atmosphere of the meeting with Cañizares is foreshadowed by the drummer's words as he presents the Wise Dog to the crowd gathered outside the hospital. Stressing the demonic quality of the scene, the narrator refers to the drummer's commands to the dog as "conjuros" (conjurations): "El primer conjuro deste día (memorable entre todos los de mi vida) fue . . . [The first conjuration of that day (which I shall remember as long as I live) was . . .]" (334). The word *conjuro* (conjuration, incantation) invokes a scenario of exorcism, in which the demons will be expelled from that tortured subject (Berganza), who has been assailed by an aimless wandering, within his identity as speaker as within his own discourse. The dispersal and oscillations of the subject are also revealed by the changes of name experienced by Berganza under his different masters. In this sense it is relevant to point at the sequence of identities assumed by the dog in the novella, as he goes from Gavilán to Barcino; back to Gavilán again; then to "perro sabio" (Wise Dog); later to Montiel; and finally, after his confrontation with the witch, to Berganza.[10]

After the drummer pronounces his third *conjuro*, an incantation that invokes the name of the famous witch La Camacha de Montilla, Cañizares materializes as if responding to the public summons of a conjurer or necromancer.[11] Her appearance, amidst an explosion of insults and disclosures, intimates the existence of a force that can no longer be contained by the narrator's discourse. It is as if Cañizares could be identified from the start by excess, namely, by an overflow of signifiers which attempts to shatter the symbolic surface of the narrative. When the avalanche of imprecations subsides, Berganza

10. This characteristic of the picaresque hero, whose story is that of a sequence of "identifications," is examined by Paul Julian Smith in "The Rhetoric of Representation in the Picaresque," in *Writing in the Margin: Spanish Literature of the Golden Age* (Oxford: Clarendon, 1988), 97.

11. On Leonor Rodríguez, called La Camacha, see Raúl Porras Barrenechea, "Cervantes, La Camacha y Montilla," in *El Inca Garcilaso en Montilla (1561–1614)* (Lima: Editorial San Marcos, 1955), 236–50; also Alvaro Huerga, "El proceso inquisitorial contra La Camacha," in *Cervantes: Su obra y su mundo*, ed. Manuel Criado de Val, Actas del Primer Congreso Internacional sobre Cervantes (Madrid Edi 6, 1978), 453–62. For the complete texts of the trials against La Camacha and other witches of Montilla (1570), see *Autos de fe y causas de la Inquisición de Córdoba*, ed. Rafael García Boix (Córdoba, 1983), 94–100.

finds himself alone with the old woman in the hospital courtyard. Night has arrived, and with it the time of revelation. Unexpectedly the witch addresses Berganza as her son: "¿Eres tú, hijo Montiel? ¿Eres tú, por ventura, hijo? [Is it you, Montiel my boy? Is it you by any chance, my son?]" (336).

Fascinated by her words, Berganza can no longer extricate himself from the old woman's power. Cañizares's voice functions as a magnet that attracts the dog toward the cave where he will witness her "unveiling," a scene that also unveils the truth about his origins. The passage evokes the image of Ensign Campuzano following Estefanía to her house to participate in her "unveiling." Riveted to Estefanía's words "porque tenía un tono de habla tan suave que se entraba por los oídos . . . [del] alma [because the tone of her voice was so soft that when she spoke she touched my very soul]" (284), Ensign Campuzano is transferred (by sound) beyond meaning, into the realm of the Other. In a parallel way, the dog becomes spellbound by the old woman's words, which carry him toward that phantasmatic scene—the primal scene of Berganza's history—which has to be "buried in silence" (338).

"Things . . . so Filthy and Loathsome"

Cañizares's discourse revolves around two themes: the scene of Berganza's birth and his conversion into a dog by the malefic offices of the famous witch La Camacha de Montilla; and the indescribable sexual pleasure of witches, especially during the Sabbaths. The witch reveals that, during these orgies, "pasan . . . cosas . . . [tan] sucias y asquerosas . . . que en verdad y en Dios . . . no me atrevo a contarlas [there occur things . . . so filthy and loathsome . . . that for the sake of truth and of God . . . I dare not tell them]" (339).

The narrative of the witch specifically addresses one of the greatest concerns of the European witch trials: namely, accusations of pacts and sexual relations with the devil. This is evidenced in the papal bull by Innocent VIII (1484), the *Malleus Maleficarum* (1487), and the works of other authorities such as Jean Bodin (1580) and Pierre De Lancre (1612). These treatises describe acts of unlimited lechery with the devil, which commonly included incestuous acts performed between the nearest possible relatives.[12] Echoing these accusations, the

12. For a discussion of the sexual relations of witches with the devil, see Rossell Hope Robbins, *The Encyclopedia of Witchcraft and Demonology* (New York: Bonanza, 1981), 461–68; the papal bull of Innocent VIII, cited ibid., 263–66; Heinrich Kramer and Jacob Sprenger, *Malleus Maleficarum* (1486), in *Witchcraft in Europe*, ed. Alan C. Kors and Edward Peters

Spanish witch trials of the fifteenth and sixteenth centuries revealed their adherence to the medieval criteria regarding witches and heretics. Indeed, if the Spanish Inquisition appears to have been more lenient toward witchcraft than were the authorities of the neighboring European countries, the fact is that—contrary to what is frequently believed—witches were persecuted and burned during the fifteenth and sixteenth centuries at Zaragoza, Calahorra, Logroño, and Navarra, among other places.[13]

Cervantes seems to be keenly aware of the most intimate aspects of the contemporary belief in witches. His account of the Sabbath and nocturnal activities of the witches not only follows the 1530 treatise by Pedro Ciruelo but also emphasizes the intense erotic pleasure achieved by these women.[14] Describing the Sabbaths, Cañizares stresses the fantastical feelings elicited by these demonic "flights": "Todo lo que nos pasa en la fantasía es tan intensamente que no hay [que] diferenciarlo de cuando vamos real y verdaderamente [Everything that happens in our imagination happens in such an intense way that it can't be distinguished from the times when we go really and truly]" (340). In the midst of her theological disquisitions, the witch returns obsessively to the compulsive pleasures of erotic life: "En medio de su ardor, que es mucho, trae un frío... que... entorpece [el alma] [In the midst of its ardors, which are many, it carries within it a chill... which... benumbs (the soul)]" (342); "Como es pecado de carne y de deleites, es fuerza que amortigüe todos los sentidos [since it is a sin of the flesh and of sensual pleasures, it must of necessity deaden all the senses]" (342); and, finally, "Como el deleite me tiene echado los grillos a la voluntad, siempre he sido y seré mala [as sensual pleasure has fettered my will, I have always been and always shall be evil]" (342).[15]

(Philadelphia: University of Pennsylvania Press, 1972), 136–44; Pierre De Lancre, *Tableau de l'inconstance des mauvais anges et démons* (Paris, 1612); and Jean Bodin, *De la démonomanie des sorciers* (Antwerp: Lyons, 1593), 295. On witchcraft in Europe, especially in Spain, see Julio Caro Baroja, *Las brujas y su mundo* (Madrid: Alianza Editorial, 1968), 96–258; and Henry Kamen, *Inquisition and Society in Spain* (Bloomington: Indiana University Press, 1985). For a psychoanalytic discussion of witches, see Ernest Jones, *On the Nightmare* (New York: Liveright, 1971), 190–236. A series of licentious acts with the devil is described in *Un documento de la Inquisición sobre brujería en Navarra* (1613), ed. Florencio Idoate (Pamplona: Diputación Floral de Navarra, 1972), 140–44.

13. Kamen, *Inquisition and Society*, 210–18.

14. See Pedro Ciruelo, *Reprovación de las supersticiones y hechicerías* (1530), ed. Alva V. Ebersole (Valencia: Hispanófila, 1978), 36–37, 45–46. On the influence of the auto-da-fé of Logroño (1610) and other witch processes on Cervantes, see Agustín de Amezúa y Mayo, *Cervantes, creador de la novela corta española*, 2 vols. (Madrid: Castalia, 1982), 2: 452–55.

15. These same words—"me tenía echado grillos al entendimiento [my will had been

Nonetheless, if these references to carnal delights appear to be couched in theological terms, the remarks of the witch about the sensual transports obtained through the "unturas" (ointments) are quite explicit:

> En untándonos con ellas . . . quedamos tendidas y desnudas en el suelo. . . . Otras veces . . . vamos al lugar donde nuestro dueño nos espera, y allí . . . gozamos de los deleites que te dejo de decir, por ser tales que la memoria se escandaliza.

> [When we anoint ourselves with them we . . . lie stretched out and naked on the ground. . . . Other times, we go where our master is waiting for us. There we . . . enjoy pleasures which I refrain from telling you about, because they are such that one's memory is scandalized.] (342)

Such powerful allusions to the sexual transports that she dares not describe "because . . . one's memory is scandalized" confers a suggestive aura to Cañizares's invitation to the dog: "Ven, hijo, verásme untar [Come, my boy, and watch me anoint myself]" (343).

Thereafter Berganza follows the witch into her room in order to watch her undress and rub the ointment over her body. Riddled with metaphors of sexual penetration, the journey into the cavernous chamber leads the dog into: "[un] aposento . . . oscuro, estrecho . . . y solamente claro con la débil luz de un candil [a dark and narrow room . . . lit only by the dim light of a candle]" (336). Indeed, the allusions to sexual possession are intensified as the anxious narrator penetrates deeper and deeper into the narrow recesses of the old woman's abode: "Entró en otro aposentillo más estrecho [He entered into another, smaller and narrower room]" (343).

A Voyage into the Womb

This is a voyage into the womb, a descent into the abyss where the "monster" lives. As if in a trance, Berganza now finds himself watching the striptease of the witch during which she massages herself, from head to toe, with the magic ointment. According to Johan Weyer, this unguent had to be rubbed well into the body, particularly over the abdomen, the upper part of the thighs, and the feet, until a warm

---

fettered]"(285)—are pronounced by Campuzano in "The Deceitful Marriage" ("El casamiento engañoso") to describe his uncontrollable desire for Estefanía.

glow was experienced.[16] Ernest Jones has also noted the sexual symbolism of the act of anointing, as intimated by the sensuous flights
of the witches and the Sabbaths.[17] Furthermore, there seems to be an
implicit connection between the ice-cold mixtures used in these ointments ("este ungüento con que las brujas nos untamos . . . compuesto
de jugos de yerbas en extremos fríos [this ointment with which we
witches anoint ourselves . . . composed of the juices of very cold
herbs]") (341), and the frigid semen attributed to the devil by common
lore.[18]

It is only after the witch lies down naked on the floor, ready to
enter into a sensual trance, that the image of the "monster" lurks out
of the shadows. We might recall here that Cañizares is first described
as a woman over seventy years old, "bruja y barbuda [a witch and a
hairy old hag]" (335–36), one certainly characterized by uncouth verbal explosions. This, however, does not warrant her conversion into
the appalling, larger-than-life creature who represents the most repulsive invention of the Cervantine *obra*.[19] We might recall here that

16. See Johan Weyer, *Histoires, disputes et discours des illusions et impostures des diables* (Geneva, 1579), cited by Jones, *On the Nightmare*, 206; and Robbins, *Encyclopedia*, 364–67.

17. Jones alludes to the evident link of mucus and semen with the movements of coitus
as the probable source of the sexual symbolism of anointing (*On the Nightmare*, 207–8).

18. For instance, Sylvine de la Plaine, condemned to be burned in Paris in 1616, declared
that the devil's "member was like that of a horse, and on insertion it was cold as ice and
ejected iced cold semen"; Robbins, *Encyclopedia*, 466–67. On witches and their relation to the
devil and hysterical attacks, see Sigmund Freud's letters to Wilhelm Fliess of January 17 and
24, 1897, letters 56 and 57 in *The Standard Edition of the Complete Psychological Works of Sigmund
Freud*, ed. and trans. James Strachey, 24 vols. (London: Hogarth Press, 1953–74), 1:242–43.
Further references to the *Standard Edition* will be abbreviated *SE*, with volume and page
number.

19. As this book was going to press, I read Carroll B. Johnson's essay "Of Witches and
Bitches: Gender, Marginality and Discourse in 'El casamiento engañoso y Coloquio de los
Perros,' " *Cervantes* 11 (1991): 7–25. Quoting a shorter version of my work, Johnson claims
that my depiction of the witch Cañizares as a sexual being presents the old woman "as the
monstrous locus of evil," a view "even more virulent," if marginally less moralistic, than
Forcione's (10). At the close of his study, Johnson reiterates that "Forcione and Garcés, who
see Cañizares as a monstrous embodiment of evil, seem to be speaking from within the
discourse of patriarchy, manifesting the hysteria provoked by the terror 'of that sex which
isn't one' " (21). In answering these claims I must say that if I speak within the discourse
of patriarchy, it is, indeed, to examine the operations that, within this very discourse, convert
the witch Cañizares into a "monstrous embodiment" of horror, not evil, as Johnson states
in his misreading of my text. Unlike Forcione, I would label the representation of Cañizares
as "beyond good and evil." My analytic exploration of the phenomenon of abjection as
represented by "The Colloquy of the Dogs" aims, instead, at exposing the "dark side" of
religious, moral, and ideological codes, the other face of human existence which has been
repressed by the sociosymbolic order. This "other-scene" leads, as Cervantes's novella seems
to suggest, back to the mother—giver of life and embodiment of death. Through Berganza's
hallucination and Campuzano's dream of a defiled, rejected maternal body, the "Colloquy"
reveals the attempt of the writer to *speak* horror. Kristeva suggests that in signifying horror,

this monstrous hallucination is a product of Berganza's mind, a vision inextricably linked to Campuzano's delirium. The witch grows into a monster, it bears stressing, only when she is transformed into a sexual being.

> Ella era larga de más de siete pies; toda era notomía de huesos, cubiertos con una piel negra, vellosa y curtida; con la barriga que era de badana se cubría las partes deshonestas, y aún le colgaba hasta la mitad de los muslos; las tetas semejaban dos vejigas de vaca secas y arrugadas; denegridos los labios, traspillados los dientes, la nariz corva y entablada, desencasados los ojos, la cabeza desgreñada, las mejillas chupadas, angosta la garganta y los pechos sumidos; finalmente toda era flaca y endemoniada.

> [She was more than seven feet tall; her bones stuck out all over, covered with dark, hairy, hard skin; her private parts were covered with the folds of skin from her stomach which was like a sheepskin and hung halfway down her thighs; her breasts were like the udder of wrinkled, dried-up cows; her lips were black, her teeth worn down, and her nose hooked and askew. With her staring eyes, her disheveled hair, her hollow cheeks, her shrunken neck and shrivelled breasts, she was as hideous and repulsive as could be.] (344)

This most gruesome description of Cañizares's cadaverous body enacts, as Forcione has maintained, a face-to-face encounter with death (*Cervantes* 75). Like a horrifying nightmare that assails the dreamer, the dark and hairy skeleton of the witch confronts the onlooker with the harrowing sight of an open sepulcher. The image evokes once more that of Ensign Campuzano in "The Deceitful Marriage" peering in horror into the wide-open trunk that Estefanía has raided: "Fui a ver mi baúl y halléle abierto y como sepultura que esperaba el cuerpo difunto... que había de ser el mío [I went to see my trunk and found it open, like a tomb awaiting a corpse, which might well have been me]" (290). The "Colloquy" represents this terrifying gap, this "void" as a living corpse. Yet this "thing" that revolts the narrator is not a human being anymore. On the frontier between monster and cadaver, the atrocious hallucination signals the margins of life, namely, the limits of being.

I propose that this "descent into the grave... [this] plunging deeper and deeper" into the "central void" of the narrative, which Forcione

---

that is, in attempting to elevate the unnameable to the power of metaphor, a reconciliation with the maternal body becomes possible.

illustrates so well (*Cervantes* 74), metaphorically enacts a voyage into the womb, a face-to-face encounter with the "void" epitomized by a woman's genitals.[20] Furthermore, I suggest that this descent into the abyss, this terrifying encounter with lack, represents the confrontation between the subject and the impossible within, that is, with that immoral, sinister void (*vide*) which, according to Kristeva, constitutes abjection (*Powers* 12).

ABJECTION: THE ABOMINATION OF THE MOTHER

Abjection, that obscure and violent revolt of being against a formidable outside or inside that threatens it, does not have a proper or definable object.[21] As defined by Kristeva, "the *abject* is not an *ob-ject* facing me, which I name or imagine" (*Powers* 1). It rather belongs within that archaic *reduplication* (other than imitation) which Freud posits "before any choice of object."[22] Not having a proper object, this archaic identification conjures up, in the process of being constituted as a subject, a simulacrum of an object which functions as a unifying image. This archaic image emerges as a discarded, "fallen" object (*objet chu*), radically excluded from meaning. The cadaver (from *cadere*, "to fall") represents the abject in its most terrifying dimension. The corpse shows me what I thrust aside in order to live: it delineates a border from which I extricate myself, as a living being (*Powers* 3–4).

Kristeva states that the abject is "experienced at the peak of its strength when that subject, weary of fruitless attempts to identify with something on the outside, finds the impossible within"—that is, when it discovers that emptiness constitutes its very being (*Powers* 5).[23] In this catastrophic confrontation with the limits of being, a frontier of loathing and repulsion is established (*Powers* 10). Echoing

20. Gossy points to the depiction of Cañizares, in Forcione's text as an illustration of "paranoid descriptions of female sexuality"; "Marriage," 70. Although I agree with Gossy's reading of this passage of Forcione's study, I would argue that the representation of the witch as that locus of horror generally associated by the sociosymbolic order with female sexuality already emerges from Berganza's → Campuzano's → Cervantes's text(s).

21. I am using the word *object* as the correlative of a *subject* in a symbolic chain. This points to the paternal agency that founds the symbolic order (the order of language) by introducing the symbolic dimension between "subject" (child) and "object" (mother); see Kristeva, *Powers*, 44.

22. Kristeva, "Freud," 25. Sigmund Freud, "Identification," in *Group Psychology and the Analysis of the Ego* (1921), SE 18:111ff.

23. I purposely refrain from identifying this vacillating "subject" as a "she" or a "he," since these operations occur when sexual difference has not yet been established.

the violence with which a body is separated from another body in order to be, the "subject" throws up what revolts it, which often includes itself as the abject (*Powers* 6–8). The "subject" thus founds its own territory bordered by the abject: the border has become an object.

Essentially different from and more violent than "uncanniness," abjection is elaborated through a failure to recognize its kin; nothing is familiar, not even the specter of a memory (*Powers* 5). In this preobjectal site or "zero state" of the subject, "the abject emerges not as an Other with whom I identify and [whom I] incorporate, but as an other that precedes and possesses me, and through such possession causes me to be" (*Powers* 10). This takes us back to the image of an archaic mother, pole of desire and hatred, of fascination and repulsion, an abject-mother not yet constituted as a forbidden object of desire. Being neither a subject nor an object, this abject-mother designates a place of regression and differentiation, an infection, like the witch Cañizares as she emerges in the central dream of the "Colloquy."

Present at La Montiela's delivery, where La Camacha officiated as midwife, Cañizares appears as a kind of metonymic mother, the only remaining witness to Berganza's birth. Her ominous inaugural salutation ("¿Eres tú, hijo, Montiel? Eres tú ... hijo?") not only identifies Berganza as her child but grants him a new name that stresses his matrilineal descent. The paternal reference, which establishes meaning and signification within the social and symbolic system, thus seems to be absent in Berganza's history.[24]

This perhaps explains the succeeding nightmare in which Cañizares appears as an apocalyptic vision of the mother. Certainly, this image does not correspond to the idealized representation of maternity, with its beautiful Madonnas of pale cheeks and rounded breasts pouring sweet milk into their children's mouths.[25] Cañizares represents, instead, a horrifying inversion of the maternal, a desecration of that saintly body which represents the highest construct of the Christian civilization regarding human conception and nurturing.[26] The soft

24. It is important to note that Berganza's original name (Montiel), derived from that of his mother's (Montiela), was given to him either by her or by the women who were present at his birth. Thus, the father was excluded from the act of naming, a curious exclusion since it was the father (or his surrogate, the priest) who was charged with naming and inscribing his children both in his lineage and in the religious (social) institutions of the city.

25. This aspect of the Virgin Mary as dispenser of milk and tears is discussed by Kristeva in her "Stabat Mater," in *Tales of Love*, 234–63.

26. Maurice Molho has also observed that the witch represents "un mirroir renversé de l'ordre naturel conçu ... par Dieu [an obverse mirror of the natural order conceived ... by

body that symbolizes creation has been transformed, by Berganza's nightmare, into a gigantic corpse whose focal point seems to be its enormous, dried-up stomach. Moreover, the depiction of Cañizares' breasts, portrayed first as "dos vejigas de vaca secas y arrugadas [two wrinkled and dried-up cows' udders]" and then as "pechos sumidos [flaccid, wrinkled breasts]" (344), suggests a complete destruction of the maternal function, a radical collapse of the image of the mother.[27]

This violent degradation of the maternal body—its desecration—is accomplished in "The Colloquy of the Dogs" through the defilement (souillure) and abomination of the feminine. In this monstrous nightmare that obsesses Berganza, Cañizares appears as a hyperbolized image of filth, as if Ensign Campuzano's syphilis had suddenly flourished on her wasted, foul-smelling body. The gruesome representation of the witch clarifies her connection to Estefanía de Caicedo and the terrible disease that devours Campuzano.[28] The debased (infectious) images of the two women recall that the primal source of decay, the "original stain" that threatens the symbolic order, has been projected since time immemorial onto the body of woman. This topography of the female body marks the borders of the pure and impure in a social or signifying system, placing pollution and waste in the site of the feminine.

In her study of biblical abomination, Kristeva explores the fundamental concern of the Old Testament with separating and defining strict identities (Powers 93) Hence, Leviticus connects the theme of menses and of woman in childbed to food prohibitions and the taboos

---

God]." See his fine introduction to his French translation of "The Deceitful Marriage" and "The Colloquy of the Dogs," "Remarques sur 'Le marriage trompeur' et 'Le colloque des chiens,' " in "Le marriage trompeur" et "Le colloque des chiens" (Paris: Aubier-Flammarion, 1976), 61.

27. Forcione's erudite note on the "gigantic, dried-up belly of the witch [where] we find inverted all the creative powers of the saintly stomach" elicits some comments. The critic interprets this "belly" as a "symbol of the Christian iconography for sin since St. Paul." Yet, as Diana de Armas Wilson has pertinently suggested, there seems to be a curious blindness on Forcione's part regarding the gender of the monster. This leads him to compare the stomach of the witch with that of Sancho Panza, whose "saintly belly" emerges as a symbol of the "creative power of bodily life." This reading obviously circumvents the image of the mother and, indeed, that of the womb as the "center of bodily creation," a description that Forcione seems to apply to the "belly" of a unisexual being; see Cervantes, 78, 79.

28. The scope of this essay does not permit me to point out the parallels between the two women. Suffice it to say that from the start, Campuzano's contagion with syphilis—his "flaqueza" (weakness)—is attributed to woman: "Salgo de aquel hospital de sudar catorce cargas de bubas que me echó a cuestas una mujer que escogí por mía [I've just come out of that hospital, after sweating out fourteen buboes I got from a woman whom for my sins I took for myself]." Peralta's response in turn links marriage to disease: "¿Luego casóse vuesa merced? [So you got married?]" (282).

concerning the sick body (Leviticus 12:22; 13–14).[29] Associated with the impure, woman is later related to leprosy—to decay and death (Leviticus 13–14). The displacement from the abomination of the maternal body (childbirth, menses) to the decaying body (leprosy) suggests that the mother's insides are associated with spoilage. The shadow of a phantasmatic mother, an obverse image of the fertile Mother Goddess, haunts these biblical passages, resurfacing constantly as a metaphor of incest.[30] Kristeva concludes that biblical abjection transposes a significant semantics in which the dietary merges with the maternal as "unclean and improper coalescence," a defilement that needs to be cut off (*Powers* 101–6).

"WE ABSORB IT WITH OUR MOTHERS' MILK"

The connection between biblical abomination and the abjection of the mother in "The Colloquy of the Dogs" remains fascinating. Exemplifying a monstrous portrayal of the mother—and of maternity itself—Cañizares also illustrates the link between biblical leprosy (sickness and decay) and the horrendous *bubas* that ravaged Europe during the seventeenth century. This link cuts across the body of woman, specifically of the mother, as Berganza signals to Cipión in one of his early expressions of abomination of the feminine: "El hacer y decir mal lo heredamos de nuestros primeros padres y lo mamamos en la leche [We inherit the tendency to do and speak evil from our first parents and absorb it with our mothers' milk]" (315). Corruption—that is, sexuality, syphilis, and sin—is thus joined from the outset to the feminine, of which the maternal is the real support. Berganza's next phrase confirms my interpretation by associating the figure of the child with that of the mother and the whore: "Y casi la primera palabra que habla [el niño] es llamar puta a su ama o madre [Almost the first word . . . (the child) utters is to call his nurse or his mother whore]" (315).

The metaphor of incestuous desire surfaces, in the metonymic con-

---

29. Because of her parturition and the blood that accompanies it, woman will be "impure" (Leviticus 13–14).

30. The insistence on the (food) taboo "Thou shalt not seethe a kid in his mother's milk," which reveals the dread of incest, is repeated throughout the Bible (Exodus 23:19, 34:26; Deuteronomy 14:21). The dietary prohibitions of Leviticus are, according to Kristeva, a screen in a still more radical separating process, one that would attempt to separate the being who speaks to his God from the fecund mother. This appalling mother is that archaic Mother Goddess who actually haunted the imagination of a nation at war with the surrounding polytheism; see Kristeva, *Powers*, 100.

nection between the child and the mother, through the whore. But the text also signals the juncture of language ("la primera palabra") with the mother's breast. The relation between the mother's milk and language has been examined by Didier Anzieu, who has referred to what he calls "l'enveloppe sonore du soi [the sound envelope of the Self]" in his studies on the formation of the Ego. The Self develops, in these early stages, through the experience of a "bath of sounds," concomitant with the experience of nursing. This bath of sounds— constituted by the mother's voice, her singing, the music she causes the child to hear—functions as a kind of sound mirror which permits the gradual articulation of language.[31] Berganza's words in the "Colloquy" reveal his association of the mother's breast (the mother's milk) and original sin, an association that connects this maternal, nurturing emblem with abomination of the feminine, specifically with the whore. These images betray the dread of incest which subtends Berganza's narrative.

Indeed, the fact that Cañizares is a witch stresses the incestuous nature of Berganza's desire, as intimated by the common accusations against witches concerning their participation in incestuous acts. Ernest Jones has indicated that both the figure of the witch and the persecution mania against these women point to the tremendous effort of the Christian church in the service of sexual repression, particularly in its horror of incest.[32] The threat of incest distinctly surfaces in the scene in which Cañizares addresses Berganza as her son, suddenly followed by her attempt to kiss him on the mouth, which makes him recoil in disgust (336). Moreover, the fact that the witch is portrayed as a giant, more than seven feet tall, suggests that this passage reenacts a phantasmatic scenario, one that reveals an archaic vision of the mother.[33]

Berganza's desire for the uncanny "object" represented by the defiled body of the witch is illustrated by his numerous attempts to bite her. These impulses, initially disguised by the narrator, are checked by the guilt (revulsion) that makes him recoil in horror from this hateful "object" of desire:

31. See Didier Anzieu, The Skin-Ego: A Psychoanalytic Approach to the Self, trans. Chris Turner (New Haven: Yale University Press, 1989), 157–73. On the formation of the Ego through a bath of sounds and the interconnectedness of visual and sound mirrors in the constitution of narcissism, see ibid., 157–73.

32. Jones, On the Nightmare, 237–38. On the devil as father substitute, see Freud, "A Seventeenth-Century Demonological Neurosis" (1925), SE 19:67–105, esp. 85–90; and also Jones, On the Nightmare, 85–90.

33. Sigmund Freud, The Interpretation of Dreams, SE 4:30.

Cada cosa destas que la vieja me decía . . . era una lanzada que me
atravesaba el corazón, y quisiera arremeter a ella y hacerla pedazos
entre dientes; y si lo dejé de hacer fue porque no le tomase la muerte
en tan mal estado.

[Every one of these things which the old woman told me . . . was
like a dagger thrust into my heart, and I should have liked to attack
her and tear her to pieces with my teeth; and if I refrained from
doing so it was only in order that death should not come to her in
the state she was in.] (341)

Melanie Klein has described the early stages of mental development, characterized by the oral-sadistic desire to devour the mother's
breast (or the mother herself). In this period, which announces the
Oedipus conflict, the child's dominant aim is to possess and destroy
the mother's body. These oral-sadistic attacks on the mother's body—
bitten or torn to pieces in fantasy—are generally directed against the
"organs of conception, pregnancy and parturition, which the child
assumes to exist in the womb, and further in the vagina and the
breasts, the fountain of milk."[34]

BERGANZA AND THE CANNIBALS

The cannibalistic impulses Klein describes are exemplified by Berganza's efforts to bite this body that both fascinates and revolts him:
"Quise morderla, por ver si volvía en sí, y no hallé parte de ella que
el asco no me lo estorbase; pero, con todo esto la así de un carcaño
y la saqué arrastrando al patio [I tried to bite her, to see if she would
recover consciousness, but I couldn't find a site on her body which
I could touch without feeling revulsion; yet, I did grab her by the
heels and drag her out into the courtyard]" (334).

The mention of the *carcaño* (the heel) as the site on the old woman's
body that Berganza grabs with his teeth elicits some comments. In
his *Tesoro de la lengua castellana o española* (1611), Sebastián de Covarrubias dedicates a long digression to the term *carcañal* "heel of the
foot." Apart from the heels of Christ, who crushed the devil's head,
and those of the Virgin Mary, which are uncontaminated from sin,
"en los demás hombres el *carcañal* se toma por la concupiscencia, y
el *fomes pecatis* que nos quedó del original, que hasta la hora de la

---

34. See "Symbol Formation in Ego Development" in *The Selected Melanie Klein*, ed. Juliet
Mitchell (New York: Free Press, 1986), 96, 74.

muerte nos pone assechanças y nos va mordiendo los çancajos [in the rest of men, the heel of the foot signifies sexual lust, and the *fomes pecatis*—literally, 'fuel for sins'—that remained from the original sin, which haunts us until the hour of death and goes around nipping at our heel bone]."[35]

We might remember at this point that, when describing his (sexual) fantasies regarding Estefanía, Ensign Campuzano uses this profoundly suggestive phrase, which sums up the intensity of his desire for the mysterious woman: "Yo que tenía entonces el juicio, no en la cabeza, sino en los carcañares [At that time, I had my brain in my heels instead of my head]" (285). The associations of the *carcaño* or *carcañal* with the most "inferior" parts of man (or woman)—"por ser el carcañal la parte postrera e inferior del hombre," according to Covarrubias—are, indeed, revealing. It bears stressing that Berganza grabs the witch precisely by her *carcaño*. Symbolizing lust, the *carcañal* points to a woman's "heel of Achilles," her genitals: "Traer rotos los carcañales se dice por afrenta a la mujer deshonesta, por lo que huella con ellos [To have fractured heel-bones is said as an insult to an unchaste woman, because of what she treads upon]."[36]

The narrative now shifts toward a sadistic scenario in which the body of the witch is crucified by innumerable pins stuck into her skin by the curious onlookers (345). Naked, riddled by pinpricks, and bitten by the dog in unnameable places, Cañizares wakes up to find herself torn apart by Berganza's teeth, which now grab her by the stomach: "Asiéndole de las luengas faldas de su vientre la zamarreé y arrastré por todo el patio: ella daba voces que la librasen de aquel maligno espíritu [Grabbing her by the long folds of her belly, I pushed her and dragged her all around the courtyard, while she cried out to be released from the teeth of such a malignant spirit]" (345).

The metaphors of incestuous desire are sustained throughout this episode, from the moment in which Berganza describes the cadaverous body of the witch. Yet this vision which terrifies Berganza also

35. The weakness of the heel of the foot as a site of sin is stressed by Psalm 49:48: "iniquitas calcanei mei circundabit mei [when the iniquity of my heels shall compass me about]."

36. Covarrubias, *Tesoro*. The belief that chastity was located in the heel bones (and could thus be controlled by one's "stirrups") is illustrated by Cervantes's novella "The Illustrious Kitchen Maid" ("La ilustre fregona"). Alluding to Constanza's chastity, the narrator states: "Pero como ella siempre andaba sobre los estribos de su honestidad y recato, a ninguno daba lugar de mirarla [But, since she was always in control of her chastity and modesty (literally, since she always walked on the stirrups of her chastity), she did not let any man look at her]"; *Novelas ejemplares*, 2:177. Notably, the Spanish language associates the loss of control in the individual with the strength of his or her heel bones: "perder los estribos" (literally to lose one's stirrups) means to lose one's temper.

elicits in him unspeakable phantasies: "Púseme despacio a mirarla, y apriesa comenzó a apoderarse de mí el miedo, considerando la mala visión de su cuerpo y la peor ocupación de su alma [I looked closely at her, and all of a sudden I was overcome by fear, as I considered the ugliness of her body and of the evil to which she was abandoning her soul]" (344). The text betrays Berganza's phantasies concerning the sexual activities of the witch with her demonic paramour—the "evil" to which Cañizares is abandoning herself in body and soul.

The next scene merges the figure of Berganza with that of the devil, who copulates with the witch (in dreams). Confronted by the furious Cañizares, who awakens to find herself naked and exposed to the eyes of the crowd, the dog claims to be the "author" of her dishonor: "Creyó, y creyó la verdad, que yo había sido el autor de su deshonra [She thought, and thought rightly, that I had been the author of her dishonor]" (345). In Spanish, since the Middle Ages, *deshonra* (dishonor) signifies rape, and "ser el autor de su deshonra [to be the author of her dishonor]" is a metaphor for sexual possession.[37] Berganza's confession therefore points to a fantazied sexual relation with the witch, with the dog taking the place of the devil—a reading enhanced by the suggestive images elicited by the allusion to Cañizares's "carcaño." In the succeeding scene, Berganza is associated with the demon and is even accused of being the devil himself: "Maligno espíritu . . . demonio . . . ¡demonio en figura de perro! [Malignant spirit . . . demon . . . the devil in the form of a dog!]" (345).

These sexual scenes find their antecedent in a previous episode that describes Berganza's adventures with a Negro slave, a passage that discloses the protagonist's attraction for another forbidden object: the body of a black woman. This black (female) body, which appears after the narrator's reference to the origins of evil, haunts Berganza and Cipión's discussion on the theme of biting. The story of the Negro

37. See the *Siete partidas* of Alfonso the Wise: "Que cualquiera que *deshonrasse* hija de Rey o su hermana, ò otra parienta, faciendole hacer maldad de su cuerpo, que hoviesse tal pena como si la matasse [Whoever rapes the daughter of the king or his sister, or any female relative of his, making her do evil things with her body, shall be punished as if he had killed her]" (*Partida* 2, *título* 14. *ley* 2). A scene in "The Call of Blood" ("La fuerza de la sangre") illustrates the use of *honra* and *(des)honra* in sixteenth-century Spain. The passage describes Leocadia relating the story of her rape to her parents: "Allí en breves palabras, les dio cuenta de todo su desastroso suceso . . . y de la ninguna noticia que traía del salteador y robador de su honra [There in brief words, she told them about the disastrous occurrence . . . and about the lack of news concerning the highway robber and thief of her honor]"; *Novelas ejemplares*, 2:83). Leocadia also exemplifies my argument regarding the "autor de su deshonra [the 'author' of her rape]": "No quiero acordarme de mi ofensor ni guardar en la memoria la imagen del autor de mi daño [I do not wish to remember my offender nor retain in my memory the image of the author of my injury]" (80).

servant exposes narrative discourse at its most chaotic, intercepted as it is by the numerous digressions that lead to the emergence of the image of the octopus. Consistently interrupted by the philosophical disquisitions and subsequent deliberations of the dogs on the proper name for the monsters' "tails," the tale of the (sexually) voracious slave is finally resumed: "Bajaba la negra ... a refocilarse con su negro [The Negress would come down ... to take her pleasure with her Negro]" (322).

Berganza's insistence on using the proper term for the *rabos* (tails) of the octopus—a word that in popular idiom refers to both the male and female genitals—acquires a special resonance in the context of the black woman's sexual activities.[38] In fact, Cipión's mention of "la asquerosidad que caus[a] el oir ... [estas cosas] en sus propios nombres [the repulsiveness caused by hearing ..(these things) alluded to in their proper names]" (319) may also extend to the black woman's sexual exploits, a subject to which Berganza returns obsessively. Amidst his descriptions of her sexual exploits, however, Berganza turns to his frenzied attacks on the black woman's body: "Una noche muy oscura ... arremetí sin ladrar y en un instante, le hice pedazos toda la camisa y le arranqué un pedazo de muslo [One very dark night ... I attacked her without barking, and in a moment, I had torn down her chemise to shreds and ripped out a piece of her thigh]" (322). These suggestive battles, secretly repeated night after night, acquire a special relevance in relation to the ensuing combats with the witch Cañizares. The cannibalistic scenes in the episode of the slave are also related to phantasmagoric sexual encounters, as verified by the use of the word *perra* (bitch) to refer to the black woman in these battles: "Yo volví a la pelea con mi perra [I went back again to the battle with my bitch]" (322). This term corresponds both to the name of the bitch and to a vernacular expression for whore.

The episode of the black servant therefore ends with the vision of a beast (a bitch). Indeed, the connections between the (sexually) voracious Negress and the devouring tentacles of the octopus—with its sexual connotations that, in turn, intimate disintegration—are signif-

---

38. On "tail" (*rabo* or *cola*) as a symbol of both male and female genitals, see Javier Herrero, "The Beheading of the Giant: An Obscene Metaphor in *Don Quijote*," *Revista hispánica moderna*, 39 (1976–77): 141–49. The associations between the *colas* or *rabos* of the octopus and uncontrolled sexual activity are enhanced by sixteenth-century Spanish literature. In his *Familiar Dialogues on Christian Agriculture* (*Diálogos familiares de agricultura cristiana*, 1589) (Madrid: Atlas, 1963), 316, Juan de Pineda refers to the octopus as a figure of lust: "No vive más el pulpo de un año porque es tan lujurioso que pierde todas sus fuerzas; ... las hembras mueren también del mucho parir [The octopus does not live more than one year because being so lustful it loses all its strength; ... the females also die from excessive parturition]."

icant. Gilbert Durand has pointed to the symbolic correlation between the spider, the hydra, and the octopus—hideous symbols of the female sexual organ. If the spider represents the devouring mother who imprisons the child in her web, the composition of the spider and the worm results in the hydra, a sort of radiating worm of the feminine element par excellence: the sea. It is in the octopus—that giant hydra which embodies the fatality of the ocean—that the overpowering pernicious presence of the feminine is manifested.[39]

These figural links elicit further associations in the light of the black woman's attempt to poison Berganza with a sponge. The allusion to the sponge as "zarazas [poison paste]" not only recalls notions of witchcraft (*maleficium*), which remind us of the witch Cañizares, but also summons the phantom of a similar aquatic creature, the squid, which poisons its enemy with a venomous black ink.[40] These images reiterate the poisonous or mortiferous representations of woman in these narratives, as embodied by Estefanía de Caicedo in "The Deceitful Marriage," by the Negro slave, and by the witch Cañizares in the "Colloquy," all of whom merge with the bestial images—the "wolves," sheep, goats, bulls, cows, horses, donkeys, serpents, cats, and dogs, among other animals—that traverse Cervantes's novella.

THE DEFEAT OF THE MONSTER

The cannibalistic (sexual) scenes of the "Colloquy" acquire a special relevance in the light of contemporary psychoanalytical theory, especially that developed by Julia Kristeva in relation to the birth of language. It is important to recall that the possibility of an archaic identification is associated by Freud to the "oral phase of the libido's organization," as if becoming as the One could be represented in terms of an oral assimilation (*SE* 18:105; "Freud" 25). Tracing the

39. Gilbert Durand, *Les structures anthropologiques de l'imaginaire* (Paris: Bordas, 1969), 115–18. The archetypal image represented by the mortal combat with the octopus reappears in Jules Verne's *Vingt mille lieues sous les mers* (*Twenty Thousand Leagues under the Sea*). The monstrous vision of the battle with the sea beast is again reproduced in Walt Disney's cinematographic transcription of Jules Verne's oeuvre.

40. The image of the octopus as a figure of multiplicity and deceit is evoked by Erasmus in his *Adagia* and repeated by Joannes Sambucus' *Emblemata, et aliquot numen antiqui operis* (Antwerp, 1564). This legend presents the octopus's (or squid's) capacity to hide in its black ink as an example of astuteness and dissimulation which deserves praise. See Nerlich's erudite article, "On the Philosophical Dimension" (285–86, n. 8). On the fear of being poisoned or devoured as related to fantazied oral attacks on the mother's breast, see Melanie Klein, "Notes on Some Schizoid Mechanisms," in *Selected Klein*, 177 and passim.

process that converts *having* into *being*, Kristeva maintains that "incorporating and introjecting orality's function is the essential substratum that constitutes man's being, namely, *language*" ("Freud" 26). This process, announced by Berganza's attempts to incorporate and destroy the mother or her substitutes, is correlative with abjection, that projective identification with a pole of desire or hatred which reflects the voyage from a zero state of subjectivity to becoming One— a subject. Yet this moment of mythic narcissism is already a search for the aquatic maternal element—the watery, reflective element in Narcissus' mirage—which permits a representation of the self ("Freud" 42).

To bridge the gap that will definitively anchor him or her in the imaginary father and in language, the speaking being must engage in a combat with the imaginary mother from whom it must break apart in order to constitute an object separate from the subject ("Freud" 41). This combat is supported by the imaginary father—the father of individual prehistory—who upholds the process of rejection against that threatening chaos which is about to turn into an abject.[41] To summarize Kristeva's arguments, primary identification seems to be "a transference to (from) the imaginary father, correlative to the establishment of the mother" as the abject ("Freud" 41). This illuminates the role of Cipión in the "Colloquy," whose function is that of an ideal other—that is, the "speaking" other with whom Berganza identifies.[42]

Supported by this ideal other that unifies him and restrains his drives through the medium of language, as shown by Cipión's recognition of the other dog as a (speaking) subject and his efforts to steer him back to the narrative, Berganza encounters the limit experience of the nonexistent. "Yo soy como eso que se llama lugar, donde todas las cosas caben y no hay ninguna fuera del lugar [I am like that which is called place, where all things coalesce and there is nothing

---

41. Freud's allusion to the "father of the individual pre-history" describes the pre-oedipal (unconscious) image of both parents merged into one; see *The Ego and the Id, SE* 19:31; and Kristeva, "Freud" 26–27.

42. On the subject of Freud's youthful prepsychoanalytic identification with the role of the listener Cipión in "The Colloquy," in which he appropriated the name of Cipión, see his letter to Martha Bernays of February 7, 1884, in *The Letters of Sigmund Freud*, ed. Ernst and Lucie Freud, trans. Tania and James Stern (New York: Basic Books, 1961), 96–98; also S. B. Vranich, "Sigmund Freud and the 'Case History of Berganza': Freud's Psychoanalytical Beginnings," *Psychoanalytic Review* 63 (1976): 73–82. For the influence of Cervantes on the development of psychoanalysis, see León Grinberg and Juan Francisco Rodríguez's essay in this volume, "Cervantes as Cultural Ancestor of Freud."

out of place]," writes Cervantes through his namesake Periandro, in the *Persiles*.[43] This "place" refers to the territory of threatening coalescence with the whole, where the I seems to speak almost at the cost of disintegrating.[44] Reminiscent of the subject's origins, *that* which is called *place* signals the limits that turn the speaking being into a separate being.

From "[ese] lugar [(that) place]" so eloquently described by Cervantes, an outside is elaborated by means of a projection from inside, as if abjection were the first authentic feeling of a "subject" in process. This outside (that which is defiled, expelled from the symbolic order: the *objet chu*) becomes the sole "object" of sexual desire—a desire for the beseeching and terrifying inside of the maternal body. In this liminal gesture, abjection takes the place of the other. Naming this outside—that is, naming it *for* an other, thus founding that distinct territory that implies a separation from the phantasmatic power of the archaic mother—leads, according to Kristeva, to the introduction of language (*Powers* 54, 61).

In this culminating experience of the subject which mimics the inaugural loss-foundation of birth, language is born. But birth, that is, the birth of the being of language, implies the overthrow and even the slaughter of the monster(s) of the abyss, from the biblical beasts that lie close to the Word and the creation of man in Genesis to the repulsive octopus or witch of Berganza's → Campuzano's → Cervantes's dreams. The Bible seems to be peopled by these unnameable monsters, related to the original chaos, as intimated by the Book of Job: "Dead things are formed under the waters, and the inhabitants thereof" (Job 26:5).[45] These "dead things" are later identified by different names—as Rahab, the Behemoth, the Leviathan, and the dragon that lives in the depths of the sea (Job 9:13, 26:12), monsters

43. Miguel de Cervantes, *Los trabajos de Persiles y Sigismunda*, ed. Juan Bautista Avalle-Arce (Madrid: Clásicos Castalia, 1970), 227.

44. Diana de Armas Wilson has keenly observed the relevance of this passage in the *Persiles*, concerning the attempt to trace the topography of "ese lugar," which she relates to Kristeva's *chora*; see Diana de Armas Wilson, *Allegories of Love: Cervantes's "Persiles and Sigismunda"* (Princeton: Princeton University Press, 1991), 148–49. Kristeva has similarly argued that the abject refers to a reiterative question: "*Where* am I?" instead of "*Who* am I?"; *Powers*, 8.

45. See the multiple allusions in the Hebrew Bible to creation as a struggle with a dragon or sea monster, identified as Rahab (Job 26:13; 38:8–11; Psalm 74:13–14; Isaiah 27:1; 51:9–10). On Genesis as an echo of the Babylonian creation epic *Enuna Elish*, which relates the battle between the primeval mother Tiamat and the male god Marduk, see Patricia Parker, "Coming Second: Woman's Place," in *Literary Fat Ladies: Rhetoric, Gender, and Property* (London: Methuen, 1987), 187–88; and Mary Nyquist, "Gynesis, Exegesis, and the Formation of Milton's Eve," in *Cannibals, Witches, and Divorce: Estranging the Renaissance*, ed. Marjorie Garber (Baltimore: Johns Hopkins University Press, 1987), 149.

defeated by the power of the Word (Yahweh). In the course of these (textual) combats with the enemy, the names of the monster(s) disappear. In fact, the Vulgate and the King James Bible reveal a reluctance to pronounce the Hebrew and Greek names of these beasts, now alluded to by the words "dragon" and/or "proud"—names attributed to Satan.

The defeat of the monster is ritually reenacted by the biblical narrative, especially in the Book of Job, Psalms, and Isaiah: "Thou has broken Rahab in pieces . . . thou has scattered the enemies with thy strong arm (Psalms 89 9–10). These texts seem to imply that if the name of the monster becomes unpronounceable, the battle with it must be at least metaphorically portrayed: "He divideth the sea with his power, and by his understanding he smitheth through the proud" (Job 26:11). The fantastic shadow of the monster reappears in the New Testament, in the suggestive scenario of Mary's conception. Here the triumph over the unnameable beast is announced by the Virgin Mary herself—a virgin impregnated by the Word: "He hath shewed strength with his arm; he hath scattered the proud in the imagination of their hearts. He hath put down the mighty from their seats and exalted them of low degree" (Luke 1:51–52).[46]

The witch, who is evidently well read, and who literally stands for the "subject" of Berganza's unconscious,[47] paraphrases the Virgin Mary's words in the poem/riddle which discloses the secret of Berganza's ability to speak: "Volverán a su forma verdadera / cuando vieren con presta diligencia / derribar los soberbios levantados / y alzar a los humildes abatidos / por mano poderosa para hacello [They will return to their true form / when they see the mighty speedily brought down / and the humble exalted / by that hand which has power to perform it]" (346).

The "mano poderosa" (powerful hand) which is enabled to perform these miracles is that of the artist, Cervantes, who emerges victorious from his encounter with the beast—this abject that threatens identity itself. Cervantes's hand has indeed revealed that the human being

46. Pamela Waley has identified the *Magnificat* as the subtext of Cañizares's prophecy in "The Colloquy of the Dogs": "Deposuit potentes de sedes, et exaltavit humildes" (Luke 1:52). See "The Unity of the 'Casamiento engañoso' and the 'Coloquio de los perros,'" *Bulletin of Hispanic Studies* 34 (1957): 200–212.

47. William J. Richardson examines the "subject of the unconscious" (the unconscious *as* subject) in "Lacan and the Subject of Psychoanalysis," in *Interpreting Lacan*, ed. Joseph Smith and William Kerrigan (New Haven: Yale University Press, 1983), 51–74. Ruth El Saffar has also argued, in this sense, that the "undesirable woman" in Cervantes literally "stands . . . for the unconscious"; see *Beyond Fiction: The Recovery of the Feminine in the Novels of Cervantes* (Berkeley: University of California Press, 1984), 14.

does not speak without the phantasm of the return to the origin, that is, without "the hypothesis of an unnameable," to adopt a vivid phrase of Kristeva's.[48] As Freud has shown, the phantasm of origins always involves an aquatic mirage, which would explain the haunting presence of the unnameable beast—the octopus—in Cervantes's novella.[49] Thus, after the representation and defeat of the monster, in the process of identification with that other—Cipión—who plays the role of a symbolic Father, Berganza gives birth to himself as subject: that is, he *speaks*.

48. See Julia Kristeva "Psychoanalysis and the Polis," in *The Kristeva Reader*, ed. Toril Moi (New York: Columbia University Press, 1986), 310.
49. Freud has established that the origins of life are always depicted in dreams (and in their correlative, fiction) as emerging from the water; see Sigmund Freud, "Symbolism in Dreams," in *Introductory Lectures on Psycho-Analysis* (1915–17), SE 15:160–61.

Notes on Contributors

ANDREW BUSH is Associate Professor of Hispanic Studies at Vassar College. He is the author of articles on various topics in Spanish, Latin American, and comparative literatures. He served as the editor of the *Revista de Estudios Hispánicos* for five years. He is currently working on a book on lyric poetry of the eighteenth and nineteenth centuries.

ANTHONY J. CASCARDI is Professor of Comparative Literature, Rhetoric, and Spanish at Berkeley, and General Editor of the Penn State series in Literature and Philosophy. Among his publications are *The Limits of Illusion: A Critical Study of Calderón, The Bounds of Reason: Cervantes, Dostoevsky, Flaubert*, and, most recently, *The Subject of Modernity*. As editor, he has published *Literature and the Question of Philosophy*. He is Co-Director for the 1993 NEH Summer Institute on Ethics and Aesthetics.

ANNE J. CRUZ teaches Spanish and Comparative Literature at the University of California, Irvine. She is the author of *Imitación y transformación: El petrarquismo en la poesía de Boscán y Garcilaso de la Vega* (1988) and has co-edited three volumes: *Renaissance Rereadings: Intertext and Context* (1988), *Cultural Encounters: The Impact of the Inquisition in Spain and the New World* (1991), and *Culture and Control in Counter-Reformation Spain* (1992). She has published widely on issues of culture and gender in Spanish Golden Age literature and is currently completing a book on the Golden Age picaresque novels.

RUTH ANTHONY EL SAFFAR is President of the Cervantes Society of America (1993–96), as well as a practicing Jungian analyst. She has been awarded fellowships from the National Endowment of the Humanities (1970–71, 1990–91), The John Simon Guggenheim Foundation (1974–75), the American Council of Learned Societies (1982), and the Newberry Library (1983). She has taught at the University of Maryland, Northwestern University, the University of Washington in Saint Louis, and at the Fundación Ortega y Gasset in Madrid. She directed summer seminars for the NEH in 1979 and 1982. She has published four books on Cervantes and edited two other collections of studies on Golden Age Literature.

CARLOS FEAL is Professor of Spanish at the State University of New York at Buffalo. His publications include *La poesía de Pedro Salinas* (1965), *Eros y Lorca* (1973), *En nombre de Don Juan: Estructura de un mito literario* (1984), and *Lorca: Tragedia y mito* (1989). He is also the editor of Miguel de Unamuno, *El resentimiento trágico de la vida: Notas sobre la revolución y guerra civil españolas* (1991).

MARIA ANTONIA GARCES is a doctoral candidate in Golden Age Spanish Literature at The Johns Hopkins University. The essay included in this volume is part of her dissertation, "The Archeology of Desire in Cervantes," a work that explores the Cervantine narrative from psychoanalytic and feminist perspectives. Her published essays include "Zoraida's Veil: The 'Other' Scene of the Captive's Tale" (*Revista de Estudios Hispánicos*, January 1989), "Coaches, Litters, and Chariots of War: Montaigne and Atahualpa" (*Journal of Hispanic Philology*, Winter 1992), and also several articles on Inca Garcilaso de la Vega and Felipe Guaman Poma de Ayala, which examine problems of marginality and linguistic colonialism in the context of Spanish-American discourse.

MARY MALCOLM GAYLORD is Professor of Romance Languages and Literatures at Harvard University. She is author of *The Historical Prose of Fernando de Herrera* and has written widely on Spanish Golden Age poetry, poetics, drama, and prose fiction. At present, she is working on two interconnected books: one concerning Cervantes and the fictions of poetics, in which she examines the fusion of fiction and theory in Cervantes's works, and the other on language, literature, and empire in Golden Age Spain, in which she looks at how imaginative literature and other discourses offer an indirect reflection of Spain's New World experience.

EDUARDO GONZALEZ is Professor of Spanish and Latin American Studies at The Johns Hopkins University and a member of the Film and Media Studies program. Besides numerous articles of comparative scope on Latin American fiction and culture, he has published *Carpentier: El tiempo del hombre* (1978), *La persona y el relato* (1985), and *The Monstered Self* (1992). His most recent book will be published by Duke University Press.

MARY S. GOSSY teaches Spanish, Comparative Literature, and Women's Studies at Rutgers University. The author of *The Untold Story: Women and Theory in Golden Age Texts* (1989), she has recently completed a book tentatively titled "Freudian Slips: Women Writing the Foreign Tongue." She is at work on a study of the idea of Spain in the European imperial unconscious.

LEON GRINBERG is Training and Supervising Analyst at the Madrid Psychoanalytic Association. He was the 1982 André B. Ballard Lecturer at the Association for Psychoanalytic Medicine, Columbia University; Visiting Professor at Tel Aviv University (1973 and 1975); and former Vice-President of the International Psychoanalytical Association. He is the author of twelve books, among them *The Goals of Psychoanalysis* (1990), *Guilt and Depression* (1992), and, in collaboration with Rebeca Grinberg, *Psychoanalytic Perspectives on Migration and Exile* (1989).

CARROLL B. JOHNSON is Professor and Chair of Spanish and Portuguese at UCLA. His books include *Matías de los Reyes and the Craft of Fiction* (1973), *Inside Guzmán de Alfarache* (1978), *Madness and Lust: A Psychoanalytical Approach to 'Don Quixote'* (1983), and *Don Quixote: The Quest for Modern Fiction* (1990), as well as numerous trenchant articles and reviews. He is working on a study of Cervantes's short fiction.

JOSHUA MCKINNEY, who translated Maurice Molho's essay for this volume, recently completed his Ph.D. in the Creative Writing Program at the University of Denver, where he served as an Associate Editor for the *Denver Quarterly*. He is currently an Assistant Professor of English at Valdosta State College in Georgia.

MAURICE MOLHO, a linguist by training, is Professor Emeritus at the University of Paris—Sorbonne. He has published on the picaresque (*Introducción al pensamiento picaresco*, 1968), on Cervantes (*Cervantes, raíces folklóricas*, 1976), on Góngora and Baroque poetics (*Semántica y poética: Góngora, Quevedo*, 1978), and is currently at work on a collection of Cervantine studies.

JUAN FRANCISCO RODRIGUEZ is Training and Supervising Analyst at the Madrid Psychoanalytical Association. He was a Professor at the John F. Kennedy University in Buenos Aires in 1970–71. He is currently teaching at the Centro de Estudios Universitarios, Universidad Complutense, Madrid. As the Main Speaker at the Second Iberian Congress, he delivered a paper titled "The Function and the Work of the Psychoanalyst." His essays include "Manic States," "The Psychoanalytic Conviction," and "The Identity of the Psychoanalyst."

GEORGE A. SHIPLEY, Associate Professor of Spanish at the University of Washington, studies experimental and anti-conventional fictions that against all odds came to be judged masterpieces. He is the author of several studies of Fernando de Rojas's *Celestina* and of the anonymous picaresque novel *Lazarillo de Tormes*. More recently, he has written a cluster of interrelated essays focused on and about the matter he treats here, Cervantes's *Don Quixote*, Part 1, Chapter 20.

PAUL JULIAN SMITH is Professor of Spanish at the University of Cambridge and author of numerous books, including *Writing in the Margin: Spanish Literature of the Golden Age* (1988), *The Body Hispanic: Gender and Sexuality in Spanish and Spanish American Literature* (1989), *Representing the Other: "Race," Text, and Gender in Spanish and Spanish American Narrative* (1992), and *Laws of Desire: Questions of Homosexuality in Spanish Writing and Film: 1960–1990* (1992). He is currently co-editing with Emilie Bergmann a volume of essays on lesbian and gay approaches to Spanish literary texts.

DIANA DE ARMAS WILSON teaches Renaissance Studies in the English Department at the University of Denver. She has been awarded three fellowships from the National Endowment for the Humanities (1982, 1985, and 1988–89). She has published *Allegories of Love: Cervantes's 'Persiles and Sigismunda'* (1991) and contributed essays to *Literary Theory/Renaissance Texts* (1986), *Critical Essays on Cervantes* (1986), and *The Ancient Novel* (1993). She was Guest Editor for the special quincentenary issue of the *Journal of Hispanic Philology* (1992) and is currently at work on a book about Cervantes and "the matter of America."

Index

Library of Congress Cataloging-in-Publication Data

Quixotic desire : psychoanalytic perspectives on Cervantes / edited by
  Ruth Anthony El Saffar and Diana de Armas Wilson.
      p.   cm.
  Includes bibliographical references and index.
  ISBN 0-8014-2823-8 (cloth). —ISBN 0-8014-8081-7 (pbk.)
    1. Cervantes Saavedra, Miguel de, 1547–1616—Knowledge—Psychology.
    2. Psychoanalysis and literature. 3. Desire in literature. I. El Saffar, Ruth S.,
1941– . II. Wilson, Diana de Armas, 1934–
PQ6358.P7Q59 1993
863'.3—dc20
                                                            93-13360